J.S. Bach
as Organist

J.S. Bach as Organist

HIS INSTRUMENTS, MUSIC, AND PERFORMANCE PRACTICES

EDITED BY

George Stauffer and Ernest May

INDIANA UNIVERSITY PRESS
BLOOMINGTON AND INDIANAPOLIS

This book is a publication of

Indiana University Press
601 North Morton Street
Bloomington, IN 47404-3797 USA

http://www.indiana.edu/~iupress

Telephone orders 800-842-6796
Fax orders 812-855-7931
E-mail orders iuporder@indiana.edu

© 1986 by Indiana University Press
First reprinted in paperback in 2000.

The paper used in this publication meets the minimum requirements of American National Standard for Information Sciences—Permanence of Paper for Printed Library Materials, ANSI Z39.48-1984.

Manufactured in the United States of America

Library Cataloging Data

J. S. Bach as organist : his instruments, music, and performance practices / edited by George Stauffer and Ernest May.
Includes index.
1. Bach, Johann Sebastian, 1685–1750—Addresses, essays, lectures.
2. Bach, Johann Sebastian, 1685–1750. Organ music—Addresses, essays, lectures.
3. Organ music—Addresses, essays, lectures.
I. Stauffer, George B., date.
II. May, Ernest, date.
ML410.B1J2   1985   786.5'092'4   84-43070
ISBN 0-253-33181-1 (cloth)
ISBN 0-253-21386-X (paper)
2 3 4 5 6 05 04 03 02 01 00

Contents

PREFACE TO THE PAPERBACK EDITION

It is a pleasure to write a preface for a paperback edition of *J. S. Bach as Organist*, issued thirteen years after the original clothbound edition. Clearly, interest in Bach's organ music has not flagged, and it is gratifying to see that these essays have retained their relevance and will now be made available in a practical format to a second generation of readers. It was our hope that *J. S. Bach as Organist* would serve as a stimulating handbook for organists, organ builders, and other aficionados of Bach's organ music; it appears that this hope has been fulfilled. It is also appropriate that the volume be reissued for the year 2000—the start of a new millennium, of course, but also the 250th anniversary of Johann Sebastian Bach's death.

The contents of *J. S. Bach as Organist* have held up well. Bach's organ works continue to enjoy tremendous popularity in concert and on recording, and the points made in the section "Bach's Organ Music" remain fully significant. Christoph Wolff's essay on Johann Adam Reinken and Johann Sebastian Bach, in particular, has spurred a full-scale re-evaluation of Bach's early years and the role that Reinken's *Hortus musicus* and other Italianate chamber works played in the evolution of Bach's compositional style. Scholars now believe that Bach was more widely acquainted with contemporary chamber and vocal music than previously thought, and that his intense involvement with this repertory, via reworkings of progressive pieces by Corelli, Albinoni, Legrenzi, Reinken, and others, led to the formulation of his own intensely contrapuntal idiom—an idiom that first emerges in his organ works.

The essays in the section "Matters of Performance Practice" have made an impact as well. The main premise in George Stauffer's essay "Bach's Organ Registration Reconsidered"—that Bach's free organ works were generally intended for one-manual performance, *organum plenum*—is no longer controversial, and one now hears the preludes, toccatas, fantasias, and fugues played this way in concert and church service as a matter of course. Robert L. Marshall's suggestion in "Organ or 'Klavier'?" that the seven "keyboard" toccatas, BWV 910–916, are organ works has also taken hold, to judge from recent compact discs that feature the pieces played effectively on the organ. In addition, Luigi Tagliavini's theory that Bach intended portions of the right-hand part of the "Grosso Mogul" Concerto transcription (and the organ solo of the Sinfonia to Cantata 146 as well) to be played an octave lower than the original model, on a 4' stop, has also met with wide acceptance.

Finally, the essays in the section "The Instruments Used by Bach" have gained new importance through recent political developments. The collapse of the Socialist regime in East Germany in 1989 and the subsequent reunification of Germany—events that were unimaginable when *J. S. Bach as Organist* appeared in 1986—have made the organs in Thuringia and Saxony readily accessible to Western visitors. This has produced a flurry of interest in the Middle German organs described by Ulrich Dähnert and Hartmut Haupt, and it has led to a complete reassessment of the instruments used by Bach—both Middle German and North German. Moreover, recent restorations of the Trost organ in the Castle Church in Altenburg and the Scherer/Frizsche/Schnitger organ in the St. Jacobi Church in Hamburg have provided a wealth of previously unknown technical details and serve to underline that a great deal is still to be learned about the instruments that Bach played and admired.

We can be certain that in the new millennium Johann Sebastian Bach and his music will fascinate new audiences and old. In the ongoing discussion of his organ works, we hope that the essays in *J. S. Bach as Organist* will serve as a ready source of information as well as a springboard to further debate.

George Stauffer and Ernest May, Spring 1999

PREFACE

This volume is the fruit of seeds sown at symposia on Bach's organ music held in recent years at Columbia University, Harvard University, the University of Nebraska (Lincoln), and the House of Hope Presbyterian Church in St. Paul, Minnesota. The present editors, together with Christoph Wolff and Peter Williams, served at various times as lecturers and panel participants at these events, whose purpose was to bring together scholars and performers to discuss the latest developments in the field of Bach organ music. By any standard, the conferences were a success: the attendance was large, the enthusiasm and interest were high, and the exchange among specialists was lively and informative.

Yet there was also a sense that something more ought to come out of these gatherings, a feeling that was articulated in the form of a question, invariably raised toward the end of a symposium, after two or three days of discourse on the most current Bach studies: "This material is fascinating—can't it somehow be made available in print?" This book is our answer to that plea. It is our attempt to set forth, for specialists as well as general readers, a representative sampling of essays by scholars, performers, and organ builders involved with recent investigations into Bach's craft.

Of course the approach of 1985, the tercentennial of Bach's birth, also served as an important catalyst. As we reach this anniversary, it seems appropriate to take stock of what has been learned recently about Bach as organist and to look at his achievements with a newly educated eye. Although we may be deluding ourselves in thinking that our perspective in 1985 is less myopic than viewpoints in the past, it seems to us that there *has* been unusual progress of late in the study of Bach and the organ. We believe it can be observed on two fronts.

First, there is the maturation of the *Orgelbewegung*, the organ revival movement. After nearly 80 years of over-reacting to nineteenth-century romanticism, organ builders and scholars are adopting more cautious, reasoned, and historically sound methods of restoring and recreating Bach's instruments. The highly successful restoration of the Huss-Schnitger organ in St. Cosmae, Stade, completed in 1975, after years of painstaking research, stands in sharp contrast to the well-intentioned but unfortunate alteration of the Scherer-Schnitger organ in the Jakobikirche, Hamburg, in 1928–30.

Second, there has been a noticeable broadening of focus in Bach research. Thirty years ago, it seemed that the majority of Bach scholars were working on the vocal compositions. The new chronology, with its extraordinary and surprising discoveries, commanded the attention of specialists. Most of Bach's cantatas were redated, and consequently his activities in Weimar and Leipzig required reinterpretation. This state of affairs is reflected in the *Neue Bach-Ausgabe*, in which vocal works represented the bulk of the initial volumes. But now that the implications of the new chronology have been assimilated, and a good number of "second-generation" monographs have been completed, scholars are returning to the instrumental works with renewed vigor, carrying with them the insights on Bach's compositional habits gained from the vocal repertoire. Study of the organ works seems to be emerging from a partial eclipse.

Current trends aside, it is beyond debate that Bach showed a more-sustained interest in organs and organ composition than in any other field of musical endeavor. As Carl Philipp Emanuel Bach pointed out to Forkel, Johann Sebastian's earliest training with his brother Johann Christoph in Ohrdruf was "fit for an organist and not much more." And to judge from the latest views on Bach's last decade, which push the composition of the B-minor Mass and the *Art of Fugue* toward the early and middle 1740s, it appears that Bach's final years, like his first, were devoted primarily to organ music—the writing of the Canonic Variations on *Vom Himmel hoch*, the transcribing of the Schübler Chorales, and the editing of the "Great Eighteen" Collection. In between his Ohrdruf study and his work of the late 1740s are over 50 years of unparalleled achievement in *Orgelkunst*.

As a much sought-after consultant and designer, Bach established new standards for the construction of organs. His examinations of new instruments—such as the test of the organ in the Johanniskirche in Leipzig, which was, to quote Agricola, "the most severe trial ever given an instrument"—set the measure for the future. Moreover, Bach's compositions themselves compelled builders to produce instruments that were more reliable and tonally progressive. The complex and variegated contrapuntal textures of Bach's works require an organ with a steady wind supply and an efficient mechanical action; the far-ranging modulatory schemes demand well-tempered rather than mean-tone tunings.

As a composer, Bach took the existing genres of his day—the North German *Praeludium*, the chorale motet, the *manualiter* fughetta, and others—to new heights and then went beyond them, inventing or codifying forms such as the prelude and fugue, the organ chorale with independent accompanimental parts, and the *pedaliter* trio. These pieces, favored by a small group of connoisseurs in the eighteenth century, form a major portion of the classical organ repertoire today. Johann Mattheson's appraisal of Bach's compositions in 1717—"I have seen things by the famous organist of Weimar . . . that are certainly such that one must esteem the man highly"—has proven to be prophetic.

As a teacher, Bach transmitted his innovative playing style and repertoire to his students. He single-handedly trained the best players of the next generation: Johann Ludwig Krebs, Johann Philipp Kirnberger, Johann Christian Kittel, his own sons Wilhelm Friedemann and Carl Philipp Emanuel, and others. "Since he had composed the most instructive pieces for clavier," said Carl Philipp Emanuel, "he brought up his students on them." In so doing, he firmly established a pedagogic method of systematic fingering and obbligato pedaling that has remained the model for good organ playing down to the present day.

And finally, in performance, the field in which he attained the greatest fame during his lifetime, Bach astounded his auditors and intimidated his fellow musicians. Rather than face Bach in an open competition, French organist Louis Marchand left town; Handel appears to have been wiser, for he judiciously avoided an encounter. Bach's public performances in Hamburg, Dresden, and Berlin helped to establish the modern organ concert (complete with reviewers, in the case of the recital in the Frauenkirche in Dresden in 1736) outside the worship service. But within the church service, too, Bach may have been an innovator in ways that we are only gradually coming to realize. Hans-Joachim Schulze recently unearthed a report from the *Dresdner Gelehrte Anzeigen* on Bach's hymn playing during a visit to the Altenburg Schlosskirche in 1739:

> Bach played the Creed in D minor, but for the second verse he lifted the congregation into E♭ minor, and for the third verse, he took them even higher to E minor. This could be accomplished only by a Bach and an organ in Altenburg.

Questions of tuning aside, this account suggests that even the twentieth century school of "razzle-dazzle," modulation-filled hymn playing must accept Bach as its founder.

In the present anthology we have tried to touch on these different aspects of Bach's life as an organist, turning first to the instruments he knew and used, continuing with the music he wrote and his methods of composition, and concluding with matters of performance practice. For the most part, the contributors have not attempted to present broad surveys, for that has been done elsewhere. Rather, they have written on specific topics that have been the focus of recent investigations. In some instances, the results of these investigations will surely open entirely new avenues of study: Christoph Wolff's reevaluation of Bach's earliest training or Peter Williams's discussion of appearance versus reality in eighteenth-century notation, for example. In other cases, the findings will certainly prove controversial: Harald Vogel's theory of mean-tone induced transpositions or Robert L. Marshall's broadening of the organ repertoire to include the six "clavier" toccatas and other works generally assigned to the harpsichord and clavichord. It is important that this material be set forth in print, for scrutiny and further debate. We hope the essays in this volume, together with the Calendar of Events, will provide edification and enjoyment for *Kenner und Liebhaber* alike.

Special thanks are due to a number of people who helped to make this volume possible: to Bruce MacIntyre, Ondine Hasson, Thomas Baker, Frigga Scott, Lynn Edwards, and Edward Pepe, who set aside their own scholarly work or performance duties in order to provide, under the pressure of tight deadlines, accurate, readable translations for a number of the foreign essays; to Christoph Wolff, who not only contributed encouragement, advice, and two articles, but also served as "middleman" between the editors and several hard-to-reach European authors; to William Scheide, who supplied photographs of Bach's personal copy of the Schübler Chorales, which rests in his collection of Bach manuscripts and prints; to James N. Settle, Dean of Humanities and the Arts, and L. Michael Griffel, Chairman of the Music Department at Hunter College, who graciously provided material support in the form of release time from teaching; and to Corodon Fuller of *Musica Vera* for overseeing the engraving of the musical examples.

George Stauffer   Ernest May
New York, N.Y.   Autumn 1984   Amherst, Mass.

ABBREVIATIONS

Bach Reader	*The Bach Reader,* edited by Hans David and Arthur Mendel, rev. ed. (New York, 1966).
BDok	*Bach-Dokumente,* issued under the auspices of the Bach-Archiv, Leipzig (Kassel and Leipzig, 1963–1979).
Berlin, DStB	Deutsche Staatsbibliothek, East Berlin.
Berlin, SPK	Staatsbibliothek Preussischer Kulturbesitz, West Berlin.
BG	*Johann Sebastian Bach's Werke (Bach-Gesamtausgabe),* issued under the auspices of the Bach-Gesellschaft (Leipzig, 1851–1899).
BJ	*Bach-Jahrbuch,* 1904–.
BuxWV	*Thematisch-systematisches Verzeichnis der Werke von Dietrich Buxtehude (Buxtehude-Werke-Verzeichnis),* edited by Georg Karstädt (Wiesbaden, 1974).
BWV	*Thematisch-systematisches Verzeichnis der Musikalischen Werke von Johann Sebastian Bach (Bach-Werke-Verzeichnis),* edited by Wolfgang Schmieder (Wiesbaden, 1950).
David	Werner David, *Johann Sebastian Bachs Orgeln* (Berlin, 1951).
Forkel	Johann Nicolaus Forkel, *Über Johann Sebastian Bachs Leben, Kunst, und Kunstwerk* (Leipzig, 1802); modern edition, edited by Joseph Müller-Blattau (Kassel, 1942).
Leipzig, MB	Musikbibliothek der Stadt Leipzig, Leipzig.
MGG	*Die Musik in Geschichte und Gegenwart,* edited by Friedrich Blume (Kassel, 1949–1979).
NBA	*Johann Sebastian Bach. Neue Ausgabe sämtlicher Werke (Neue Bach-Ausgabe),* issued under the auspices of the Johann-Sebastian-Bach-Institut, Göttingen, and the Bach-Archiv, Leipzig (Kassel and Leipzig, 1954–).
NBA, KB	*Neue Bach-Ausgabe, Kritischer Bericht*
Peters Edition	*Johann Sebastian Bach's Kompositionen für die Orgel,* edited by Friedrich Conrad Griepenkerl and Ferdinand Roitzsch (Leipzig, 1844–1852).
Spitta	Philipp Spitta, *Johann Sebastian Bach* (Leipzig, 1873–1879); English translation by Clara Bell and J. A. Fuller-Maitland (London, 1889).

In the present volume, musical keys are designated by the use of capital letters for major (as in the Prelude in D, BWV 532/1) and small letters for minor (as in the Toccata in d, BWV 565).

The Instruments Used by Bach

He not only understood the art of playing the organ, but he also knew the construction of organs from one end to the other. . . . No one could draw up or judge dispositions for new organs better than he.

—Obituary of 1754

ULRICH DÄHNERT

Organs Played and Tested
by J. S. Bach

Eisenach (1685–95)

Johann Sebastian Bach's first model as an organist must surely have
been his famous uncle, Johann Christoph Bach (1642–1703), who
played at St. George's Church in Eisenach from 1665.[1] Johann Christoph was a very strong player and must also have been quite knowl-
edgeable in the area of organ design and construction. The old organ
at St. George's was in poor condition and sometimes became virtually
unplayable. Johann Christoph struggled to have it rebuilt[2] and, in
1679, submitted a detailed plan for its reconstruction to the Town
Council. That body, however, appears to have taken its time approv-
ing the project. A four-manual instrument was eventually built by
Stertzing of Ohrdruf, but it was completed only after Johann Christoph's death. It was tested by C. F. Witt from Gotha on June 22, 1707.
Adlung later remarked that the organ needed repair. It was rebuilt
several times during the eighteenth century and no longer exists. One
can imagine that the struggles over this instrument contributed to
Johann Sebastian's lifelong interest in the field of organ design and
construction.

Ohrdruf (1695–1700)

The organ played by Bach's older brother Johann Christoph
(1671–1721) at St. Michael's Church in Ohrdruf was a two-manual instrument with *Rückpositiv*. This instrument, which is thought to have
been defective and incomplete,[3] is perhaps the one on which Johann
Sebastian learned the rudiments of organ playing.

Lüneburg (1700–1703)

While Bach was a student at St. Michael's School in Lüneburg, his interest in the organ was probably stimulated by Georg Böhm, the famous organist at St. John's. Both Lüneburg organs—at St. Michael's and St. John's—were old and fragile. The pedal of the instrument at St. John's was permanently coupled to the manual and had but one stop, an Untersatz 16', whose lower range descended only to F.[4] Perhaps Bach was influenced by Balthasar Held, an organ builder who cared for the large organ in St. Michael's as well as for the *positiv* and the harpsichord in the Choir of the Church and the Regal at the School. It is not known whether Bach attempted to gain access to the organs in nearby Celle.

Sangerhausen (1702) and Weimar (1703)

In August 1702, Bach applied unsuccessfully for the post of organist at the Jacobikirche in Sangerhausen.[5] In March 1703, he went on to Weimar as a court musician—probably a violinist—in the private chapel of Duke Johann Ernst, the brother of the reigning Duke Wilhelm Ernst.[6] It is possible that Bach occasionally substituted in the castle chapel for the aging court organist Johann Effler.

Arnstadt (1703–1707)

In the summer of 1703, Bach traveled to the "New Church" in Arnstadt.[7] In 1581 a fire had destroyed the Bonifatiuskirche, and when the church was rebuilt in the second half of the seventeenth century, it was given its new name. For a long time there was no organ in the church. On October 17, 1699, a contract was signed with the organ builder Johann Friedrich Wender of Mühlhausen, who had been recommended by Deacon Fischer of St. Blasius in Arnstadt. Work began slowly, and the instrument was finally completed on July 3, 1703. Near the end of June or the beginning of July, Bach tested the organ. The exact words of his report have not been preserved, but judging from a deposition by the Town Council of Arnstadt, his evaluation seems to have been positive. Bach inaugurated the two-manual instrument and was subsequently offered the organist's position. The appointment was officially approved on August 9, 1703. In terms of the organ itself, the specifications of the contract and the finished instrument do not coincide, and hence we cannot be sure of the original stoplist. The contract provided for 21 stops, but the instrument was enlarged to 23 stops. The range of the manuals was to be CD–c'''; the pedal, CD–c', d'.[8] The original console, which is housed today in the Bach Museum in Arnstadt, has 49 notes in the manuals, CDE–d''', and 25 notes in the pedal, CDE–d', with D as the upper key. The contract shows the following stop list:

Oberwerk (Untermanual):	*Brustwerk (Obermanual):*	*Pedal:*
Prinzipal 8' (tin, in the case)	Prinzipal 4' (tin, in the case)	Prinzipal Bass 8' (tin, in the case)
Viol da Gamba 8' (tin?)	Stillgedackt 8'	Subbass 16' (wood)
Quintadena 8'	Spitzfloet (2'?)	Posaun Bass 16'
Grobgedackt 8'	Quinta 3'	Hohlfloet 8' (g–d?)
Quinta 6' (open)	Sesquialtera	Cornet Bass 2' (according to the estimate of 1701, but not in the contract)
Octava 4'	Nachthorn 4' (capped)	
Mixtur 4 ranks	Mixtur 3 ranks	
Cymbel 2 ranks	Manual coupler	
Gemshorn 8'	Pedal coupler	
Trompete 8'		
Tremulant		
Glockenaccord		

(metal bracket spanning Quintadena 8' through Trompete 8')

In the *Oberwerk*, the Cymbal was changed to three ranks; in the *Brustwerk*, the mixture was altered to four ranks, and an Octava 2' and Glockenaccord were added beyond what was called for in the contract. Seven stops from the Wender organ have been preserved: Gemshorn 8', Quintadena 8', Grobgedackt 8', Viol da Gamba 8', Octava 4', Stillgedackt 8', and Nachthorn 4'.[9]

Lübeck (1705–1706)

When Bach traveled from Arnstadt to Lübeck to hear the famous Buxtehude and to be present at his Abendmusiken, he was without doubt interested in the organs of Buxtehude's church, St. Mary's.[10] The three-manual organ at St. Mary's was originally built in 1516–18 by Bartholt Hering. Jacob Scherer added to it, in 1637–41 Friedrich Stellwagen renovated it, and in 1704 Otto Diederich Richborn made additional changes. By this time the organ had fifteen reeds, including a Grossposaune 32'. The smaller Totentanz organ must also have been of interest to Bach, but unfortunately we have no specific information about his association with it or with the larger instrument in the church.

Langewiesen (1706)

The organ in Langewiesen near Gehren was built in 1706 by Johann
Albrecht of Coburg. Bach tested the instrument, but his findings are
not preserved in writing, and there is no additional information about
this organ.[11]

Mühlhausen (1707–1708)

After the Mühlhausen organist Johann Georg Ahle died on December 2, 1706, Bach applied for the vacant post at St. Blasius. He
auditioned successfully around April 24, 1707, and was installed on
June 15. Since he found the condition of the two-manual organ, consisting of *Oberwerk, Rückpositiv*, and Pedal, most unsatisfactory, he
made a proposal to the Church Council for a thorough renovation.[12]
(This proposal shows great similarity to the one his uncle Johann
Christoph Bach made for the organ at St. George's in Eisenach on October 30, 1679.[13]) The parish elders approved the proposal in a meeting on February 21, 1708, and entrusted Bach with supervising and
guiding the work of organ builder Johann Friedrich Wender. Bach's
proposal called for the construction of three new powerful bellows to
supplement the four old ones, which were to be adapted to yield
greater wind power. As a result, it would be possible "to play with one
stop or with all the stops together without a change in pressure." For
the Pedal Bach wanted a 32' Subbass or a so-called Untersatz made of
wood, which would give the entire instrument the best "gravity."
   The Posannenbass was to be built "with new and larger pipes, and
the pipe mouths were to be designed differently so the stop could
produce a more solid tone (a better gravity)." For the Pedal, a
Glockenspiel (with 26 bells at 4' pitch) was planned, at the request of
the parishioners, but it was never built. In the *Oberwerk*, the Trompete
8' was to be replaced by a Fagott 16', "which would serve for many
new ideas and sounds very delicately." Instead of the Gemshorn, "a
Viol di Gamba 8', which would complement the Salicional 4'" should
be installed in the *Rückpositiv*, and "instead of the Quinta 3' a Nasat 3'
should be added. . . . Between the *Brustpositiv* and the *Oberwerk* there
must be a coupler. And finally, after a complete tuning of the whole
organ the tremulant must be regulated, so that it flutters at the proper
rate." The range of the manuals was 50 notes, CD–d'''; the pedal, 26
notes, CD–d'.

For the new *Brustpositiv* Bach had the following stops in mind:

In the case, 3 Principals, namely:
1. Quinta 3' ⎤
2. Octave 2' ⎥ of good 14-ounce tin
3. Schalemoy 8' ⎥
4. Mixtur 3 ranks ⎦
5. Tertia, with which, by drawing a few other stops, one can produce a fine and complete Sesquialtera.
6. Fleute douce 4'; and finally a
7. Stillgedackt 8', which accords perfectly with concerted music and, made of good wood, should sound much better than a metal Gedackt.

On June 25, 1708, Bach submitted his resignation at Mühlhausen in order to accept a post at the court chapel of Duke Wilhelm Ernst. Bach may have returned to Mühlhausen on Reformation Day 1709, when the renovation of the organ had been completed. He may have dedicated the organ with a work possibly composed for the occasion, the chorale fantasia *Ein feste Burg*, BWV 720, which requires three manuals and pedal.[14] In two lost manuscripts[15] "Fagotto" was written above the beginning of the left hand, and above the beginning of the right hand on the *Brustpositiv* was noted "Sesquialtera."

This instrument, perhaps tested and dedicated by Bach, consisted of 37 stops divided among *Oberwerk, Brustpositiv, Rückpositiv,* and Pedal. Each of the three divisions had a Sesquialtera; on the *Brustwerk* it was produced by combining the Tertia and the Quinta. The Pedal was exceptionally full, including an Untersatz 32', a Rohrflötenbass 1', and the reeds Posaune 16', Trompete 8', and Cornetbass 2'.

Weimar (1708–17)

The organ in the castle chapel of Weimar, built by Ludwig Compenius in 1658, had been rebuilt in 1707–1708 by J. Conrad Weishaupt of Seebergen near Gotha shortly before Bach arrived.[16] All that is known about its stop list is that it had a Subbass that had been built over and above the original estimate. While the chapel and the cupola were being renovated in 1712, the organ could not be played. In 1714, the organ was rebuilt by Nicolaus Trebs, probably according to Bach's sketch. Gottfried Albin Wette's stop list of 1737 reads:

Zum Obern Clavier, C–c‴ [17]
1. Principal 8', tin *
2. Quintadena 16', metal *
3. Gemsshorn 8', metal *

Im Untern Clavier, C–c‴
1. Principal 8', tin
2. Viol di Gamba 8', metal
3. Gedackt 8', metal *

4. Grobgedackt 8', metal
5. Quintadena 4', metal
6. Octava 4', metal
7. Mixtur 6 ranks, metal
8. Cymbel 3 ranks, metal*
9. A Glockenspiel "und Spiel-
   Register dazu"

Im Pedal, C–e'
1. Gross Untersatz 32', wood
2. Sub-Bass 16', wood
3. Posaun-Bass 16', wood*
4. Violon-Bass 16', wood
5. Principal-Bass 8', metal
6. Trompeta-Bass 8', metal
7. Cornett-Bass 4', metal

4. Trompete 8', metal*
5. klein Gedackt 4', metal
6. Octava 4', metal
7. Wald-Flöthe 2', metal*
8. Sesquialtera 4 ranks "in Octava,
   aus 3 und 2 Fuss"

Accessories
Tremulant for the Hauptwerk
Tremulant for the Unterwerk
Oberwerk to Pedal coupler
Manual coupler
Cymbel Stern

*From the Compenius organ of
   1658.[18]

Reinhold Jauernig has speculated that this specification may reflect the organ as reconstructed in 1719–20 under the direction of Court Organist Johann Martin Schubert (see note 16). As early as 1712–13 a Glockenspiel had been added, possibly on Bach's advice. In 1715 a new Glockenspiel from Nürnberg was obtained. According to Spitta[19] the castle church organ of Weimar was tuned in cornett pitch (high choir pitch). It was later rebuilt several times, and the new organ of 1756 was tuned to chamber pitch. Bach may also have been familiar with the organ located in the Church of St. Peter and St. Paul in Weimar, built by Christoph Junge[20] in 1685, and played by his relative Johann Gottfried Walther. The 25 stops of this organ, probably equipped with spring chests, were distributed over *Oberwerk, Rückpositiv*, and Pedal.[21]

Taubach (1710)

The organ in the village church of Taubach near Mellingen was built in 1709–10 by Nicolaus Trebs, and we can be almost certain that Bach designed its stop list.[22] On October 26, 1710 (the nineteenth Sunday after Trinity), Bach tested the instrument in the presence of church officials at a festive dedication service. Bach's written evaluation of February 16, 1711, states:

> Whereas Mr. Heinrich Trebs, the bearer, an organ builder experienced in his art, requests me to give him a testimonial concerning the work he has done in this principality, I have neither been able nor desired to refuse him since he merits it too well; accordingly I assure the gracious reader of this letter that he has applied his most praiseworthy

industry to the work he has done in these parts, and I, as one appointed to inspect the same, have found that both in the fulfillment of the contract and in subsequent work he has proven himself a reasonable and conscientious man, for he made us the lowest price and he afterwards performed the work agreed upon with the greatest industry.[23]

The stop list contained the following:

Manual:		Pedal:	
1. Principal	4' of good tin	1. Sup Bass	16' of wood
2. Gedact	8' of wood	2. Wald-Flöth Bass	2' of metal
3. Quinta	3' of metal	3. Principal Bass	8' of wood
4. Octava	2' of metal		
5. Tritonus	1-3/5' of metal	Stern, Cymbel	
6. Superoctav	1' of metal	Tremulant	
7. Mixtur	3 ranks of metal	Pedal coupler	
8. Quintathön	8', half metal and half wood	2 bellows 9 feet long and 4-1/2 feet wide	

Weissenfels (c. 1713)

It can be assumed that Bach was familiar with the organ in the castle chapel of the Augustusburg in Weissenfels, built by Christian Förner of Wettin in 1673.[24] It consisted of 30 stops, on spring chests, distributed among *Oberwerk, Brustwerk,* and Pedal (with an unusually high range ascending to f'). The wind was generated in three wedge bellows, each 9 feet long and 4-1/2 feet wide. Both the Toccata in F, BWV 540, with its second pedal solo reaching f', and the Vivaldi concerto transcription in a, BWV 593, which requires an e' in the third movement (mm. 86–97), could have been played on the Weissenfels organ.

Halle (1713–1716)

Bach traveled to Halle near the end of November 1713 in order to inform himself about the plans for the new large organ to be built by Christoph Contius of Halberstadt[25] in the Liebfrauenkirche and to compete for the organist post in this church. The contract with Contius for the organ had been signed October 1, 1712, and the construction of the instrument stretched from Easter 1713 to Easter 1716. The Church Council elected Bach organist on December 13, but he eventually declined the offer early in 1714.[26] In April 1716, Thomaskantor Johann Kuhnau of Leipzig, Kantor Christian Friedrich Rolle of Quedlinburg, and Bach were asked to test the completed three-manual, 65-stop organ. The examination lasted from April 29 till May 1.[27] In a written evaluation, the examiners found fault with the low wind pressure of the ten bellows, which "only drives the wind gauge to the 32nd or 33rd degree." They also raised objections about the voicing, especially in the reeds. Contius promised to attend to all pipes found to be out of tune and to adjust the temperament and voicing of various pipes found unsatisfactory by the examiners. At the time of the test the following items had not yet been installed: two tremulants, two stars, a movable sun on the *Oberwerk*, and the bird song. Many years later, on April 16, 1746, Wilhelm Friedemann Bach assumed the organist's post at the Liebfrauenkirche, succeeding Gottfried Kirchhoff, who had been a student of Zachow. The Halle instrument, like most Bach organs, has not been preserved.

Erfurt (1716)

The construction of the three-manual, 39-stop organ in the Church of St. Augustine, Erfurt,[28] was begun by Johann Friedrich Stertzing.[29] Stertzing however, went to Kassel in 1714 to succeed Johann Wenderoth as court organ builder, and Johann Georg Schröter was brought in to continue the work in Erfurt. The completed instrument was examined by J. S. Bach and the organ builder Johann Anton Weise of Arnstadt. In their report of July 31, 1716, both examiners expressed appreciation for Schröter's work.[30] Unfortunately, the disposition was altered in 1753 by Hartung of Schlossvippach.

Köthen (1717–23)

It is to be regretted that very little can be said about the organ in the Agnuskirche in Köthen, an instrument with which Bach was no doubt familiar. The Pedal—which supposedly ranged to f'—had eight stops; the *Hauptwerk* and *Rückpositiv* apparently had ten stops each.[31] The range of the manuals was allegedly 49 keys, CD–d'''; the pedal, CD–d'e'f'.[32]

Leipzig (1717)

On the invitation of the University in Leipzig, Bach traveled from Köthen to give his expert opinion about the new large organ in St.

Paul's, built by Johann Scheibe. According to Paul Rubardt,[33] the stop list was designed by organ builder Horatio Casparini of Breslau; that explains its similarity to Casparini's instrument at St. Peter and Paul in Görlitz.[34] Wilhelm Stieda writes: "The organ builder Casparini of Breslau was not present in Leipzig, though he gave his advice from afar as an experienced expert in the field and was reimbursed for his consultation."[35]

The initial work order to Johann Scheibe dates from as early as September 1710.[36] The instrument was built on the west choir loft, utilizing parts of the old organ, which had been located on the south loft. The Nikolai organist, Daniel Vetter, supervised the work. Construction was completed on November 4, 1716. The finished instrument had three manuals and 54 stops, distributed over *Hauptwerk, Brustwerk, Hinterwerk* (or *Seitenwerk?*), and Pedal.[37] Fourteen of the stops (ranging from 16' to 1') were in the Pedal division. The Principalbass 16' and Gross Quintadenbass 16' were borrowed from the *Hauptwerk*, as were the Octava 8', Octava 4', Quinta 3', and Mixtur V-VI. The presence of only four reeds[38]—Chalumeau 8' (capped and soft) on the *Hauptwerk*, Sertin 8' (capped and sharply voiced) in the *Hintenwerk*, Posaunenbass 16' and Trompeta 8' in the Pedal—and the absence of a 32' stop do not seem to be consistent with Bach's sound ideal. In his evaluation of December 17, 1717,[39] Bach criticized the "structure, which is too closely confined and would make repair difficult, should it become necessary." It must be noted, however, that Scheibe had not constructed the organ case.

Bach found the conventional major parts of the organ, such as wind chests, bellows, pipes, and roller boards, acceptable as far as workmanship was concerned. However, he recommended that the wind pressure be equalized throughout to avoid sudden changes. He may have regretted the lack of the two reeds—Schallmey 4' and Cornet 2'—which had to be omitted, according to an order from the University of Leipzig. In their place, an Octava 2' (in the *Brustwerk*) and an Hohlflöte 2' (in the *Hintenwerk*) were installed. A few minor defects, made apparent by unequal voicing, could be taken care of immediately by the organ builder by changing the speech of the lowest pipes in the Posaune and Trompete from a coarse, noisy tone to a clear, firm one and by adjusting the remaining unsatisfactory pipes in a similar fashion. Bach requested another complete tuning when the weather was more suitable and pointed out that "the touch of the organ should be somewhat lighter and the keys ought not to go down so far." The old *Brustwerk* wind chest, with its one-piece sound board

and short octave, had to be replaced with a new one. Bach recommended that the organ builder be reimbursed for the additional work
required.

Hamburg (1720)

We can assume that Bach was deeply impressed by North German
organs, and in particular by the four-manual instrument with sixteen
reeds at St. Catherine's in Hamburg.[40] The renowned Johann Adam
Reinken played there and maintained the organ conscientiously.
From the Obituary of 1754 we know that even in his youthful
Lüneburg days Bach traveled to Hamburg to hear the famous
organist.[41] In 1720, Bach played for members of the City Council and
other dignitaries for two hours on the St. Catherine's organ, renovated
in 1670 by Johann Friedrich Besser of Braunschweig. According to a
later report, Bach was "greatly admired by his audience." For almost
half an hour he improvised in many different ways on the chorale *An
Wasserflüssen Babylon*.[42] Reinken listened with great pleasure and com-
mended Bach on his performance. The excellent 58-stop instrument
had a short octave in the manuals and the Pedal (which had an F♯,
however). The manuals ranged up to c‴; the pedal to d′. According to
his student Johann Friedrich Agricola, Bach spoke of no other organ
with as much admiration and high praise as he did of the instrument
in St. Catherine's.[43] Bach was a great friend (connoisseur) of reeds and
applauded their beauty and variety of tone color. Of great importance
to Bach also was the "gravity" of the 32′ stops, which he found to be of
the very finest quality. Bach claimed that the 32′ Principal and 32′ Posaune in the Pedal spoke evenly and clearly down to the lowest C. The
Principal, he said, was the only one of that size that he knew to be so
excellent. Agricola assumed that the St. Catherine's organ was no
more than a large half-step above French chamber pitch.[44]

The purpose of Bach's trip to Hamburg in 1720 was his audition for
the organist post at St. Jacobi, which had become vacant after the
death of Heinrich Frese.[45] The four-manual, 60-stop organ, completed in 1693 by Arp Schnitger, seems to have been as compatible
with Bach's sound ideal as the similarly designed instrument at St.
Catherine's. The Principal chorus of the *Hauptwerk* was almost the
same on both organs; at St. Catherine's, the mixture had ten ranks; at
Jacobi, six to eight ranks. The flute chorus and color stops at St.
Catherine's consisted of Bordun 16′, Spitzflöte 8′, and Querflöte 8′; at

St. Jacobi, Spitzflöte 8', Viola da Gamba 8', Rohrflöte 4', and Flachflöte 2'. In addition, both organs had Quintadena 16', Rauschpfeife II, and Trompete 16'. At St. Catherine's, the Principal chorus on the *Oberwerk* contained only Principal 8' and Scharff VI; at St. Jacobi, it was much stronger. Flutes from 8' to 2' and three reeds were present in both cases. The *Brustwerk* at St. Catherine's had a Dulcian 16' and a Regal 8'; at St. Jacobi, there was a Trechterregal 8' and a Dulcian 8'. The *Rückpositiv* of both organs was lavishly designed; among the stops were Sesquialteras and three reeds (at St. Jacobi, Dulcian 16', Bärpfeife 8', and Schalmey 4'). The Pedal division included seventeen stops at St. Catherine's and fourteen at St. Jacobi, including Principal 32', Posaune 32', Cornet 2', Nachthorn 2', and Rauschpfeife III. At St. Jacobi, the Pedal and *Rückpositiv* had broken octaves (c♯ and d♯ were lacking); *Hauptwerk*, *Oberwerk*, and *Brustwerk* had short octaves.[46] The manuals ranged to c''', the pedal to d'. The Jacobi organ is still tuned a whole tone above 440Hz.[47] Perhaps the original temperament, like the Arp Schnitger *Positiv* in Niew Scheemda,[48] was a modified mean-tone, similar to the Schlick temperament. We can be virtually certain that Bach improvised at St. Jacobi, but we do not know why he left Hamburg without waiting for a formal audition (though his departure may have had something to do with the fact that a "contribution" appears to have been required to attain the organist post).

Leipzig (1723–50)

The stop lists of the three-manual organs at St. Nikolai and St. Thomas were probably more compatible with Bach's sound ideal than the 47-stop Scheibe organ at St. Paul's. The large St. Nikolai organ was built by Johann Lange and reconstructed in 1693–94 by Zacharias Thayssner of Merseburg.[49] Johann Scheibe worked on the large St. Thomas organ in 1721–22.[50] Both instruments consisted of *Oberwerk*, *Brustwerk*, *Rückpositiv*, and Pedal and were well supplied with reed stops. From remarks by Agricola, it is clear that Bach was by no means an opponent of the *Rückpositiv*, unlike Jacob Adlung, who rejected it with exaggerated fanaticism.[51]

On the St. Nikolai organ, the Principal chorus was based on an 8' Principal in the *Oberwerk*; in the *Rückpositiv* as well as the *Brustwerk* it was based on a 4' Principal. The foundation stops were a Quintadena 16' in the *Oberwerk*, Gedackt 8' in the *Rückpositiv*, and Quintadena 8' in the *Brustwerk*. The Mixtures were grouped in the following fashion: *Oberwerk*, six ranks; *Rückpositiv*, four ranks; *Brustwerk*, three ranks. Each of the three divisions included a Sesquialtera 1-3/5'.

The St. Thomas organ had a fully developed Principal chorus with a 16' Principal as the foundation and a six-, eight-, ten-rank Mixture in the *Oberwerk*, which also contained a Quintadena 16', Spielpfeife 8', and Sesquialtera II. The incomplete Principal chorus in the *Rückpositiv* consisted of Principal 8', Rauschpfeife II,[52] and Mixture IV. The *Brustwerk* included (besides the Principal 4') a two-rank Cymbal, which was most likely used in combination with the two Regales. In addition, it also contained a Sesquialtera 1-3/5'. According to Spitta,[53] who quotes Rust, Scheibe added a Sesquialtera to the *Rückpositiv* in the 1721–22 rebuilding.

Stopped flutes and a few isolated strings up to the 2' range were well represented in both organs—for example, Waldflöte 2' in the *Oberwerk* of the St. Nikolai organ; and Gemshorn 2' in the *Brustwerk* and Violin 2' and Schallflöte 1' in the *Rückpositiv* of the St. Thomas organ. As regards reeds, the St. Nikolai organ had a Fagott 16', probably with cyclindrical resonators and mild tone color,[54] and a Trompete 8' in the *Oberwerk*; a Schalemey 4' in the *Brustwerk*; and a Bombard 8' in the *Rückpositiv*. The St. Thomas organ had a Regal 8' and Geigenregal 4' in the *Brustwerk*, probably taken over from Johann Lange; and in the *Rückpositiv*, Krumbhorn 16' and Trommet 8'. Both organs had a complete chorus of four reeds in their Pedal divisions: Posaunenbass 16', Trompetenbass 8', Schallmeyenbass 4', and Cornet 2'. The resonators of these reeds were tin plated. The labials were represented only by a Subbass 16' in both instruments plus an Octavbass 4' at St. Nikolai. Neither the manuals nor the Pedal divisions of either instrument were lacking in suitable cantus firmus stops, which could also be used as obbligato voices in cantatas and passions.

Störmthal (1723)

From Leipzig Bach traveled to nearby Störmthal to test the fourteen-stop, one-manual organ built by Zacharias Hildebrandt. He found it a fine and substantial instrument,[55] but, unfortunately, his written evaluation has not been preserved. The dedication of the organ took place on November 2, 1723,[56] with Bach conducting his cantata *Höchsterwünschtes Freudenfest*, BWV 194.

Gera (1724)

In June 1724[57] Bach ventured to Gera to examine the two organs built by Johann Georg Finke, Sr., at the Salvatorkirche and at the town church, St. John's.[58] The first was a small instrument, probably completed in 1722, but nothing is known about its stop list. The second instrument, at St. John's, apparently built between 1722 and 1724, was a large three-manual, 43-stop organ with eight reeds. On June 25 it was examined and dedicated by the famous "Cantor Capellmeister Bach." According to Ferdinand Hahn, Bach declared this large organ to be quite successful. The stop list[59] showed striking similarity to the organ at the town church, "Zur Gotteshilfe" in Waltershausen, built by Heinrich Gottfried Trost. Like the organ in Waltershausen, the organ in Gera was "equipped with two large stars in each side." Five wedge bellows supplied the organ with the required wind. The instrument had mixtures containing third-sounding ranks, a trait also seen in other organs in Thuringia. The nicely varied stop list, with its multi-colored voices and considerable number of reeds, apparently appealed to Bach and probably matched his sound ideal. Unfortunately, both St. John's and its organ fell victim to a fire in 1780.

Dresden (1725, 1731, 1736)

Bach had his best opportunity to become acquainted with Silbermann organs in Dresden, at St. Sophie and at the Frauenkirche. On September 19 and 20, 1725, he played the organ at St. Sophie in the presence "of the local virtuoso musicians of the court and city."[60] The three-manual organ of 30 stops showed French influence in the stop list and included five reeds.[61] Like most Dresden organs of the eighteenth century, it was tuned to chamber pitch (approximately 415.5 Hz); the organs in Leipzig during Bach's time were tuned to choir pitch. Six years later, on the day following the première of Johann Adolf Hasse's opera *Cleofide* (September 14, 1731), Bach performed again at St. Sophie at 3:00 in the afternoon in the presence of all the court musicians and virtuosi.[62] Five years later, on December 1, 1736, he performed from 2:00 to 4:00 P.M. on the new organ in the Frauenkirche in the presence of "His Excellency the Russian Ambassador Baron von Keyserling and many other persons and artists."[63]

The Frauenkirche's three-manual, 43-stop Silbermann organ,[64] with its seven reeds and its Untersatz 32′ in the Pedal, may have impressed

Bach a great deal, though it is possible that he had reservations about certain aspects of its design. Agricola, who studied with Bach in Leipzig shortly after the Dresden trip,[65] expressed the following:

> Genuine Connoisseurs do not find much fault with Silbermann's organs, except for the unvaried stop lists, the obstinate temperament, and finally his weak Mixtures and Cymbels, which don't possess enough sharpness and clarity, especially for large churches. These three things he could have altered easily. On the other hand, specialists admire the outstanding meticulous workmanship, the quality and durability, the great simplicity of the interior mechanism, the unusually magnificent and full voicing, and the light action, which is easily playable.[66]

The uniformity of Silbermann's stop lists was a result of French influence. Concerning the temperament, Christian Ernst Friderici found fault with the fact that "Ab, C#, and B were hardly usable."[67] The Mixtures and the Cymbels, especially, are lacking the necessary high register, and that is why the *plenum* is deficient not in volume but in pungency.

Stöntzsch (1731)

On November 2, 1731, Bach traveled to Stöntzsch, near Pegau on the outskirts of Leipzig, to examine the organ in the Mauritiuskirche, which had been enlarged to twelve stops by the schoolteacher Johann Christoph Schmieder of Mölbis.[68] It originated from a small five-stop organ with a Dulcian-Regal 8′ and a Zimbelstern, built in 1678 by the school janitor and organist, Georg Öhme, in Gatzen.[69] Since only six stops and the two bellows had been completed by November, Bach tested the organ a second time, on February 4, 1732, after the remainder was finished. In his evaluation, Bach apparently had high praise for the instrument, but unfortunately his report is no longer extant. The original stop list can hardly be reconstructed, for the organ has been changed many times and has lost its former character. The Manual had a Principal 4′ in the facade, and perhaps a Gedackt 8′ (wood), a Gedackt 4′ (wood), a Quinte or Nasat 2-2/3′, an Octave 2′, and a Mixture III. The Pedal had a Subbass 16′ and Principalbass 8′, both of wood. Originally, there may have been reeds in the Manual and the Pedal. The instrument was tuned approximately a whole tone above 435 Hz. Since 1967 the organ has been located in the town church in Hohnstein.

Kassel (1732)

On September 21, 1732, Bach arrived in Kassel in order to test the organ of the Freyheitskirche of St. Martin. The original organ in the church had been built by Hans Scherer, Jr., and his brother Fritz from 1610 to 1614. The work was continued over a century later by the court organ builder Johann Friedrich Stertzing and was completed after his death by Nicolaus Becker of Mühlhausen.[70] The three-manual, 33-stop organ had an *Oberwerk*, an upper *Positiv*, a *Rückpositiv*, and a Pedal division.[71] Stertzing and Becker increased the number of stops and added a Posaune 32' in the Pedal, where only a 16' Posaune had existed before. The complete stop list, which had been altered between 1730 and 1732, is not known. The report by Bach has not been preserved, but he seems to have found fault with the wind supply, for in 1733 the bellows were installed in a lower position. The difficulties apparently arose from the addition of the two 32' Pedal stops, which required a great deal of wind. On Sunday, September 28, 1732, Bach played the organ dedication before a large gathering of the public.[72] This instrument is no longer extant.

Mühlhausen (1735)

In the beginning of June 1735, Bach went to Mühlhausen with his son Gottfried Bernhard, who had applied for the organist position at St. Mary's.[73] Sebastian was asked to give his opinion on the condition of the organ in the church, a request he fulfilled without remuneration. The three-manual, 60-stop instrument, which included fourteen reeds,[74] had been struck by lightning and needed extensive renovations, but it was hoped that isolated stops, such as the Principal 8', could be salvaged. Bach recommended Zacharias Hildebrandt of Leipzig to the Town Council, but the contract was awarded to Johann Friedrich Wender and his son Christian Friedrich, of Mühlhausen. The work was completed in 1738. The renovated organ, with a manual range CD–c''' and pedal range CD–d', consisted of only 43 stops, seven of which were reeds. In the *Hauptwerk*, the Principal chorus, ranging from a Principal 8' to Octave 2' and Mixtur VI, was well represented, as were the flutes and mutation stops. The Scharfe Cymbal III was probably used in conjunction with the 16' Basson and the Trompete 8'. The Principal choruses of the *Oberwerk* and the *Rückpositiv*, both based on 4' Principals, were incomplete. The *Oberwerk* had a reed "sordino," a muted Trompete 8'. Sesquialteras were available on the *Oberwerk* (Quinte 2-2/3' and Tertia 1-3/5') and the *Rückpositiv* (two ranks). The twelve-stop Pedal was exceptionally full: Posaune 32' and 16', Trompete 8', Cornettin 2', and flues from Principal 16' (in the case) and Untersatz 16' to Spitzflöte 2' and Rohrflöte 1'. Among the accessories were "two chamber couplers [*Kammerkoppeln*], one for large and the other for small chamber pitch throughout the entire organ." Whether Bach played a role as advisor is not known.

Altenburg (1739)

In September 1738 (or 1739?), Bach played the two-manual organ at the Castle Church in Altenburg built by Tobias Gottfried Heinrich Trost. He judged the construction durable and the quality of each voice lovely and very successful.[75] The instrument had 36 stops (including five reeds) distributed over two manuals and Pedal. In addition, there were five transmissions from the *Hauptwerk* to the Pedal and a Glockenspiel from c' to c''' on the *Hauptwerk*.[76] The tuning came rather close to equal temperament, with the exception of major thirds on B♭ and D♯, which were not consistent with Neidhardt I.[77]

Bad Berka (1742–43)

At the beginning of his last decade, Bach designed a stop list for a two-manual, 28-stop organ.[78] The stop list was discovered by Hans Löffler around 1931 in an organ manuscript from Thuringia dating from 1798.[79] It contained the following registers:

Hauptwerk		*Brustwerk* (=*Oberwerk*)		Pedal	
1. Principal	8'	1. Principal	4'	1. Subbass	16'
2. Quintadena	16'	2. Quintadena	8'	2. Principalbass	8'
3. Flöte	8'	3. Gedackt	8'	3. Hohlflöte	4'
4. Gedackt	8'	4. Nachthorn	4'	4. Posaune	16'
5. Gemshorn	8'	5. Quinte	2-2/3'	5. Trompete	8'
6. Gedackt	4'	6. Oktave	2'	6. Cornet	4'
7. Oktave	4'	7. Waldflöte	2'		
8. Quinte	2-2/3'	8. Tritonus	(=Terz		
9. Nasat	2-2/3'	9. Zimbel	1-3/5')		
10. Oktave	2'		3 ranks		
11. Sesquialtera	2 ranks				
12. Mixtur	5 ranks			Manual and Pedal	
13. Trompete	8'			couplers	

The design differs noticeably from a Silbermann stop list. First, there is a Quintadena 16' and numerous 8' stops in the *Hauptwerk*. Second, there is a five-rank Mixture in the manuals, a stop that Silbermann would never have made stronger than four ranks. And most of all, the strong Pedal, complete to the 4' stop, is rarely seen in Saxony in the eighteenth century. This stop list was realized in 1742–43 in Bad Berka, near Weimar, by Heinrich Nicolaus Trebs, his son Christian Welhelm, and their apprentice Johann Christian Immanuel Schweinefleisch.

Leipzig (1743)

In 1743 Bach and Zacharias Hildebrandt were commissioned to test the two-manual, 22-stop organ at St. John's, Leipzig, built in 1742–43 by Johann Scheibe.[80] The instrument was subject to one of the strictest tests ever performed on an organ and was declared to be free of fault by both Bach and Hildebrandt.[81]

Zschortau (1746)

On August 7, 1746, the ninth Sunday after Trinity, Bach tested the one-manual, thirteen-stop organ in the church of Zschortau near Delitzsch, built by Johann Scheibe in 1745–46.[82] The dedication took place the same day. In his evaluation,[83] Bach remarked that all aspects of the contract had been well carried out, and, aside from a few minor faults, which were corrected by Scheibe during the test, no major defects were found, not even in the four additional stops that were added beyond the contract:

1. Quinta Thön (wood)   16'
2. Viola di Gamba (wood)   8'
3. Fleute Travers (wood)   4'
4. Super Octava (metal)   1'
5. A draw-down mechanism between the manual and the pedal . . .

According to Paul Rubardt,[84] these four stops may have been included as a result of Bach's advice.

Naumburg (1743–46)

When the Town Council of Naumburg decided on August 26, 1743, to have a completely new instrument built for St. Wenzel's church, it requested an evaluation by the "Director Musices" in Leipzig.[85] (We know this from a letter by Bach to the Naumburg Town Council, written on July 24, 1748, in which he asked that his son-in-law Johann Christoph Altnikol be considered as an applicant for the vacant organist position at the church.[86]) When Bach submitted his evaluation, he may have also recommended Hildebrandt as a builder. In any case, it can also be assumed that Bach had considerable influence in the drafting of the stop list. The three-manual organ includes 53 stops, among which are eight reeds. Each division includes a fully developed Principal chorus, based on a Principal 16' in the *Hauptwerk* and the Pedal, and Principal 8' in the *Oberwerk* and *Rückpositiv*.

The *Hauptwerk* also contains a 16' Quintadena, as in large North German organs. Gedeckts, flutes, and other color stops are well represented through to 2' pitch. The *Rückpositiv* includes two strings, Viol di Gamba 8' and Fugara 4', made of tin and somewhat narrowly scaled, becoming a bit wider at the top. The Pedal Violon 16' is of wood, and the Violon 8' is of metal; both are conically shaped. The *Hauptwerk* is equipped with a Sesquialtera II; the *Oberwerk* with a Quinta 2-2/3' and Tertia 1-3/5'; and the Pedal has a metal Nachthorn 2', which is especially suitable for cantus firmus playing. The *Hauptwerk* reeds are a Bombart 16', made of wood in the lower register and of metal in the higher register, and a Trompete 8', made of metal. The *Oberwerk* has a Vox Humana 8' in the approximate shape of a Doppelkegelregal. The *Rückpositiv* has a Fagott 16' in the form of a Dulcian, as in Divi Blassii at Mühlhausen, where it was located in the *Hauptwerk*. The Pedal is outfitted with four reeds: Posaune 32' and Posaune 16', both of wood, and Trompete 8' and Clarin 4', both of tin. The Naumburg organ was originally tuned to choir pitch and was tempered according to Neidhardt,[87] whose temperament had already been advocated by Bach's predecessor in Leipzig, Johann Kuhnau. The official test of the organ was carried out by Bach and Gottfried Silbermann on September 27, 1746.[88]

Potsdam (1747)

On May 8, 1747, Bach played the organ in the Heiliggeistkirche in Potsdam while visiting Frederick the Great. It is to be lamented that nothing is known about this instrument, which was used in Bach's last documented public concert.

(TRANSLATED BY ERNEST MAY AND FRIGGA SCOTT)

NOTES

1. See the comments on Johann Christoph Bach in J. S. Bach's Obituary (BDok III, no. 666; *Bach Reader*, pp. 215–16).
2. David, pp. 11–12, 78.
3. E. Lux, "Das Orgelwerk in St. Michaelis in Ohrdruf," BJ 1926:145–55; Hans Löffler, "J. S. Bach und die Orgeln seiner Zeit," in *Bericht über die 3. Tagung für deutsche Orgelkunst in Freiberg in Sachsen* (Kassel, 1928), p. 123; Ernst Flade, "Bachs Stellung zum Orgel- und Klavierbau seiner Zeit," in *Bericht über die wissenschaftl. Bachtagung der Gesellschaft für Musikforschung* (Leipzig, 1950), p. 406; David, pp. 12–14 and 79.
4. Michael Praetorius, *Syntagma musicum II: De organographia* (Wolffenbüttel, 1619; reprint Kassel, 1958), p. 170; P. Smets, editor, *Die Dresdener Handschrift, Orgeldispositionen* (Kassel, 1931), nos. XLV and XLVI; Charles Sanford Terry, *Bach: A Biography* (London, 1933), chapter 3; Löffler, in *Bericht über die 3. Tagung*, p. 123; Gustav Fock, *Der junge Bach in Lüneburg* (Hamburg, 1950), p. 81; David, pp. 14–16 and 80–81.
5. David, p. 19; BDok I, no. 38.
6. David, p. 20; Reinhold Jauernig, "Johann Sebastian Bach in Weimar," in *Johann Sebastian Bach in Thüringen: Festgabe zum Gedenkjahr 1950* (Weimar, 1950), pp. 51–52.
7. Spitta I, pp. 218–21; Terry, *Bach*, pp. 60–75; Hans Löffler, "J. S. Bachs Orgelprüfungen," BJ 1925: 93; Karl Müller, "J. S. Bach in Arnstadt," in *Johann Sebastian Bach in Thüringen*, pp. 30–46; David, pp. 20–22 and 83–84; BDok IV, nos. 54–57; Annemarie Niemeyer, Alwin Friedel, and Karl Müller, *265 Jahre Arnstädter Bach-Orgel* (39. Deutschen Bachfest der Neuen Bachgesellschaft: Weimar, 1964); Hans Klotz, *Über die Orgelkunst der Gotik, der Renaissance und des Barock* (Kassel, 1975), pp. 379–80.
8. Klotz, *Über die Orgelkunst*, p. 379.
9. Niemeyer, et al., *265 Jahre*, p. 10.
10. Smets, no. XLIV; David, pp. 24–27 and 85–86.
11. BDok I, no. 83; David, p. 27; Wilhelm Martini, "Die Gehrener Bache," in *Johann Sebastian Bach in Thüringen*, p. 216.
12. BDok I, no. 83; *Bach Reader*, pp. 58–60; Joh. Lorenz Albrecht, in Jakob Adlung, *Musica mechanica organoedi* (Berlin, 1768), vol. I, p. 260; Spitta I, pp. 350–53; Terry, *Bach*, pp. 74–81; Löffler, BJ 1925: 93 and 99–100; Löffler, in *Bericht über die 3. Tagung*, pp. 125 and 130; Gotthold Frotscher, "Zur Problematik der Bach-Orgel," BJ 1935: 107–21; Hermann Keller, *The Organ Works of Bach* (New York, 1967), pp. 19–21 and 237–38; Ulrich Dähnert, "J. S. Bach's Ideal Organ," *The Organ Yearbook* I(1970): 34; Klotz, *Über die Orgelkunst*, pp. 380–83; David, pp. 27–29, 35, 70–71, 86–87; Ernest Zavarsky, "J. S. Bachs Entwurf für den Umbau der Orgel in der Kirche Divi Blasii und das Klangideal der Zeit," in *Bach-Studien 5* (Leipzig, 1975), pp. 83–92.
13. David, p. 11.
14. Spitta I, pp. 394–95; Keller, *Organ Works*, p. 175; Klotz, NBA IV/3, KB, pp. 45–47.
15. Königsberg 15839 and Plauen III.B.a.No.4, according to NBA IV/3, KB, p. 46; see also Peter Williams, *The Organ Music of J. S. Bach* (Cambridge, 1980–84), vol. II, pp. 260–63.
16. Jauernig, "J. S. Bach in Weimar," pp. 49–105; David, pp. 29–33 and 88.
17. In Klotz, *Über die Orgelkunst*, p. 381, the compass is given as manuals, C–c‴; pedal, C–d′. Dietrich Kilian (in NBA IV/5–6, KB, vol. I, p. 185) has

concluded, however, that the pedal compass was, in fact, C–e′.

18. David, p. 88; Thekla Schneider, "Die Orgelbauerfamilie Compenius," in *Archiv für Musikforschung* II(1937): 75.

19. Spitta I, pp. 380 and 794; Albert Schweitzer, *J. S. Bach* (Leipzig, 1948), p. 95; Jauernig, "J. S. Bach in Weimar," p. 95; David, p. 33.

20. Johann Gottfried Walther, *Musikalisches Lexikon* (Leipzig, 1732; reprint: Kassel, 1953), p. 333; Paul Rubardt, in *Kamenzer Orgelbuch* (Kamenz, 1953), p. 16.

21. Smets, no. CIL (p. 70); Adlung, *Musica mechanica organoedi*, vol. I, p. 281; David, pp. 34 and 89.

22. David, pp. 35–36 and 90; Paul Rubardt, "Zwei originale Orgeldispositionen J. S. Bachs," in *Festschrift Heinrich Besseler zum sechzigsten Geburtstag* (Leipzig, 1961), p. 496; Jauernig, "J. S. Bach in Weimar," pp. 82–87.

23. BDok I, no. 84; *Bach Reader*, p. 64.

24. Adlung, *Musica mechanica organoedi*, vol. I, p. 282; David, pp. 34 and 91; Klotz, *Über die Orgelkunst*, pp. 381–82.

25. Spitta I, pp. 508–16 and 802–803; Löffler, BJ 1925: 94; Löffler, *Bericht über d. 3. Tagung*, p. 126; David, pp. 36–37 and 91–92.

26. BDok II, nos. 62–63; *Bach Reader*, pp. 65–68.

27. BDok I, no. 85; *Bach Reader*, pp. 71–74. For the stop list, see David, pp. 91–92. Terry, *Bach*, gives May 3 as the day of the dedication. See also BDok II, no. 76.

28. Adlung, *Musica mechanica organoedi*, vol. I, p. 218; David, pp. 39, 73–74, and 93; Ferdinand Carspecken, *Fünfhundert Jahre Kasseler Orgeln* (Kassel, 1968), p. 120.

29. Johann Friedrich Stertzing was the son of Georg Christoph Stertzing, who from 1696 to 1707 had constructed the large four-manual organ at St. George's, Eisenach, according to the specification drawn up by Johann Christoph Bach, J. S. Bach's uncle. Among its unusual features were the Cornet 2′ and Bauerflöte 1′ in the Pedal. However, contrary to J. S. Bach's Mühlhausen organ specification, St. George's had no Fagott 16′ in the *Hauptwerk*.

30. BDok I, no. 86; *Bach Reader*, pp. 74–75.

31. David, pp. 41–42.

32. See NBA IV/5–6, KB, vol. I, p. 186.

33. Rubardt, in *Festschrift Heinrich Besseler*, pp. 496 and 503n5.

34. See Ulrich Dähnert, *Historische Orgeln in Sachsen* (Leipzig, 1980), pp. 132–34.

35. Wilhelm Stieda, "Der Neubau der Pauliner Kirche in den Jahren 1710–12," *Schriften des Vereins für die Geschichte Leipzigs* XXII(1958): 75–79.

36. However, the contract was not concluded until May 11, 1711.

37. Smets, no. LXXVI; *Sammlung einiger Nachrichten* (Breslau; 1757), p. 55 (see Albrecht in Adlung, *Musica mechanica organoedi*, vol. I, p. 251); Dähnert, *Historische Orgeln*, pp. 183–84; Spitta II, pp. 117–22; David, pp. 43–45 and 94–95.

38. Rubardt, in *Festschrift Besseler*, p. 503n5.

39. BDok I, no. 87; *Bach Reader*, pp. 76–78.

40. Smets, nos. XXVI/XXVII; Dähnert, *The Organ Yearbook* I(1970): 22 and 33; David, p. 82; Gustav Fock, "Die Hauptepochen des norddeutschen Orgelbaus bis Schnitger," in *Orgelbewegung und Historismus* (Berlin, 1958), p. 44; Fock, "Zur Geschichte der Schnitger-Orgel in St. Jacobi," in *Die Arp-Schnitger-Orgel der Hauptkirche St. Jacobi Hamburg: Festschrift* (Hamburg, 1961), pp. 9–20; Klotz, "Joh. Seb. Bach und die Orgel," *Musik und Kirche* 32 (1962): 50.

41. *Bach Reader*, p. 217.

42. *Bach Reader*, p. 219.

43. Johann Friedrich Agricola, in Adlung, *Musica mechanica organoedi*, vol. I, p. 66, note to section 104; p. 187, note to section 267; p. 288nα.

44. Ibid., p. 288nα.

45. Walther Vetter, *Der Kapellmeister Bach* (Potsdam, 1950), p. 144.

46. Heinz Wunderlich, "Die Schnitger-Orgel der Hauptkirche St. Jacobi zu Hamburg und ihre Bedeutung für die Orgelbewegung," in Fock, *Die Arp-Schnitger-Orgel . . . Festschrift*, p. 30.

47. Ibid, pp. 29 and 33.

48. Bernhardt H. Edskes, in *Arp Schnitger en zijn werk in het Groningerland* in *Publikaties van de Stichting Groningen Orgelland*, no. 1 (1969), p. 35.

49. Spitta II, pp. 116–17 and 770; David, pp. 53–54 and 97; Dähnert, *Historische Orgeln*, pp. 180–81.

50. Spitta II, pp. 111–16, 769–70, and 870–72; David, pp. 51–53 and 96; Dähnert, *Historische Orgeln*, pp. 184–86.

51. Adlung, *Musica mechanica organoedi*, vol. I, pp. 179, 289; vol. II, pp. 8, 19, and 22.

52. According to Jakob Adlung, *Anleitung zu der musikalischen Gelahrtheit* (Erfurt, 1758), p. 453, Rauschpfeif is a compound stop following Principal scaling, which usually consists of Quint 3' and Octav 2'.

53. Spitta II, pp. 113 and 769–70; Dähnert, *Historische Orgeln*, p. 185.

54. Adlung, *Anleitung*, p. 413, section 150; Adlung, *Musica mechanica organoedi*, vol. I, pp. 90 and 92.

55. Spitta II, pp. 194–95; Paul Rubardt, *Alte Orgeln erklingen wieder* (Leipzig, 1936), p. 13; Rubardt, in *Joh. Seb. Bach: Das Schaffen des Meisters im Spiegel einer Stadt* (Leipzig, 1950), p. 103; David, pp. 56 and 99; Ernst Flade, *Gottfried Silbermann* (Leipzig, 1953), pp. 115 and 200; Dähnert, *Der Orgel- und Instrumentenbauer Zacharias Hildebrandt* (Leipzig, 1962), pp. 30–33, and 158–64; Dähnert, *Historische Orgeln*, p. 258; BDok II, nos. 163 and 164.

56. The Tuesday following Trinity XXIII.

57. BDok II, nos. 183 and 183a.

58. Terry, *Bach*, p. 159; Löffler, "J. S. Bach in Gera," BJ 1924: 125–27; Löffler, BJ 1925: 95; Löffler, in *Bericht über die 3. Tagung*, pp. 127 and 131; Ferdinand Hahn, *Geschichte von Gera* (Gera, 1855); David, p. 57.

59. Adlung, *Musica mechanica organoedi*, vol. I, p. 229; David, pp. 99–100.

60. BDok II, no. 193.

61. For the specifications, see Ernst Flade, *Gottfried Silbermann* (Leipzig, 1953), p. 109; Dähnert, *Die Orgeln Gottfried Silbermanns in Mitteldeutschland* (Leipzig, 1953), pp. 195 and 197; Dähnert, *Historische Orgeln*, p. 86. On the *Hauptwerk*, it was possible to compose a *Grand jeu*: Trompete 8', Clarin 4', Cornet V, and a wide-scaled Terz, along with the open and stopped flutes.

62. BDok II, nos. 294 and 294a.

63. BDok II, no. 389; *Bach Reader*, p. 151.

64. Smets, no. CXIV, Dähnert, *Die Orgeln Silbermanns*, p. 206; Dähnert, *Historische Orgeln*, pp. 69–70; David, pp. 61–62.

65. Löffler, BJ 1953: 22; also in *Johann Sebastian Bach in Thüringen*, pp. 176 and 181.

66. Adlung, *Musica mechanica organoedi*, vol. I, p. 212; quoted in Dähnert, *The Organ Yearbook* I(1970): 23.

67. Karl-Marxstadt, Stadtarchiv, Cap.IV, Sect.II no. 29, B1.50a, ad 9 (letter of April 25, 1766 from Friderici to the Superintendent, Bürgermeister, and Town Council of Chemnitz).

68. Löffler, BJ 1925: 95; Rubardt, *Alte Orgeln*, p. 19; Rubardt in *Joh. Seb. Bach: Das Schaffen des Meisters*, p. 104; David, pp. 58–59 and 101; Dähnert, *Historische Orgeln*, pp. 156–58; BDok II, no. 298.

69. Pegau, Pfarrarchiv, Rechnungsbuch Stöntzsch, 1661–1715, p. 249.

70. David, pp. 59–60; Carspecken, pp. 53–55; BDok II, nos. 315–18; *Bach Reader*, pp. 127–28.

71. Praetorius, pp. 183–84; Smets, no. CIV (p. 54); Carspecken, pp. 51–52.

72. NBA IV/5–6, KB, vol. II, pp. 363–65.

73. Löffler, BJ 1925: 96; Löffler, in *Bericht über die 3. Tagung*, p. 125; David, pp. 60–61; BDok II, nos. 365 and 393.

74. Smets, no. XLVIII; Johann Lorenz Albrecht, in Adlung, *Musica mechanica organoedi*, vol. I, p. 259; David, pp. 102–103.

75. BDok II, no. 453.

76. See the discussion in David, pp. 62–63. For the specifications, see Dähnert, "Geschichte der Schlosskirchen-Orgel in Altenburg," *The Organ Yearbook* X (1979): 55–57; Dähnert, *Historische Orgeln*, pp. 20–25; and Felix Friedrich, "Johann Sebastian Bach und die Trost-Orgel zu Altenburg. Bemerkungen zur Problematik der 'Bach-Orgel,'" BJ 1983: 107.

77. Ulrich Dähnert, in *Musik des Ostens*, vol. 9 (Kassel, 1983), p. 235.

78. Rubardt, in *Festschrift Heinrich Besseler*, p. 498.

79. Löffler, "Ein unbekanntes Thüringer Orgelmanuskript von 1798," *Musik und Kirche* III (1931): 140. The manuscript, once in the possession of the Eisenach collector Manfred Gorke, is now in the Bach-Archiv Leipzig.

80. BDok II, no. 519; Agricola, in Adlung, *Musica mechanica organoedi*, vol. I, p. 251n; Dähnert, *Hildebrandt*, pp. 85–86 and 103; Dähnert, *Historische Orgeln*, pp. 177–78; David, p. 98.

81. BDok III, no. 740.

82. BDok II, no. 545; David, pp. 64, 75–76, and 104; Dähnert, *Historische Orgeln*, pp. 285–86.

83. BDok I, no. 89; *Bach Reader*, pp. 173–74.

84. Rubardt, in *Festschrift Heinrich Besseler*, p. 496.

85. Dähnert, *Hildebrandt*, pp. 86–102 and 189–99; Dähnert, *The Organ Yearbook* I (1970): 27 and 35.

86. *Bach Reader*, p. 181.

87. Dähnert, *Hildebrandt*, pp. 115–16; Dähnert, *The Organ Yearbook* I (1970): 28; see also Johann Kuhnau to Johann Mattheson (Leipzig, December 8, 1717), in *Critica Musica*, vol. II (Hamburg, 1725; reprint Amsterdam, 1964), pp. 233–39.

88. BDok I, no. 90; BDok II, nos. 546 and 547; *Bach Reader*, p. 174.

HARTMUT HAUPT

◈

Bach Organs in Thuringia

Bach's connections with the organ were manifold. He was not only a practicing artist and composer for the instrument but also an authoritative consultant on organ design and construction. His appraisals, tests, and recommendations document this ability.[1] It was Bach who dared to express the rising new style and tonal ideals. His strong artistic personality, whose effects can still be felt today, overcame obstacles and resistance. His registrations were far ahead of his time and were not generally accepted until the nineteenth century.[2] When Bach was but 21, he surprised and shocked his Arnstadt audience with new sounds. His daring chorale harmonizations and rich style of playing confused the clergy as well as the congregation and left the bellows blower struggling for air. However, the magic of his playing and his "unusual combinations of voices" were difficult to resist. By the nineteenth century he had become a legend, to judge from C. F. D. Schubart's romanticized description of his prowess at the organ: "He executed fast passages in the pedal with greatest accuracy; changes in registration were carried out so smoothly that the listener was caught up in the whirlwind of his wizardry."[3]

As a performer, Bach set high standards for himself and expected the same of instruments. His organ tests usually began by "pulling all the sounding stops and playing the instrument with its fullest possible tone." Jokingly he would explain that, above all, he must know if the finished instrument had "good lungs."[4] He then tested various combinations of stops and "displayed each register according to its character in the greatest perfection."[5]

Bach's recommendations for organs can be outlined briefly as follows:

1. The sound of the organ must possess depth. Bach apparently liked low sonority and seemed to have had a special predilection for the 32' range in the pedal.

2. There should be a sufficient number of 8' and 4' registers on the manuals, including colorful foundation stops such as Viol di gamba, Salicional, and other solo labial 8' stops with pleasant sounds that would blend well among themselves.

3. Stops reinforcing the third should be present in order to add variety to the organ ensemble.

4. The organ must be capable of achieving a *plenum*.

5. There must be an adequate wind-generating capacity and a sufficient air reserve, in order to avoid sudden changes in wind pressure. This requirement resulted in Bach's request for larger bellows, and larger cross-sections but shorter connections for the windways.

6. Bach tolerated, if not even endorsed, a Glockenspiel on the organ.

This list of recommendations has been culled from various sources, for Bach requested these items at different locations and times. The only project we can trace in detail is the two-manual organ in the Church of St. Blasius in Mühlhausen, which Johann Friedrich Wender rebuilt in 1708–1709 according to Bach's specifications and under his supervision.[6] In the specifications, which show certain correspondences to Werckmeister's recommendations,[7] Bach made the following specific demands:

1. Addition of a 32' Untersatz in the Pedal, "which will give the instrument depth and the best gravity"; rebuilding of the Pedal Posaune 16', "enabling greater depth and gravity"; and replacing the Trompete 8' with a Fagott 16' in the upper manual.

2. Addition of a *Brustwerk* as a third manual to give the organ a more complete sound.

3. Addition of a Viol di gamba 8' in the upper manual (in place of a Gemshorn 8'), which "will blend admirably" with the Salicional 4' on the *Rückpositiv*; a Stillgedackt 8' on the new *Brustwerk*, to be made of good quality wood and which will sound much better than a metal Gedackt.

4. A new Tertia, included in the *Brustwerk* to complement the Sesquialteras of the *Oberwerk* and *Rückpositiv*.

5. Correction of the insufficient wind supply. Three new strong bellows are to be added for the manuals. The four old ones are to be used to produce the necessary wind for the 32' stop and the bass

stops. The old bass wind chests are to be "supplied with such wind conduction so that one stop alone or all the stops together can be sounded without a change in wind pressure—something which has not been possible in the past and yet is very necessary."

6. Addition of the Glockenspiel with 26 bells (desired by the parishioners).

In his organ-related travels through Thuringia, Bach had contact with a number of builders: Wender, Finke, Schröter, Trebs, and Trost. And at the following locations, he either tested the organ, played for a special occasion, or was regularly employed:

Ohrdruf, St. Michael's (small organ). Bach probably practiced here while he studied with his older brother Johann Christoph.

Ohrdruf, St. Michael's (large organ). Bach probably witnessed the rebuilding of this instrument.

Arnstadt, St. Bonifatius. Examination of the new instrument in 1703 and employment immediately following.

Langewiesen, Town Church. Examination of the new organ in 1706.

Mühlhausen, St. Blasius'. Organ rebuilt in 1708–1709 according to Bach's recommendations.

Weimar, Castle Church. Court organist 1708–17. The organ was rebuilt in 1714, probably according to Bach's recommendations. A Glockenspiel was included.

Weimar, Town Church. Bach possibly played here while the organ at the Castle Church was being rebuilt.

Taubach, Town Church. Examination and acceptance of the new organ in 1710.

Erfurt, St. Augustine. Examination and acceptance of the new organ in 1716.

Gera, St. John's. Examination and acceptance of the new organ in 1724.

Gera, St. Salvator. Examination and acceptance of the new organ in 1724.

Mühlhausen, St. Mary's. Examination and recommendation to rebuild the instrument in 1735.

Altenburg, Castle Church. Examination of the new organ in 1739.

Unfortunately, of these Thuringian instruments played by Bach, only the Altenburg organ, built in 1735–39 by T. G. H. Trost, exists today.[8] It was subjected to numerous changes but has now been re-

stored according to Trost's original specifications by the organ-building firm VEB Eule Bautzen.[9] The organ at St. Blasius' in Mühlhausen
is no longer in its original form. Its condition was greatly regretted by
no less than Albert Schweitzer, who was instrumental in the movement to rebuild the organ. The reconstruction was finally undertaken
by VEB Potsdamer Schuke-Orgelbau, together with the Mühlhausen
organist Heinz Sawade, and was completed in 1958.[10]

Since only one of the Thuringian organs that Bach is known to have
played has survived, it is of interest to study other instruments in
Thuringia that may reflect his requirements and recommendations.
One example is the organ in the Castle Church of Eisenberg, originally built around 1685 by Christoph Donat of Leipzig according to
ideals and concepts common in pre-Bach times. Approximately 50
years later, however, a number of changes were made by Trost. They
correspond to many of Bach's recommendations for other instruments, and considering his close ties with Trost, may even stem from
his advice:[11]

1. Trost achieved depth and gravity through changes in the Pedal
(a Subbass 16' was reconstructed of wood instead of metal, and an Octavbass 8' replaced a Schalmey 4').

2. The 8' labial stops of the *Oberwerk* were enriched by adding a
Flauto traverso "with a pleasing sound."

3. A richer ensemble was achieved by adding a rank reinforcing the
third in the Mixture of the *Oberwerk*.

4. A fuller and more rounded tone quality was produced by rescal-
ing most of the stops.

5. The entire air supply system was rebuilt, allowing full chords to
be played without causing deficiencies in the wind.

These changes are reminiscent of Bach's recommendations for rebuilding the St. Blasius organ in 1708. A reconstruction of the Eisenberg instrument according to the original specifications is planned.

It seems most likely that Bach knew of and observed Trost's largest
and most important project, the organ at Waltershausen (1722–1730),
and followed its completion with interest. Research by VEB Eule
Bautzen concerning the original specifications shows that Bach's ideas
and principles are reflected in parts of this organ as well. In this three-
manual, 46-stop instrument:

1. Depth and gravity are achieved with the 32' stop in the Pedal
and three 16' stops in the *Hauptwerk*.

2. Colorful stops at 8′ and 4′ pitch are abundant (Viol di gamba 8′, Fugara 8′, Flöte dupla 8′, Schweizerflöte 8′, Unda maris 8′, Salicional 4′, Geigenprincipal 4′, Fleute douce 4′) and can be used soloistically or in combination.

3. Third-sounding ranks (in Mixtures) are present.

4. The air supply is sufficient to play the *plenum*.

5. Two Glockenspiels are included in the stop list.

This organ approaches the type of instrument envisioned in the Romantic era. It, too, is presently being considered for restoration.

Glockenspiels are abundant in Thuringian organs of the eighteenth century, and it may be that Bach approved and used this stop. An instrument built by J. G. Schröter in Klettbach, still in virtually its original condition, has a Glockenspiel with 26 notes playable from the *Oberwerk*. Hence one can hear a 26-note Glockenspiel almost like the one desired by the parishioners at St. Blasius'.

Research on Bach's influence in Thuringian organ building continues, and certainly new discoveries lie on the horizon. Bach's spirit and influence remain strong today, and the surviving organs from his epoch are treasured as guiding beacons from an enlightened era.

(TRANSLATED BY FRIGGA SCOTT AND ERNEST MAY)

NOTES

1. See Werner David, *Johann Sebastian Bachs Orgeln* (Berlin, 1951).

2. See Winfried Schrammek, "Versuch über J. S. Bachs Vorstellungen von Orgelbau, Orgeldisposition und Orgelregistrierung," *Bach-Studien* 7, edited by Reinhard Szeskus (Leipzig, 1982), pp. 192–211.

3. BDok III, no. 903.

4. BDok III, no. 801; *Bach Reader*, p. 276.

5. BDok III, no. 666; *Bach Reader*, p. 223.

6. BDok I, no. 83; *Bach Reader*, pp. 58–60.

7. Peter Williams, "J. S. Bach—Orgelsachverständiger unter dem Einfluss Andreas Werckmeisters?" BJ 1982: 131–32.

8. For an account of Bach's contact with this instrument, see BDok II, no. 453.

9. Described in Felix Friedrich et al., *Geschichte und Rekonstruktion der Trost-Orgel in der Konzerthalle Schlosskirche Altenburg* (Altenburg, 1978). See also Ulrich Dähnert, "Geschichte der Schlosskirchen-Orgel in Altenburg," *The Organ Yearbook* 10 (1979); and most recently, Felix Friedrich, "Johann Sebastian Bach und die Trost-Orgel zu Altenburg. Bemerkungen zur Problematik der 'Bach-Orgel,'" BJ 1983: 101–108.

10. For a discussion of the Mühlhausen organ specification, see Ernest

Zavarsky, "J. S. Bachs Entwurf für den Umbau der Orgel in der Kirche Divi Blasii und das Klangideal der Zeit," in *Bach-Studien* 5, edited by Rudolf Eller and Hans-Joachim Schulze (Leipzig, 1975).

11. See Ulrich Dähnert, "Die Donat-Trost-Orgel in der Schlosskirche zu Eisenberg in Thüringen," *Walcker-Hausmitteilungen* 31 (July 1963).

HARALD VOGEL

❧❧

North German Organ Building of the Late Seventeenth Century

Registration and Tuning

The development of the North German organ proceeded in an unbroken line from the late Middle Ages to the "golden era" of Arp Schnitger and his school. Without entirely relinquishing the tonal characteristics of earlier periods, a new style was launched, assimilating particularly Dutch Renaissance influences and the ingenious scaling and construction techniques of Gottfried Fritzsche and his followers. Starting with the Gothic *Blockwerk* and its intense Principal sound, North German organ builders of the sixteenth century gradually added *Rückpositiv, Oberwerk (Oberpositiv)* and *Brustwerk*. After 1600 the "multiple choir" arrangement of these various divisions became the aesthetic ideal. The large pedal towers constructed on either side of the main case, developed by the Scherer family and its circle, were a special feature of this style. With the introduction of 32′ facade pipes in the seventeenth century, these towers grew to monumental proportions. It was not just in its outward appearance, however, that the North German organ reflected both old and new; the continuous re-use of existing stops also contributed to the unusual synthesis that had been achieved. It is small wonder that the organ literature of North Germany shows a stylistic pluralism unparalleled in the seventeenth century. Since there are so few registration indications present in actual compositions, however, it is essential to begin a discussion of registrational practices by examining four basic categories of sound available on the North German organ:

1. The *plenum* (the cylindrical open pipes of the Principal chorus, from the facade pipes to the high-pitched mixtures). This *plenum*

sound, with its doublings of ranks reinforcing the octave and fifth, was an inheritance from the Gothic *Blockwerk*. It was fortified, especially in the mid-seventeenth century, by the addition of high-pitched ranks as well as ranks stressing the third (usually in the form of Sesquialtera or Tertian). This desire to strengthen the *plenum* was a result of the increasing use of the organ to accompany congregational singing. (In the sixteenth century, there had been no connection whatsoever between organ playing and congregational singing.) Increasingly during the seventeenth century, reed stops were added to the North German *plenum*, first in the Pedal and then in the manuals. (These reeds were smoother and blended better with the *plenum*.) The development of a colorful *plenum* enriched with reeds and "third" ranks reached its peak in the work of Schnitger and his school.

2. The vocal quality of the principals (especially in the praestants, or facade pipes). The concept that each pipe should tonally approximate the human voice, with a speech of differentiated consonants and vowels, was a legacy of the Renaissance organ ideal. While Italian organ building from the sixteenth century onward concentrated almost entirely on the vocal quality of the *Principale* (8'), North German organ building retained this vocal ideal primarily in the foundation principals at 16', 8', and 4' pitches.

3. The instrumental character of the "consort" registers (primarily the reed and flute stops). These stops imitate the sound of existing instruments and bear the names of their models—Dulcian, Krummhorn, Blockflöte, Posaune, etc. It is possible to register a homogeneous consort sound corresponding to a complete family of instruments, ranging from bass to soprano. Or one can realize the mixed consort sound by using stops from different families on different keyboards. These purely instrumental tone colors are a legacy from the late sixteenth and early seventeenth centuries, when organ builders displayed a special delight in experimenting with new timbres. The consort ideal was carried to an extreme in the famous Compenius organ at Fredriksborg Castle, Denmark, built in 1610. Schnitger retained the late-Renaissance and early-Baroque sounds in his instruments. By contrast, many of his contemporaries—especially in Central Germany—sought not the greatest possible tonal variety but tonal unity with variety achieved through dynamics.

4. The mutation stops (individual ranks at the fifth or third, as well as compound stops). Mutation stops produce a remarkably colorful sound, one especially useful for solo registrations. This practice of

coloring a solo registration with the so-called *Aliquots* (mutations) apparently originated around 1500 in organ building along the Rhine.

The blending potential of stops of all types is of fundamental importance to North German registrational practice. Principals, flutes, reeds, and mutations can be drawn together without hesitation. This blending ability was significantly strengthened by the pure-third mean-tone, or "Praetorian," temperament in common use in the seventeenth century. It should be noted, however, that all available registers were never combined into a *tutti*. The sensitive wind supply alone would have made such a *tutti* unthinkable. While the flexible wind endowed the sound with a breathing quality, it would have been too unsteady with all the stops drawn. In any event, the *tutti* is no louder than a carefully chosen selection of *plenum* stops (principals and reeds)—it is simply thicker and less clear. Indeed, the principle of economy is very important in the registration of the North German repertoire. The desired sound is best achieved with the smallest possible number of registers. (Doubling of ranks at the same pitch is possible, but chiefly at 16' or 8' pitch. Higher-pitched stops of dissimilar scaling react differently to the changes of wind pressure inherent in the old wind system and can, therefore, sound out of tune with one another.)

In contrast to the Catholic countries, where the organ repertoire developed largely in the form of versettes of limited duration, the Protestant North fostered the dissolution of liturgical forms, making it possible for the organ literature to achieve much greater independence. That resulted in the creation of autonomous musical forms. Freedom of tonal imagination no doubt led the North German organists away from codifying registrations, in a manner similar to that of their French contemporaries of the seventeenth and eighteenth centuries.

For us to understand the possibilities of North German registrational practices, the different stylistic layers of the repertoire must be correlated with the above-mentioned categories of sound. The *plenum* was specifically reserved for thick, chordally oriented compositions (for example, the *Modus ludendi pleno organo . . .* published at the end of Samuel Scheidt's *Tabulatura Nova* of 1624). There is no evidence that the *plenum* was ever used in the performance of complicated polyphony. References to the sixteenth-century motet style (for example, in Praetorius and Antegnati) indicate time and time again the central role of the "vocal" principal sound, particularly at 8′ pitch. Likewise, the many references to consort registrations in Michael Praetorius' description of organ stops in *De Organographia* assign no role to the *plenum*. In Scheidt's registrational indications in the *Tabulatura Nova*, mixtures are only mentioned in a discussion of solo registrations. In strict polyphony, the *plenum* sound confuses the intervals between voices. It also destroys the identity of each voice in terms of range; with the repetition of the high mixture ranks, all voices sound almost equally "high."

However, at the same time that the *plenum* was being relegated to a secondary role in the "consort organ" described so thoroughly by Praetorius in *De Organographia*, it was experiencing a major revival in seventeenth-century North Germany because of its connection with congregational singing. As a result of its new function in the church service, the *plenum* became the center of tonal interest in the late seventeenth and the eighteenth century. Moreover, an attempt was made to develop a new organ polyphony—one that could be performed with the *plenum*. While the precursors of this development can be found among seventeenth-century North German composers, it was J. S. Bach who first succeeded in combining the musical concept of strict polyphony with the true tonal identity of the organ, the *plenum*. Indeed, the art of *plenum* polyphony reached its peak in his work.

The antique North German organs make it apparent, however, that both the vocally oriented polyphonic music of the sixteenth century and the instrumentally oriented consort music of the seventeenth century are noticeably harmed by the use of strong mixtures. An examination of the relationship between polyphony and *plenum* is therefore crucial for understanding the registrational practice of any period, because each generation seems to have exhibited a different attitude toward the use of the *plenum* sound. One misconception of the twentieth century is that mixtures render every polyphonic work clear and precise. The mid-twentieth century's extreme attraction to the *plenum* can be understood on the one hand as a reaction to the infrequent use of mixtures in the late-nineteenth and the early-twentieth century, and on the other as an expressionistic love of dissonance. The imposition of equal temperament further detracts from a most important characteristic of the North German *plenum*—its blending quality, which is achieved in spite of strongly voiced and high-pitched ranks. Fortunately, many antique organs in North Germany are tuned in non-equal temperaments. A fundamental guideline for North German registrational practice is the principle that the more complicated and consistently polyphonic the work, the fewer the stops that should be used.[1]

Within the toccata-like sections of the North German *stylus phantasticus* repertoire, it is very important to alternate between the contrasting *plena* of the *Rückpositiv* and *Hauptwerk* (sometimes of the *Brustwerk*, as well). In this way large blocks of sound are clearly set apart and gain increased spatial depth. Alternating the pedal with contrasting manual *plena* adds still another dimension in works such as the *Praeludium* in D, BuxWV 139, of Buxtehude (mm.13–16) or the *Praeludium* in d of Lübeck (mm.35–40). The fugal sections can be registered with a wide variety of consort sounds (reed stops, especially, can be exploited here). Because of the great blending quality of the North German reeds, they can be registered not only singly but also in combination with principals or flutes or in the *plenum*. This arrangement applies equally to the reeds with full-length resonators (Trompet, Posaune, Schalmei, Cornet) and to those with half-length (Regal, Krummhorn, Dulcian, Vox Humana). In a reed *plenum* (based on a low-pitched reed stop such as the Trompet 16' or 8' or the Dulcian 16', with the principal chorus including the mixture), each individual voice in the polyphony retains its identity much more than in a pure principal *plenum*. The reed *plenum* is thus especially useful for many of the final fugues of the North German *Praeludia*, which, with their simpler rhythms, exhibit strong homophonic tendencies. In all fugues, the bass voice should be at the same pitch level as the rest of the voices, regardless of whether it is played in the manual or in the pedal.[2]

The chorale fantasias, with their various solo and echo sections, are perhaps the most elaborate of the North German compositions. In this genre there are no limits on the organist's tonal fantasy and imagination—there is nothing to link a particular sound with a particular musical form or texture, as there is in the French repertoire of the time. The sources for these works offer only a few registrational indications. The chorale fantasias of Scheidemann, Buxtehude, Tunder, Reinken, and Lübeck frequently have an underlying symmetrical structure, which often suggests a balanced registrational scheme to a modern performer.[3] Changes of color occur in the North German chorale fantasias and variation sets more frequently and more rapidly than in any other organ repertoire of the Baroque period. Quick shifts in registration cannot be accomplished on a seventeenth-century organ by the performer alone. In some cases, the stop knobs are out of the organist's reach, on the outer edges of the *Rückpositiv* case. In addition, sliders can be very difficult to move, especially in humid weather. Spring chests also prevent the performer from changing registrations quickly, for the stop knobs have to be carefully hooked into place. Indeed, the North German repertoire seems to presuppose the presence of registrational assistants. Church records show that organ balconies were heavily frequented. Arp Schnitger, for instance, complained again and again that there were too many people in the organ loft.[4] In the Italian and French traditions, by contrast, registrational changes could be easily accomplished without assistance. The stops were smaller, they could be moved with little effort, there were far fewer registers, and they were easily taken in at a glance by the performer. (In Italian organs there were even mechanical combination devices!) In the organ works of Bach, the tonal aesthetic seems to be based not on variety, as it is in the North German repertoire, but on the complete unity of form and sound. Registration changes within a Bach work are, therefore, exceptional.

In the last decades of the seventeenth century Arp Schnitger dominated organ building in Protestant northern Europe. The "classical" North German organ that he developed was extremely economical in terms of its technology. Its outward appearance reflected its design. It had an extensive and varied disposition, and it displayed extraordinary tonal finesse. The Schnitger school, which continued building instruments in this tradition well into the eighteenth century, was not at all influenced by the developments in Central Germany that precipitated new trends in the organ literature. In many ways, the organ style of J. S. Bach could not have developed in North Germany. It was founded on the organ-building aesthetic of Central Germany, particularly Thuringia. Outwardly, at least, the organ in Central Germany departed completely from the *Werkprinzip*, which had so strongly governed the building of Schnitger and his North German contemporaries. The *Rückpositiv* disappeared, the Pedal division retained its old position behind the Manual division (the two were not separated by rear case walls), and the Manual divisions were no longer segregated by cases.

Also of crucial significance to the Central German style was the move away from mean-tone, Praetorian temperament to the well-tempered system. In mean-tone (of which there are many versions), pure major thirds are purchased at the cost of limiting the number of playable keys. The major thirds built on B, F♯, C♯, and G♯ are so strongly dissonant that they cannot be used. In this system the range of the so-called church modes may not be exceeded. In well-tempered tuning, on the other hand, all keys are usable. The most-distant keys (those with many accidentals) are tense and agitated, while the traditional keys sound relaxed and well blended. In some of the possible well-tempered tunings, the tonic chords of C major, G major, and F major are the same or very close to the analogous chords in mean-tone. There are also considerable differences between the well-tempered systems and the equal-tempered system used today, in which all intervals in all keys are exactly the same. Andreas Werckmeister was one of the principal advocates of the well-tempered tuning system, and he had a particularly strong effect on organ building in Thuringia.

Unfortunately, for the late seventeenth-century North German repertoire of Lübeck, Buxtehude, Reinken, Bruhns, and Böhm, there are absolutely no manuscript copies—much less autographs or printed editions—authorized by the composers. Virtually all the extant sources come from Central Germany or Scandinavia. No other organ repertoire is based on such a dubious transmission, and the total absence of autographs, which must have been in tablature, is most curious. The best manuscripts for most of the North German repertoire are of the same provenance as those for the works of J. S. Bach and J. G. Walther, a fact that demonstrates the interest of these later composers and their students in the music of their predecessors. However, the translation of a repertoire originally written in tablature for mean-tone organs into modern eighteenth-century notation for well-tempered organs may well have resulted in distortions. Upon examining the range of modulation in the North German repertoire, one finds that only the works of Buxtehude, Lübeck, and Bruhns exceed the limits imposed by the mean-tone system. Furthermore, even works in "remote" tonalities only rarely modulate beyond six keys, the modulatory range of mean-tone. For example, in the *Praeambulum* in E by Lübeck and the *Praeludium* in E, BuxWV 141, of Buxtehude, the tonal center, E major, lies not in the middle but on the edge of the mean-tone system. If transposed to an appropriate mean-tone key, C major, the works no longer exceed the limits of the mean-tone system. (It is interesting to note in this regard that Bach's early organ toccata, BWV 566, which in terms of themes and use of several toccata-like elements can be seen as an "Homage to Lübeck," has been handed down to us not only in E major but in C major as well, that is, in high well-tempered and low mean-tone versions.)

By transposing compositions of Buxtehude, Lübeck, and Bruhns from E minor to D minor, D major to C major, F♯ minor to D minor, A major to G major, and B♭ major to G major, the limits of the mean-tone system are rarely overstepped. The exceptions are mostly in the works of Buxtehude.[5] The organ repertoire around 1700 was considerably enriched by this process of transposing a low mean-tone version to a higher well-tempered version,[6] and it is very likely that the well-tempered "modernization" of a part of the North German literature contributed to eighteenth-century interest in these works. Buxtehude was openly sympathetic to the ideas of Werckmeister and complained during his tenure as organist that his instrument in the Lübeck Marienkirche did not receive a major renovation. His works sometimes overstep the limits of mean-tone, even after having been transposed back to an appropriate mean-tone key. Hence it is possible that the well-tempered versions of his organ music were authorized or worked out by the composer himself.[7]

The complicated transmission of the seventeenth-century North German organ repertoire resulted from an equally complicated historical situation. The "classical" North German organ of the Schnitger school, based on mean-tone tuning and *Chorton*, was best suited to the accompaniment of congregational singing and to organ literature that was confined to restricted modulatory possibilities. Nevertheless, some of the toccatas and *Praeludia* of Buxtehude, written in the monumental North German *stylus phantasticus*, overstepped the modulatory bounds of mean-tone, and the continuation of this style demanded the use of well-tempered tunings. However, the well-tempered system was rejected in North Germany at this time, and hence the avant-garde free works of the North German repertoire could not continue to evolve there. Instead, a new organ aesthetic developed elsewhere, in Central Germany, where mean-tone and the *Werkprinzip* were abandoned in favor of the well-tempered system. But even in Central Germany there was resistance to well-tempered tuning. Gottfried Silbermann, for instance, could not bring himself to use it in his organs. As a result, no specific literature exists for his instruments, nor for the North German organs of the first half of the eighteenth century. These organs served mainly to accompany congregational singing, a function based largely on improvisation.

The process by which part of the North German repertoire came from Hamburg and Lübeck to the Weimar circle of J. S. Bach and J. G. Walther may never be clarified beyond the report by Walther himself, who stated (in a letter of August 6, 1729) that he obtained his collection of Buxtehude's works "from Werckmeister and from Buxtehude's own autographs in German tablature."[8] Such well-tempered versions of the repertoire, emanating from Central Germany and Scandinavia, are all that have survived. While the disappearance of the original mean-tone versions is indeed curious, it may be explained by the fact that the radical change around 1700 toward writing and performing in all keys was not adopted in North Germany. Not until the middle of the eighteenth century were the North German organs tuned in well-tempered systems, and by then it was too late to ensure the continuation of the seventeenth-century tradition. Instead, it was J. S. Bach and his associates and students who carried on the tradition of the North German masters. It was in this circle that the compositions of Buxtehude, Lübeck, Bruhns, and their contemporaries were copied, exchanged, and transmitted to posterity.

(TRANSLATED BY LYNN EDWARDS AND EDWARD PEPE)

NOTES

1. Moreover, it is not always necessary to base the registration on the normal 8' pitch. A piece may also be registered an octave higher or lower (at 4' or 16'). A 16' foundation is recommended for manual *plenum* registrations, especially in works that have an obbligato pedal line. Sixteen-foot stops are available in North German organs even on subsidiary manuals. For example, the *Rückpositiv* of the Schnitger organs in Cappel and Lüdingworth have 16' stops (in both cases a Dulcian), even though the divisions are based on 4' Principals.

2. Indeed, the common belief that the pedal should always be at 16' pitch, as in the works of J. S. Bach, does not apply to the North German repertoire. Because of the rich variety of stops in the North German Pedal divisions, consort registrations can be created at all pitch levels. For example, it is possible to register all voices at 4' pitch. When the Pedal and Manual are registered at the same pitch level, problems created by voice crossings between Pedal and Manual (bass and tenor) are usually avoided.

3. Such a balanced registration is demonstrated in the author's recording (*Organa 3004*) of Lübeck's chorale fantasia *Ich ruf zu dir, Herr Jesu Christ*, which begins with a solo *plenum* (based on 16'), moves to a Sesquialtera solo (based on 8'), then to a consort-like combination of Krummhorn and Trechterregal, back to the Sesquialtera solo, and finally to the original 16' *plenum* solo.

4. See Gustav Fock, *Arp Schnitger und seine Schule* (Kassel, 1974), p. 89.

5. For a proper understanding of the use of transposition, one must also consider the question of pitch. In North Germany all instruments were in *Chorton* (high pitch), which was a half to a whole tone higher than today's standard. In Central Germany, on the other hand, *Kammerton* (low pitch) was also common, and it was a half step lower than today's standard. *Chorton* is thus

between a whole tone and a minor third higher than *Kammerton*. To approximate the original pitch, therefore, the North German repertoire must be transposed up when it is performed on the lower-pitched Central German instruments. To demonstrate this process, let us return to the *Praeambulum* of Vincent Lübeck, which has come down to us in an E-major version. Played on a *Chorton* organ, in the original C-major version, the *Praeambulum* sounded approximately at the pitch of modern D major. (That can still be experienced at the Cosmae organ in Stade.) Performed on a *Kammerton* organ in the well-tempered E-major version, the same *Praeambulum* would have sounded approximately at the pitch of modern E♭ major.

6. There are very few examples in the seventeenth-century mean-tone repertoire of compositions in E major, A major, B♭ major, E minor, or F♯ minor. The only exceptions to this rule are works conceived for instruments with subsemitones (split keys).

7. It is quite different with Lübeck, who was a more conservative composer than Buxtehude. With appropriate transpositions back to mean-tone keys, Lübeck's works no longer exceed the limits of mean-tone and can, therefore, be seen as the last examples of a genuine mean-tone repertoire. On the other hand, Lübeck's works certainly push the mean-tone system to its very limits. In the manner of the *stylus phantasticus*, he employs very dramatic chords, including the diminished-seventh chord, a particularly dissonant sound in mean-tone (see m.26 of the *Praeambulum* in c, and mm.151, 156, and 159 of the *Praeambulum* in C [E]).

8. BDok II, no. 263.

JOHN BROMBAUGH

Bach's Influence on Late Twentieth-Century American Organ Building

In the broad spectrum of organ literature, Bach's music represents one of the largest portions of the current repertoire. Furthermore, it comes from a person who was a comprehensive genius—a composer who did not limit himself to a narrow sphere of activity, a musician who has never been surpassed. Bach's musical ideas have been very influential in leading many organ builders beyond constructing organs in the "Neo-Baroque" style, which developed during the course of the twentieth century in Europe and America.[1] After all, *musical* sounds have to be the reason why Bach—and those who influenced him, such as Nicolas de Grigny—gave us such a wealth of wonderful compositions. From my familiarity with Charles Fisk and his work, I know that his ultimate interest in building new organs was the assumption that those instruments could make music. As an organ builder, that is my own stimulus, so I shall describe several factors pertinent to obtaining that music.

Although tracker action became a required norm as early as the 1926 Freiburg Conference (it was not deemed necessary by Schweitzer in 1906),[2] subsequent experience has shown that tracker action alone does not produce the desired musical result. Among the various other requirements of the German *Orgelbewegung* were: the *Werkprinzip*, lower wind pressures controlled by stabilizers (*Schwimmers*) in the wind chests, the use of high-tin-content alloys, the elimination of nicking in flue pipes, the elimination of leather on reed shallots, the reintroduction of higher-pitched stops such as Mixtures, and

41

the use of various newly invented, extremely high-pitched Zimbels. Some or all of these features were lacking in the organs that were the impetus to many significant composers, including J. S. Bach. For example, although tin-alloyed pipes are commonly found in historic instruments neighboring a geographic line between Paris and Vienna, the pipes in the oldest extant organs in northwestern and southern Europe are made with an alloy high in lead content and hammered. Thin tin foil was often applied—it was cemented to the lead with duck egg white—to enhance the appearance of the front pipes, but it was not viewed as a musical requirement. Voicing was done on wind pressures of about 90 mm (water column), which was high by Neo-Baroque standards, though low by late-Romantic measure; and that lead to relatively high cut-up pipe mouths that gave a special *vocale* sound (as opposed to the more "instrumental" sound of tin pipes).

Study of the actual instruments in Thuringia,[3] the region of Bach's early professional experience, brings forth examples that are quite different from either the North German[4] or the Silbermann[5] organs that have so often been heralded as standards for Bach. Among their specialities were 32' Subbass and 16' Posaune registers, mild string sounds like the wooden Violonbass 16' in the Pedal and the Viol di Gamba 8' for the manuals, and Glockenspiels. There are interesting similarities between the early eighteenth-century Thuringian organs and mid-nineteenth-century American instruments.[6] Both tend to be wide and rather deep, with minimal enclosure. The second-manual wind chests were often in the lower part of the case at the sides of the keyboards or behind the *Hauptwerk*. The Pedal wind chests were near the floor behind the manual divisions, as was the norm for Silbermann and, occasionally, for such Schnitger work as Cappel and Uithuizen. *Rückpositivs* were rare. But reeds in a wide variety—including 2' Pedal Cornetts—were common, so we find a dissimilarity to both Silbermann and American styles. Though Mixtures, Cornets, and Sesquialteras were common (thus differing from the later American organs), their composition followed a Central German style that differed from the entire Dutch–North German *plenum* tradition.

The question of the *plenum* is of great significance, for many twentieth-century builders (myself included) have taken too much from the ancient Dutch–North German (e.g., Niehoff and Scherer) or French concepts to suit the musical needs of Bach. His works represent the peak of late polyphonic writing, requiring not only the radiation of a collage of sounds from an organ but also that individual voice lines be heard clearly. It means that we must give our utmost attention to the *plenum* structure needed for his music, since Bach used the *plenum*—which is unique to the organ among all musical instruments—to an unprecedented degree. The unison pitch must be strong to establish the voice lines. As a further aid, the newer German reeds could also be added to the Principal *plenum* without the domination that is normal in historic French organs. Finally, the Mixtures must be in tune, and the interference between their individual ranks and needs of the temperament must not cause difficulty—a problem that is aggravated by both mean-tone and equal temperament.

Gottfried Fritzsche set new standards for Mixtures in North Germany when he moved to Hamburg in 1629. These ideas are best exemplified for us today in the organ of the Jacobikirche in Hamburg, which he rebuilt in 1635. He had come from Meissen and apparently was a student of Hans Lange, a disciple of the Beck and Compenius families in Central Germany, a group whose work was to influence instruments built in Bach's home region. The Principal *plenum*, including the Mixtures, from Beck and Fritzsche was capable of letting the complex polyphonic voice lines be heard in ways not encouraged by the older, northwest European format. And Fritzsche also delighted in the musical potential of Quintadenas. When used at 16' pitch below an 8' Principal, they give a sense of depth to the *plenum* without losing the sense of unison pitch needed for Bach's compositions. A *plenum* in the new style was capped by a single compound stop, such as a Mixture or a Scharff, to which a Sesquialtera, Tertian, or small Cimbel might be added. There was a trend to use more tin in the new pipe alloys, which gave a brighter, lighter sound than that produced by lead pipes. This choice was especially important for the small, high-pitched pipes found in the Octave 2' and in the Mixtures. The compound stops generally had doublings in many of their pitches, which increased the stability of tuning and speech—something that is nearly impossible when a Mixture, Scharff, and Octave 2' exist on the same wind chest.

Andreas Werckmeister, the noted organ authority and friend of Buxtehude, published the first edition of his *Orgel-Probe* in 1681. This document contained material on musical temperaments, a topic treated even more thoroughly in his *Musicalische Temperatur* of 1691. *Orgel-Probe* may have been the first attempt at suggesting a departure from the mean-tone tuning that had become standard for keyboard instruments throughout Europe after the mid-sixteenth century; but it is also possible that the treatise simply records practices that had already been tested and proven. From newly acquired archival data showing that a large sum was spent tuning the Marienkirche organs in Lübeck in 1683, we may hypothesize (though not prove) that a change to one of Werckmeister's new temperaments may have taken place at that time.[7] In any case, the modulations in Buxtehude's compositions often go far beyond the possibilities of mean-tone forms. In fact, some of his music is impossible in mean-tone, even when transposed to keys other than those in which we find it published today. In Bach's case, however, the desire for the flexibility of well-tempered tuning (there is no evidence that *wohl-temperiert* implied modern equal temperament!) for his keyboard music is well established and nicely exemplified in an organ work such as the Toccata in F, BWV 540 (especially the final cadence), when we hear it with either a Werckmeister or Kirnberger temperament.

In 1709–10, shortly after completing his journeyman's experience with Thierry in Paris, Andreas Silbermann built an organ that is still extant at Marmoutier (Alsace) and has an exquisite manual action for its *Grand orgue*. Like most other historic builders, he used very simple suspended action systems, similar to those depicted by Dom Bédos in his treatise of 1766.[8] This action has the incredible ability to handle the complex ornamentation found in the Classical French literature, and though it cannot be proven that such actions are necessary for the best performance of Bach's compositions, in the opinion of the present engineer-turned-organ builder, they are certainly the best commonsense models for better organs today.

Arguments abound for the organs of Andreas's younger brother, Gottfried Silbermann, being the ideal for Johann Sebastian Bach's music. The experience of Gottfried's apprenticeship to Andreas in Alsace, his move back to his Saxon homeland, and his reportedly wild character merged to produce a builder with a unique style. Certain French concepts are especially noticeable in the reeds of the second instrument Gottfried built for the Freiberg Dom, near his birthplace. After its completion, however, he developed a form of reed making more like the usual Central German practice, and this feature remained more or less unchanged throughout the rest of his career. Gottfried Silbermann's Pedal Posaune 16′ generally had full-length wooden resonators and shallots cast of lead with a leathered face. The musical result was quite similar to equivalent, but differently constructed, stops made by Schnitger's shop. Gottfried Silbermann's Trumpets had a bright but full sound and were often found as 8′ stops in the Pedal. Except on large organs, Silbermann tended to provide few other reeds—remarkably contrary to the requirements Bach placed in his recommendations when acting as a consultant or to the enthusiasm he displayed for the many reeds at the Catherinenkirche in Hamburg when he paid his final visit to Reinken in 1720. Though a quasi-French concept remained in his Mixture-Cimbel layouts, Gott-fried Silbermann's Mixture compositions are basically good for main-taining polyphonic clarity in Bach's music (despite Agricola's negative comments), and the relationships ("forceful and penetrating," "sharp and cutting," "delicate") Silbermann set up between the various divi-sions are compatible. In a mechanical sense, he produced organs of possibly the highest quality to be found, though his architectural style was unexciting. His pipe making, both in execution and in quality of material, was unusually good, certainly better than the run-of-the-mill Schnitger work. But his high-tin *plenum* produced a sound that is al-most overbearingly sharp at times, as one can experience in his 1741 Grosshartmannsdorf organ. This sharpness contrasts with the mildness found in French building of the time and also with the re-markable work of his apprentice Zacharias Hildebrandt.

Silbermann consistently used keyboards with a compass of CD−c‴ for his manuals and CD−c′ for his pedals. Although this manual com-pass is satisfactory for all of Bach's organ music except some instances of d‴ in the Fantasia in g, BWV 542/1, and the *Art of Fugue* (if it is considered organ music), the absence of pedal notes above c′ makes Silbermann's pedal boards unsatisfactory for a great number of Bach's compositions. Clearly the instruments that inspired Bach's works went at least to d′ and occasionally even to f′ in the pedals. Arp Schnitger's organs, incidentally, had a pedal compass to d′, but both manuals and pedal usually had a short bass octave that would not support Bach's music adequately.

The large weighted wedge bellows, developed a century or so be-fore Bach's lifetime, became common throughout Europe as the prin-cipal way to generate and stabilize the wind provided to the pipes. In older organs, the wind supply "problem" precluded the use of more than a few stops simultaneously. In his *Orgel-Probe*, Werckmeister dis-cusses wind supply first in terms of individual stops, then of pairs, then of groups of three, four, etc., and finally in terms of the full organ.[9] In his recommendations for rebuilding the organ in St. Blasius' Church in Mühlhausen, Bach expressed the need for "such wind conduction that one stop alone and also all the stops together can be used without alteration of the pressure, which has never been possible in the past [with this particular instrument] and yet is very necessary."[10] This result had to be achieved within the basic technology of the wedge-bellows system (reservoirs were not introduced until later) by adding more bellows and by skillfully designing the wind ducts, check valves, and wind chests. Werckmeister describes having "recently seen the work of an eminent builder which first collects the wind from all bellows in one spacious wind trunk. From this channel, individual wind ducts connect with each wind chest, thus the wind is steady." [11]

When integrity is given to the various styles desired today, we are faced with an insurmountable conflict, if we wish to provide cohesion in an organ that has all the desired stylistic possibilities. The new Fisk instrument at Stanford University is a unique example in virtually all organ-building history of a pipe organ that can provide two quite different temperaments, a mean-tone and a well-tempered form. And adjacent to this instrument is a late-Romantic American organ that can provide a totally different sound and handle an area of the organ literature for which most listeners would consider the new Fisk unsuited. Thus Stanford represents a remarkable solution to an organ question not unlike the separation and specialization often observable in our wider musical culture. However, just how far we can go in providing such specialization within the organ domain remains to be seen. Current studies show more and more that no single organ style is totally correct to handle even the entire corpus of Johann Sebastian Bach's organ music. So we will be in even more trouble if we expect to accommodate the work of other fine composers with an "all-purpose" instrument that copies and merges several styles.

In conclusion, my recommendation is that we follow the example of virtually every historic builder by making new instruments that are coherent in themselves. We Americans can make our most significant contribution to the history of the organ if we just remember that, above all, the organ is expected to be a musical instrument. If its sound can attract and increase the interests of the general public as well as that of musicians and composers, it will have fulfilled its purpose in much the same manner as the organ of Johann Sebastian Bach's time. Certainly we can give this composer no finer tribute!

(DEDICATED TO THE MEMORY OF MY TEACHER IN ORGAN
BUILDING, CHARLES FISK)

NOTES

Research for this paper was partially funded by a grant from the Seattle Chapter of the American Guild of Organists.

1. For a summary of developments in the first half of the twentieth century, see Poul-Gerhard Andersen, *Organ Building and Design* (London, 1969).

2. See *Bericht über die Freiburger Tagung für deutsche Orgelkunst* (Kassel, 1928); Albert Schweitzer, *Deutsche und französische Orgelbaukunst* (Leipzig, 1906); and Bernhard Billeter, "Albert Schweitzers Einfluss auf den europäischen Orgelbau am Beginn des 20. Jahrhunderts," *Acta Organologica* 15 (1981): 168–79.

3. These instruments are described in Werner David, *Johann Sebastian Bachs Orgeln* (Berlin, 1951). See also Ulrich Dähnert, "Johann Sebastian Bach's Ideal Organ," *The Organ Yearbook* 1 (1970): 20–37; as well as his *Der Orgel- und Instrumentenbauer Zacharias Hildebrandt* (Dresden, 1960); and Winfried Schrammek, *Bach-Orgeln in Thüringen und Sachsen* (Leipzig, 1985).

4. Concerning North German organ building, see Gustav Fock, "Hamburgs Anteil am Orgelbau im niederdeutschen Kulturgebiet," *Zeitschrift des Vereins für Hamburgische Geschichte* 28 (1939): 289–373; and Fock, *Arp Schnitger und seine Schule* (Kassel, 1974).

5. The most recent Silbermann study is Werner Müller, *Gottfried Silbermann: Persönlichkeit und Werk* (Leipzig, 1982). See also Müller's *Auf den Spuren von Gottfried Silbermann* (Kassel, 1968) and Ulrich Dähnert, *Die Orgeln Gottfried Silbermanns in Mitteldeutschland* (Leipzig, 1953).

6. See Orpha Ochse, *The History of the Organ in the United States* (Bloomington, Indiana, 1975).

7. According to Kerala J. Snyder, "From Account Books to Performances: Buxtehude at the Marienkirche in Lübeck" (abstract printed in *Abstracts of Papers Read at the Forty-seventh Annual Meeting of the American Musicological Society, Boston, Massachusetts, 12–15 November, 1981*, p. 52).

8. Dom François Bédos de Celles, *L'Art du facteur d'orgues* (Paris, 1766–1778); English translation by Charles Ferguson (Raleigh, 1977).

9. *Orgel-Probe* (2d ed., 1698), chap. 12; see Gerhard Krapf's translation of this treatise under the title *Werckmeister in English* (Raleigh, 1976).

10. *Bach Reader*, p. 59. For a study of the connections between Werckmeister and Bach, see Peter Williams, "J. S. Bach—Orgelsachverständiger unter dem Einfluss Andreas Werckmeisters?" BJ 1982: 131–42.

11. *Werckmeister in English*, pp. 21–22.

MARIE-CLAIRE ALAIN

Why an Acquaintance with Early Organs Is Essential for Playing Bach

It is no longer possible for the organist of our epoch to ignore the practice of early instruments. In the realm of performance, the pursuit of historical authenticity has finally dethroned the old belief that instrumental technique is in a constant state of progress. It has taken many years for musicians to realize that each period of music history possesses a manner of execution intimately connected with the instruments of its day. The idea is now firmly established that in past eras one played *differently* on organs of a *different* construction. This evolution, which took place during the nineteenth and twentieth centuries, by no means constitutes an improvement in playing style, it simply reflects the birth of another type of organ (or perhaps several other types of organs) for which another type of literature was written.

At the time of J. S. Bach's death, the organ was already the "black sheep" of the keyboard instrument family. With the new possibilities of dynamic expression offered by the *forte-piano*, performers soon forgot the nuances of "touch" preached by the early masters. The last defender of the organ as it was played in the Baroque might well be Mendelssohn, with his *École d'Orgue* (the original title of the Organ Sonatas, Op. 65).

It is noteworthy that Mendelssohn often went to Rötha to play on the marvelous Gottfried Silbermann organ in St. Georgen, an instrument that still exists today. If one studies the slurring marks printed in a faithful edition of Mendelssohn's organ works (the Henle Edition or the Lea Pocket Score; most others are untrustworthy), one notices that the composer demands that his interpreter have a real sense of articulating musical sentences on a mechanical-action keyboard.

At the same time that Mendelssohn's collection was published, the first Barker lever and tubular pneumatic actions appeared. Soon the *Récit* division was enclosed in an expressive box operated by the organist's foot, in an effort to imitate the crescendos and sforzandos of the piano. The sense of "touch" died, and the appetite for virtuosity grew. New works were written for an instrument that was easier to handle. The Romantic organ was born; in the evolution of performance, it changed according to country and school of playing. But the art of performing early music was lost at the same time, as was knowledge of ornamentation and Baroque registration. Musicians constantly believed that to improve the music of the past they had to adjust it to the "nouvelle mode." One school recommended a solemn legato, another an exaggerated articulation—the former standardizing the duration of note values, the latter ignoring accents and strong beats. All these schools aimed only at giving life to a keyboard rendered inert by the use of an intermediary (pneumatic or electric) between the performer's finger and the valve controlling the admission of air into the pipe.

With the advent of electricity, the aberration became even more shocking. Performers indulged in musical "pointillism": the temptation to reorchestrate a fugue by Bach became too great. Even the famous Schönberg indulged in such fantasies in his orchestration of the Prelude and Fugue in E♭, BWV 552. Then why not change the style for each exposition of the theme? The "piston mania" facilitated all sorts of sonorous fantasies and changes of keyboards—intimate decrescendos for episodes and brash crescendos for conclusions.

Even as I write these lines many young organists are still being trained according to techniques derived from the unnatural traditions I have described. Few conservatories of music offer a course of organ study that enables them to get a clear idea of the performance style of past centuries. Bach, Couperin, and Scarlatti are still played on the modern grand piano!

That is why an acquaintance with early organs—or good copies of them—is essential for every performer concerned with authenticity. A quick visit during the course of a trip is not enough; it is necessary to practice regularly on this type of instrument in order to accomplish the complete musical and technical retraining the instrument requires.

With this style of practice, the organist experiences new elements of performance: *mechanical aspects*, derived from the use of the instrument; and *musical aspects*, derived from the above but also from the new aural and intellectual demands made on the performer.

The mechanical aspects of early organs appear at first to be negative:

1. Because the air is unstable, it is impossible to play fast without distorting the sound.

2. Because the keys are short, substitution is difficult. Often it produces a break or a cessation of the sound.

3. Because the pedal board is short (it usually does not extend very far under the keyboards), it is difficult to use the heels in pedal playing, except in the very low or very high range.

4. Because the draw knobs for the stops are far from the keyboards, they are difficult to manipulate.

5. The shove coupler cannot be used while one is playing. Not only would it be difficult to manipulate but one would risk breaking the mechanism.

6. The air supply is not sufficient for all the stops—the flutes, the principals, and the reeds—to be played simultaneously without a drop in wind pressure.

All these idiosyncracies lead us to search for solutions to the problems thus created. The solutions can be found only in giving up a number of old habits, which we can now detail:

1. An organ constructed for a specific building is supposed to be adapted to the acoustics of that site. We cannot adopt a pre-determined tempo but must listen to the organ and the way it reacts. For those who know how to listen, the organ will impose its own tempo, one related to its breathing. We ought to be wary of metronomical tempos.

2. We must reappraise our fingerings. Most of the time, substitution is useless. Giving it up greatly facilitates playing and produces the breathing that is necessary to musical discourse.

3. The same applies to the pedal. By abandoning the general use of the heels, one produces an articulation that resembles the bowing of a cello.

4. We ought not change the registration during a work unless the score explicitly indicates it (there are no more than five or six such examples in all of Bach's compositions).

5. Do not engage the coupler while playing. We should at least wait until the piece gives us the occasion to do so (for example, at the end of the Passacaglia in c, BWV 582, after the Neapolitan sixth chord, m. 285).

6. We must study the registrations of the time. In the Baroque period, the *plenum* generally consisted of only a single stop at each pitch: 8', 4', 2', Mixture, Cymbel. Only with Silbermann does one see the Principal 8' doubled by a Bourdon 8', and later the Octave 4' by a Flute 4' (registration instructions for Grosshartmannsdorf, 1741; registration instructions for Fraureuth, 1742).

The musical aspects of early organs that follow are:

1. Contrary to the belief derived from the experience of bad restorations, a well-built (and well-restored) early organ is *not* hard to play. It is a "classical" mechanism, with which the organist can forget 130 years of pneumatic and electric actions and learn anew how to make music with one's fingers. With daily practice on a sensitive tracker instrument one can rediscover all the nuances of "touch" that the classical treatises recommend. One can then sense the necessity of the correctly placed accent and the musical phrase modeled on vocal pronunciation or the bowing of string instruments.

2. The use of early fingering is a consequence of the above, but it must be viewed as a natural necessity. Good position of the hands and feet will always result in a comfortable performance. I have noticed that switching from Romantic fingerings to more straightforward early fingerings results in a great simplification of my entire positioning on the manuals, and abandoning the excessive use of the heels leads to a better equilibrium on the pedal board.

3. If we admit that our fingers are producing the music and its expression, then let us search, from the beginning, for the best registration for a given piece. If the *plenum* has beauty, it is unnecessary to outline the theme of a fugue in the tenor—or to insist on a decrescendo by changing keyboard, or to include a final crescendo—except by emotional intensity. Bach was too skilled an organist and too inspired a composer not to provide variety within unity. What is the exposition of a fugue other than a gigantic crescendo?

Listen to the Fugue in g, BWV 542/2, for instance. The exposition proceeds: one voice (soprano), two voices (soprano and alto), three voices (the tenor is added), and finally four voices (the bass enters, the manual voices move to a high range). After the counter-exposition and the cadence in the relative key, the pedal comes to a stop. Why change keyboards at this point, when the piece has only three, and then only two, voices? Isn't the decrescendo contained in the counterpoint itself? All the more so because Bach, with unique mastery, then reintroduces the voices one by one in their strongest register, in order to make them sound at their best, thus contributing to the sonorous (as well as formal) buildup of ascending passages—indeed, in a crescendo. Why chop the work into pieces, under the pretext of creating color, when the composer has already taken care of all that, within the possibilities of a single *plenum*? Of course one must assume that the organ has a good *plenum*. When it is lacking, one must choose a registration that gives a sense of the perfect balance between counterpoint and dynamic feeling.

For me, it was the "clarity"—the possibility of hearing clearly all the voices in a counterpoint—of the German *plenum*, in North as well as East Germany, that was the determining factor. It caused me, at the beginning of my career, to turn away from all the schools in which I had been trained.

4. To understand the phenomena (still mysterious) of registration in Bach, one must certainly become acquainted with as many as possible of the instruments that Bach knew or could have known.

We must take into account that Bach often changed jobs. He did not compose for a single organ but rather for a goodly number of them, generally instruments belonging to other people. The organs in Lübeck (Marienkirche), Hamburg (Katharinenkirche), Halle (Liebfrauenkirche), and Naumburg (Wenzelkirche) are, in this respect, more instructive than the mediocre, two-manual instruments in Arnstadt or Weimar.

We must remember, too, that this unparalleled virtuoso appeared in public over a period of almost 50 years, and that the organ in Germany from 1700 to 1750 was in a state of evolution (indeed, perhaps Bach was a leading force in this evolution). Bach began playing on an instrument close to Praetorius; he gave his last inaugural concerts on instruments containing an Unda Maris and Cornets "à la française." In his recommendations for reconstructing the Blasiuskirche organ in Mühlhausen, he himself praised the potential of such stops for realizing "neue inventiones."

If the great organs of Arp Schnitger enlighten us on Bach's youthful works and the initial Weimar years, it is to the organs of Central Germany that we must turn for the works of his maturity. When Silbermann returned from France in 1710, Casparini and Hildebrandt were producing their greatest instruments, from 1700 (Görlitz) to 1747 (Naumburg). The organ of the Prelude and Fugue in b, BWV 544; the Prelude and Fugue in e ("Wedge"), BWV 548; and *Clavierübung* III is an instrument in a state of transition. The organ of the Frauenkirche in Dresden (1736) is very different from the organ in the Freiberg Cathedral (1714), even though both are signed "Gottfried Silbermann."

The performer of Bach must seek nourishment in this sonorous universe, in this remarkably lively evolution of the organ between 1700 and 1750. On a Silbermann organ all registers are beautiful. Perhaps that is why Bach did not wish to designate any specific stops for his works.

In conclusion, we can speak only of the pleasure of the ear. There is a velvety quality of sound in the speech of an early organ pipe that even the most beautiful modern copy cannot equal. The organ has aged, it is becoming more melodious, more musical with time.

We must play on early instruments to find authenticity. But when it is combined with the delight that is gained by hearing under our fingers the sharp brilliance of a Schnitger or the luminous transparency of a Silbermann, it is no longer a question of obligation. It is a question of joy, inspired by the discovery of a sonorous realm, the real world of J. S. Bach, perhaps even improved by the passing of some 300 years of music making.

(TRANSLATED BY ONDINE HASSON)

Bach's Organ Music

*In his secular compositions he disdained every-
thing common, but in his compositions for
organ he kept himself infinitely more distant
from it, so that here, it seems to me, he does not
appear like a man, but as a true disembodied
spirit, who soars above everything mortal.*

—*Johann Nicolaus Forkel* (1802)

CHRISTOPH WOLFF

•⋗§⋖•

Johann Adam Reinken and Johann Sebastian Bach

On the Context of Bach's Early Works

More than 100 years ago Philipp Spitta endeavored to place the musical beginnings of the young Bach in proper perspective, taking as his point of departure a chronological ordering of compositional repertoire he classified as early works. He succeeded not only in presenting a multitude of fundamental observations on biographical and stylistic matters—perceptions that have remained valid up to the present day—but also in offering an exemplary, discriminating, and, in its basic features, still unsurpassed synopsis of musical currents in Germany in the closing years of the seventeenth century.[1] Since Spitta's day, Bach research, especially in the last three decades, has somewhat filled in the picture of Bach the young composer as sketched by Spitta, expanding new aspects and modifying numerous details in the process.[2]

However, it seems that no other creative period of Bach's life presents so many unsolved problems, and the list has been expanding rather than shrinking as a result of more recent research.[3] The central questions continually revolve around the establishment of an authentic body of works, the chronology of the compositions, and the direct and indirect spheres of musical influence that might have affected the young Bach. These critical questions are so closely intertwined that they cannot be treated separately. Moreover, the acute lack of firm biographical and compositional dates makes a broader approach to the matter all the more necessary.

I

Except for his older brother Johann Christoph of Ohrdruf, "under whose guidance"—run the words of the Obituary[4]—"he learned the fundamentals of clavier playing," Bach does not appear to have had a real teacher. But certainly the three renowned North German organists, Johann Adam Reinken, Dietrich Buxtehude, and Georg Böhm, must be counted among the decisive mentors of the young Bach—and not simply in the broad general sense. Böhm, organist of St. John's Church in Lüneburg, may well have served in some ways as Bach's instructor, at least in part, in the years after 1700. Although the biographical sources say nothing in this regard, one suspects that C. P. E. Bach had good reason to use the phrase "his Lüneburg teacher Böhm"[5] with regard to his father's training. Emanuel subsequently corrected the passage, neutralizing it to read "the Lüneburg organist Böhm,"[6] perhaps to extol his father further as a self-taught genius. In any event, there were personal bonds between Bach and Böhm. These ties lasted into the Leipzig years and were still strong enough in 1727 that Bach was able to turn to the aging Böhm and enlist him as an agent for the sale of the individual prints of his second and third partitas, BWV 826 and 827.[7]

Bach's personal encounter with Dietrich Buxtehude did not take place until the middle of the Arnstadt period. During the winter of 1705–1706, Bach spent several months in Lübeck in order "to listen to" the master; this stay, as the Obituary put it, was "not without profit."[8] The Lübeck trip must have made a very strong impression on Bach, for he himself stated (according to the Arnstadt protocol of February 21, 1706) that the journey had enabled him "to comprehend one thing and another about his art."[9] Since the beginnings of Bach research, the Buxtehude encounter has been taken as one of the decisive biographical and stylistic turning points, especially with regard to the chronology of the organ works—whether for the better or the worse will be discussed shortly.

The third and eldest of this completely congenial North German trio of organists, Johann Adam Reinken, was ranked below his Lüneburg colleagues in terms of significance for Bach by Spitta and, as a rule, by those writing since. The noticeable downplaying of Reinken's role and importance might be explained by the fact that at the time Spitta was writing the first volume of his Bach biography, he was not aware of the direct link between Bach and Reinken's music; not until later was Spitta able to identify the sonata and fugue arrangements from

Reinken's *Hortus musicus*, BWV 954, 965, and 966, in a special essay, "Umarbeitungen fremder Originale." [10]

Even though the precise circumstances of the relationship between the aged Reinken, the organist of St. Catherine's in Hamburg, and Bach, who was nearly two generations younger and a student at St. Michael's School in Lüneburg, remain for the most part in the dark, Reinken represents a major, perhaps even *the* major, figure in young Bach's life. It is worth noting that Reinken is the only one of the three great North German organists to be mentioned in two prominent places in the Obituary. One may view that as an indication of the weight his name carried in the Bach household. It is certainly no more than a fortunate coincidence that after the early Lüneburg–Hamburg contact still another encounter took place, in 1720, between Bach, now elevated to Cöthen *Kapellmeister*, and the 97-year-old Reinken, on the occasion of Bach's competing for the organist's post at the Jacobikirche in Hamburg. [11] Although that may have been fortuitous happenstance, it underlines an affinity clearly felt on both sides. The reaction of the venerable Reinken to Bach's organ playing ("I thought that this art was dead, but I see that it lives on in you" [12]), passed down in the Obituary, can hardly be overrated. [13] For in fact Bach was—and not only from Reinken's perspective—the only organist of rank in his generation who not only preserved the traditions of the seventeenth century but developed them further. For Bach, Reinken's pronouncement must have been more than a simple "compliment." He must have sensed the historical significance of the phrase. Indeed, Bach probably even shaped its precise formulation, since he himself was undoubtedly the primary preserver and disseminator of the Reinken citation and therefore was responsible for its inclusion in the annals of music history. By 1752, when Johann Joachim Quantz was able to write that "the art of organ playing, which had been received from the Netherlanders, was carried quite far . . . by the above named [among them Froberger, Pachelbel, Reinken, Buxtehude, and Bruhns]" and that it "had in recent times been brought to its greatest perfection by the admirable Johann Sebastian Bach," [14] it appears that Reinken's prophetic words had become historical fact.

While the short reunion of Reinken and Bach in 1720 may be viewed as no more than a noteworthy meeting of a special nature, the earlier encounter, during Bach's Lüneburg period, must be rated as a much more momentous event, one that could not have failed to influence the young musician, thirsty for experience and searching for direction. An attempt to discuss the early Reinken–Bach tie must enter the realm of hypothesis, for documentary sources are lacking. The Obituary gives no more than a pithy confirmation: "From Lüneburg he journeyed occasionally to Hamburg in order to hear the then-famous organist of St. Catherine's Church, Johann Adam Reinken." [15] The more anecdotal report in Friedrich Wilhelm Marpurg's *Legenden einiger Musikheiligen* (1786) adds nothing substantial to the account, though Reinken is expressly described as a "solid organist and com-poser." It also mentions that Bach "traveled frequently" to Hamburg and that the unanticipated discovery of a ducat made possible "a new pilgrimage to Herr Reinken." [16]

It is significant that the Obituary, in its generally succinct sketch of Bach's Lüneburg years, singles out Reinken for mention, not Böhm or August Braun, the Kantor of St. Michael's. One cannot exclude the possibility that the allusion to Reinken alone corresponds to his im-portance within Bach's family and student circle. From Bach's perspec-tive in Ohrdruf, St. Michael's School in Lüneburg probably repre-sented an immediate and realistic goal with economic security—but no more than that. The Hamburg scene, by contrast, may have repre-sented the true ideal and a future goal, one that was being pursued at the same time by Handel. Perhaps Lüneburg, with Böhm, offered Bach an additional bonus. On the one hand, Böhm was an attractive organ teacher *sui generis*.[17] On the other, he could also offer Bach an introduction to the North German organ school and especially to Reinken, whose fame as an organist was equal to Buxtehude's, if not even greater.[18]

Bach's several or even frequent "pilgrimages" to Hamburg to hear Reinken, perhaps as early as his Ohrdruf years, parallel the educa-tion of his cousin and one-time schoolmate at the Ohrdruf Lyceum, Johann Ernst Bach. Johann Ernst remained at the Lyceum until April 1701 and then "visited Hamburg for a half-year at great expense, in order to improve his understanding of the organ." [19] Lüneburg may have offered Johann Sebastian better possibilities for subsistence—with a long-range contact with Hamburg thrown into the bargain—than the more financially taxing route taken by his cousin. Just how long Bach received his modest income as a member of the Mettenchor at St. Michael's is unknown; documentation exists only for the begin-ning of 1700.[20] Gustav Fock has already established that Bach could hardly have remained in the first class at St. Michael's School beyond Easter 1702.[21] Moreover, his candidacy for the organist's post at the Jacobikirche in Sangerhausen in the summer of 1702[22] suggests that his ties to Lüneburg were loosening. How these ties may have been

viewed after he had lost—in the words of the Obituary—"his unusually fine soprano voice,"[23] is an open question. But without a doubt
numerous opportunities for employment as an instrumentalist were
open to him. That he was even considered for the post in Sangerhausen
testifies to his qualifications as an organist, a skill he must have developed to a passable level in Lüneburg.

II

A number of reference points and analogies enable us to estimate—at
least in broad outline—Bach's musical development between the ages
of fifteen and eighteen. The invitation from the Arnstadt Church
Council for the eighteen-year-old Bach to test and inaugurate the
Wender organ in the New Church[24] can only be taken as a sign of unusually high esteem. The false title given to Bach on the honorarium
receipt, "Court Organist to the Prince of Weimar"[25] underlines the
reputation of the young virtuoso; and one might assume that his professional abilities in 1703 considerably exceeded the skills he had acquired in Ohrdruf up to the beginning of the year 1700. It also seems
that he had long since overcome the original disparity with his elder
brother Johann Christoph, whose professional development was similar to Sebastian's. Johann Christoph began his studies at age fifteen
with Pachelbel in Erfurt, a tutelage that three years later led to an
organist position at St. Thomas's Church in Erfurt.[26] The external
chronology is the same, but the differences in circumstances are striking: Johann Sebastian did not spend a journeyman period with a
single master, but rather took part in an academic program that fath-
omed and explored what must have been for its time a very attractive
German organ scene. At the conclusion of this independent tutorial
period came the assumption of a well-paying organist post with a new
instrument.[27] The younger brother must have outstripped the older at
a very early point, even though the latter was termed "optimus ar-
tifex" in the Ohrdruf funeral register.[28] The description in the Obituary of the acceptance of the ten-year-old orphan into his brother's
household is significant: "Little Johann Sebastian's love of music was
uncommonly great even at this tender age. In a short time he had
mastered all the pieces that his brother had voluntarily set before
him."[29] His desire to learn was difficult to keep in bounds: the story of
the secret copying of the book "full of clavier pieces by the most famous masters of the day, Froberger, Kerll, and Pachelbel"[30] serves as a
striking example.

Corrections are needed in the portrait of the years 1695–1700 as projected by Friedrich Blume, which claims by way of summary, that the period elapsed "without leaving us the smallest clue about Bach's musical progress."[31] And certainly it is inappropriate to reduce, as Spitta did, the relationship between Johann Sebastian and Johann Christoph Bach to the transmission of "Pachelbel's creations and artistic spirit."[32] On the contrary, as the offspring of a musical family, Johann Sebastian had most certainly achieved musical and instrumental polish even before he was ten years old, else why would the decision to send him on his way toward professional training be made as early as 1695? That decision may have been comparable to the one Bach made in 1720, the tenth year of the life of his own son Wilhelm Friedemann, when Johann Sebastian began writing the *Clavierbüchlein*.

Johann Christoph must have wished, above all, to pass on to his brother what had been suggested to him by his own training. The anxiously guarded book copied by Sebastian contained works by Pachelbel, Kerll, and Froberger as repertoire to be emulated, and in a sense it must have represented Johann Christoph's own musical ambitions. The book as well as the copy made by Sebastian "by moonlight" during the course of six months are lost.[33] However, one can get an idea of the type of repertoire involved from the 1692 tablature book of Johann Valentin Eckelt.[34]

Eckelt, born in 1673, was two years younger than Johann Christoph Bach. Both boys studied with Pachelbel in Erfurt, and Eckelt took the occasion to assemble a tablature book[35] whose basic contents are written in Pachelbel's hand.[36] The compositions are principally those of Pachelbel and Froberger (most of the latter were apparently purchased from Pachelbel[37]). In addition, there are pieces by Philipp Heinrich Erlebach, Andreas Nicolaus Vetter, Johann Caspar Kerll, Johann Philipp Krieger, and, mainly toward the end, a large number of anonymous pieces, evidently compositions by Eckelt himself.[38] The "core" of the volume—especially the pieces by Pachelbel and Froberger—is probably roughly the same as the repertoire entrusted to Johann Christoph Bach. It includes the following works edited in DTB[39] and DTO:[40]

Johann Pachelbel:

Toccatas, Preludes, Fugues and Ciacona (DTB IV/1, Part 1: nos. 1, 4, 5, 7–9, 11, 20, 23, 25, 26, 31, 41, 42)

Chorale Preludes (DTB IV/1, Part 2: nos. 5, 11, 26, 60)
Suites (DTB II/1: nos. 16, 33b)

Johann Jacob Froberger:

Ricercar (DTO 21: no. 7)
Canzonas (DTO 13: no. 6; DTO 21, no. 4)
Capriccios (DTO 21: nos. 12, 18)
Toccatas (DTO 21: nos. 23–25)
Fantasia (DTO 21: no. 7)
Capriccio, Prelude, and Fugue (DTO 21: Doubtful Works, pp. 125–26)

The repertoire of the Eckelt tablature book was probably somewhat smaller than that assembled by Johann Christoph Bach and differed in some respects. However, it offers welcome insights into the knowledge of contemporary keyboard literature, the level of technical skill, and the rudiments of composition that Johann Sebastian might have possessed by the time he departed for Lüneburg.

The copying and playing of works by recognized masters also signified for Bach, as for other budding musicians of the day, the study of *exempla classica* of composition. Thus, we can assume that toward the end of the Ohrdruf period, at least, he was studying composition through the models available to him. Ever since Spitta, there has been a pronounced tendency to grant no importance whatsoever to this aspect of the Ohrdruf period. For instance, Spitta says of the Fugue in e for clavier, BWV 945: "Of all the Bach fugues I know, this is the most immature and can hardly have been composed later than the Ohrdruf years." [41] However, this fugue shows none of the characteristics that would be expected of a work written under the influences of the Pachelbel circle. Moreover, it has recently been shown to be an inauthentic piece. [42] Thus one must search for new and more reliable traces of Bach's earliest compositional activity, if they have survived. They probably are to be found in works such as the Canzona in d, BWV 588, or the Fantasia in C, BWV 570, two pieces handed down (perhaps in revised form) in the two large collections assembled shortly after 1700 by Johann Christoph Bach, the so-called *Möllersche Handschrift* and the *Andreas-Bach-Buch*. [43]

In his Lüneburg years, Bach was probably entrusted with an entirely new repertoire of keyboard works, but there is no concrete evidence that he had already been exposed to North German music through his brother. It seems more likely that the handsome assemblage of North German keyboard music, as represented in the

Möllersche Handschrift and the *Andreas-Bach-Buch*, was placed into the hands of Johann Christoph by his younger brother, and not vice versa. The *Möllersche Handschrift* and the *Andreas-Bach-Buch* are, in fact, principal sources for the transmission of music by Reinken, Buxtehude, Bruhns, and Böhm—something that must be credited to the Bach brothers, perhaps especially to the young Sebastian.

Bach's first direct access to North German organ music probably came through Georg Böhm. But it should not be overlooked that Böhm's organ in St. John's Church, like the other instruments in Lüneburg, was then in deplorable condition and did not allow true obbligato pedal playing. An appraisal by Arp Schnitger in 1683 is also relevant for the period 1700–1702:

> The organ in St. John's is in a very bad state of repair. The wind chests are old and completely unserviceable. The keyboards go no higher than a^2 in the treble and completely lack lower semi-tones. The pedal is coupled to the middle clavier and has only a Sub-Bass 16', and therefore can provide no real gravity, since it is so dependent on manual stops. . . .[44]

It was not until 1712–14 that Matthias Dropa added two pedal towers to the organ, from plans drawn up by Böhm.[45] Thus the relatively small number of pedal pieces by Böhm would seem to stem from the time after 1714. In light of this situation, it appears more plausible that Böhm's direct influence on the young Bach was less in the area of the specifically North German manner of pedal playing than in the sphere of French-derived manual repertoire. Böhm's chorale partitas and clavier suites stand out in this regard. It is surely no accident that the works by him preserved in the *Möllersche Handschrift* and the *Andreas-Bach-Buch* are almost exclusively clavier suites. Clavecin music by LeBegue in the *Möllersche Handschrift* points to the French connection. Bach was exposed to it in Lüneburg through Böhm and, in a more general way, through the Braunschweig-Lüneburg court, which was dominated by the "Frantzösischer Geschmack." The Obituary speaks not of *trips* by Bach to the relatively faraway Celle, but only of his "hearing several times a then-famous Capelle maintained by the Duke of Zelle." [46] This Capelle could have made music in the Lüneburg town castle,[47] among other places, for that edifice had been chosen to be the dowager's estate of Duchess Eleanore d'Olbreuse after 1700.

If Lüneburg offered Bach only limited opportunities for an intensive encounter with North German organ style, then the trips to Hamburg and Lübeck must be given greater emphasis. Ever since

Spitta, Bach's successful trip from Arnstadt to Lübeck around the turn of the year 1705–1706 and his several-months' stay with Dietrich Buxtehude have been assigned the key role in this regard, even though the plausibility of this idea is not obvious. The thesis that the Lübeck trip was of crucial importance for Bach's understanding of Buxtehude's organ style rests on two premises: that Bach's visit was chiefly concerned with Buxtehude's organ music, and that Bach was only vaguely familiar with Buxtehude's organ music before 1705–1706. But even his choice of date for his trip, Advent 1705, suggests that Bach expected to attend concerts of Abendmusik arranged by Buxtehude.[48] Unfortunately, of the two oratorio-like Abendmusik works that were performed in St. Mary's on December 2–3, 1705, *Castrum Doloris*, BuxWV 134, and *Templum Honoris*, BuxWV 135, only the printed texts have survived,[49] so that the precise musical impressions Bach received must remain illusive. Since Buxtehude's Abendmusik ranked as the most significant church music program in Protestant circles of the day, it must have held a strong attraction for Bach. The wording of the Obituary, that Bach traveled to Lübeck in order "to listen" to Buxtehude and stayed "for almost a quarter of a year, not without profit," [50] is certainly neutral. But it suggests that during the extended stay Bach must also have profited from Buxtehude, the master of organ playing. However, the influence of Buxtehude's vocal writing should not be overlooked in Bach's earliest vocal works, written soon after the Lübeck trip. Buxtehudian qualities stand out most clearly in the "Actus Tragicus" (Cantata 106, *Gottes Zeit ist die allerbeste Zeit*), especially in the sections based on chorale melodies (above all in the closing segment, "Durch Jesum Christum, Amen"). One cannot exclude the possibility that for its conception as well as its performance, this unusually elaborate and grandly wrought composition had as its musical model the funeral music for Emperor Leopold, *Castrum Doloris*, BuxWV 134.[51]

To say that Bach's reception of Buxtehude's organ music culminated in the middle of the Arnstadt period means that the Lüneburg years are essentially excluded from consideration and that Reinken's role, in particular, is rated very low. Such a viewpoint has serious consequences for the chronology of Bach's early keyboard music. The few surviving original sources for this repertoire (the autographs of the Prelude and Fugue in g, BWV 535a; the organ chorale *Wie schön leuchtet der Morgenstern*, BWV 739; and the 23-measure fragment of a chorale prelude on the same melody, BWV 764) elude exact chronological placement, but can be assigned with certainty to the period "before

1707." [52] The autograph of the Prelude and Fugue in g is found in the
Möllersche Handschrift,[53] and that of the organ chorales on *Wie schön
leuchtet der Morgenstern*[54] is closely connected to the *Möllersche Handschrift* and the *Andreas-Bach-Buch* in turn. Nothing speaks against placing all three compositions in the years before the Lübeck trip. At the
same time, the chorale preludes might claim chronological priority
over the Prelude and Fugue. However, all three works breathe a special North German spirit and, therefore, belong to Bach's compositional involvement with corresponding models. But since BWV 739,
especially, with its extensive virtuosic echo passages is indebted to
a Reinken model rather than to a Buxtehude one (Reinken's only
surviving organ chorales, *An Wasserflüssen Babylon* and *Was kann uns
kommen an für Not*, show numerous stylistic parallels[55]), the organist of
St. Catherine's in Hamburg moves into the foreground as a decisive
mediator and catalyst for Bach during his formative years.

III

It was certainly to Bach's advantage to attempt to establish ties with
Reinken from Lüneburg, for Reinken was the senior and most widely
recognized representative of the North German organ school. Spitta
acknowledged, with good reason, that Böhm may have bridged the
gap between the generations, although the oft-mentioned student—
teacher relationship between Böhm and Reinken has eluded verifica-
tion up to the present day. In any case, before accepting his post in
Lüneburg in 1698, Böhm had resided in Hamburg for at least five
years, a circumstance that gives a solid basis to his connection with the
Hamburg scene.[56] In the organ of St. Catherine's, Reinken possessed
the largest, most famous, and most beautiful instrument in North
Germany. Buxtehude never had anything comparable at his disposal.[57]
In a description of the legendary 32' pedal stops of the St. Catherine's
organ, Johann Friedrich Agricola referred specifically to Bach's ad-
miring appraisal of the instrument.[58] Bach's encompassing knowledge
of instruments, the foundation for which must have been laid by the
ongoing repairs on the organs in Eisenach, Ohrdruf, and Lüneburg,
could have received a decision rounding out from the Hamburg
experiences.

To a young musician such as Bach, Reinken offered direct access
to the main repertoire of North German organ music, its principles,
and its manner of performance. Included in the repertoire available
through Reinken was the encompassing and certainly most consider-

able *oeuvre* of Buxtehude, for the close connection between Buxtehude and Reinken—something not touched upon by Spitta and later Bach biographers—has recently been demonstrated.[59] And thus one can proceed with the assumption that even during his Lüneburg years, Bach could have studied Buxtehude's organ works. The Lübeck trip of 1705–1706 would then be viewed as the culmination, not the beginning, of a long, intensive involvement with matters of organ writing. Because of the paucity of reliable documentation, the details remain unclear. Nevertheless, Bach's involvement with specific North German compositional models (clearly seen in the Toccata in E, BWV 566, for instance) should be shifted to the early Arnstadt period, if not even earlier.

Without a doubt, Reinken represented a versatile and colorful musical personality of a special sort. He was a virtuoso of high order and an esteemed organ expert. He was a founding member of the Hamburg opera and sat on its directorate, thereby assuming an important role in the musical life of the city. At the same time, he also possessed theoretical interests and clearly had an encompassing professional knowledge of the musical literature.[60] In this respect, Reinken must have appeared incomparably more fascinating to the young Bach than Buxtehude or Böhm. While the Bach–Reinken relationship escapes a closer description, Bach's arrangements of Reinken's sonata movements, BWV 954, 965, and 966, offer a few confirmable clues, at least. The very fact that Bach did not arrange any works by a North German composer other than Reinken, not even by Buxtehude or Böhm, underlines Reinken's significance for the student at St. Michael's, Lüneburg.

Spitta first identified the Reinken arrangements and linked them with Bach's visit to Hamburg in 1720,[61] a dating that by and large has remained unchallenged. But the provenance of the sources as well as comparison with other fugue arrangements suggest that the compositions spring from Bach's early years. Of course, that does not mean that the arrangements had to originate under Reinken's eye during Bach's Lüneburg period. In truth, it seems more reasonable to suppose that they were written during the period of Bach's general encounter with Reinken and that they should be seen in direct connection with Bach's own course of self-study in counterpoint. This view gains support from C. P. E. Bach. In 1775, he borrowed an appropriate phrase from the Obituary to characterize his father's early training: "Through his own study alone he became, even in his youth, a pure and strong fugue writer,"[62] and indeed he advanced principally "through the observation of the famous and profound composers of the time."[63]

Bach's arrangements from Reinken's *HORTUS MUSICUS/recentibus aliquot flosculis/SONATEN,/ALLEMANDEN,/COURANTEN,/SAR[A]-BANDEN,/et/GIQUEN/Cum 2. Violin. Viola* [da Gamba]. *et Basso/continuo* . . . ("MUSICAL GARDEN/of fresh little flowers/SONATAS/ALLE-MANDES/COURANTES/SARABANDES/and/GIGUES/ for 2 violins, viola [da gamba], and Basso continuo . . .") (Hamburg, n.d. [1687]),[64] involve the following works listed in Table 1.

TABLE 1

BWV 965	BWV 966	BWV 954
Sonata 1ᵐᵃ (in a)	Sonata 11ᵐᵃ (in C)	Sonata 6ᵗᵃ (in B♭)
Adagio	Lento	
Allegro	Allegro	Allegro
Solo. Largo-Presto	Solo. Largo-Allegro	
Allemand 2ᵈᵃ. Allegro	Allemand 12ᵐᵃ. Allegro	
Courant 3ᵗⁱᵃ		
Saraband 4ᵗᵃ		
Gique 5ᵗᵃ		

The individual movements are numbered from 1 to 30 in the original print of *Hortus musicus*, but are grouped into six tonally enclosed trio sonatas with suite appendixes. While BWV 965 encompasses an entire sonata with suite, BWV 966 includes the Sonata in C and the ensuing Allemande, and BWV 954 is limited to the imitative Allegro section of the Sonata in B♭. To all appearances, this sequence corresponds to the course of Bach's study through arranging: he begins with the transcription of a complete sonata but then concentrates increasingly on the contrapuntal movements. Bach's arrangements of the noncontrapuntal movements consist of richly figured but generally exact clavier transcriptions of Reinken's instrumental originals. The gigues and allegro movements, by contrast, are not simply expanded but are actually newly composed. Bach's own interest extends to the unfolding of the imitative allegro movements in the sense of a formal fugue. Hermann Keller[65] and Ulrich Siegele[66] have analyzed Bach's Reinken transcriptions from various points of view, and they stress the structural similarity and chronological proximity to the fugues of *Well-Tempered Clavier* I. However, their discussions are based on Spitta's dating of the works in connection with Bach's Hamburg trip of 1720. New discoveries regarding the manuscript sources of the arrangements force one to abandon this dating and think through the style of the pieces once again.

The earliest source for BWV 965 and 966 is in the collection Berlin, DStB *P 803*, where the arrangements are entered in the hand of Johann Gottfried Walther (probably around 1712 at the latest).[67] BWV 965 and 966, together with BWV 954, are also transmitted in the manuscript Berlin, SPK *P 804*, along with other early works by Bach written out by Johann Peter Kellner some time after 1725.[68] Since the manuscripts from which Walther and Kellner made their copies (perhaps Bach's autographs?) have not survived, there is no firm evidence for a more precise dating of the arrangements. They surely stem from before 1710, and probably even earlier. Speaking in favor of this early date is the direct stylistic connection with Bach's fugue compositions after Italian trio-sonata models: Fugue in b, BWV 579, after Corelli, Op. 3, no. 4 (Rome, 1689); Fugues in A, b, and C, BWV 950, 951/951a, and 945, after Albinoni, Op. 1, nos. 3, 8, and 12 (Venice, 1694); and Fugue in c, BWV 574/574a/574b, after Legrenzi, Op. 2, no. 11, "La Mont' Albana" (Venice, 1655).[69]

The similarities of genre (Reinken's sonatas represent a North German variant of the Italian trio sonata, standing between the Legrenzi type and the Corelli and Albinoni models[70]) already point to a distinct link, implying that Bach became occupied with the chamber music of the passing seventeenth century, together with its performance practices, when this repertoire was still current.[71] A bit of chronological evidence for the early dating of Bach's Italian transcriptions can be gleaned from the sources, for the early version of the Legrenzi Fugue, BWV 574b, is handed down in the *Andreas-Bach-Buch*.[72] The *Andreas-Bach-Buch* also contains open scores of the first two Trio Sonatas from Albinoni's Op. 1. The sister manuscript, the *Möllersche Handschrift*, contains an arrangement of a Reinken fugue[73] made by Peter Heidorn, which completes the chain of circumstances that appears to confirm the North German origin of this sort of keyboard transcription of instrumental sonatas. This situation seems to be an early parallel to the Netherlands origin of the concerto transcriptions for keyboard instruments.[74] In this case, Reinken would seem to be the logical connecting link.

Thus Bach's arrangements of Reinken's works must be grouped with his arrangements of Italian trio sonatas, especially with regard to the technical, formal, and stylistic evolution of the Bach keyboard fugue as it unfolded before 1710.[75] In this context the following theoretical considerations—in which the musical analysis must necessarily remain cursory—can be set forth:

1. The term *arrangement* for a fugue fashioned by Bach from a trio-sonata movement is misleading and, in truth, inappropriate. Without exception, one is dealing with a new composition, based on given thematic materials, generally thematic combinations with fixed countersubjects. Bach's approach, which results in fully altering the structural and formal proportions of the original, can be sensed even from a simple comparison of the expansiveness of the new compositions with the sonata models: the arrangements of Reinken's music are almost twice as long as the pieces on which they are based (BWV 965 = 85 mm., the Reinken movement = 50 mm.; BWV 966 = 97 mm., the Reinken original = 47 mm.; BWV 954 = 95 mm., the Reinken original = 50 mm.). The arrangement of the Corelli work goes even further and is almost three times the length of its model (BWV 579 = 102 mm., the Corelli movement = 39 mm.).

2. Although the young Bach immersed himself in the composition of suites in the French manner (including the corresponding models by Böhm and Reinken), when it came to writing contrapuntal movements he relied primarily on Italian style. The basis for this tendency was established with his early schooling in the Pachelbel tradition. This development took a decisive turn, however, as Bach strove to achieve a synthesis of the North German archetype (expansive form) and the Italian ideal (clear thematic profile, closed disposition)—and indeed under the influence of trio-sonata practice. In the process, additional qualities entered into Bach's keyboard fugues that did not stem simply from the tradition of keyboard music. It is precisely in this connection that the influence on Bach of the older Italian sonata and concerto style (especially the elements of *ritornello*, episode, and sequence techniques) must be reappraised, in order to differentiate it from the influence of the newer Italian writing of the Vivaldian stamp, which did not take hold until Weimar.

3. In his keyboard fugues Bach develops principal structural components from the model of the contrapuntal trio-sonata movement. To these components belong especially:

a. Consistent and logical part writing.

b. The production of an independent, closed movement. The concept of the fugue as a movement, not a section, makes possible the form-pair later so greatly preferred by Bach, the prelude and fugue.

c. The development of motivically unified contrapuntal fabric. See,

EXAMPLE 1

Reinken

EXAMPLE 2

EXAMPLE 3

EXAMPLE 4

for instance, Examples 1 and 2, where the closing figuration of Reinken's theme (m. 4) is refashioned by Bach into an independent imitative motive (m. 24 and elsewhere), or Examples 3 and 4, where the running motion of the theme is, in contrast to Reinken's original, expanded contrapuntally.

d. The differentiation of thematic exposition and episode. Reinken's contrapuntal sonata movements are episode-free, while the Italian counterparts display episodes without exception (although they are sometimes extremely short). Bach appropriates episodic technique for his Reinken fugues and uses it to expand the pieces.

e. The expansion of sequential patterns, especially through the setting of thematic expositions in other keys. Sequential schemes, which also belong to the North German keyboard idiom, are employed in the modulatory manner of the Italian trio sonata (see Example 5).

4. Bach strives to endow his subjects and countersubjects with a pronounced rhythmic and melodic contour, which finds its clearest precedent in Corelli's works (see Example 8 below). In Examples 6 and 7, Reinken's countersubject, which is consistently maintained, is varied by Bach and treated in a nonuniform manner—a sign of an experimental phase reflected throughout BWV 965, 966, and 954.

5. As a critical feature of his fugues modeled after trio-sonata movements, Bach relies on the logical and systematic use of double counterpoint. The procedure of voice exchange found in three-voice movements is thereby extended to four- or five-voice textures. In so doing, Bach avoids the systematic use of permutation technique—employed above all by Reinken (Table 2)—as well as the asymmetrical ordering of entries, often seen, for instance, in Corelli (Examples 8 and 9).

6. The permutation and voice-exchange techniques of Reinken furnish the models for Bach's thematic expositions in double counterpoint, which are, however, handled much more flexibly (including modulation to distant keys). The expansion of the fugue through a new harmonic dimension and the extension of the form through strategically placed episodes appear to have been among Bach's early goals. In 1759 Marpurg reported a conversation with Bach concerning these techniques:

> Just consider his fugues. How many ingenious transpositions of the principal subject, how many splendidly assorted subsidiary ideas you will find there! I myself once heard him, when during my stay in Leipzig I was discussing with him certain matters concerning the fugue, pronounce the works of an old and hard-working contrapuntist dry and wooden, and certain fugues by a more modern and no less great contrapuntist—that is, in the form in which they are arranged for clavier—pedantic; the first because the composer stuck continuously to his principal subject, without any change; and the second because, at least in the fugues under discussion, he had not shown enough fire to reanimate the theme by interludes.[76]

Permutation technique, used consistently, allows neither episodes nor harmonic digressions—essential elements of Bach's instrumental fugues, but not of his vocal fugues. His involvement with permutation technique in a number of early keyboard works,[77] however, appears to precede his development of the vocal permutation fugue, as it first appears in Cantata 71 of 1708.[78] This clearly contradicts the con-

EXAMPLE 5

EXAMPLE 6

EXAMPLE 7

TABLE 2

Reinken: Sonata in a, Allegro

```
Vl. 1    a  b       a  b
Vl. 2       a  b       a  b
B.c.           a  b       a
           v  i  v  i  v  i
```

This scheme is repeated exactly in the second half of the movement. NB: in BWV 965 (Bach's arrangement of the movement) the thematic entries are likewise limited to the tonic (i) and dominant (v). Double counterpoint is not maintained strictly.

Reinken: Sonata in C, Allegro

```
Vl. 1    a  b   ⌐a  b⌐
Vl. 2       a  b       a  b
B.c.           a  b       a
           V  I  V  I  V  I
```

The segment marked with a bracket is repeated five times. NB: BWV 966 (Bach's arrangement of the movement) includes thematic entries in b and c as well as the tonic (I) and dominant (V). Double counterpoint is not maintained strictly.

Reinken: Sonata in Bb, Allegro

```
Vl. 1    a  b       a  b
Vl. 2       a  b       a  b
B.c.           a  b       a
           V  I  V  I  V  I
```

The scheme is repeated in the fashion of the Sonata in C. NB: BWV 954 (Bach's arrangement of the movement) also includes thematic entries in d, g, Eb, C, and F (including a diminution of the theme in inversion!). Double counterpoint is not carried out strictly.

ventional view that Bach's permutation fugue is a specifically vocal phenomenon.[79]

The new dating and briefly sketched reappraisal of the Reinken fugues within the broad and narrow context of Bach's early works raises questions that are not well served by hasty answers. Rather, they lead to the plea that the youthful and first master periods of Bach be thought through once again, in terms of both biography and musical style. The reassignment of compositions long dated 1720 to a time nearly half a generation earlier signifies that one must grant the young Bach a greater measure of compositional craft and artistic discipline than has been done in the past.

But above all, Bach's fugues after Reinken, Corelli, Albinoni,

EXAMPLE 8

EXAMPLE 9

Legrenzi, and perhaps other still-to-be-identified masters offer a concrete look into that sphere of intense "study" that made Bach, according to the testimony of Carl Philipp Emanuel, "even in his youth a
pure and strong fugue writer." At a very early point, there emerge
elements of the most characteristic and essential parameters of Bach's
compositional art:[80] the probing elaboration, modification, and transformation of a given musical *res facta* originating from himself or another composer, with the aim of improvement and further individu-
alization. Bach's Reinken fugues reflect both of these goals. They are
more expansive and represent more perfect realizations of a new idea
of fugal genre, yet at the same time they carry a more personal stamp
than do their original models.

NOTES

This article first appeared as "Johann Adam Reinken und Johann Sebastian Bach: Zum Kontext des Bachschen Frühwerks," BJ 1985: 99–118. It is reprinted here, in translation and with emendations by the author, by permission.

    1. Spitta, vol. I, book I, sections IV–VII.

    2. See the figure sketched in Friedrich Blume, *Der junge Bach* (Wolfenbüttel and Zurich, 1967); Gustav Fock, *Der junge Bach in Lüneburg. 1700 bis 1702* (Hamburg, 1950); Elke Krüger, *Stilistische Untersuchungen zu ausgewählten frühen Klavierfugen Johann Sebastian Bachs* (Hamburg, 1970); Hartwig Eichberg, "Unechtes unter Johann Sebastian Bachs Klavierwerken," BJ 1975: 7–49; Peter Williams, *The Organ Music of J. S. Bach* (Cambridge, 1980–84), vols. 1 and 2.

    3. See the discussion by Christoph Wolff, "Probleme und Neuansätze der Bach-Biographik," in *Bachforschung und Bachinterpretation heute*, edited by Reinhold Brinkmann (Kassel, 1981), pp. 21–31; abbreviated English translation in *Proteus* 2 (1985): 1–7.

    4. Assembled by C. P. E. Bach and Johann Friedrich Agricola in 1750 and printed in 1754; BDok III, p. 81.

    5. Letter to Forkel, January 13, 1775, in BDok III, p. 288.

    6. Facsimile in *Bach Urkunden . . . Nachrichten über Johann Sebastian Bach von Carl Philipp Emanuel Bach*, edited by Max Schneider (Leipzig, 1917); BDok III, p. 290.

    7. A newspaper announcement of September 19, 1727 states that the two partitas "may be obtained . . . not only from the author, but also . . . 3) from Herr Böhm, organist at St. John's in Lüneburg . . ."; BDok II, no. 224.

    8. BDok III, p. 82.

    9. BDok II, p. 19.

    10. *Bachiana I*, in *Allgemeine Musikalische Zeitung*, 1881, no. 47–48. Reprinted in Philipp Spitta, *Musikgeschichtliche Aufsätze* (Berlin, 1894), pp. 111–20.

    11. BDok II, no. 102.

    12. BDok III, p. 84.

    13. On this occasion, Bach performed in Hamburg "before the Magistrate and many other distinguished persons of the town, on the fine organ of St. Catherine's, for more than two hours, to their general astonishment. The aged organist of this church, Johann Adam Reinken, who at that time was nearly a hundred years old, listened to him with particular pleasure. Bach, at the request of those present, performed *ex tempore* the chorale *An Wasserflüssen Babylon* at great length—almost a half-hour—and in different ways . . . . Particularly on this Reinken paid Bach the following compliment: 'I thought that this art. . .' ."

    14. Johann Joachim Quantz, *Versuch einer Anleitung die Flöte traversiere zu spielen* (Berlin, 1752); BDok III, p. 18.

    15. BDok III, p. 32.

    16. BDok III, pp. 423–24.

    17. One can also not exclude the possibility that Böhm, who was born in the vicinity of Ohrdruf and raised near Gotha, had ties to the Bach family that Johann Sebastian could only take advantage of in Lüneburg.

    18. Johann Gottfried Walther (in *Musicalisches Lexicon*, Leipzig, 1732) speaks of the "two extremely renowned organists, Herren Reinken and Buxtehude";

Johann Mattheson (in *Critica Musica*, Hamburg, 1722, p. 517) writes of Reinken's organ playing: "of the things in which he was versed, one knew nothing comparable in his time."

19. Karl Müller, "Der junge Bach," in *Arnstädter Bach-Buch*, 2d ed., edited by Karl Müller and Fritz Wiegand (Arnstadt, 1957), p. 63.

20. BDok II, no. 5.

21. Fock, *Der junge Bach in Lüneburg*, p. 100.

22. BDok I, no. 38.

23. BDok III, p. 82.

24. BDok II, no. 7.

25. Ibid.

26. On the life of Johann Christoph Bach see Hans-Joachim Schulze, "Johann Christoph Bach (1671–1721), 'Organist und Schul Collega in Ohrdruf', Johann Sebastian Bachs erster Lehrer," BJ 1985: 55–81.

27. J. S. Bach's beginning salary at Arnstadt exceeded his brother's highest income. See BDok II, p. 12; and Ferdinand Reinhold, "Die Musik-Bache in Ohrdruf," in *Festschrift zum Bachjahr 1950* (Ohrdruf, n.d.), p. 14.

28. Reinhold, p. 14.

29. BDok III, p. 81.

30. Ibid.

31. Blume, p. 7.

32. Spitta, vol. I, p. 186.

33. See Robert Hill, "The Lost Clavier Books of the Young Bach and Handel," in *Bach, Handel, Scarlatti: Tercentenary Essays*, edited by Peter Williams (Cambridge, 1985).

34. Formerly *Mus. ms. 40 035* of the Preussische Staatsbibliothek in Berlin, now preserved in the Biblioteka Jagiellońska, Cracow. The source had not been accessible since World War II. I should like to thank the director of the library, Dr. J. Pierozyński, for allowing me to examine the manuscript for the first time during my stay in Cracow in 1981 and for placing a microfilm of it at my disposal.

35. See the article "Eckelt" by Walter Blankenburg, in *Die Musik in Geschichte und Gegenwart*, vol. III (1954), column 1091–93.

36. I should like to thank Hans-Joachim Schulze for his help in identifying Pachelbel's handwriting.

37. An entry on the recto side of leaf 18 reads: "The music to the chorales I bought from him."

38. A thorough discussion of the Eckelt tablature book must remain the object of a future study.

39. Max Seiffert, ed., *Denkmäler der Tonkunst in Bayern* II/1 (1901); IV/1 (1903).

40. Guido Adler, ed., *Denkmäler der Tonkunst in Österreich* 13 (1899); 21 (1903).

41. Spitta, vol. 1, p. 220.

42. Eichberg, pp. 14–17. New perspectives on Bach's early compositional activities are provided by the organ chorales of the Neumeister Collection (Yale Univesity, *ms. LM 4708*), edited by Christoph Wolff (New Haven and Kassel, 1985); and Wolff, introduction to the facsimile edition, *The Neumeister Collection of Chorale Preludes from the Bach Circle* (New Haven, 1985).

43. The contents of both sources are given in NBA IV/5–6, KB (edited by Dietrich Kilian, 1978), pp. 98–106 (*Möllersche Handschrift*) and 122–31 (*Andreas-Bach-Buch*). For a detailed discussion of the repertoire of the two

manuscripts as well as the identification of the principal copyist see Hans-Joachim Schulze, *Studien zur Bach-Überlieferung im 18. Jahrhundert* (Leipzig, 1984), pp. 30–56.

44. Gustav Fock, *Arp Schnitger und seine Schule* (Kassel, 1974), p. 104.

45. Ibid., p. 105.

46. BDok III, p. 82; see also Hans-Joachim Schulze, "Der französische Einfluss im Instrumentalwerk J. S. Bachs," in *Studien zur Aufführungspraxis und Interpretation von Instrumentalmusik des 18. Jahrhunderts*, Book 16, edited by Walter Blankenburg (1981), pp. 57–63.

47. The Herzögliches Schloss am Markt, built in 1693–96 by D. A. Rossi after a French model. Today it is the Land- und Amtsgericht.

48. Bach did not return to Arnstadt from this journey of three-to-four months until shortly before February 7, 1706.

49. See Georg Karstädt, *Thematisch-systematisches Verzeichnis der musikalischen Werke von Dietrich Buxtehude* ("BuxWV"; Wiesbaden, 1974), p. 132.

50. BDok III, p. 82.

51. The proposed date of 1707 for Cantata 106 connecting it with the memorial service for Bach's uncle Tobias Lämmerhirt, who died on August 10 of that year (see Alfred Dürr, *Die Kantaten von Johann Sebastian Bach*, 2d ed. [Kassel, 1971], p. 611), is questionable. Bach would have had to finish the composition between the day of death and the memorial service. This period was not enough time for "an ingenious work, which has seldom been equaled by great masters and with which the twenty-two year old, with a single stroke, swept all his contemporaries behind him" (ibid., pp. 611–12). It is more likely that Bach wrote the "Actus Tragicus" on "advance notice," so to speak, creating a carefully worked-out presentation piece for some opportune occasion.

52. Georg von Dadelsen, *Beiträge zur Chronologie der Werke Johann Sebastian Bachs* (Trossingen, 1958), p. 75.

53. In Hans-Joachim Schulze, *Studien zur Bach-Überlieferung*, it is dated "scarcely before 1705" (assuming a relatively late reception of Buxtehude's style by Bach), from which corresponding inferences are drawn for the chronology of the *Möllersche Handschrift*.

54. See also Russell Stinson, "Bach's Earliest Autograph" (résumé in *Abstracts of Papers Read at the Forty-eighth Annual Meeting of the American Musicological Society, University of Michigan, Ann Arbor, 1982*), unpublished.

55. J. A. Reincken, *Sämtliche Orgelwerke*, edited by Klaus Beckmann (Wiesbaden, 1974), pp. 4–21 and 22–37.

56. See the article "Böhm" by Hugh J. McLean, in *The New Grove Dictionary of Music and Musicians* (London, 1980), vol. 2, pp. 852–53.

57. Reinken's organ had 58 stops, distributed among four manuals and pedal. For Buxtehude, the large organ in St. Mary's had 54 stops (on three manuals and pedal); however, in 40 years Buxtehude did not succeed in obtaining an overdue "thorough renovation" of the instrument. See Friedrich W. Riedel, *Quellenkundliche Beiträge zur Geschichte der Musik für Tasteninstrumente in der 2. Hälfte des 17. Jahrhunderts* (Kassel, 1960), p. 189.

58. BDok III, no. 739: "In the organ of St. Catherine's Church in Hamburg there are 16 reeds. The late Kapellmeister, Herr J. S. Bach in Leipzig . . . could not praise the beauty and variety of tone of these reeds highly enough" (1768).

59. See Christoph Wolff, "Das Hamburger Buxtehude-Bild. Ein Beitrag zur musikalischen Ikonographie und zum Umkreis von Johann Adam Reinken," in *800 Jahre Musik in Lübeck*, edited by Antje Kathrin Grassmann and Werner Neugebauer (Lübeck, 1982), pp. 64–79.

60. His library contained, among other things, treatises by Zarlino and Poglietti (see Riedel, p. 190) as well as Frescobaldi's Second Book of Toccatas (see Wolff, "Das Hamburger Buxtehude-Bild," p. 76).

61. Spitta, vol. I, p. 431.

62. BDok III, no. 803.

63. BDok III, p. 82.

64. The only extant complete copy is located in Berlin, DStB.

65. Hermann Keller, "Über Bachs Bearbeitungen aus dem 'Hortus musicus' von Reinken," in *Kongressbericht Basel 1949*, pp. 160–61.

66. Ulrich Siegele, *Kompositionsweise und Bearbeitungstechnik in der Instrumentalmusik Johann Sebastian Bachs* (Neuhausen-Stuttgart, 1975), pp. 11–22.

67. Hermann Zietz, *Quellenkritische Untersuchungen an den Bach-Handschriften P 801, P 802, und P 803 aus dem "Krebsschen Nachlass" unter besonderer Berücksichtigung der Choralbearbeitungen des jungen J. S. Bach* (Hamburg, 1969), p. 216.

68. Paul Kast, *Die Bach-Handschriften der Berliner Staatsbibliothek* (Trossingen, 1958), pp. 48–49.

69. The title of BWV 574b in the *Andreas-Bach-Buch* is *"Thema Legrezianum. Elaboratum per Joan. Seb. Bach."* Robert Hill recently identified the thematic source of Bach's Legrenzi fugue, and I am grateful to him for having shared that information with me. He will report on his discovery in BJ 1986.

70. Reinken's sonatas are much more indebted to Italian trio-sonata style than are the chamber sonatas of Buxtehude, for instance.

71. It is possible that Bach also tried his hand at composing chamber music at this time, even though no trace of that activity has survived unless one places the Fugue in g for violin and continuo, BWV 1026, in the early period (the piece is also handed down in *P 803* in Walther's hand). The style of the Fugue does not speak against an early date.

72. The fact that the Legrenzi Fugue survives in three different versions strongly suggests that the remaining fugues on themes by other composers also went through several stages of refinement. That would certainly reflect their role as study pieces.

73. The original has not survived. It is not from *Hortus musicus*.

74. See Hans-Joachim Schulze, "J. S. Bach's Concerto Arrangements for Organ—Studies or Commissioned Works?" *The Organ Yearbook* 3 (1972): 4–13.

75. See the discussion in Joseph Müller-Blattau, *Geschichte der Fuge*, 3d ed. (Kassel, 1963), pp. 66–78.

76. BDok III, pp. 144–45. Translation from *Bach Reader*, p. 257.

77. Note, for instance, the use of permutation technique in the fugue of the Passacaglia in c for organ, BWV 582, which in some sources (including the earliest manuscript copy, in the *Andreas-Bach-Buch*) is called "fuga cum subjéctis." The structure of the Passacaglia fugue follows a strict permutation scheme:

Measure

	169	174	181	186	192		198	209	221	234	246	256	272
soprano		a	b	c	—	|	c	b	c	—	a	—	a
alto	a	b	c	—	a	|	b	a	b	c	—	b	b
tenor	b	c	—	a	b	|	a	c	—	a	b	c	—
bass			a	b	c	|		a	b	c	a	c
harmonic plan	i	v	i	v	i	|	III	VII	v	i	v	iv	i

See the discussion in Christoph Wolff, "Zur Architektur von Bachs Passacaglia," *Acta organologica* 3 (1969): 183–94.

78. Werner Neumann, *J. S. Bachs Chorfuge. Ein Beitrag zur Kompositionstechnik Bachs*, 2d ed. (Leipzig, 1950), pp. 14–15.

79. See also Carl Dahlhaus, "Zur Geschichte der Permutationsfuge," BJ 1959: 95–110.

80. See also Christoph Wolff, "'Die sonderbaren Vollkommenheiten des Herrn Hofcompositeurs'—Versuch über die Eigenart der Bachschen Musik," in *Bachiana et alia musicologica. Festschrift Alfred Dürr zum 65. Geburtstag* (Kassel, 1983), pp. 356–62.

ERNEST MAY

The Types, Uses, and Historical Position of Bach's Organ Chorales

The genre organ chorale can be defined as a polyphonic prolongation, elaboration, or working out of a chorale tune on the organ. In Bach's time, the organ chorale enjoyed a variety of functions. It could be used as a prelude to a congregational chorale, as an *alternatim* piece, as an interlude between verses, as an independent work in the service, or as a concert piece. The chorale tune was usually presented in its entirety in one voice, or motives drawn from it formed the basis of a polyphonic texture, or both.[1]

Bach was born into a rich tradition of organ-chorale writing, a tradition that provided an indispensable context for his remarkable contribution to the genre. The Dutch Calvinist organist Jan Pieterszoon Sweelinck created one of the two earliest forms of the Baroque organ chorale, the chorale variation, by combining the style of the English secular keyboard variation with the sacred chorale melodies (see Table 1, which summarizes, in diagram form, the present discussion). Sweelinck normally wrote four variations (for two to four voices) to a set, usually presenting the chorale tune in long notes and placing motivic, patterned, or sequential figuration in the other parts. Since organ music was excluded from the Calvinist services, Sweelinck's chorale variations must have been intended for performance at his frequent organ concerts. Further development stems from Sweelinck's leading German pupils: Samuel Scheidt, whose monumental *Tabulatura Nova* (1624) is a major landmark in the repertoire; and Heinrich Scheidemann, who invented the free chorale fantasia by introducing toccata elements into the other very early form of Baroque organ chorale, the chorale motet. Dietrich Buxtehude, who was influenced by both

81

Scheidt and Scheidemann, wrote chorale fantasias and complete sets
of chorale variations, but his 30 short chorale preludes constitute his
principal contribution to the development of the genre. Each of his
short chorales can be regarded as the reduction of a set of variations
to a single prelude, probably intended to introduce the congregational chorale in the service. The chorale is usually set in the soprano,
with ornamented expressive vocal embellishments, and accompanied
by modest lower parts in such a way as to convey the affect of the chorale text. Clearly, certain pieces by Buxtehude served as models for
similar works by Bach.[2]

In Central Germany, the chorale motet was compressed into the chorale fughetta by reducing the multiple points of imitation to a single
fugue. A set of 44 such pieces was composed by Bach's relative Johann
Christoph Bach of Eisenach. Johann Pachelbel also developed a distinctive Central German chorale prelude style, in which a generally
strict, unadorned cantus firmus is set against nonmotivic counterpoint, but with each phrase of the chorale introduced by pre-imitation
in the accompanying voices. By the early eighteenth century, the North

TABLE 1

The Evolution of the Baroque Organ Chorale

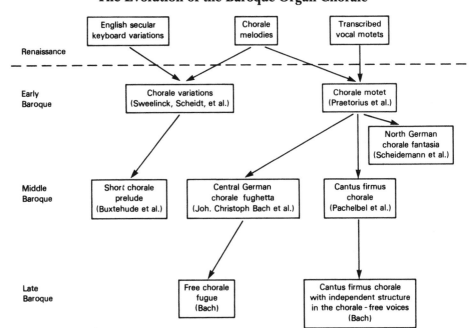

and Central German styles exerted equal influence, as demonstrated in the works of Georg Böhm, Georg Philipp Telemann, Johann Gottfried Walther, Georg Friedrich Kauffmann, and, of course, J. S. Bach.

Bach's great collections—the *Orgelbüchlein*, the Schübler Chorales, the "Great Eighteen" Chorales, the chorales from *Clavierübung* III, and the Canonic Variations on *Vom Himmel hoch*—clearly represent the artistic culmination of the organ chorale, and it is possible, though simplistic, to view everything else as either an antecedent or a derivative of these masterpieces. For some years after 1750 organ chorales were still being composed by Bach students Johann Ludwig Krebs, Gottfried August Homilius, Johann Peter Kellner, Johann Philipp Kirnberger, Johann Friedrich Agricola, and others, but by 1800, newly composed organ chorales were rare.

Organ chorales are generally classified according to the treatment of the chorale tune: accompanimental setting, chorale motet, chorale variation, melody chorale, cantus firmus chorale, ornamental chorale, chorale canon, chorale fantasia, chorale fughetta, and chorale fugue.[3] Most of these types exist in either short form (without interludes between lines of the chorale) or long form (with interludes). In the majority of cases, the treatment of the chorale melody itself is rather strict, although a free approach is certainly possible.

Such a typology, based on the handling of the chorale alone, is adequate for classifying the majority of Bach's compositions. However, a number of his most fully developed pieces, mostly those in the cantus firmus category, offer a clear, independent structure in the chorale-free voices. The large setting of *Vater unser im Himmelreich*, BWV 682, from *Clavierübung* III, is a most astonishing example of this technique: a full-scale trio-sonata texture is combined with a chorale canon. Traditionally, this structure would be classified as a chorale canon with trio-sonata accompaniment. However, the reverse description is equally valid: a trio sonata to which a chorale tune has been added in canon. For such works, the musical significance of the chorale tune is equaled by an independent formal structure in the chorale-free voices (the so-called accompaniment): canon (e.g., the Canonic Variations), invention (e.g., *Wo soll ich fliehen hin*, BWV 646), fugue (e.g., *Wir glauben all' an einen Gott*, BWV 680), trio sonata (e.g., *Vater unser im Himmelreich*, BWV 682), or ritornello (e.g., *Kommst du nun, Jesu, vom Himmel herunter*, BWV 650). The combination of such structures with the traditional chorale tunes was a major innovation by Bach and demands a categorization of its own.

Congregational Singing and Bach's Accompanimental Settings

The best place to begin our survey of Bach's organ chorales is with his accompanimental settings. During the sixteenth and the early seventeenth century, congregational chorales were sung relatively slowly, in octaves and without accompaniment. It is possible that the organist improvised an introduction, interludes between verses, or *alternatim* verses. Organ accompaniment was introduced around 1600. The first hymnbook to offer the melodies with a figured-bass accompaniment (rather than simple four-part harmonizations for the choir) appeared in 1640. By the end of the seventeenth century, however, organ support was the usual (but not universal) style of performance.[4]

In the first half of the eighteenth century, an organist's responsibilities for congregational chorale singing were at least to introduce and accompany it, and possibly to play interludes between verses or to alternate verses with the congregation. All these functions were normally improvised. Considerable differences in local liturgies and performance customs, as well as significant variation in the pitch level and melodic shape of the chorale tunes themselves, made standardization of the repertoire impossible. Obviously, it was inefficient to commit such improvisations to paper except as exemplars for teaching purposes or repertoire for organ concerts. Part of an organist's training was to learn to improvise chorale accompaniments from a figured bass or to improvise organ chorales in the service in response to local needs and in conformity with local practice. Thus, the organ chorales that survive in manuscripts and some printed editions are intended— like the pieces in Bach's *Orgelbüchlein* ("in which a Beginner at the Organ is given Instruction in Developing a Chorale in many diverse ways . . .")—more as instruction in improvisation than as pieces actually destined for a specific liturgical function. Local exigencies prevented an automatic interchange of organ chorales from place to place.

It is not possible to recreate the local congregational chorale accompaniment requirements at Arnstadt, Mühlhausen, or Weimar. There are, however, some clues provided by the censuring of the 21-year-old Bach by the Arnstadt Consistory:

> Reprove him for having hitherto made many curious *variationes* in the chorale, and mingled many strange tones in it, and for the fact that the congregation has been confused by it. In the future, if he wished to introduce a *tonus peregrinus*, he was to hold it out, and not to turn too

quickly to something else, or, as had hitherto been his habit, even play a *tonus contrarius.* In addition, it was quite disagreeable that hitherto no concerted music had been performed, for which he was responsible, because he did not wish to get along with the students; accordingly he was to declare himself as to whether he was willing to play for figured music as well as chorales sung by the students. . . .[5]

From this reproval, it can be deduced, first, that Bach's position required him to accompany congregational chorales in a relatively simple manner. Certain chorale preludes—*Wer nur den lieben Gott lässt walten,* BWV 690; *Christ lag in Todesbanden,* BWV 695; *Jesu, meine Freude,* BWV 713; *Nun freut euch, lieben Christen g'mein,* BWV 734; and *Valet will ich dir geben,* BWV 736—are followed by simple figured-bass settings of the chorale tune, which, undoubtedly, served as a guide to the organist for improvising an accompaniment to congregational singing. *Herr Gott, dich loben wir,* BWV 725, if authentic, offers a rare example of a straightforward but fully realized five-part accompaniment to the *Te Deum.*

Second, the Consistory made it clear that, on occasion, Bach challenged and confused the Arnstadt congregation with free accompaniments. The surviving pieces that fit the Consistory's description of Bach's performance are the following:

BWV	Title	Source[6]
715	*Allein Gott in der Höh' sei Ehr'*	Berlin, SPK, *P 804* (Kellner)
722a	*Gelobet seist du, Jesu Christ* (improvisation sketch)	Berlin, DStB, *P 802* (J. T. Krebs)
722	*Gelobet seist du, Jesu Christ*	Leipzig, MB, *Ms. 7* (Preller)
726	*Herr Jesu Christ, dich zu uns wend'*	Berlin, SPK, *P 804* (Kellner)
729a	*In dulci jubilo* (improvisation sketch)	Berlin, DStB, *P 802* (J. T. Krebs)
729	*In dulci jubilo*	Leipzig, MB, *Ms. 7* (Preller)
732a	*Lobt Gott, ihr Christen* (improvisation sketch)	Berlin, DStB, *P 802* (J. T. Krebs)
732	*Lobt Gott, ihr Christen*	Leipzig, MB, *Ms. 7* (Preller)
738a	*Vom Himmel hoch* (improvisation sketch)	Berlin, DStB, *P 802* (J. T. Krebs)
738	*Vom Himmel hoch*	Leipzig, MB, *Ms. 7* (Preller)

The source situation does not preclude a pre-Weimar origin for these pieces.[7] It demonstrates, moreover, that Bach continued to use these works—especially the four Christmas chorales BWV 722, 729, 732, and 738—well into the 1740s as pedagogic examples of accompanying a congregational chorale with free interludes.

Third, the reproval mentions that the organist was to play along with the students when they sang chorales. Simple four-part settings, fully written out, would have been appropriate for this task. The chorales that follow *Ich hab' mein' Sach' Gott heimgestellt*, BWV 707 and 708, offer examples of such vocal settings, apparently intended to be played by the organist.

For Mühlhausen and Weimar, there is no further information about congregational singing or accompaniment. In Weimar, chorales were undoubtedly sung by the choir, since the Court Chapel did not have a congregation in the usual sense. Had Bach accepted the position at the Liebfrauenkirche in Halle, which was offered to him in 1714, one of his duties would have been

> To take care to accompany attentively the regular chorales and those prescribed by the Minister, before and after the Sermons on Sundays and feast days, as well as at Communion and at Vespers and on the eves of holidays, slowly and without unusual embellishment, in four or five parts, on the Principal, to change the other stops at each verse, also to use the fifths [*quintaden*] and the reeds [*Schnarr Wercke*], the stopped flute [*Gedackte*], as well as syncopations and suspensions, in such manner that the Congregation can take the organ as the basis of good harmony and unison tone, and thus sing devoutly and give praise and thanks to the Most High.[8]

For Leipzig there exists an autograph sketch on the back of the title page of Cantata 61 for the order of service. Although the Cantata was written in 1714, the outline of the service appears to date from 1723, when the work was reperformed:[9]

1) Preluding
2) *Motetta*
3) Preluding on the Kyrie, which is performed throughout in concerted music
4) Intoning before the altar
5) Reading of the Epistle
6) Singing of the Litany
7) Preluding on the Chorale
8) Reading of the Gospel
9) Preluding on the principal composition
10) Singing of the Creed
11) The Sermon
12) After the Sermon, as usual, singing of several verses of a hymn
13) Words of Institution
14) Preluding on the composition. After the same, alternate preluding and singing of chorales until the end of the Communion, *et sic porro*.

This sketch confirms two usual functions of "preluding on the chorale": as a prelude to a congregational chorale, and alternating verses during the Communion. However, since Bach was not the organist in Leipzig, and since most of his organ chorales had already been composed by the time he left Weimar, it cannot be assumed that any of his pieces (with the possible exception of those in *Clavierübung* III) were written in response to the requirements of the Leipzig service.

In summary, then, the proceedings of the Arnstadt Consistory, the written-out free accompaniments in the manuscript collections of organ students J. T. Krebs, Kellner, and Preller (all of whom had access to the early autographs of Bach's organ works[10]), the offer from Halle, and the sketch of the Leipzig liturgy give us an idea of the general context within which Bach's organ chorales were composed. They also provide specific examples of how Bach went about realizing the basically improvisatory tasks required of all church organists of the period. The lack of detailed liturgical information for Arnstadt, Mühlhausen, and Weimar, however, is a considerable impediment to the creation of a reliable chronology for Bach's organ chorale production.[11]

The Chorale Motet and Its Derivatives

One of the two earliest forms of organ chorale is the chorale motet, so-called because it imitates the vocal chorale motets of the early seventeenth century. In its strict form, the chorale motet presents each line of the chorale in imitation, producing a series of fugal entries on the successive lines of the chorale tune. The most extraordinary example of this form, Bach's six-voice setting of *Aus tiefer Not*, BWV 686, from *Clavierübung* III, is a strict realization of this plan, as is the four-voice setting of the same chorale, BWV 687, in the same collection. The very early pieces that Bach wrote in this form are somewhat freer.

Pre-Weimar

BWV 705	*Durch Adams Fall ist ganz verderbt*	Breitkopf Collection[12]
BWV 707	*Ich hab' mein' Sach' Gott heimgestellt*	Breitkopf Collection
BWV 724	*Gott durch deine Güte*	*Andreas-Bach-Buch* (Leipzig, MB, *III.8.4*; tablature)
BWV 737	*Vater unser im Himmelreich*	Den Haag *4.G.14*

Leipzig[13]

BWV 669	*Kyrie, Gott Vater in Ewigkeit*	*Clavierübung* III
BWV 670	*Christe, aller Welt Trost*	*Clavierübung* III
BWV 671	*Kyrie. Gott heiliger Geist*	*Clavierübung* III
BWV 686	*Aus tiefer Not* (a 6)	*Clavierübung* III
BWV 687	*Aus tiefer Not* (a 4)	*Clavierübung* III

Chorale Fantasia

The chorale fantasia, developed when Scheidemann and other North German composers (including Reinken and Buxtehude) introduced toccata elements into the chorale motet, quickly emerged as a virtuosic showpiece. The basic structural plan of the fantasia is to present each line of the chorale twice, once ornamented in the soprano and once unornamented in the bass. Strict imitation is rare, while bravura passage-work, motivic fragmentation, and echo effects are common. Bach's three modest contributions to the genre are all early. The source for BWV 739, *P 488*, appears to be Bach's earliest autograph manuscript. BWV 720 may be associated with the rededication of the organ in St. Blasius' in Mühlhausen.[14]

Pre-Weimar

BWV 718	*Christ lag in Todesbanden*	Berlin, SPK, *Mus. ms. Autogr. Krebs 2*
BWV 720	*Ein' feste Burg ist unser Gott*	Den Haag *4.G.14*; Kö *15839*; Berlin, DStB, *P 802*; *Plauener Orgelbuch*
BWV 739	*Wie schön leuchtet der Morgenstern*	Berlin, SPK, *P 488*; *Möllersche Handschrift* (Berlin, SPK, *Mus. ms. 40644*)

From the report in the Obituary of 1754, it would appear that Bach's greatest chorale fantasia was improvised and never written out:

> During this time, about the year 1722, [Bach] made a journey to Hamburg and was heard for more than two hours on the fine organ of the Catharinen-Kirche before the Magistrate and many other distinguished persons of the town, to their general astonishment. The aged Organist of this Church, Johann Adam Reinken, who at that time was nearly a hundred years old, listened to him with particular pleasure. Bach, at the request of those present, performed extempore the chorale *An Wasserflüssen Babylon* at great length (for almost a half-hour) and in different ways, just as the better organists of Hamburg in the

past had been used to doing at the Saturday vespers. Particularly on this, Reinken paid Bach the following compliment: "I thought that this art was dead, but I see that in you it still lives." This verdict of Reinken's was the more unexpected since he himself had set the same chorale, many years before, in the manner described above . . . and this fact . . . was not unknown to our Bach.[15]

Chorale Fughetta

If the chorale fantasia can be regarded as a North German expansion of the chorale motet into a concert piece, then the chorale fughetta can be regarded as a Central German reduction of the same genre into a brief prelude to congregational singing. J. S. Bach's production in this form is considerable.

	Pre-Weimar	
BWV 696	*Christum wir sollen loben schon*	Breitkopf Collection
BWV 697	*Gelobet seist du, Jesu Christ*	Breitkopf Collection
BWV 698	*Herr Christ, der ein'ge Gottes Sohn*	Breitkopf Collection
BWV 699	*Nun komm', der Heiden Heiland*	Breitkopf Collection
BWV 701	*Vom Himmel hoch da komm' ich her*	Breitkopf Collection
BWV 702	*Das Jesulein soll doch mein Trost*	Breitkopf Collection
BWV 703	*Gottes Sohn ist kommen*	Breitkopf Collection
BWV 704	*Lob sei dem allmächt'gen Gott*	Breitkopf Collection
BWV 712	*In dich hab' ich gehoffet, Herr*	Breitkopf Collection
BWV 716	*Allein Gott in der Höh sei Ehr'*	Berlin, SPK, *P 1160*
	Leipzig	
BWV 672	*Kyrie, Gott Vater in Ewigkeit*	*Clavierübung* III
BWV 673	*Christe, aller Welt Trost*	*Clavierübung* III
BWV 674	*Kyrie, Gott heiliger Geist*	*Clavierübung* III
BWV 677	*Allein Gott in der Höh' sei Ehr'*	*Clavierübung* III
BWV 679	*Dies sind die heil'gen zehn Gebot'*	*Clavierübung* III
BWV 681	*Wir glauben all' an einen Gott*	*Clavierübung* III
BWV 685	*Christ, unser Herr, zum Jordan kam*	*Clavierübung* III

The chorale fughettas from the Breitkopf Collection (which are transmitted as a group in Brussels *Ms. II.3919*, Part I) probably represent a lost collection of pieces that Bach may have used to introduce congregational chorales at Arnstadt or Mühlhausen.[16] (Since these works are not transmitted through the Weimar sources, it would appear that hymns were not introduced by fughettas in Weimar.) Thirty to 40 years later, Bach wrote a series of much more ambitious chorale fughettas for *Clavierübung* III that represent the artistic culmination of the form. Historically, however, these final contributions to the genre are retrospective works. Their function, if any, is unclear.

Free Chorale Fugue

A number of pieces derive from the general idea of the chorale motet but have been traditionally viewed as being closer to the fugue than to any other organ chorale classification.

	Pre-Weimar	
BWV 733	*Meine Seele erhebt den Herren* (*Fuga sopra il Magnificat*)	Berlin, SPK, *Mus. ms. 12014*
	Weimar	
BWV 661	*Nun komm', der Heiden Heiland*	"Great Eighteen" Collection
	Leipzig	
BWV 680	*Wir glauben all' an einen Gott*	*Clavierübung* III
BWV 689	*Jesus Christus, unser Heiland*	*Clavierübung* III

These works are not fugues in the usual sense, for the pedal never participates in fugal discourse. In BWV 733 and 661 it is used to present the unadorned cantus firmus. In BWV 680 it is given a rising *ostinato* figure, unrelated to the chorale tune. In BWV 689, the pedal is dispensed with altogether. The *manualiter* setting a 4, titled "Fuga" in the original print of *Clavierübung* III, displays a more thoroughgoing fugal development than do the fughettas in the collection.

To summarize: the chorale motet and its derivatives were relatively old, practical forms, in which Bach may well have improvised a great deal more than he composed. *Clavierübung* III includes Bach's best written-out representatives of these types of organ chorales.

The Chorale Variation

After Sweelinck invented the chorale variation as a concert piece, the form was developed further and apparently introduced into the church service by his pupils Scheidemann and Scheidt, who may have used it for introductions to congregational singing or for *alternatim* verses. Buxtehude, Pachelbel, and Böhm were leading choralevariation composers in the cultural milieu in which Bach grew up. The fact that Böhm was organist at the Johanniskirche in Lüneburg while Bach was a student at St. Michael's Choir School in the same city makes Böhm's influence especially plausible.

	Lüneburg (Böhm's influence?)	
BWV 766	*Christ, der du bist der helle Tag*	Darmstadt, *Ms. 73*
BWV 767	*O Gott, du frommer Gott*	Berlin, DStB, *P 802* (J. T. Krebs)
	Weimar	
BWV 627	*Christ ist erstanden*	*Orgelbüchlein*
BWV 656	*O Lamm Gottes unschuldig*	"Great Eighteen" Collection
BWV 711	*Allein Gott in der Höh sei Ehr'* (bicinium)	Breitkopf Collection
BWV 768	*Sei gegrüsset, Jesu gütig*	Berlin, DStB, *P 802*; Kö *15839*; Carpentras; Leipzig, MB, *III.8.17*; Brussels, *W.12.102*
	Leipzig	
BWV 769	*Vom Himmel hoch da komm' ich her*	Original Print; Berlin, DStB, *P 271* (autograph)

In light of the fact that in his youth Bach must have been cognizant of the many chorale variations by Böhm, Pachelbel, and Buxtehude, his output in this form appears small. It seems clear that the organ posts at Arnstadt, Mühlhausen, and Weimar did not require or encourage the production of such works. Of course, the much later Canonic Variations on *Vom himmel hoch*, BWV 769, was written for a special secular purpose (the acceptance into Mizler's Society for the Musical Sciences) and represents a degree of theoretical speculation that completely transcends the usual connotations of the term *organ chorale*.

The Short Chorale Preludes

The short chorale prelude developed by Buxtehude had considerable usefulness for Bach, for he devoted a major collection, the *Orgelbüch-*

lein, to exploring its potential. The *Orgelbüchlein* manuscript[17] was
ruled in advance for 164 pieces, following the order of a still unknown Thuringian hymnbook (apparently not the Weimar hymn-
books of 1708 or 1713). Bach began by copying into the manuscript
previously composed pieces and then added newly written works. But
he finished only one-third of the project and overlooked or bypassed
a handful of previously composed short chorales: *Wer nur den lieben
Gott lässt walten*, BWV 690; *Herr Jesu Christ, dich zu uns wend'*, BWV
709; *Ach Gott und Herr*, BWV 714; *Erbarm' dich mein, o Herre Gott*,
BWV 721; *Herzlich tut mich verlangen* BWV 727; *Liebster Jesu, wir sind
hier*, BWV 730 and 731. He later composed a few more short chorales
for the notebooks of Wilhelm Friedemann Bach (1720) and Anna
Magdalena Bach (1722 and 1725): *Wer nur den lieben Gott lässt walten*,
BWV 691 and 691a; *Jesus, meine Zuversicht*, BWV 728; and *Jesu meine
Freude*, BWV 753.

Melody Chorale

By far the most prevalent subtype among Bach's short preludes is the
melody chorale, which is, by definition, a short form. The chorale
tune appears as a continuous melody in the soprano, and there are no
interludes between lines. It is accompanied by contrapuntal parts.

	Before 1714	
BWV 690	*Wer nur den lieben Gott lässt walten*	Breitkopf Collection
BWV 721	*Erbarm' dich mein, o Herre Gott* (imitation of Busbetzky?)	Berlin, DStB, *P 802* (J. G. Walther)
BWV 727	*Herzlich thut mich verlangen*	Berlin, DStB, *P 802* (J. T. Krebs); Den Haag *4.G.14*
BWV 730	*Liebster Jesu, wir sind hier*	Leipzig, MB, *Poel. 39*
	1713–16	
BWV 599	*Nun komm', der Heiden Heiland*	*Orgelbüchlein*
BWV 601	*Herr Christ, der ein'ge Gottes-Sohn*	*Orgelbüchlein*
BWV 602	*Lob sei dem allmächtigen Gott*	*Orgelbüchlein*
BWV 603	*Puer natus in Bethlehem*	*Orgelbüchlein*
BWV 604	*Gelobet seist du, Jesu Christ*	*Orgelbüchlein*
BWV 605	*Der Tag, der ist so freudenreich*	*Orgelbüchlein*
BWV 606	*Vom Himmel hoch, da komm' ich her*	*Orgelbüchlein*

BWV 607	*Vom Himmel kam der Engel Schar*	*Orgelbüchlein*
BWV 609	*Lobt Gott, ihr Christen, allzugleich*	*Orgelbüchlein*
BWV 610	*Jesu, meine Freude*	*Orgelbüchlein*
BWV 611	*Christum wir sollen loben schon*	*Orgelbüchlein*
BWV 612	*Wir Christenleut'*	*Orgelbüchlein*
BWV 613	*Helft mir Gottes Güte preisen*	*Orgelbüchlein*
BWV 616	*Mit Fried' und Freud' ich fahr' dahin*	*Orgelbüchlein*
BWV 617	*Herr Gott, nun schleuss den Himmel auf*	*Orgelbüchlein*
BWV 621	*Da Jesus an dem Kreuze stund'*	*Orgelbüchlein*
BWV 623	*Wir danken dir, Herr Jesu Christ*	*Orgelbüchlein*
BWV 625	*Christ lag in Todesbanden*	*Orgelbüchlein*
BWV 626	*Jesus Christus, unser Heiland*	*Orgelbüchlein*
BWV 628	*Erstanden ist der heil'ge Christ*	*Orgelbüchlein*
BWV 630	*Heut' triumphieret Gottes Sohn*	*Orgelbüchlein*
BWV 631a	*Komm, Gott Schöpfer*	*Orgelbüchlein*
BWV 631	*Komm, Gott Schöpfer*	*Orgelbüchlein*
BWV 632	*Herr Jesu Christ, dich zu uns wend'*	*Orgelbüchlein*
BWV 635	*Dies sind die heil'gen zehn Gebot'*	*Orgelbüchlein*
BWV 636	*Vater unser im Himmelreich*	*Orgelbüchlein*
BWV 637	*Durch Adams Fall ist ganz verderbt*	*Orgelbüchlein*
BWV 638	*Es ist das Heil uns kommen her*	*Orgelbüchlein*
BWV 639	*Ich ruf' zu dir, Herr Jesu Christ*	*Orgelbüchlein*
BWV 640	*In dich hab' ich gehoffet, Herr*	*Orgelbüchlein*
BWV 642	*Wer nur den lieben Gott lässt walten*	*Orgelbüchlein*
BWV 643	*Alle Menschen müssen sterben*	*Orgelbüchlein*
BWV 644	*Ach wie nichtig, ach wie flüchtig*	*Orgelbüchlein*

Leipzig

| BWV 683 | *Vater unser im Himmelreich* | *Clavierübung* III |

Short Ornamental Chorale

The short ornamental chorale is similar to the melody chorale, for the
chorale tune is presented without interludes. The difference lies in

the fact that the tune is heavily ornamented. Bach composed only a
few examples of this subcategory.

		Before 1713	
BWV 709	*Herr Jesu Christ, dich zu uns*		Leipzig, MB, *III.8.10*;
	wend'		Breitkopf Collection
BWV 731	*Liebster Jesu, wir sind hier*		Leipzig, MB, *Poel. 39*

		1713–16	
BWV 614	*Das alte Jahr vergangen ist*		*Orgelbüchlein*
BWV 622	*O Mensch, bewein' dein'*		*Orgelbüchlein*
	Sünde gross		
BWV 641	*Wenn wir in höchsten Nöten*		*Orgelbüchlein*
	sein		

		Köthen	
BWV 691a	*Wer nur den lieben Gott lässt*		*Clavierbüchlein* for Wilhelm
	walten		Friedemann Bach (1720)
BWV 753	*Jesu, meine Freude*		*Clavierbüchlein* for Wilhelm
	(fragment)		Friedemann Bach (1720)

		Leipzig	
BWV 691	*Wer nur den lieben Gott lässt*		*Clavierbüchlein* for Anna
	walten		Magdalena Bach (1725)
BWV 728	*Jesus meine Zuversicht*		*Clavierbüchlein* for Anna
			Magdalena Bach (1722)

The *Orgelbüchlein* settings *Das alte Jahr*, BWV 614, *O Mensch bewein'*,
BWV 622, and *Wenn wir in höchsten Nöten*, BWV 641, are among the
most subjective pieces in the genre. The presence of BWV 691a, 691,
728, and 753 in the private instructional books of the Bach family
demonstrates that the long-standing practice of using the organ chorale as household music was still observed.

Short Chorale Canon

The chorale canon is a somewhat more complicated version of the
melody chorale. The chorale tune, supported by accompanying contrapuntal voices, is set in canon, without interludes between lines.

		Before 1713	
BWV 714	*Ach Gott und Herr*		Berlin, DStB, *P 802* (J. L.
			Krebs)

		1713–16	
BWV 600	*Gott, durch deine Güte*		*Orgelbüchlein*
BWV 608	*In dulci jubilo*		*Orgelbüchlein*
BWV 618	*O Lamm Gottes unschuldig*		*Orgelbüchlein*

BWV 619	*Christe, du Lamm Gottes*	*Orgelbüchlein*
BWV 620	*Christus, der uns selig macht*	*Orgelbüchlein*
BWV 624	*Hilf Gott, dass mir's gelinge*	*Orgelbüchlein*
BWV 629	*Erschienen ist der herrliche Tag*	*Orgelbüchlein*
BWV 633	*Liebster Jesu, wir sind hier*	*Orgelbüchlein*
BWV 634	*Liebster Jesu, wir sind hier*	*Orgelbüchlein*

In dulci jubilo, BWV 608, is a particularly striking example of Bach's mastery of this form: not only the chorale but also the accompanying voices are canonic.

Short Chorale Fantasia

In dir ist Freude, BWV 615, obviously belongs with the other short chorale preludes of the *Orgelbüchlein*, for it is built around the through-composition of the chorale tune in the soprano. Nevertheless, it is the only short prelude type in which the motivic counterpoint thoroughly penetrates the chorale melody itself, giving the impression of a fantasia. For this reason, it cannot be classified in any of the other categories and must occupy a unique position.

Bach's interest in the short chorale prelude was so concentrated in the years 1713–16, with little activity in the form before and after, that it seems most likely that the pieces had some specific function during that period. It is possible that for some liturgical reason, Bach suddenly needed to write out what he normally improvised during services in the Weimar Court Chapel. But it is also possible that he required examples of improvisatory art for his growing circle of organ students. Once he had created a sufficient body of didactic material it was, perhaps, a waste of time and paper to write out what normally was improvised for a particular service.

Long Chorale Preludes without Independent Structure in the Chorale-Free Parts

Long Cantus Firmus Chorale

A cantus firmus chorale can be defined as a long form in which the chorale tune is presented in sustained notes, often in the pedal, with its successive phrases separated by interludes. Bach inherited this form from the previous generation—especially from Böhm, Buxtehude, and Pachelbel—and went on to transform it greatly. However, a few pieces simply imitate the Böhm-Buxtehude-Pachelbel type of cantus firmus chorale, in which the chorale-free parts accompany and sometimes imitate the melody.

	Very Early	
BWV 700	*Vom Himmel hoch, da komm' ich her* (Pachelbel influence)	Breitkopf Collection; Leipzig, MB, *Ms. 3*
BWV 723	*Gelobet seist du, Jesu Christ* (Pachelbel influence)	Leipzig, MB, *Poel. 39*
BWV 741	*Ach Gott, vom Himmel sieh' darein* (J. C. Bach influence?)	Breitkopf Collection
	Weimar	
BWV 656	*O Lamm Gottes unschuldig*	"Great Eighteen" Collection
BWV 657	*Nun danket alle Gott* (Pachelbel influence)	"Great Eighteen" Collection
BWV 665	*Jesus Christus, unser Heiland* (Böhm influence?)	"Great Eighteen" Collection
BWV 666	*Jesus Christus, unser Heiland* (Pachelbel influence)	"Great Eighteen" Collection
BWV 667	*Komm, Gott Schöpfer*	"Great Eighteen" Collection
BWV 735a	*Valet will ich dir geben* (Buxtehude or Böhm influence?)	*Plauener Orgelbuch*; Den Haag *4.G.14*; Kö *15839*
BWV 736	*Valet will ich dir geben* (Pachelbel influence)	Leipzig, MB, *Poel. 39*
BWV 766/7	*Christ, der du bist der helle Tag* (Böhm influence)	Darmstadt, *73*
BWV 768/10	*Sei gegrüsset, Jesu gütig*	Berlin, DStB, *P 802*; Leipzig, MB, *III.8.17*
	Leipzig?	
BWV 668	*Vor deinen Thron tret' ich* (Pachelbel influence)	"Great Eighteen" Collection

Long Ornamental Chorale

Bach's long ornamental chorale preludes without independent structure in the accompaniment are similar to the cantus firmus chorales above, except that the melody itself is elaborately embellished in a manner derived from Böhm and Buxtehude. These works are masterpieces of subjective, introspective expression.

		Weimar
BWV 652	*Komm, heiliger Geist, Herre Gott*	"Great Eighteen" Collection
BWV 659	*Nun komm', der Heiden Heiland*	"Great Eighteen" Collection
BWV 662	*Allein Gott in der Höh' sei Ehr'*	"Great Eighteen" Collection

Long Chorale Preludes with Independent Structure in the Chorale-Free Voices

Bach made a significant innovation in the form and underlying idea of the organ chorale by strengthening and contrasting the "accompanying" voices to the point where they developed an independent motivic and formal structure. The results of this breakthrough are clearest in the six Schübler Chorales, in which the ritornellos contrast sharply with the chorale tunes. However, if we survey the entire corpus of Bach's chorales, a body of works composed over a period of nearly 50 years, it becomes clear that hints and actual manifestations of an independent accompanimental structure appeared quite early. For example, the *Fantasia super Komm, heiliger Geist*, BWV 651a, and the fugal setting of *Nun komm', der Heiden Heiland*, BWV 661a, both from around 1710–14,[18] consist of strong polyphonic structures based on independent motives to which chorale tunes are added. From this time at the latest, then, Bach's continuous struggle to surpass his models resulted in a structurally expanded concept of the organ chorale.[19] However, this effort also led Bach away from the strict forms toward the more flexible designs of invention, trio, and ritornello aria.

Invention with Added Chorale Tune

		Type of chorale treatment	Number of voices	Location of chorale
		Pre-Weimar?		
BWV 694	*Wo soll ich fliehen hin*	c.f.	3	Bass (pedal)
BWV 695	*Christ lag in Todesbanden*	c.f.	3	Alto
BWV 710	*Wir Christenleut'*	c.f.	3	Bass (pedal)

		Weimar		
BWV 660a	*Nun komm', der Heiden Heiland*	ornamental	3	Soprano
BWV 717	*Allein Gott in der Höh' sei Ehr'*	c.f.	3	Soprano
		Leipzig		
BWV 646	*Wo soll ich fliehen hin*	c.f.	3	Alto (pedal)
BWV 675	*Allein Gott in der Höh' sei Ehr'*	c.f.	3	Alto

Trio with Added Chorale Tune

		Weimar		
BWV 655a	*Herr Jesu Christ, dich zu uns wend'*	c.f.	3	Bass (pedal)
BWV 658a	*Von Gott will ich nicht lassen*	c.f.	4	Tenor (pedal)
BWV 664a	*Allein Gott in der Höh' sei Ehr'*	c.f.	3	Bass (pedal)
		Leipzig		
BWV 676	*Allein Gott in der Höh' sei Ehr'*	c.f.	3	Soprano 1 & 2
BWV 678	*Diess sind die heil'gen zehn Gebot'*	canon	5	Tenor 1 & 2
BWV 682	*Vater unser im Himmelreich*	canon	5	Soprano & tenor
BWV 684	*Christ, unser Herr, zum Jordan kam*	c.f.	4	Tenor (pedal)
BWV 688	*Jesus Christus, unser Heiland*	c.f.	3	Tenor
BWV 647	*Wer nur den lieben Gott lässt walten*	c.f.	4	Tenor (pedal)

Ritornello with Added Chorale Tune

		Pre-Weimar?		
BWV 734	*Nun freut euch, lieben Christen g'mein*	c.f.	3	Tenor
		Weimar		
BWV 653b	*An Wasser- flüssen Babylon*	ornamental	5	Soprano
BWV 654a	*Schmücke dich, o liebe Seele*	ornamental	4	Soprano
BWV 663a	*Allein Gott in der Höh' sei Ehr'*	ornamental	4	Tenor
		Leipzig		
BWV 645	*Wachet auf, ruft uns die Stimme*	c.f.	3	Tenor
BWV 648	*Meine Seele erhebt den Herren*	c.f.	4	Soprano
BWV 649	*Ach bleib' bei uns, Herr Jesu Christ*	c.f.	3	Soprano
BWV 650	*Kommst du nun, Jesu, vom Himmel herunter*	ornamental	3	Alto (pedal)

These works can be viewed as two- or three-voice pieces in freely imitative or ritornello form, constructed in such a way that the chorale tune can be presented simultaneously with the piece itself. The impression is that of two rather different but complementary musical events taking place at the same time (BWV 650 and 684 are exemplary in this regard). In two cases (BWV 678 and 682), this idea is further intensified by presenting the chorale melody as a two-part canon, together with an independent trio in the "accompanying" parts. BWV 678 and 682, along with the Canonic Variations on *Vom Himmel hoch*, BWV 769, represent the culmination of Bach's canonic art, and all three imply speculative associations with theology and numerology.[20] As such, they are incomparable. However, these large canons are also works that, to paraphrase Bach's nemesis Johann Adolph Scheibe,[21] can be regarded as turgid, excessively artful, and potentially confusing to the ear. This alleged defect hardly applies to the remainder of the group, however, which includes several of the most popular masterpieces in the organ repertoire.

NOTES

1. From Ernest May, "Organ Chorale," in *Harvard Dictionary of Music*, 3d ed., edited by Don M. Randel, forthcoming. For a detailed bibliography, see Robert L. Marshall's article on the same subject in *The New Grove Dictionary of Music and Musicians*, vol. 4, pp. 329–38; and Peter Williams, *The Organ Music of J. S. Bach* (Cambridge, 1980–84), vol. 2, pp. 341–46. General background to this topic is presented in Friedrich Blume, *Protestant Church Music: A History* (New York, 1974), and Manfred Bukofzer, *Music in the Baroque Era* (New York, 1947). The present author's dissertation, "Breitkopf's Role in the Transmission of J. S. Bach's Organ Chorales," Princeton University, 1974; and Peter Williams, *The Organ Music of J. S. Bach*, 3 vols. (Cambridge, 1980–84), form the foundation for the present study.

2. *Nun komm', der Heiden Heiland*, BWV 659, for example, must surely be an expanded imitation of Buxtehude's prelude on the same tune, BuxWV 211.

3. See, for example, Robert L. Tusler, *The Style of J. S. Bach's Chorale Preludes* (Berkeley and Los Angeles, 1956).

4. In addition to the references listed above, see Georg Rietschel, *Die Aufgabe der Orgel im Gottesdienst bis in das 18. Jahrhundert* (Leipzig, 1893; reprint, Hildesheim, 1971).

5. *Bach Reader*, p. 5.

6. This column lists the most important source (or sources) for each chorale and the copyist involved (if known). The library sigla are as follows (see also Williams, vol. 2, pp. 335–40):

Berlin, DStB = Deutsche Staatsbibliothek, Berlin, East
Berlin, SPK = Staatsbibliothek Preussischer Kulturbesitz, Berlin, West
Brussels = Bibliothèque Royale de Belgique
Carpentras = Carpentras (Vaucluse), Bibliothèque Inguimbertine
Darmstadt = Hessische Landesbibliothek, Darmstadt
Den Haag = Gemeente Museum, The Hague
Kö = Universitätsbibliothek, Königsberg (now Kaliningrad)
Leipzig = Musikbibliothek der Stadt Leipzig, Leipzig

A summary of the source situation for Bach's major collections is presented in May, "Breitkopf's Role," and in Williams.

7. To complicate matters, however, both BWV 715 and 725 include a low E♭, a note that was not available at Arnstadt (though it was available at Mühlhausen and Weimar).

8. BDok II, no. 63; *Bach Reader*, pp. 65–66.

9. *Bach Reader*, pp. 70 and 429; BDok I, no. 178.

10. See Ernest May, "J. G. Walther and the Lost Weimar Autographs of Bach's Organ Works," in *Studies in Renaissance and Baroque Music in Honor of Arthur Mendel*, edited by Robert L. Marshall (Kassel and Hackensack, N.J., 1974), pp. 264–82.

11. In this connection, the lack of specific knowledge about the hymnals in use at Arnstadt, Mühlhausen, and Weimar is particularly regrettable.

12. There are compelling reasons to use the title "Breitkopf Collection" in reference to the organ chorales BWV 690–713, 734, 741, 748, 759, 760, and 761 rather than "Kirnberger Collection," which is employed in BG and BWV. The so-called Kirnberger Collection manuscript, Berlin, SPK, *AmB 72a*, turns out not to have been written by Kirnberger at all but to have been ordered by him through the mail from Breitkopf in Leipzig. See May, "Breitkopf's Role," esp. chapters IV and V; and May, "Eine neue Quelle für Bachs einzeln überlieferte Orgelchoräle," BJ 1974: 98–103.

13. See Christoph Wolff, *Der stile antico in der Musik Johann Sebastian Bachs: Studien zu Bachs Spätwerk* (Wiesbaden, 1968), esp. pp. 96–97.

14. See Spitta, vol. 1, pp. 394–97; and Williams, vol. 2, pp. 260–63.

15. *Bach Reader*, p. 219.

16. See May, "Breitkopf's Role," pp. 123–37; and George Stauffer's discussion of *plenum* registration for these pieces in the present volume, pp. 195–200.

17. See the recent facsimile edition of the autograph, with an introduction by Heinz-Harald Löhlein (Leipzig, 1981).

18. See Hermann Zietz, *Quellenkritische Untersuchungen an den Bach-Handschriften P 801, P 802 and P 803 aus dem "Krebs'schen Nachlass" unter besonderer Berücksichtigung der Choralbearbeitungen des jungen J. S. Bach* (Hamburg, 1969), pp. 137–38, as well as Williams, vol. 2, pp. 124–27.

19. Werner Breig's "The 'Great Eighteen' Chorales: Bach's Revisional Process and the Genesis of the Work" in this volume offers an in-depth study of the *Fantasia super Komm, heiliger Geist, Herre Gott*, BWV 651a/651, and the ornamental chorale *An Wasserflüssen Babylon*, BWV 653b/653a/653, fully consistent with these conclusions.

20. The Canonic Variations on *Vom Himmel hoch* is discussed at length in chapters 2 and 3 of Ludwig Prautzsch, *Vor deinen Thron tret ich hiermit: Figuren and Symbole in den letzten Werken Johann Sebastian Bach* (Neuhausen-Stuttgart, 1980).

21. *Bach Reader*, p. 238.

WERNER BREIG

❦

The "Great Eighteen" Chorales
Bach's Revisional Process and the
Genesis of the Work

It is a hallmark of Bach's last decade that along with the composition of several monumental works conceived in this period—the Goldberg Variations, Canonic Variations on *Vom Himmel hoch*, *Musical Offering*, and *Art of Fugue*—he was also occupied in assembling, completing, and editing many earlier pieces. Among these earlier works which in a sense are "indirectly" tied to Bach's final years, are the *Well-Tempered Clavier*, vol. II, the *Symbolum Nicenum* of the B-minor Mass, the Schübler Chorales, and the collection stemming from the revision of organ chorale preludes of the Weimar period—a collection that Wilhelm Rust, in the *Bach-Gesamtausgabe*, gave the title "Achtzehn Choräle von verschiedener Art" and that has come to be known in English as the "Great Eighteen" Chorales.

Certainly in earlier periods of his life, Bach returned to old compositions, to their grouping into collections, and to their more or less thorough revision into "Fassungen letzter Hand."[1] But in the late Leipzig years, this musical activity assumed a special position, for it seems to have presented Bach with compositional problems quite different from those he faced in the original works from that time. The original works were large, monothematic pieces with cyclical structures[2]—something new and perhaps singular in music history—and characterized by canonic writing.[3]

The "secondary" works have nothing to do with these problems, despite certain generic ties. Yet Bach's objective in refining and assembling these pieces cannot be assessed without attempting to see how they fit, one way or another, into his late compositional practice. The question seems obvious: Are there recognizable connections between the revisional procedures used for the earlier compositions and the stylistic characteristics that emerge in the late ones?

For an investigation of this question, a comparison of the late-Leipzig versions of the "Great Eighteen" Chorales with their Weimar originals proves to be especially fruitful. The late-Leipzig versions have been preserved in Bach's autograph, Berlin, DStB *P 271*.[4] The Weimar originals—which survive almost without exception—have been handed down chiefly in copies by Johann Gottfried Walther, Johann Tobias Krebs, and others.[5] Thus the source situation—often problematic for Bach's keyboard works—permits a reliable and thorough investigation of the revisions. But more important, perhaps, is the fact that in this case Bach's revisions were not influenced by exterior considerations, such as adaptation for another instrument (in the Schübler Chorales, for instance; or somewhat earlier, in the harpsichord concertos). Rather, they were motivated by purely compositional concerns.

The following investigation attempts to shed light on Bach's revisional process and the genesis of the "Great Eighteen" Chorale collection by focusing on two pieces: *Fantasia super Komm, heiliger Geist, Herre Gott*, BWV 651, and *An Wasserflüssen Babylon*, BWV 653. These works, along with their earlier forms, BWV 651a, 653a, and 653b, are unusually noteworthy, for Bach did far more than change details. He reconsidered his fundamental compositional concept.

Fantasia super Komm, heiliger Geist, Herre Gott

The Fantasia is transmitted in two forms: one is 48 measures long, the other 106. The shorter version, BWV 651a, is preserved in copies from the Weimar period; the longer one, BWV 651, appears in the late-Leipzig autograph (*P 271*) and in manuscripts derived from this source. Hans Klotz, who edited the "Great Eighteen" Chorales for the NBA, came to the conclusion that BWV 651a is "certainly not the later abridgment of a copyist, but Bach's original composition." Klotz based his opinion above all on two considerations: First, the differences between BWV 651a and 651 are typical of those encountered in other chorale preludes written in Weimar and reused in Leipzig. Second, the segments added to BWV 651, in comparison with the rest of the work, show "a stronger hand" and "relatively freer writing."[6]

Among later commentators, Hermann Zietz obviously sides with Klotz's interpretation.[7] Peter Williams, on the other hand, sees another explanation of the work's evolution as at least imaginable if not even more likely. Like Klotz, Williams views the short version as authentic, but he questions whether it is the original one:

> Since the evidence of the sources cannot be regarded as conclusive, it may be doubted that BWV 651a was later "enlarged" to BWV 651; the integration achieved in BWV 651 may suggest that the two versions are contemporary. Thus BWV 651a could be a shortened version of BWV 651; this is not suggested by the sources, nor is it denied by them.[8]

It is true that the sources do not allow a more certain conclusion to be made about the work's genesis, and that is why Klotz turned to style criticism for his arguments. Thus it seems all the more necessary to return once again to the musical text of the two versions to discern which order of composition seems the more logical.

We can begin by observing the course of the cantus firmus, which is presented in the pedal. The chorale, set out in Example 1 in the bass range of the pedal, has a text of eight lines arranged in rhyming couplets (marked I–VIII) and a concluding two-fold Halleluja (IX–X).[9] Characteristic of the melody is the large proportion of repetition: lines II and VI, and III and VII are identical; lines IV and VIII have the same beginning; and lines I and V, and VIII and X have the same conclusion.

The correspondences within the chorale melody are highlighted in Example 1 by the use of repeat marks. The notation allows the differences between BWV 651 and 651a to be seen at a glance. While BWV 651 presents the chorale in its entirety, BWV 651a makes use of a truncated version, created by leaving out the repetitions, including the first endings (that is, mm. 44–88 and 89–103). BWV 651a, therefore, employs only lines I, II, III, and VIII of the chorale. Both BWV 651 and 651a, however, include an expansion of the cantus firmus voice at the beginning (through the use of a pedal point) and the end (through the use of a harmonically elaborated cadence).

In both versions, the basic compositional concept of Bach's chorale prelude is this: the cantus firmus is presented in the pedal in long, held notes, while the three upper voices weave imitative material whose substance is drawn from the chorale melody. In the large version of the Fantasia, mm. 1–88 (presentation of chorale lines I–VIII) are dominated by a theme derived from line I of the chorale, which we can call the principal theme (in Example 2a, the chorale notes are marked with an *x*). In the closing section a second important idea

EXAMPLE 1

(I) Komm, hei - li - ger Geist, Her - re Gott,
Lich - tes Glast

(II) er - füll mit dei - ner Gna - den Gut
(VI) zu dem Glau - ben ver - Sam - melt hast

(III) dei - ner Gläub - gen Herz, Mut und Sinn,
(VII) das Volk aus al - ler Welt Zun - gen.

(IV) dein brün - stig Lieb ent - zünd in ihn'.
(VIII) Das sei dir, Herr, zu Lob ge -

(V) O Herr, durch dei - nes sun - gen.
le - lu - ja.

(IX) Hal - le - lu - ja,   (X) Hal -

EXAMPLE 2

enters; it is based on line IX of the chorale, and we will name it the
Halleluja theme (Example 2b).

The Fantasia could have evolved in one of two ways:

Hypothesis 1. Only the short, 48-measure version is of Weimar origin. Bach then constructed the Leipzig version from it, by repeating
mm. 12–43 and by composing the *Prima volta* segment, mm. 44–54,

and the Halleluja segment, mm. 89–103. This expansion is shown in the diagram below.

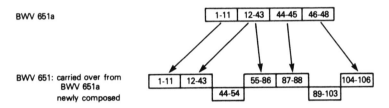

Hypothesis 2. A complete, 106-measure version of the Fantasia, no longer extant, already existed in Weimar. From this *Urfassung* came the surviving Weimar version, through abridgments, as well as the existing late-Leipzig version, through refinements.

The key to unlocking the history of the work might well rest in the segments that appear only in the large version. If the first hypothesis is correct, these segments were newly composed in Leipzig. But if the second one is true, they belong to the original concept of the work but were eliminated to create a shorter arrangement.

Let us examine first mm. 44–54, which include the close of line IV, an expansive interlude, and the beginning of line V. In mm. 46–47 we find two exceptional—for this work—presentations of the principal theme. In m. 46 the second half-measure of the principal theme is transformed into two-part texture. In m. 47 the incipit of the principal theme (in the alto) is surrounded by a chordal accompaniment (in the soprano and tenor), in place of the contrapuntal fabric that appears elsewhere (see Example 3).

EXAMPLE 3

In addition, at the beginning of line V of the chorale the accompanimental voices present a variant of the principal theme that has not appeared up to this point: while previously the second half of the second measure of the principal theme had the diastematic shape of Example 4a, it now assumes a new form (Example 4b), which anticipates the Halleluja theme of mm. 89–106.

EXAMPLE 4

One might well say that these observations are of little consequence. But we would have no need to inspect such details if we were not concerned with the history of the work. For this question, the piling up of anomalies—to which one can perhaps add the striking harmonic excursion of m. 47—leads to the suspicion that mm. 44–54 were not composed in the same flow of invention as the music that surrounds this segment.

The second segment belonging solely to the large version also shows anomalous elements. Here the Halleluja theme (see Example 2b) appears for the first time. It is quite closely related to the end of the principal theme. In fact, since this new idea encompasses only a half measure, one has the impression—in the segment in which it dominates—of an acceleration at the conclusion. The closing segment, from m. 98 on, is five-voiced and brings together all the important thematic elements in a narrow space: the cantus firmus with its long notes, the principal theme, the Halleluja theme (including its newly introduced inversion), and the suspension motif from the interludes at mm. 26–27, 49–51, and 69–70. It is a stretto in the spirit of Johann Gottfried Walther's definition: "One or several themes are brought together in a very short space, and follow smartly one upon the other."[10] Its similarity to the "alla stretta" measures at the close of the "canone al rovescio" of the Canonic Variations on *Vom Himmel hoch* is obvious.

In view of all these elements, it seems unlikely that Bach initially composed a piece with the dimensions of BWV 651 and then derived a truncated version, BWV 651a, from it. BWV 651a distinguishes itself from BWV 651 not only through its brevity, but also through the unusual homogeneity of its upper voices, a style of writing that is closely related to the two Weimar free organ preludes, the Toccata in d ("Dorian"), BWV 538/1, and the Toccata in F, BWV 540/1. That this unity would have resulted from abridging a more variegated version is difficult to imagine, especially since the excisions could not be determined by the upper voices, but rather by the course of the predetermined cantus firmus. A further observation can be added: the cancelling of the long repeat, mm. 44–88, would be an understandable way of making the piece shorter and hence "more pleasing" to the listener. But the dropping of the highly impressive, climactic Halleluja section would not.

Thus, we must conclude that Bach wrote the short version first and later, apparently only during the last Leipzig years, created the long form that is handed down to us in *P 271*. What does this evolutionary process signify?

The *Fantasia super Komm, heiliger Geist, Herre Gott* documents a basic tendency of Bach's chorale preludes written after the Weimar period: the abandonment of composing the entire fabric "after the cantus firmus" in favor of creating a self-supporting structure in the accompanimental voices. The architectonic concept of the present work is the ongoing unification of the upper parts through the use of a principal theme—and not a principal theme that changes from chorale line to chorale line, but one that remains the same and permeates the entire piece. The cantus firmus, by contrast, appears to be not so much a determinant of the form as an additional layer in the musical fabric.

One difficulty in realizing this compositional goal lies in the length of the cantus firmus and the resulting predetermined length of the prelude, which stands in a problematic relationship to the concise thematic material of the upper voices. In the initial Weimar realization of his plan, Bach attempted to avoid the danger of overstressing the upper-voice theme by shortening the cantus firmus from ten to four lines. Line IV was reinterpreted into line VIII, and the concluding Halleluja (lines IX and X) was left out. The prelude attained a length of 48 measures with 24 entrances of the theme. The precarious balance between the richness of the principal theme and the compass of its execution was thereby happily stabilized.

But in so doing, the composer infringed on a traditional principle of organ-chorale writing, which calls for the complete presentation of the arranged melody. It was an infringement almost without parallel in Bach's organ music based on chorales. In *Allein Gott in der Höh sei Ehr*, BWV 664, the chorale melody is cited in an abbreviated form. This case is hardly comparable, however, for the work is a special type of chorale prelude, namely, an organ trio. The quotation of the first two lines of the chorale at the close has merely the function of a coda.[11]

The one true parallel to BWV 651a is the Weimar Whitsunday work, Cantata 172, *Erschallet, ihr Lieder, erklinget ihr Saiten*, composed for May 20, 1714. The fifth movement of this composition is a dialogue between the Soul (soprano) and the Holy Spirit (alto) over a basso continuo. The oboe enters as a fourth voice, playing a richly embellished version of the chorale *Komm, heiliger Geist, Herre Gott*. In this chorale quotation, the first eight lines are coalesced into four, just as they are in BWV 651a: I, II (=VI), III (=VII), and VIII (in contrast to BWV 651a, the Halleluja lines are not omitted). The cause of the shortening here stemmed from the need to limit the length of the movement, a restriction imposed primarily by the length of the text.

One suspects that this cantata movement not only represents a parallel to BWV 651a for the modern observer but may actually have laid the groundwork of the organ chorale for the composer himself. That is to say, Bach may have taken the procedure of quoting only part of the chorale from the cantata, where it was not problematic, and transferred it to the organ chorale. That this transferral was possible without essential loss of meaning can be explained by Bach's new concept of form in the Weimar organ chorales: the accompanying voices have such a strong coherence—thanks to the use of an all-pervasive, unifying theme—that the chorale melody can be "added" as a free citation, joining the other material just as it does in the cantata. One can easily imagine that the organ chorale was also composed for performance on Whitsunday 1714. The source material does not contradict this conjecture.[12]

But why would Bach approach anew the problem he had averted in Weimar and expand the piece to more than double its original length by presenting the cantus firmus in its full form? Perhaps the challenge of setting the entire chorale held a certain artful fascination for him, especially given the restriction of retaining, almost as a souvenir, the motivic material he had penned years earlier in Weimar.

The note-for-note repetition of two-thirds of the musical text of the original version could hardly be avoided in the expansion: to alter the settings of the cantus firmus segments would only have trivialized the effect of a concept based on the desire for unity. To compensate for the resulting redundancy, Bach introduced moments of harmonic or contrapuntal contrast into the segments that had to be newly composed. Just how successful his solution to the final form of the chorale prelude is can be sensed from our analysis.

Whether redundancy and variety could be brought into an even balance cannot be demonstrated by objective means. Surely the new arrangement belongs to those of Bach's organ works to which Albert Schweitzer's term "majestic monotony" applies.[13] And certainly Hans Klotz is correct when he points to the daring nature of the concept, which stretches "to the very limits what is possible with the use of a single, short theme."[14]

The decision to expand the piece may have resulted from something beyond the aesthetic consideration of redundancy and variety. Johann Nikolaus Forkel's comment in a review of the Goldberg Variations goes to the heart of the matter: "As all his works created at this time were models of art, these variations, too, became such under his hand."[15] Bach's striving to create "models of art" resulted in a series of works that illustrate the principles of various genres and therefore can be taken as compositional examples of the highest order. If we turn to our piece, we can say that the *idea* of this special work was indeed evident in the Weimar composition, but not yet a *concept*, a *genre*. Only when the chorale melody was presented in its full form, not in "convenient" segments, could the work qualify as a representative "model of art."

An Wasserflüssen Babylon

An Wasserflüssen Babylon has been handed down in three forms: a five-part version, BWV 653b, and a four-part version, BWV 653a, both from the Weimar period; and a revision of the four-part version, BWV 653, appearing in the Leipzig manuscript *P 271*. Of the two Weimar versions, the four-part was viewed by Philipp Spitta as the original and the five-part as a later arrangement. Spitta speculated that the five-part version, with its special demand on pedal playing, was fashioned especially for Bach's "1720 trip to Hamburg, where he won the high regard of the venerable Reincken for his realization of the chorale *An Wasserflüssen Babylon*."[16]

Hans Klotz, on the other hand, declared the genesis to be the opposite: "The bass part of BWV 653a is obviously a compromise between the two bass parts of BWV 653b. Moreover, BWV 653a is more rhythmically pronounced than BWV 653b."[17] Klotz's observations are confirmed, if one studies the relationship of the two arrangements in detail.[18] We will return to this evidence later.

The chorale prelude *An Wasserflüssen Babylon*, in all three guises, belongs to a group of pieces in the "Eighteen Chorales" in which a duple melody is arranged into a triple pattern. The motivic cell of the transformation, extended into various forms, is the following:

Rhythm of the chorale:[19]   𝄴 𝅗𝅥 | 𝅘𝅥 𝅘𝅥 𝅘𝅥 𝅘𝅥 | 𝅘𝅥 𝅘𝅥 𝅗𝅥

BWV 653 $\frac{3}{4}$ ♩♩♩ | ♩♩ | ♩♩ | $\overset{\frown}{\text{♩·}}$

Through this metamorphosis, the prelude acquires the character of a sarabande,[20] which Bach used in a series of vocal works to produce the affect of mourning (the final choruses of the St. John and St. Matthew passions, for instance).

The original version is a five-voice organ chorale with a florid soprano melody, played by the right hand on a solo manual. The four accompanimental voices are divided evenly between a secondary keyboard and the pedal. The underlying compositional plan is clear: the complete chorale melody is presented in the right hand. Against it, the counter voices weave material drawn from lines I and II of the chorale (this is especially true of the soprano of the accompaniment, which has nonthematic material in only nine of the work's 77 measures). Although it shares certain properties with the *ritornel* type of chorale prelude of the Böhm circle, this working out of the idea is Bach's. The poetical concept behind the compositional approach could be loosely termed "litany-like lament."

The decision to have two soprano parts, one for the cantus firmus and one for the most important accompanimental voice, led directly to five-part texture, for a completely rounded sonority could be achieved only through the presence of two voices in the middle range.

In the four-part version that originated in Weimar, BWV 653a, the cantus firmus is shifted to the tenor and the pedal is reduced to one voice, corresponding mostly to the original lower bass part but occasionally borrowing from the upper one as well. The first and second lines of the chorale are given a sharper rhythmic profile (see Example 5). The new layout sets in greater contrast the litany-like repetition of the first two chorale lines and the presentation of the entire chorale, now sounding as a solo voice in the tenor. The rhythmic sharpening, too, makes the difference between chorale and free material more obvious. Thus the four-voice version seems to present the compositional idea of the prelude more clearly than does the five-voice setting.

On the other hand, one cannot overlook certain compositional irregularities that result from dropping the fifth part. Bach seems to have considered them tolerable (they survive to some extent even in the final version), although he surely would have avoided them in a piece composed *ex novo*. Thus, during the pauses of the cantus firmus in BWV 653a one finds unusually large gaps. Sometimes these gaps extend to two octaves between the alto and the bass, an area that was

filled by the upper pedal part in BWV 653b. (How Bach would otherwise handle the disposition of voices in a four-part piece with cantus
firmus in the tenor can be seen in *Allein Gott in der Höh' sei Ehr'*,
BWV 663.)

In BWV 653a there are numerous passages with only two-note harmonies. In BWV 653b the second pedal part almost always supplies
the missing third voice at these spots. Bach must have viewed such
empty-sounding chords as acceptable, but he may also have attempted
to compensate for them by improving the linear element, i.e., by
sharpening the rhythm. In a number of cases in the Leipzig version
(the beginnings of mm. 5, 17, 59, and 63), Bach restored the missing
third note by altering the alto voice.

Perhaps the four-voice version should not replace the five-voice one
but stand as an alternate arrangement. From a pedagogical viewpoint,
there would certainly be an advantage to showing how the same compositional procedure could be carried out in four as well as in five
voices. In Johann Gottfried Walther's copy, Berlin, DStB *P 802*, and
the Leipzig Mempell-Preller manuscript (which probably emanates
from *P 802*[21]), the two versions exist side by side. The four-voice
arrangement is labeled "alio modo."

The two Weimar versions of *An Wasserflüssen Babylon* exhibit the
same compositional concept carried out in different sonorous man-
ners. In the five-part texture, the two thematic layers are distinguished
by contrasting registers; in the four-part texture, the layers are distinguished by wide intervallic separation and stronger linear movement.
Of the two, the five-part arrangement is more balanced and more
evenly shaped. At many points, the four-part version undeniably reveals its origin as a reduction of the five-part setting.

Bach's decision to take the four-part version, BWV 653a, as the
model for his Leipzig revision, BWV 653, was probably not made because of the quality of the realization of BWV 653a (indeed, the reworking reveals its weaknesses all the more, as will be shown). Rather,
he must have viewed the four-part version as the more appropriate
vehicle for realizing his compositional ideal.

That is certainly true of the individual parts. In the 1740s, after completing *Clavierübung* III, Bach must have approached *An Wasserflüssen
Babylon* from a different perspective than before. He undoubtedly
weighed the relationship between the five-part texture of the original
version and the role each voice plays in the piece. *Clavierübung* III,
with its emphasis on polyphonic writing, displays a distinct tendency
toward economy in this respect. The move to more than four voices

was consistently made only when each voice had a valid, defined role in the contrapuntal structure. This principle is obvious in the large settings of *Kyrie, Gott heiliger Geist; Dies sind die heiligen zehn Gebot; Vater unser im Himmelreich;* and *Aus tiefer Not schrei ich zu dir.* Compared with these pieces, the five-voice *An Wasserflüssen Babylon* seems less "strong": the contrapuntal function of its individual voices is too casual. Although the five-part texture is not without an element of sonorous luxury, the compositional principle of the piece could be expressed better with four voices (except for the conclusion, see below). That may explain in part why Bach used the four-voice setting as his point of departure in Leipzig. To be sure, this decision called for an intensive reworking of the details of the piece. One senses the extent of this reworking from the fact that only sixteen of the 83 measures of the Leipzig version have been taken over without change from the four-part Weimar model.

To begin with, in *An Wasserflüssen Babylon*, Bach carried the rhythmic sharpening of the first two chorale lines in the accompaniment still another step, turning the ♩♩♩ figures into ♩. ♩♩ (see Example 5). In addition, he improved a multitude of details.

EXAMPLE 5

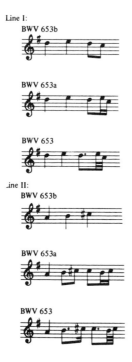

Line I:
BWV 653b

BWV 653a

BWV 653

_ine II:
BWV 653b

BWV 653a

BWV 653

Two sections of the work illustrate Bach's revisional procedure especially well. The first begins two measures before the entry of line V
of the chorale. The three versions of this passage are presented in
Example 6. (In the two four-part versions, the tenor [solo manual]
and bass [pedal] are both notated on the bass staff, for the sake of
convenience.)

Let us consider first the alterations in the four-part Weimar version

EXAMPLE 6

BWV 653

from the five-part version. The cantus firmus, aside from its move to
the tenor, remains the same except for the addition of a trill in m. 36.
The soprano and alto of the accompaniment are embellished (in
mm. 33, 34, and 36) through the addition of sixteenth notes, as mentioned above. Moreover, the conclusion of m. 37 is retouched: the
lengthening of the upbeat a' in the soprano produces a more distinct
entry of the chorale motive and establishes a more satisfactory relationship with the cantus firmus.

The most substantial change, of course, occurs in the pedal part,
which is reduced to one voice. In m. 33, beat 2, the bass moves to the
upper voice in order to avoid an empty sound at the end of the measure. Measure 34, as a consequence, must be reformulated, to make a
smooth bridge to the pedal point G. The shortening of the pedal
point, however, lessens the effective standstill of harmonic movement.
The striking depth of the pedal in m. 33 of the five-part version is presented as an afterthought in m. 37 of the four-part setting. Thus we
have the initial transformation, which Bach apparently viewed as
satisfactory.

Now let us consider the Leipzig arrangement. The rhythmic sharpening that permeates the late version requires no comment. Of primary interest to us are the special changes in our passage, which Bach
made to avoid difficulties in the earlier version, but which he now
found disturbing.

In m. 34 the step b'–c" in the alto had become an incorrectly resolved dissonance in relation to the c in the modified pedal part. In
the Leipzig version the dissonance is corrected by moving the alto

downwards, b'−a'. In m. 35 the omission of the upper bass voice left
no rhythmic subdivision on the first beat, and, with the cadencing of
the pedal, produced the effect of an unwarranted cessation. In the
Leipzig version the alto is made more rhythmically and melodically
active, at the same time restoring to the passage the ductus of the
eliminated pedal part. In m. 36 the modification of the first quarter
note of the chorale voice necessitated the rhythmic sharpening of
the alto.

In m. 37, beat 1, the relationship between the chorale and the soprano accompanimental voice was already precarious in the initial
version of the piece. It seemed hardly capable of emendation, however, for both voices were bound to the chorale. The reduction of the
accord on the second quarter note of the four-part Weimar version
only highlighted the problem. In the Leipzig version Bach solved the
difficulty by breaking up the pauses between the two chorale-based
lines with an unthematic insertion, which somewhat enhanced the
clarity of the chorale voice and considerably improved the sonority of
the passage.

The conclusion of the piece serves as a second example. In the last
six measures of the original version, all four upper voices weave thematic material over the pedal point G. In the second version, the loss
caused by deleting the upper pedal part could not be overcome without resorting to supplementary resources. Thus at the end of BWV
653a, at m. 76, the fifth voice is reintroduced, with a thematic citation
in the pedal. This device produced an effective close, but it also created the feeling of an unmotivated addition, especially since the note
eb' is no longer connected to a descending chromatic line, as it was in
BWV 653b. Setting *all* the measures after m. 73 in five-voice texture
would have produced a satisfying close to the work, of course, but it
probably conflicted too much with Bach's self-imposed compositional
constraints.

The solution adopted in Leipzig was to enlarge the piece by six
measures. After a false cadence in m. 77, the bass and soprano each
quote the first chorale line, which actually overcompensates for the
lost tenor entry of the original five-part version.

The conclusion gains from the newly composed measures in other
ways as well:

1. Since the bass ultimately passes its role of sustaining voice to the
tenor, the important emphasis on the subdominant, C major, can be
fully realized. In the five-part version, the subdominant was only

suggested over the pedal point; in the first four-part version, it was omitted altogether. (The progression G^7–C of the final version is therefore all the more effective, since it has not been heard before in the piece.)

2. At the close of the *Urfassung*, the last line of the chorale sounds in the soprano, the uppermost voice of the movement. After the chorale-carrying voice was transferred to the tenor in the second Weimar version, the role of the highest part was taken over by the soprano of the accompaniment, which, as the only nonthematic voice other than the bass, provided a somewhat neutral final flourish. In the Leipzig revision, the soprano is given the last word with a citation of the first chorale line. This chorale line, acting as a sort of *idée fixe* for the entire piece, provides a fitting conclusion that also enables the final chord to be capped with an expressive third.

3. Quite astounding and admirable, finally, is the solution that Bach found in the Leipzig version for the harmonic problem of the concluding measures. The strong emphasis on the subdominant in mm. 79–80 requires counterbalancing with a clear articulation of the dominant; but that would collide with the long-held concluding note of the chorale in the tenor. There is clearly a potential conflict between harmonic logic, which the dominant demands, and contrapuntal logic, which dictates g as the final note. Bach's ingenious solution is to move the cantus firmus voice into the lower octave in the penultimate measure. On the one hand, it temporarily creates room for a harmonic change; on the other hand, the final note of the chorale melody is not essentially abandoned, but rather embellished by the scale descending from g to G. The critical leading tone, f♯, is assigned to an added second pedal part, whose shape recalls line II of the chorale.

With the new harmonic direction went the elimination of the minor sixth, e♭, which had been a special feature of the concluding plan in both Weimar versions. It has already been suggested that the minor sixth had lost some of its impetus in the second Weimar version, with the removal of its chromatic predicate. Indeed, perhaps we can now view the concluding measures of the five-part *Urfassung* with a bit of distance. Certainly, no one would criticize this close if it had not been rendered problematic by the incomparably beautiful and convincing conclusion of the Leipzig version. Viewed in light of Bach's final refinement, however, one gets the impression that the use of the minor sixth in the Weimar arrangements was expressive and strong but that it did not set the proper "tone" for the entire piece and for the chorale melody that serves as its foundation, especially since the *major* sixth is so heavily stressed in the chorale. So in this passage, at least, Bach seems to have ruled against his original compositional instincts.

To summarize: from our observations of two selected chorale preludes from the Leipzig manuscript of the "Great Eighteen" collection, we can point to several characteristics of Bach's revisional process:

1. In the *Fantasia super Komm heiliger Geist, Herre Gott*, the endeavor to create a purer genre of chorale prelude, a "model of art," in which the structure of the cantus firmus and the length of the work are appropriately proportionate to one another.

2. In *An Wasserflüssen Babylon*, the principle of economy of contrapuntal means, i.e., the number of voices, with regard to the compositional concept.

3. In *An Wasserflüssen Babylon*, the attempt—introduced in the Weimar revision but more pronounced in the Leipzig refinement—to endow all parts with a sharper thematic profile.

4. The improvement of detail, in both pieces, lifted to a new plane, where exceedingly increased sensitivity is shown to correcting the smallest inconsistency in the musical fabric.

In these factors we see distinct parallels to the general tendencies of Bach's composition in his late-Leipzig years, when his interest in expansive thematic invention and colorful sonority receded. Bach concentrated instead on the exploration and subsequent development of small thematic nuclei.

In Bach's Leipzig revisions the "Great Eighteen" Chorales retain the colorful musical conception, full of fantasy, that they carried with them from the time of their origin. Thanks to circumstance, this conception was reevaluated and refined in terms of a new compositional ideal—that of Bach's last Leipzig years. As a result, these "Fassungen letzter Hand" bear a reflection of Bach's late works.

(TRANSLATED BY GEORGE STAUFFER)

NOTES

The present essay stems from the study "Zu Bachs Umarbeitungsverfahren in den 'Achtzehn Chorälen'," in *Festschrift Georg von Dadelsen*, edited by Thomas Kohlhase and Volker Scherliess (Neuhausen-Stuttgart, 1978). With the kind permission of Hänssler-Verlag, the study appears here in a thoroughly revised and expanded form. The revision, especially the reworking of the first section, was stimulated by the appearance of Peter Williams's three-volume work, *The Organ Music of J. S. Bach*, in which the genesis of BWV 651 and 653 is discussed anew and the findings of the *Kritischer Bericht* of the *Neue Bach-Ausgabe* IV/2 were placed in question. Thus it appeared necessary to examine the history of these two pieces once again, on a somewhat broader basis. I wish to express my gratitude to George Stauffer, who not only assumed the task of translating the present article but also proved to be a critical and helpful reader.

1. See Georg von Dadelsen, "'Die Fassung letzter Hand' in der Musik," *Acta Musicologica* 33 (1961): 1–14.
2. See Werner Breig, "Bachs Goldberg-Variationen als zyklisches Werk," *Archiv für Musikwissenschaft* 32 (1975): 243–65; and Breig, "Bachs 'Kunst der Fuge': Zur instrumentalen Bestimmung und zum Zyklus-Charakter," BJ 1982: 103–23.
3. See Christoph Wolff, "Bach's 'Handexemplar' of the Goldberg Variations," *Journal of the American Musicological Society* 29 (1976): 224–41; and Wolff, "Bachs Kanonkunst—neue Perspektiven," *Bachwoche Ansbach 1977*, pp. 43–50.
4. The "Great Eighteen" Chorales, BWV 651–68, together with the Trio Sonatas, BWV 525–30, and the revised version of the Canonic Variations on *Vom Himmel hoch*, BWV 769a, make up the contents of *P 271*, which is mostly autograph. The handwriting of the chorales points to the years 1744–48. Bach himself assigned no title to the group BWV 651–68. When Rust edited the chorales for vol. XXV² of the *Bach-Gesamtausgabe*, he called them "Achtzehn Choräle von verschiedener Art, auf einer Orgel mit 2 Clavieren und Pedal vorzuspielen," a title analogous to that of the Schübler Chorales ("Sechs Choräle von verschiedener Art . . ."). In his new edition for the NBA (IV/2, *Die Orgelchoräle der Leipziger Originalhandschrift*, 1958; KB, 1957), Hans Klotz grouped BWV 651–67 together under the heading "Siebzehn Choräle," viewing BWV 668, the fragmentary copy of Bach's "Funeral Chorale," *Vor deinen Thron tret ich hiermit*, as a separate work, since it is divided from BWV 651–67 in *P 271* by the late version of the Canonic Variations. Here the adopted title "Eighteen Chorales" is maintained, for BWV 668 appears to belong with the remaining chorales. All are revisions of Weimar works; and BWV 667, *Komm, Gott Schöpfer, Heiliger Geist*, like BWV 668, is drawn from the *Orgelbüchlein*. See Christoph Wolff, "J. S. Bachs 'Sterbechoral'—Kritische Fragen zu einem Mythos," in *Studies in Renaissance and Baroque Music in Honor of Arthur Mendel*, edited by Robert L. Marshall (Kassel and Hackensack, NJ, 1974), pp. 283–97.
5. The early versions as well as the Leipzig revisions are published in NBA IV/2. On the chronology of the pieces, see the KB to NBA IV/2 as well as Georg von Dadelsen, *Beiträge zur Chronologie der Werke J. S. Bachs* (Trossingen, 1958), p. 127; and Hermann Zietz, *Quellenkritische Untersuchungen an den Bach-Handschriften P 801, P 802 und P 803 . . .* (Hamburg, 1969).
6. NBA IV/2, KB, p. 64.
7. Zietz, p. 140.
8. Peter Williams, *The Organ Music of J. S. Bach* (Cambridge, 1980–1984), vol. 2, p. 131.
9. The inclusion of the text in Example 1 should in no way suggest that a detailed expression of the words is presented in the organ composition. It is

given merely to help illustrate the structure of the chorale. The chorale can be traced back to the antiphon *Veni sancte Spiritus*. Strophe 1 stems from the fifteenth century; strophes 2 and 3 were added by Martin Luther (first printed in the Erfurt *Enchiridion*, 1524).

10. Johann Gottfried Walther, *Musicalisches Lexicon* (Leipzig, 1732), p. 582.

11. It may be that at a later point Bach was not entirely satisfied with the partial citation of the chorale in this trio. One might view the trio on the same melody in *Clavierübung* III, BWV 676, in which the entire chorale is presented in the course of the movement, as an indirect "correction" of the "Great Eighteen" arrangement.

12. The entering of BWV 651a into the manuscript Berlin, DStB *P 802* by Johann Tobias Krebs cannot have taken place before 1714, for the copy of the *Orgelbüchlein* chorale *O Mensch, bewein dein Sünde gross*, BWV 622, which occurs a few pages before BWV 651a in *P 802*, was only composed in 1714, according to Heinz-Harald Löhlein. See *Johann Sebastian Bach, Orgelbüchlein*, facsimile edition edited by Heinz-Harald Löhlein (Kassel, 1981), Foreword, p. 9.

13. Albert Schweitzer, *J. S. Bach* (Leipzig, 1908), p. 256. Schweitzer uses the phrase in reference to the Toccata in F, BWV 540/1, and the Prelude in C ("9/8"), BWV 547/1.

14. NBA IV/2, KB, p. 64.

15. Johann Nikolaus Forkel, *Über J. S. Bachs Leben, Kunst, und Kunstwerke* (Leipzig, 1802); modern edition by Joseph Müller-Blattau (Kassel, 1950), p. 68.

16. Spitta I, p. 606. Spitta's source for this conjecture was the Obituary of Bach printed in 1754. See the *Bach Reader*, p. 219, or BDok III, p. 84.

17. NBA IV/2, KB, p. 67.

18. This conclusion is not self-evident however; Peter Williams feels that the position of BWV 653b as the original version of *An Wasserflüssen Babylon* is confirmed "neither by the sources nor by its musical character" (Williams, vol. 2, p. 137).

19. Compare the rhythm of the chorale in Bach's four-part harmonization, BWV 267, for example. The *Urfassung* of the melody stems from Wolfgang Dachstein. It was joined with the text *An Wasserflüssen Babylon* (a rhymed version of Psalm 137) and published for the first time in *Teutsch Kirchenampt* (Strassburg, 1525).

20. The rhythmic transformation of chorales into dances was later systematized by Johann Mattheson "in order to further underline the unusual strength of the poetic accent." See Johann Mattheson, *Der vollkommene Capellmeister* (Hamburg, 1739), pp. 161–66.

21. See NBA IV/2, KB.

CHRISTOPH WOLFF

Bach's Personal Copy of the
Schübler Chorales

During the editing of the original Bach prints for the *Bach-Gesamtausgabe*, only one of the composer's personal copies, or *Handexemplare*, was known to exist: that for the "Six Chorales of Diverse Kinds," the so-called Schübler Chorales, BWV 645–50. Friedrich Conrad Griepenkerl brought it into consideration for the first time in vols. VI and VII of his edition of the organ works published by Peters in 1847. Wilhelm Rust also used it for his editorial work on vol. 25/2 of the *Bach-Gesamtausgabe* in 1878.

Since that time Bach's personal copies of almost all the other original prints have been located and identified,[1] so that the *Handexemplar* of the Schübler Chorales must relinquish its position of singularity. But despite its relatively early utilization by Griepenkerl and Rust, it never really lost its significance, especially because of the unusually encompassing and instructive additions and corrections it contains. On the contrary, the *Handexemplar* of the Schübler Chorales attained an almost legendary fame, for it disappeared without a trace in the 1850s and was considered a lost source, unavailable to Bach research, for more than a century.

Rust, who had inspected the Schübler print in 1852, while it was owned by Siegfried Wilhelm Dehn in Berlin (Dehn had obtained it from Griepenkerl's estate), lamented its later disappearance in his Foreword to vol. 25/2 of the *Bach-Gesamtausgabe*: "Whoever is now the fortunate owner, is anyone's guess."[2] In the summer of 1975 Bach's personal copy of the Schübler Chorales came to light once again in the international book dealers' market. The generosity of the present

121

owner[3] has made possible new study and appraisal of this long-vanished "relic."

I

Indeed, "precious relic" was the term used for the *Handexemplar* of the Schübler Chorales by Philipp Spitta, while he had access to it for a brief time in 1882 through arrangements made by Joseph Joachim.[4] In two letters that accompany the print today, Spitta attempted to clarify the provenance of the copy and to confirm its identity as the Griepenkerl-Dehn source. His primary concern was to determine whether a second *Handexemplar* might exist. Spitta's initial letter runs as follows:

> Berlin W., Burggrafenstr. 10
> 30.1.82
>
> My Esteemed Sir,
>
> My friend Professor Joachim has shown me the original print of the six Bach chorales, of which you are the owner. In the annotations written in ink I perceive Bach's own hand, and I believe, as you do, that you are in possession of a precious relic.
>
> What also arouses my special interest is the following circumstance. There was once a copy of the six chorales with Bach's handwritten corrections throughout. Griepenkerl, the editor of the Bach instrumental works at Peters in Leipzig, owned it. After Griepenkerl's death, it went into the possession of Professor S. W. Dehn here in Berlin, who apparently still possessed it in 1852. Thereafter it disappeared.
>
> Is your copy the one owned by Griepenkerl? Certain facts lead me to doubt that it is. I would be very grateful to you, Esteemed Sir, if you could tell me what you know about the past fortunes of your relic. Joachim said to me that you obtained it from Princess Czartoryska, who in turn received it from the Duke of Aumale in Paris. He couldn't specify, however, how and when these transactions took place.
>
> In looking forward to receiving helpful particulars from you, I am
>
> With high esteem,
> Yours respectfully,
> PHILIPP SPITTA
> Prof.

Apparently this letter, whose addressee was not named, went unanswered, for a half year later Spitta again picked up his pen:

Berlin W., Burggrafenstr. 10
14.6.82

My Esteemed Sir,

In January of this year Professor Joachim, upon returning from Krakow, brought me a copy of the six organ chorales of Bach belonging to you—a copy which contains corrections in the hand of the master. This print awakened a great interest in me, for at the beginning of the '50s just such a print was owned by Prof. Dehn in Berlin. In the meantime, this print has disappeared. It seems quite possible that Dehn's copy is identical with yours. In order to enter into greater certainty on the matter, I turned to you in a letter of January 30 with the request for further information. My letter remains unanswered. Might I be so bold as to approach you once more about this matter. I do not conceal the fact that I run the danger of appearing to be importunate. I find an excuse solely in the circumstance that this concerns a master to whose life and works I have dedicated a portion of my own.

Professor Joachim mentioned to me that the print was given by the Duke of Aumale (perhaps after it had been owned by Chopin) to Princess Czartoryska in Warsaw, who in turn presented it to you. It is very important to me to ascertain when, by chance, this may have happened, and if the transmission of the manuscript can perhaps be traced back even further, and if the title page was already lost, as it came into your hands. Anything else you might be able to say about it would be of great interest to me.

As soon as I know that this letter has safely reached its address, I will hurry to return the precious relic to you.

With high esteem,
Yours faithfully,
PROFESSOR DR. SPITTA

Sometime thereafter Spitta must have received a response, which may have been lost, for he returned the source to its Polish owner. Spitta's remarks and conjectures about the print's change of owners give us the occasion to go briefly into the question of its provenance. Joachim's information appears to be reliable. To judge from his report, Henri Eugène Philippe Louis d'Orléans, Duke of Aumale (1822–97), gave the *Handexemplar* to Marcelline Czartoryska, née Princess Radziwill (1817–94), a student of Chopin's and a much-celebrated pianist. From her it went to the unnamed recipient of the two Spitta letters, a citizen of Krakow.[5] We do not know when or how the print came into the Duke's hands. One can rule out Joachim and Spitta's hypothesis that it came via Chopin, for the pianist died in 1849, just a few months after Griepenkerl, and it is beyond question that the print went from Griepenkerl's estate to Dehn's collection without detour. Since it was still in Dehn's possession in 1852, according to Rust, it could only have changed ownership once again between this date and the year of Dehn's death, 1858.

During the last years of his life, Dehn gave away various items from his valuable collection. On October 1, 1857, for instance, he presented the manuscript of the "Small" Magnificat, BWV Anh. 21, attested to be a Bach autograph, to the Russian composer Alexis von Lwoff.[6] Since at that time Dehn was on bad terms with the *Bach-Gesellschaft*, it would not be surprising if he wished to keep the Schübler *Handexemplar* out of its reach by passing it on to a foreigner. Possibly Dehn intended to give it to the pianist Czartoryska, so that the Duke of Aumale would have served chiefly as a "middleman." This theory is compelling, since Dehn's contacts with eastern Europe were very close at all times. Thus he was united in a warm friendship with Glinka; Anton Rubinstein was one of his composition students; and he gave the supposed Magnificat autograph to a Russian musician.

The details of the travels of the Schübler print after its separation from the Dehn library will probably never be clarified. And in the long run, they are of little significance to the actual value of the score. It is unfortunate, however, that the first page of the *Handexemplar* has been lost.[7] It was still present, with the title of the collection on the front side and the beginning of the musical text on the back, when Rust inspected the source in 1852, but it was absent by the time Spitta looked at it in 1882. The title side may have contained lines of dedication or other remarks about earlier owners. The initial page may have been removed because it was an especially attractive collector's item, or in order to "hush up" the lineage of the copy in question.

II

With regard to the provenance of the *Handexemplar*, the first century after Bach's death is incomparably more important than the period after 1852. Up to 1852 the line of descent seems to be clear and without gaps. In 1750 the print was inherited by Carl Philipp Emanuel Bach, who sold it in 1774 to Johann Nicolaus Forkel. Griepenkerl procured it from Forkel's estate in 1819, and after his death in 1849 it went to Dehn along with other "Griepenkerliana." According to an exchange of letters between C. P. E. Bach and Forkel on the occasion of the sale of the Schübler print, the *Handexemplar* of the Schübler Chorales was bound with the *Handexemplar* of *Clavierübung* III. In a letter to Forkel on August 26, 1774, Emanuel wrote: "Find hereby enclosed the two volumes, the correct payment for which I heartily thank you. To the back of one you will find bound the six printed chorales."[8] In an earlier letter he had already indicated that the print of *Clavierübung* III was "the copy which he [J. S. Bach] used to have for his own use."[9] But when was Bach's personal copy of the Schübler Chorales separated from the volume obtained by Forkel, and what happened to his personal copy of *Clavierübung* III? In the 1819 catalogue of Forkel's estate, the two are still listed together:

> (Clavierübung) 3 Thl. Consisting of diverse preludes on chorales for the organ, in 4. Bound to it are 6 chorales for an organ with 2 manuals and pedal.[10]

Ever since the publication of Georg Kinsky's bibliographical study of the Bach original prints,[11] it has been assumed that Bach's *Handexemplar* of *Clavierübung* III is the copy in the Staatsbibliothek Preussischer Kulturbesitz in West Berlin, *DMS 224676(3)*, which went to the Berlin State Library via Georg Poelchau. A connection between Forkel and Poelchau cannot be verified, however. As far as we know, Forkel did not own a second copy of *Clavierübung* III, and, as it has been unequivocally demonstrated, the Forkel copy mentioned above was obtained by Griepenkerl. It is inconceivable that the question of provenance was not taken up anew by Manfred Tessmer in the *Kritischer Bericht* of the *Neue Bach-Ausgabe*, vol. IV/4, where the Berlin copy (Source Al) is unambiguously labeled "with all certainty . . . stemming from J. S. Bach's estate."[12]

Also overlooked is the fact that the print of *Clavierübung* III, once owned by Rust and now in the Musikbibliothek der Stadt Leipzig under the signature *PM 1403*, has a more striking and significant clue about the provenance of the Schübler *Handexemplar*. On the pasteboard binding, covered with brown paper with parchment edges and corners, there is a faded ink notation in Griepenkerl's hand:

> Third Part/of the/Claiver-Übung/and/Six Chorales/NB: the corrections in the 6 chorales are in J. S. Bach's/own hand.[13]

This print, therefore, is the true *Handexemplar* of the composer, and we can disqualify the Berlin copy. The binding also shows traces that it was originally fashioned for thicker contents. Hence the Schübler Chorales were probably removed after Griepenkerl's death, possibly so that the two prints could be sold separately.[14]

There remains one interesting detail. The back flyleaf of the Leipzig

binding,[15] which appears to stem from the second half of the eighteenth century, bears a Berlin watermark: a crowned double eagle
with breastplate; in the breastplate, F(ridericus) R(ex). From this watermark we can conclude that C. P. E. Bach had the two prints of organ
chorales stemming from his father's estate bound together during his
years in Berlin.

III

Bach's handwritten additions and corrections in his personal copy of
the Schübler Chorales have been very carefully described and evalu-
ated by Griepenkerl and above all by Rust. Five categories can be
distinguished:

1. Corrections of printing errors. Examples: the erasure of a tie in
m. 2 of *Meine Seele erhebt den Herren*, BWV 648 (Plate 1, top); correction of the first note in m. 2 of *Kommst du nun, Jesu, vom Himmel
herunter*, BWV 650 (d″ instead of c″; Plate 2, top); correction of the last
two notes in m. 15 of the same piece (c″–b′ to b′–a′; Plate 2, bottom).

Meine Seele erhebt den Herren,
BWV 648, mm. 1–7

Meine Seele erhebt den Herren,
BWV 648, mm. 8½–10½

Bach's Personal Copy of the Schübler Chorales
(William Scheide Collection, Princeton, NJ)

PLATE 1

Kommst du nun, Jesu, vom Himmel herunter,
BWV 650, mm. 1–4

Kommst du nun, Jesu, vom Himmel herunter,
BWV 650, mm. 12–17

Bach's Personal Copy of the Schübler Chorales
(William Scheide Collection, Princeton, NJ)

PLATE 2

2. Filling in of accidentals and articulation marks. Example: legato indications in mm. 1–5 of *Meine Seele erhebt den Herren* (Plate 1, top).

3. Improvement of readings. Example: modification of the arpeggiated figure in m. 2 of *Kommst du nun, Jesu* (Plate 2, top). See also below.

4. Performance and registration indications. Examples: indication of how the voices are to be distributed, on manual or pedal (Plate 1, top; Plate 2, top and bottom); indication of the pitch of stops to be used ("Ped. 4 F. u. eine 8tav tiefer" ["Pedal 4 foot and an octave lower"]; Plate 2, bottom) as well as degree of prominence ("destra forte" ["right hand forte"]; Plate 1, bottom).

5. Clarification of the rhythmic notation. Example: indication of rhythmic sharpening in m. 13 and of triplets in m. 16 of the middle voice of *Kommst du nun, Jesu* (Plate 2, bottom).[16]

This is not the place to enumerate the small details that were overlooked in Bach's time or to enlarge upon Rust's critical report in vol. 25/2 of the *Bach-Gesamtausgabe*. Nevertheless, several observations of a general nature should be made.

Bach's handwriting, which can be seen most clearly in the written comments, appears to stem from the last years of his life and may even be one of the latest preserved samples of his script. It exhibits the distinctive features delineated in Bach's late handwriting by Georg von Dadelsen.[17] For instance, the discontinuity of the ductus is unmistakable. The segregation of the individual letters within words and the uneven slant of the letters is striking. See, for example, the *s* leaning strongly to the right, followed by the *i* leaning strongly to the left in "Sinistra" (Plate 2, top). Along with this go the clublike corrections of the noteheads (see especially Plate 2, top). The absolute *terminus ante quem non* for the completion of the Schübler Chorale print is the second half of 1746.[18] In all likelihood, however, the edition was not issued before 1748.[19] Thus Bach's handwriting characteristics may reflect the period 1748–50, possibly even 1749–50.

The state of m. 2 of the chorale *Meine Seele erhebt den Herren* (Plate 1, top) allows us to draw certain inferences about the manuscript (now lost) from which it was engraved. The reading *ante correcturam* is shown in Example 1. The tie between the third and fourth notes is

EXAMPLE 1

engraved (and appears in all other copies of the Schübler print), but during the "filling-in process" it was changed by Bach into an articulation sign. The printing mistake most certainly goes back to a handwritten model and can be explained in the following way: The handwritten model was apparently copied from the autograph score of Cantata 10, *Meine Seel' erhebt den Herren*, written in 1724. The fifth movement of this work represents the original, aria form of the organ chorale prelude. In Bach's score of Cantata 10 (now in the Library of Congress, Washington, D.C., under the designation *ML 30.8b.B2M4*), the articulation mark in m. 2 is misplaced to the degree that it can easily be misinterpreted as a tie. Such an error would certainly not be made by Bach. Thus the handwritten manuscript of the Schübler Chorales used in the production of the print must have been made by a copyist, at least for this piece. Bach must have given the copyist instructions to write out the movement without articulation marks, for the mistake in m. 2 of the print can only be explained as a misunderstood tie. Similar errors traceable to copying mistakes are found in other places in the print. A further sign of copyists at work is the layout of the voices, which are taken over in a mechanical way from the cantata scores, with the result that the parts in the individual preludes are often set out in a manner poorly suited to the organ (see Plate 2, top and bottom). One can thus conclude that Bach was probably not closely involved in the printing of the six chorales. This assumption adds strength to the time-honored belief that the prelude *Wo soll ich fliehen hin*, BWV 646, also represents a movement drawn from a cantata score. Hence in this piece we have a fragment of a lost work.

The corrections in the print, taken as a whole, show that Bach scrutinized the text of the Schübler Chorales not only in terms of orthography and mistakes of secondary consequence but also from the standpoint of a composer giving his work a critical appraisal. An especially characteristic example can be seen in m. 2 of the prelude *Kommst du nun, Jesu* (see Plate 2, top), where Bach used the correction of a printing mistake as an opportunity to ponder anew the motivic consequences of the arpeggiated figure in the right hand. The three different readings given in Example 2 document the metamorphosis of the motive.

EXAMPLE 2

Reading 1 represents the passage as written for solo violin in the chorale setting from Cantata 137, *Lobe den Herren*, of 1725. Reading 2 corresponds to the uncorrected state of the organ prelude, in which neither the first note nor last two notes can be viewed as a revision of Reading 1. Rather they are printing and copying mistakes respectively.[20] Reading 3, finally, gives Bach's last version of the text, as found in the *Handexemplar*. The initial shape of the sixteenth-note figure, as

EXAMPLE 3

set forth in m. 1, was repetitive, with a repeated d″ as the top tone (shown in Example 3).

This shape was initially maintained in m. 2, with a repeated a″ as the top tone (see Readings 1 and 2, in Example 2), but then softened into a more melodically flexible version (Reading 3). The highest tone now moves down, b″–a″–g″, complementing the movement of the bass. As his personal copy of the Schübler Chorales aptly demonstrates, when Bach set his indefatigably self-critical hand in motion, there seemed to be no such thing as an "untouchable" text, whether manuscript or print.

(TRANSLATED BY GEORGE STAUFFER)

NOTES

This essay originally appeared as "Bachs Handexemplar der Schübler-Choräle," BJ 1977: 120–29. It is reprinted here, in translation and with several emendations by the author, with permission.

1. Around 1890 Bach's personal copy of *Clavierübung* II surfaced in Dresden (today it is in the British Library, London, under the call number *K.8.g.7*). See Walter Emery, NBA V/2, KB (1981). In 1975 the *Handexemplar* of the Goldberg Variations emerged (now in the Bibliothèque nationale, Paris, call number *Ms. 17669*). See Christoph Wolff, NBA V/2, KB (1981); and Wolff, "Bach's *Handexemplar* of the Goldberg Variations: A New Source," *Journal of the American Musicological Society* 29 (1976): 224–41. Richard Douglass Jones presents arguments in NBA V/1, KB (1978), that the copy of *Clavierübung* I in the British Library, London (Hirsch Collection *III.37*), is Bach's *Handexemplar*. On the supposed and actual composer's copy of *Clavierübung* III, see section II below. For a related discussion on Bach's personal copies of his original editions see also Christoph Wolff, "Textkritische Bemerkungen zum Originaldruck der Bachschen Partiten," BJ 1979: 65–74.

2. BG 25/2 (1878): xv. In the mid-1950s at the Bach-Archiv in Leipzig a certain Aleksander Ewert from Poland was known as the owner of the *Handexemplar* in question. The original itself, however, was never seen (oral communication from Hans-Joachim Schulze).

3. William H. Scheide, of Princeton, obtained it from Albi Rosenthal, a bookdealer in Oxford, England. Special thanks go to Mr. Scheide for his kind permission to examine the source and for providing the author with photographs of it.

4. Joseph Joachim was at that time director of the Musikhochschule in Berlin; Spitta had served the Musikhochschule as deputy director since 1879.

5. Perhaps the pianist and music historian Franciszek Bylicki, a student of Czartoryska (conjecture of Albi Rosenthal, Oxford).

6. See Hans-Joachim Schulze, "Das 'Kleine Magnificat' BWV Anh. 21 und sein Komponist," *Musikforschung* 21 (1968): 44.

7. In its present, unbound state, Bach's *Handexemplar* of the Schübler Chorales has the following structure:

> (title page; musical text, page 1)
> (musical text, pp. 2–3)
> (musical text, pp. 4–5)
> (musical text, pp. 6–7)
> (musical text, pp. 8–9)
> (musical text, pp. 10–11)
> (musical text, pp. 12–13)
> (musical text, p. 14; reverse side, blank)

The pages were printed singly in oblong format (plate size: 17 × 28 cm). The appropriate pages were then glued together at the left vertical margins to form double pages. Finally, the double pages were folded and arranged in the manner shown above.

8. BDok III, no. 793.

9. BDok III, No. 792.

10. *Verzeichnis der von dem verstorbenen Doctor und Musikdirector Forkel in Göttingen nachgelassenen Bücher und Musikalien* (Göttingen, 1819), p. 136; no. 59.

11. *Die Originalausgaben der Werke Johann Sebastian Bachs* (Vienna, 1937; Hilversum, Netherlands, 1968), p. 60.

12. NBA IV/4, KB (1974), p. 16. This view is also promulgated in the commentary to BDok III, no. 792, as well as in Wolff, "Bach's *Handexemplar* of the Goldberg Variations," n.1.

13. Tessmer presents this copy of the print as Source A6 in the KB of NBA IV/4 without a more-detailed description. Peter Krause, in his catalogue *Originalausgaben und ältere Drucke der Werke Johann Sebastian Bachs in der Musikbibliothek der Stadt Leipzig* (Leipzig, 1970), clearly delineates the transmission of the copy from Griepenkerl to Rust (p. 77), but does not report Griepenkerl's remark on the cover and the descent of the print from Forkel's estate. In the Foreword to vol. VI of the Peters Edition of the organ works (1847), Griepenkerl noted: "Nos. 2 and 3 [that is, *Clavierübung* III and the Schübler Chorales] are original editions from Forkel's estate and are now in my possession." The copy *PM 1403* contains no striking autograph entries, but merits closer inspection in this regard. The Peters Facsimile Edition, edited by Christoph Wolff (Leipzig, 1984), is based on this copy.

14. Kinsky's comments (*Die Originalausgaben*, p. 60) on the Berlin copy—"Its present condition shows that a second print was bound to it and later cut out of the binding: the *Handexemplar* of the organ chorales" remain enigmatic and could not be substantiated by Tessmer (KB to NBA IV/4).

15. The front flyleaf has not survived.

16. The alignment of the sixteenth notes and the triplets in mm. 16, 26, etc., is misleading in the recently published NBA IV/1 (1983; pp. 99–100), edited by Heinz-Harald Löhlein. The sixteenth notes of the pedal are placed after the third note of each group of triplets, implying that the sixteenth notes are to be interpreted at face value, that is, as dotted figures falling after the last note of each triplet group. To judge from the manner in which such pas-

sages are aligned in other Bach works (the Prelude in c, BWV 546/1, for example, where in manuscripts stemming from the Bach circle the sixteenth notes are placed directly above or below the third note of each triplet group) and from contemporary performance practices, it seems most likely that the sixteenth notes would be interpreted as the last third of a triplet figure, played in time with the triplets of the left hand.

17. Georg von Dadelson, *Beiträge zur Chronologie der Werke Johann Sebastian Bachs* (Trossingen, 1958), pp. 113–18.

18. See the commentary to BDok I, no. 175.

19. Arguments for the appearance of the Schübler Chorales after the publication of the *Musical Offering* (1747), which was also printed by Schübler, are presented in Christoph Wolff, NBA VIII/1, KB (1976), pp. 108–109.

20. Since the original score of Cantata 137, from which the manuscript copy for the print must have been made, is no longer available, one cannot ascertain if lack of clarity in the autograph was responsible for the error-ridden Reading 2 (see the case of the original score of Cantata 10, described above). Of the manuscripts used for writing out the Schübler transcriptions, only one besides the autograph score of Cantata 10 (the model for *Meine Seele erhebt den Herren*, BWV 648) has survived: the original score for Cantata 6 (the model for *Ach bleib' bei uns, Herr Jesu Christ*, BWV 649), preserved in West Berlin, SPK, under the designation *P 44*.

GEORGE STAUFFER

᪥

Fugue Types in Bach's Free Organ Works

In 1788 an anonymous German critic, writing in the *Allgemeine deutsche Bibliothek*, launched a spirited defense of Bach's fugue composition.[1] Four years earlier, Charles Burney had published a pamphlet declaring Handel a better fugue writer than Bach. Now the German critic, a musician obviously well acquainted with Bach's works,[2] refuted Burney's remarks point by point. He lauded Bach's craft, noting the superiority of the part writing, the greater diversity of styles, and the subtler combination of strict and free, learned and *galant*. But above all, he extolled Bach's gift for fashioning fugues with singing lines and deep expression, rather than formulaic themes and pedantic counterpoint: "He, the deepest savant of contrapuntal arts (and even artifice), knew how to subordinate art to beauty."[3]

With this remark, the critic put his finger on the problem we face when trying to categorize Bach's free organ fugues. Certainly the great variety of style, the melodic invention, and the deep expression place these pieces, in which Bach chose his themes "at will,"[4] among the most appealing and accessible fugues in Western music. But at the same time, the subordination of art (and even artifice) to beauty renders them exceedingly difficult to classify. We can take the traditional approach of most of the monographs dealing with Bach's organ music and analyze the works in terms of "art." That is, we can examine the treatment of theme (simple fugue, double fugue, counter fugue, etc.) and look closely at specific contrapuntal procedures (double counterpoint, inversion, augmentation, etc.). While this analysis may heighten our appreciation of the works, it does not explain their unique character, the quality the German critic referred to as "beauty."

Although Bach expressed disdain for the "textbook" fugues of his day[5] and certainly went far beyond the models available to him, he relied heavily on a number of conventional fugue types when penning his pieces. The choice of fugue type determined the nature of the work: it dictated the appropriate thematic material and contrapuntal gesture and stood behind such fundamental compositional decisions as shape of the subject, meter, number of voices, presence or absence of "learned" devices, and length and placement of episodes. In a word, the selection of fugue type was among Bach's most fundamental compositional decisions, one that decided from the outset what sort of "beauty" a particular piece would have.

In a probing article on Bach's fugue writing, Stefan Kunze has outlined a number of fugue types that appear in the *Well-Tempered Clavier*.[6] Two of the genres he treats are relevant to our discussion, for they also emerge in the free organ works: *Spielfugen* and dance fugues. To them we can add two other types: allabreve fugues and art fugues. Each of the four genres has its own special characteristics—characteristics that frequently have important implications for performance practice.

Spielfugen

By far the most prominent fugue type in Bach's free organ works is the *Spielfuge*. The term does not readily translate into English. The phrase "instrumental fugue," which is sometimes used, is misleading, for it is not instrumental music, reproduced literally, that serves as the basis for *Spielfugen*,[7] but rather the figural play of the instrumental idiom. Kunze presents the best succinct description of the *Spielfuge* when he defines it as "the large family of fugues in which the rich tradition of instrumental virtuosity and figural play is subjected to the rules of fugue."[8] Among the free organ works, we find at least twelve fugues that fall into this category:

	Meter	Number of Voices
Fugue in C, BWV 531/2	C	4
Fugue in D, BWV 532/2	C	4
Fugue in g, BWV 535/2	C	4
Fugue in G, BWV 541/2	C	4
Fugue in g, BWV 542/2	C	4
Fugue in e ("Wedge"), BWV 548/2	¢	4

Fugue in c, BWV 549/2	¢	4
Fugue in G, BWV 550/2	¢	4
Fugue from the Toccata in d, BWV 565	¢	4
First fugue from the Toccata in E, BWV 566	¢	4
Fugue in c, BWV 575 (*manualiter*, until the close)	¢	3
Fugue in g, BWV 578	¢	4

These works are distinguished from other fugues in their reliance on instrumental gestures. In Bach's time, *Spielkunst* ("instrumental art") was usually discussed in terms of its contrast with *Singkunst* ("vocal art"). In his comparison of vocal and instrumental melodies, Johann Mattheson touched on a number of elements that are critical to what might be called the *"Spiel"* style:

> Instrumental melody has more fire and freedom than vocal melody. . . .
>
> Vocal melody does not have the same kind of jumps as instrumental. If one compares Vivaldi's concertos, especially the so-called *L'Estro harmonico*, with the cantatas of Buononcini, one will no longer have the slightest doubt about this. . . .
>
> Vocal melodies must be fashioned with the nature of breathing in mind, while in instrumental pieces this is not necessary.
>
> Instruments allow more artful writing than voices. Many-beamed notes, arpeggios, and all sorts of broken figuration. . . . are easily executed on instruments. . . .[9]

All these qualities—fire and freedom, disjunct melodic motion, long-winded phrases, and artful figurations—play a central role in Bach's *Spielfugen* for organ. They emerge at the very outset in the principal themes. The subject of the Fugue in g, BWV 535/2 (Example 1a), is typical. Composed of black notes and possessing a strong chordal stamp, it contains a number of wide leaps (ascending sixths and fourths, and a fifth and a tritone descending), two sets of repeated notes (on e♭″ and d″), and two different repeated patterns (marked *x* and *y* in Example 1a). These two patterns imply harmonic sequences that are later used expansively in the episodes of the work. In an analysis, the theme can be viewed as the instantaneous embellishment, in the instrumental manner, of a simpler melodic idea, given in Example 1b. The half notes of Example 1b become the object of ornamental diminution: first, the e♭″ of m. 2 and the d″ of m. 3 are elaborated through eighth-note repetition; then, in m. 4, d″ and c″ are

EXAMPLE 1

embellished through faster-moving neighbor-note sixteenths. The acceleration toward the end of the theme creates a climactic effect and establishes the unit of pulse, the sixteenth note, which becomes the norm for the rest of the work.

Acceleration and immediate embellishment are found in the subjects of many other *Spielfugen*: the Fugues in G, BWV 550/2 and 541/2, the Fugue in c, BWV 549/2, and, most strikingly, the "Little" Fugue in g, BWV 578. Repetition of notes also occurs frequently, especially in pieces whose themes are based on the North German *repercussio* idea: the Fugues in G, BWV 550/2 and 541/2 (in which the North German *repercussio* is "Vivaldi-ized"), and most notably in the initial fugue of the Toccata in E, BWV 566, in which the eighth-note motives of the opening bar are elaborated with sixteenth-note figurations in the three measures that follow (Example 2a).

Sequential motivic repetition is found in all the *Spielfugen* subjects and hence appears to be a basic feature of the genre. In the theme of the Fugue in g, BWV 542/2, two motives, x and y, are arranged in an alternating pattern, $x x y x y x$ (Example 2b), producing a subtle element of balance that suggests the periodic phrasing of the later Classical era.[10] Sometimes the repetition is taken to extremes, as in the Fugue in D, BWV 532/2, where the initial motive is repeated four times and the second motive five (or ten, if one divides the motive into units of four, rather than eight, sixteenth notes; Example 2c). This *repetitio ad extremum* accounts for the jocularity of the subject, which is, in a sense, a parody of *Spielfuge* melodic conventions.

The qualities seen in the *Spielfuge* themes continue in the material that follows the initial exposition. The sixteenth-note motion (or eighth-note, in the Prelude in G, BWV 550/2, in ¢), established by the end of the subject, continues unabated, producing the bravura "perpetuum mobile" effect of many pieces. The extreme "breathlessness" of works such as the Fugue in C, BWV 531, the Fugue in G, BWV 550/2, or the Fugue in D, BWV 532/2, echoes Mattheson's description

EXAMPLE 2

of instrumental melodies, in which human respiration is of no concern. The composer is free to indulge in an unending string of the "many-beamed notes" that are a part of instrumental writing.

From the standpoint of formal structure, it becomes clear, as the *Spielfugen* unfold, that episodes are of great importance. They appear frequently, often becoming longer and more complex as the pieces progress. The sequential motives of the subjects are commonly used as the basis for elaborate digressions, in the manner of instrumental *Fortspinnung* (the Fugue in C, BWV 531/2, or the Fugue in c, BWV 549/2) or, in later works, in the fashion of concerto solos (the Fugue in g, BWV 542/2, or the "Wedge" Fugue in e, BWV 548/2). Progressions implied in the subjects are now fulfilled, sometimes in lengthy circle-of-fifth sequences, replete with the "arpeggios and all sorts of broken figurations" described by Mattheson. In works such as the Fugue in g, BWV 542/2, or the "Wedge" Fugue in e, the episodes seem to "take over" the middle of the piece, to such a degree that the reappearance of the subject is almost like an intrusion, a parenthetical reminder telling us that the composition is, after all, a fugue.

The elaboration of motives in episodic passages sometimes becomes so exuberant that it spills over into the restatements of the subject itself. In the Fugue in g, BWV 542/2, for instance, the eighth notes

EXAMPLE 3

of the first measure are embellished when the theme reappears at mm. 44 and 100 (see Example 3).[11] Such ornamentation reflects the improvisatory practices of instrumental music. Equally outgoing is the treatment of the pedal, which is handled in a virtuoso manner quite antithetical to vocal style.

All these aspects point to the fact that *Spielfugen* are the "freest" of Bach's organ fugues. Episodic digressions are as interesting as the expositions—if not even more so. Invertible counterpoint, sometimes applied rigidly in early works (the Fugue in g, BWV 578, or the fugue from the Toccata in E, BWV 566), is ubiquitous, perhaps because its active, reiterative nature makes it compatible with the repetition and "reveling in the notes" that are so much a part of the *Spiel* idiom. But "learned" devices such as stretto, augmentation, and inversion play little role in these works.[12] Even the thematic expositions are casual: in the Fugue in D, BWV 532/2, and the Fugue in g, BWV 578, the subjects "migrate" from one voice to another,[13] breaking the laws of strict fugal writing.

With regard to texture and meter, the instrumental play of the *Spielfugen* takes place in a relatively "neutral" context. Except for the Fugue in c, BWV 575 (which is *manualiter* up to its pedal-point conclusion), all the *Spielfugen* display four-part texture. Five-part writing is reserved for the more *recherché* vocal-derived pieces, which we will discuss shortly. And the predominant meter is 4/4, calling for a straightforward *tempo ordinario* interpretation. In the words of Bach's Weimar colleague Johann Gottfried Walther, *tempo ordinario*, notated with the meter signature ₵, designates that "all notes are to be executed in their natural and normal value."[14] That is, the quarter note is assigned a duration close to that of the human heartbeat, $\quarternote = 72$.[15]

Dance Fugues

Dance fugues are closely related to *Spielfugen*, for they also exhibit instrumental qualities. What sets them apart is their dependence on specific dance idioms, which has a decisive effect on such elements as meter, melodic material, and structure. Among Bach's free organ fugues we find seven examples of this genre:

	Meter	Number of voices	Dance type
Fugue in A, BWV 536/2	3/4	4	minuet
Fugue from the Passacaglia in c, BWV 582	3/4	4	passacaglia
Second fugue from the Toccata in E, BWV 566	3/4	4	gigue
Fugue in a, BWV 543/2	6/8	4	gigue
Fugue from the Toccata in C, BWV 564	6/8	4	gigue
Fugue in G ("Gigue"), BWV 577[16]	12/8	4	gigue
Fugue from the Pastorale, BWV 590[17] (*manualiter*)	6/8	3	gigue

The fact that only three dance types are represented, the minuet, the passacaglia, and the gigue, rather than the half dozen or so that appear in the fugues of the *Well-Tempered Clavier*,[18] suggests that transferring dances to the organ was not an easy matter. Many techniques common to dance music do not work well on the organ. *Style brisé*, for instance, loses much of its effect when realized through pipes rather than strings. Also, the treatment of texture presents difficulties. In his dance fugues for clavier, Bach consistently employs three-part texture,[19] appropriately light for dance music. But on the organ he had to escalate to four voices in order to use the pedal,[20] thereby producing a thicker, heavier texture not entirely suitable to the dance idiom. In the four early chorale partitas, BWV 766–68 and 770, and the Pastorale in F, BWV 590, Bach skirted this problem by dispensing with the pedal in dance movements (except in the opening section of the Pastorale, in which the pedal acts as an appropriate drone).

In view of these difficulties, the most logical choice for an organ fugue was the French gigue. Its texture was more contrapuntal than *brisé*; it usually commenced with a fugue-like point of imitation; and although it called for a light texture, like other dances, it quite often possessed disjunct themes that were admirably suitable for pedal performance. Hence it is not surprising that almost all of Bach's dance fugues for organ are gigues.

The subjects of the fugues reflect the dance types on which they are based. The theme of the Fugue in A is a symmetrical, eight-measure melody, divided into balanced segments of 2 + 2 + 4 mm. As one would expect in a minuet, the accent shifts back and forth from the first beat of the measure to the second (see the arrows in Example 4a). The theme of the Passacaglia fugue consists of two four-measure

units, 4 + 4, outlining the harmonic movement from I → V, V → I
and stressing the downbeat of each bar. The subjects of the gigue
fugues are also emphatic, with constant emphasis on the strongest
beats of each measure (the first and third quarter notes in 3/4; the first
and fourth eighth notes in 6/8; the first and seventh eighth notes in
12/8[21]). In the Fugue in a, BWV 543/2, the principal accents are
stressed initially through duration (the eighth notes in m. 1) and then
through the change in figural pattern (see Example 4b). In the fugue
from the Toccata in C a more subtle approach is taken. The hemiola
found at the cadences of gigues is incorporated into the subject itself,
whose first six measures sound as if they were written in 3/4, with
three accents per measure, rather than 6/8, with two accents per measure. The ambiguity is not clarified until m. 7, when the correct pulse
of 6/8 is established (see Example 4c). This element of rhythmic sophistication is not found in the other 6/8 fugues and seems to reflect
Bach's increasingly skillful handling of the dance idiom. The themes
of the dance fugues show the same tendency toward triadic shapes,
melodic leaps, and motivic sequences as the *Spielfugen* subjects. The
themes of the fugue from the Toccata in E and the "Gigue" Fugue in
G contain dotted rhythms often associated with the gigue.[22]

The regular accents and sequential motives of the dance subjects

EXAMPLE 4

are carried over into the episodes, imbuing them with a strong stamp of periodicity. For instance, in the "Gigue" Fugue, the half-measure-long motives of the theme return in the episodes, where they serve as the material for long sequences, both singly (as at mm. 41–44) and in pairs (as at mm. 52–56, where the pairs are marked *f* and *p* in many scores). In the fugue of the Toccata in C the blocklike construction is also emphasized by the carefully spaced appearances of the pedal, lending still another level of symmetry to the work.

In the case of the Fugue in A, which may well be Bach's first attempt at writing a *pedaliter* dance, the symmetrical elements of construction are *too* pervasive. The opening 56 measures are composed of small four- and eight-bar units: 8 + 8 + 4 + 8 + 4 + 8 + 4 + 4 + 8. The effect of such a design is stultifying. The work is too "square," too predictably periodic. This tendency can also be observed to a lesser extent in the fugue from the Toccata in E and the "Gigue" Fugue in G.

As was true in *Spielfugen*, the episodes in dance fugues are long and elaborate, with much instrumental *Fortspinnung*. In the expositions, permutation technique and invertible counterpoint are used to a lesser degree than in *Spielfugen*, perhaps because the contrapuntal rigidity of these procedures, if combined with the natural repetitiveness of the dance themes, would make the writing too mechanical. The potential danger of applying invertible counterpoint too zealously can be observed in the fugue of the Passacaglia in c, in which the blocklike presentation of thematic expositions is not relieved until the concluding measures.[23] Learned devices, too, are conspicuously absent. It is the strong rhythmic element rather than contrapuntal manipulation that gives the dance fugues their compelling forward momentum. In the second fugue of the Toccata in E, rhythm carries the piece forward even when the writing sags.

Although the pedal is treated in the virtuoso *Spielfuge* tradition, one can observe an effort to modify its use in order to make the dance fugues more playable. In the second pedal section (mm. 95–151) of the Fugue in a, BWV 543/2, the complete subject is avoided in the pedal, even though it appeared earlier in a special version for the feet (m. 26). The point of entrance for the second pedal section in the "Gigue" Fugue is unclear. In most manuscripts, the pedal enters at m. 63 (see the Peters Edition). Part writing, however, would call for its emergence seven bars earlier, at m. 57 (see the BG).[24] In the Pastorale in F, the dance fugue "pedal dilemma" is solved, as mentioned above, by eliminating the use of the feet altogether.

The meters of the pieces mirror the appropriate dance models: 3/4 for the minuet-like Fugue in A; 3/4 for the passacaglia fugue; 6/8 and 12/8 for the gigue fugues. The 3/4 of the second fugue from the Toccata in E stands out from the others. It is an unusual gigue meter for Bach, not appearing in any of his gigues for clavier. The source seems to be the "old-fashioned" 3/4 gigues of the North German composers of an earlier generation,[25] whose music Bach emulated during his Lüneburg and early Arnstadt years.

From the standpoint of performance, the presence of dance idioms separates this group of pieces from *Spielfugen*. While the *Spielfugen* call for *tempo ordinario* and an unaffected instrumental articulation, the dance fugues demand a more-specialized approach. The fugue of the Passacaglia in c requires the firm, stately pace associated with the passacaglia dance. As a minuet-like piece in 3/4, the Fugue in A seems to call for a moderate tempo and a reasonably light articulation. According to Mattheson, the minuet has "no other affect than a moderate mirth."[26] Bach originally notated the piece in 3/8 (in BWV 536a), but changed his mind during a subsequent revision.[27] The 3/8 meter might have implied *too* fast a tempo and *too* light an articulation.

The concern for a more moderate tempo and a "weightier" touch is seen in the gigue-derived fugues as well. Bach notated them in 3/4, 6/8, and 12/8, avoiding the lighter chamber meters of 3/8, 6/16, and 12/16, which appear in his gigues for clavier. In discussing 6/16, Johann Philipp Kirnberger, who studied with Bach in Leipzig (see note 21), explained how 6/16 differs from 6/8, using the Fugue in F from *Well-Tempered Clavier* II as an example. He noted that if the subject of the well-tempered fugue, which is in 6/16, is written out in 6/8,

> the tempo is no longer the same, the gait is much more ponderous, and the notes, particularly the passing notes, are emphasized too much. In short, the expression of the piece suffers and is no longer the one given by Bach. If this fugue is to be performed correctly on the keyboard, the notes must be played lightly and without the least pressure in a fast tempo.[28]

For the gigue fugues that Bach wrote for organ, the opposite would seem to hold true. Since they are notated in 3/4, 6/8, and 12/8, the notes would be played with some weight and a bit of pressure, and in a slower tempo than called for by the lighter chamber meters of 3/8, 6/16, or 12/16. Bach avoided these meters, perhaps because he deemed them too light and precipitous for the organ.[29]

Allabreve Fugues

In sharp stylistic contrast to *Spielfugen* and dance fugues are a number of works that can be placed under the rubric "allabreve fugues." As Christoph Wolff has shown, Bach's allabreve pieces are related to the *stile antico*, the classical sixteenth-century vocal style of Palestrina,[30] and outwardly they display many features of Renaissance *prima prattica*. But they are not *stile antico* in the purest sense, for they also incorporate certain elements of instrumental writing, as we shall see. Among Bach's free organ works, we find five allabreve fugues:

	Meter	Number of Voices
Fugue in f, BWV 534/2	¢	5
Fugue in d ("Dorian"), BWV 538/2	¢	4
Fugue in F, BWV 540/2	¢	4
Fugue in C, BWV 545/2	¢	4
Fugue in c, BWV 546/2	¢	5

To this list we might cautiously add the Fugue in c, BWV 537/2 (also in ¢; for four voices), whose middle section is based on a white-note allabreve theme.

Wolff points out that Bach probably did not derive his allabreve keyboard style directly from sixteenth-century vocal music but modeled it on an existing Baroque tradition, seen in the allabreve instrumental fugues and ricercars of Frescobaldi, Froberger, Kerll, Pachelbel, and others. Bach's allabreve fugues exhibit the stylistic duality seen in the works of these composers: the Renaissance vocal style serves as the fundamental prototype, especially for the expositions. But more-personal elements are added, such as instrumental figurations, which commonly come to the fore in the episodes. Wolff's survey of Bach's allabreve writing, applied to our group of organ fugues, can be summarized as follows:[31]

1. On the surface, the fugue subjects resemble Renaissance vocal themes. They are composed chiefly of white notes, in allabreve meter. They move mostly in conjunct motion, at least initially, and they commonly contain suspensions (see the subject of the Fugue in C, BWV 545/2; Example 5a). The suspensions are especially apparent in the theme of the "Dorian" Fugue in d, where they form a five-fold chain (marked *x* in Example 5b). The allabreve subjects generally lack the type of repetitive sequences that characterize the instrumental-derived

EXAMPLE 5

Spielfuge and dance fugue themes. But unlike true sixteenth-century vocal subjects, in which linear considerations predominate, allabreve themes show a strong chordal orientation. Even striking leaps, usually of diminished or augmented intervals, reflect an underlying chordal design (see the Fugue in f, BWV 534/2; Example 5c).

2. In allabreve fugues there is a strong tendency to present two themes. The more austere "church" style was more receptive to multiple subjects than were the virtuoso *Spielfuge* or dance fugue idioms. A true double fugue, the Fugue in F, BWV 540/2, presents its two subjects in separate expositions before combining them contrapuntally. The Fugue in c, BWV 537/2, also has two distinct themes, but they are segregated from one another in a *da capo* format. The Fugue in c, BWV 546/2, creates the impression of a double fugue, though the second theme does not have a real exposition of its own. In each work, the two subjects are created with a strong sense of contrast in mind. One theme is quasi *stile antico*, with white notes and vocal qualities, whereas the other is instrumental in nature, with black notes and keyboard figurations (see the Fugue in F, BWV 540/2, in which the first theme [Example 6a] is vocal, and the second theme [Example 6b] is instrumental). The dual nature of the themes also underlines the distinction between allabreve style and true *stilo antico*. The latter could not accommodate instrumental writing.

3. As the allabreve fugues unfold, vertical considerations are most important. The frequent circle-of-fifths progressions and the chains

EXAMPLE 6

of parallel thirds and sixths that appear in the episodic sections are but two indications of this feature. In real *stile antico* the orientation is horizontal: when thematic material is absent, excitement is created chiefly through syncopation and suspension. Moreover, unlike true *stile antico* pieces, in which the *integer valor* is maintained throughout, and unlike *Spielfugen* or dance fugues, in which a motor rhythm is established at the outset, the allabreve fugues show a gradual increase in motion. The black notes—or, more specifically, the eighth notes—take possession of the texture as the work progresses and provide an accelerated conclusion.

While the allabreve fugues generally have more expositions of the subject than do *Spielfugen* or dance fugues, the concentration of thematic material is not so great as in *stile antico* (compare, for example, the Credo of the B-minor Mass). In addition, the frequently appearing episodes have an instrumental stamp: they commonly contain instrumental motives and sequences, and become longer and more digressive during the course of the work. The vocal style is restored only with the return of the fugue subject. A striking example occurs at m. 121 of the Fugue in c, BWV 546/2, where a digression lasting nineteen measures, dominated by a purely instrumental figuration, seems almost out of context with the vocal-oriented material that surrounds it (Example 7).

EXAMPLE 7

In addition to these principal characteristics of Bach's allabreve writing, as outlined by Wolff, three other aspects pertaining to the free organ fugues should be mentioned. The first is the tendency toward heavier, five-part texture, as seen in the Fugue in f, BWV 534/2, and the Fugue in c, BWV 546/2, and briefly in the "Dorian" Fugue in d (at m. 164, where a fourth manual voice mysteriously enters for three bars). The thicker texture was associated with the more serious Renaissance vocal style and was never used by Bach for *Spielfugen* or dance fugues (this textural distinction is even more marked in the clavier repertoire, where *stile-antico*–derived fugues are written in four or five parts and *Spielfugen* and dance fugues in three). The second aspect is the high degree of chromaticism, which results from the elaboration of the conjunct motives of the themes. In *Spielfugen* and dance fugues chromaticism is used chiefly for momentary diversion, but in allabreve fugues, especially those in the minor mode, it is a fundamental thread of the contrapuntal fabric. The third feature is the subdued treatment of the pedal. In *Spielfugen* and dance fugues the pedal is handled in a *bravura* manner, whereas in allabreve fugues pedal virtuosity seems to be dutifully avoided. In several instances, when restrained fugues follow especially outgoing preludes an anticlimax results. This effect is most apparent in the "Dorian" Toccata and Fugue and the Toccata and Fugue in F, BWV 540.[32]

In sum, allabreve fugues are tied to the *stile antico* but show a degree of hybridization. The *stile antico* foundation, however, suggests that the works require a different manner of performance from *Spielfugen* and dance fugues. The allabreve meter, with the eighth note as the smallest value, points to a somewhat weightier, more earnest articulation. According to Kirnberger,

> It is to be noted about this meter (2/2, or rather *alla breve*, which is always designated by ¢ or ₵) that it is very serious and emphatic, yet is performed twice as fast as its note values indicate, unless a slower tempo is specified by the adjectives *grave, adagio*, etc.[33]

This instruction leads us to suspect that allabreve fugues are to be performed at a tempo roughly proportional to *tempo ordinario*. But the notes are to be played more "seriously and emphatically," which is to say, they should probably be given more "weight" than those of other fugue types.

Art Fugues

The "art fugue" is a less-common fugue type in Bach's free organ works. Wilhelm Friedrich Marpurg uses this term, citing it as a special category of the strict fugue or *fuga obligata*:

> A *strict fugue*, or *fuga obligata*, is a fugue in which nothing other than the theme is elaborated. That is to say, the theme, after the initial exposition, comes back, entry after entry, if not the entire time, then most of it. All the remaining counterpoint and interludes are drawn from the theme or counter theme, which are subjected to fragmentation, augmentation, diminution, and various types of motion. . . .
>
> If such a strict fugue is well worked out, and also incorporates all sorts of other artifice . . . one labels such a piece with the Italian name *ricercare* or *ricercata*, or calls it an *art fugue* or *master fugue*.[34]

The art fugue is distinguished by two principal characteristics. First, its chief purpose, as Marpurg implies, is contrapuntal display. After a concise exposition, the theme is subjected to such fugal devices as inversion, contrary motion, and stretto. Because the subject is fashioned for polyphonic elaboration, it often lacks the direct musical "appeal" of the subjects of other fugue types. In an art fugue, it is not the immediate effect of the theme that counts but the way the theme fulfills its potential for contrapuntal manipulation.[35]

Second, because the focus in an art fugue is on the subject and its treatment, episodes tend to be of secondary importance. As we have seen, in other fugue types, even allabreve fugues, episodes are an essential part of the structural plan, sometimes even overshadowing expositions. In an art fugue, episodes have a distinctly subsidiary function; the principal theme keeps returning, "entry after entry," as Marpurg puts it. Consequently, episodes are short and infrequent and serve mainly to link the thematic expositions in as succinct a fashion as possible. Therefore the lengthy chains of instrumental sequences that go hand in hand with the extended episodes of *Spielfugen* and dance fugues are uncommon. In addition, the textural and stylistic differentiation of exposition and episode, a hallmark of Bach's other fugue types, is noticeably subdued.

Bach's most extensive assemblage of art fugues is found in *Art of Fugue*, as we might expect. In the free organ repertoire, a number of works show learned devices: the Fugue in G, BWV 541/2, concludes with stretto; the Fugues in c (BWV 546/2), F (BWV 540/2), c (BWV 537/2), and b (BWV 544/2) each have two subjects. But only two pieces display the concentrated contrapuntal artifice of the art fugue:

	Meter	Number of voices
Fugue in C, BWV 547/2	¢ or c[36]	5
Fugue in c (incomplete), BWV 562/2	6/4	5

The Fugue in C, BWV 547/2, is an art fugue *par excellence*. The concise theme, which appears more than 50 times in the work, is treated in a multitude of ways: normal *rectus* imitation (mm. 1–26), inversion (mm. 27–34), contrary motion with stretto (mm. 34–48), and, finally, augmentation *rectus* and *inversus* combined with stretto *rectus*, *inversus*, and *moto contrario* (mm. 48–72).[37] In many organ fugues, Bach reserves the lowest pedal entry of the theme for the conclusion. In the Fugue in C he goes even further, withholding the pedal altogether until m. 49, when it appears with the subject in augmentation. This delayed entry of the pedal would not work in another fugue type; it would seem a compositional shortcoming (as it does in the early Fugue in c, BWV 549/2). Within the context of an art fugue, however, the technique makes marvelous sense. As the fifth voice and the lowest-pitched part, the pedal brings the fugue to a textural climax. As an augmentation of the theme, its appearance brings the work to a contrapuntal climax as well.

Almost the entire piece is devoted to the exposition of the subject. There are few real episodes and only a smattering of instrumental-derived sequences. The strongest cadences are used to denote the end of one exposition and the beginning of another (mm. 8, 15, 27, 37, and 48); in a different fugue type, such cadences would mark the boundary between exposition and episode. So much exposition and so little episode produce the dense writing characteristic of an art fugue.

The same compression of material occurs in the Fugue in c, BWV 562/2, which unfortunately is handed down in an incomplete state.[38] To judge from the fragment that survives, the work was planned as an art fugue. The first 22 measures are devoted to a concise exposition of the theme in five parts. This exposition concludes on a half cadence, and a second exposition begins immediately. In the second exposition, of which only five measures survive, the fugue theme is presented in close stretto, in five parts. Thus the fugue shows the use of contrapuntal artifice very early on, and there is a noticeable lack of episodic material and the change of texture normally accompanying it. Both features point to the art-fugue idiom.

How did the piece continue, if, indeed, it went on? Dietrich Kilian has suggested that a second subject might have been introduced to produce a double fugue.[39] There is also the possibility, in light of the early introduction of stretto, that Bach wished to explore the potential of the given subject alone. He took this approach in the Fugue in E, BWV 878/2, from *Well-Tempered Clavier* II, which begins in precisely the same manner as the organ fugue (opening exposition, ending on a half cadence, followed by a stretto exposition) and continues with various types of stretto combinations and then diminution.

What makes the Fugue in c all the more fascinating is its date. Schmieder, drawing from Spitta, assigned the work to "Weimar, between 1712 and 1716 (or first in Cöthen?)."[40] More recently, Georg von Dadelsen, working with Bach's handwriting, convincingly gave it a later date, between 1735 and 1744–46.[41] Thus Bach probably wrote the work during the period of his most intense involvement with contrapuntal artifice, while he was working on the *Well-Tempered Clavier*, vol. II (which contains a greater number of "learned" fugues than does vol. I), *Clavierübung* III, the B-minor Mass, and *Art of Fugue*.[42] For this reason, it is all the more lamentable that this rare example of an art fugue for organ is incomplete.

Conclusion

In light of our survey, we might pose the question: Why did Bach turn so often to the *Spielfuge* in his free organ works? One factor may be the medium: the organ, with its clear, incisive, mixture-filled *plenum*, was ideally suited to reproducing instrumental figurations. To judge from the repertoire as it survives, Bach seems to have concentrated on the *Spielfuge* before expanding to other fugue types. This choice may reflect the fact that he started his career as a keyboard player. He seems not to have moved to vocal and instrumental composition until the Mühlhausen and Weimar years.

Then, too, his early success as a virtuoso organist may have played a part. Starting with his Arnstadt years, Bach was frequently requested to examine and inaugurate new instruments and to present public organ concerts. Contemporaries who heard him play on such occasions describe his technique with astonishment and awe.[43] Certainly the *Spielfugen*, with their captious melodies and virtuoso manual and pedal writing, would have served as perfect vehicles for technical display. Manuscript marginalia support this view. Copies of the Fugue in g, BWV 542/2, carry the remark that the work is "the very best pedal piece by Bach."[44] A copy of the Fugue in D, BWV 532/2, warns: "Please Note: in this fugue one really has to kick the feet around a lot."[45] Such remarks bear witness to Bach's inclination, in his early and middle years, to compose works with "fire," as Mattheson said of the *Spiel* idiom.

As Bach grew older, however, he seems to have become interested in more severe genres—allebreve and art fugues—and in combining various fugue types in a single work. In the Fugue in F, BWV 540/2, and the Fugue in c, BWV 537/2, he joined allabreve and *Spielfuge* themes. But in the "St. Anne" Fugue in E♭, BWV 552/2, from *Clavierübung* III, a work to which we now turn by way of conclusion, he took an additional daring step, creating a triple fugue of diverse idioms. The opening fugue (mm. 1–36, in ¢), with its white-note theme (Example 8a), five-part texture, dense concentration of material, horizontally oriented lines, and suspension-filled episodes, is a true *stile antico* piece.[46] The ¢ meter of the original edition is not a mistakenly uncrossed ¢, as has been suggested.[47] Rather, it is the eighteenth-century "large 4/4 meter," used in place of 4/2. As Kirnberger described it:

> Large 4/4 time is of extremely weighty tempo and execution and, because of its emphatic nature, is suited primarily to church pieces, choruses, and fugues.[48]

The second fugue (mm. 37–81, in 6/4), with its winding black-note theme (Example 8b), motor rhythm, four-part texture, and sequential episodes, seems to be a type of *manualiter Spielfuge*. The rhythmic ambiguity of the theme (is the subject in 3/2 or 6/4?) is clarified only with the entrance of the accompanying voices—a playful gesture appropriate for the genre.[49] The third fugue (mm. 82–117, in 12/8), with its incisive downbeat theme (Example 8c), gigue meter and rhythms, sequential episodes, and periodic construction, is a dance fugue. But its texture is five-part, not four, as one would expect in a dance fugue. Bach obviously introduced this innovation in order to bestow the entire piece with an element of textural balance:

Section	Meter	Number of Voices
stile antico fugue	¢ (4/2)	5
Spielfuge	6/4	4
dance fugue	12/8	5

EXAMPLE 8

This textural symmetry is echoed in *Clavierübung* III as a whole, since the "St. Anne" Prelude, BWV 552/1, the work that opens the collection, also begins and ends with five-part writing.

Finally, the combining of the *stile antico* subject with the themes of the two other fugues makes the entire Fugue in E♭, in a sense, an art fugue. But it is an art fugue carried to a new level of sophistication. The union that takes place is not simply contrapuntal, but stylistic. The amalgamation of three fugue types—with differing meters, textures, rhythmic accents, and methods of expansion—represents an unprecedented reconciliation of vocal and instrumental styles in a fugal context. In the "St. Anne" Prelude, Bach accomplished the seemingly impossible feat of uniting two diametrically opposed genres, the French ouverture and the Italian concerto.[50] By achieving a similarly astonishing synthesis in the "St. Anne" Fugue, Bach produced a fitting partner for the prelude. At the same time, he created a work that acts as an appropriate *summa* to his lifelong exploration of the free organ fugue.

NOTES

I should like to thank my Hunter College colleague L. Michael Griffel for reading the initial draft of this essay and offering helpful suggestions on numerous points.

1. Reprinted in BDok III, no. 927, and *Bach Reader*, pp. 280–88.
2. The anonymous writer was probably C. P. E. Bach, but that cannot be proved conclusively. See the commentary to BDok III, no. 927.
3. BDok III, p. 440.
4. In the eighteenth century, fugues were divided into two general families: chorale fugues, whose themes were drawn from chorale melodies, and

free fugues, whose themes were chosen at will ("nach Gefallen"). See Johann Mattheson, *Der vollkommene Capellmeister* (Hamburg, 1739), p. 474, item 33.

5. Friedrich Wilhelm Marpurg reported: "I myself once heard him, when during my stay in Leipzig I was discussing with him certain matters concerning the fugue, pronounce the works of an old and hard-working contrapuntist *dry and wooden*, and certain fugues by a more modern and no less great contrapuntist—that is, in the form in which they are arranged for clavier—*pedantic*; the first because the composer stuck continuously to his principal subject, without any change; and the second because, at least in the fugues under discussion, he had not shown enough fire to reanimate the theme by interludes." BDok III, pp. 144–45; translation from *Bach Reader*, p. 257.

6. Stefan Kunze, "Gattungen der Fuge in Bachs Wohltemperiertem Klavier," in *Bach Interpretationen*, edited by Martin Geck (Göttingen, 1969), pp. 74–93.

7. Although Bach does come close to mimicking instrumental works in certain mature pieces, such as the "Wedge" Fugue in e, BWV 548/2.

8. Kunze, p. 90.

9. Mattheson, *Der vollkommene Capellmeister*, pp. 203–208. These and other differences are outlined in part II, chapter 12, "Vom Unterschiede zwischen den Sing- und Spiel-Melodien."

10. Bach's arrangement of the motives in the fugue subject was determined in part by the Dutch folk song on which the subject is based, *Ik ben gegroet* (see BDok II, no. 302). Yet Mattheson's version of the same theme (printed in *General-Bass-Schule*, 1731, p. 34, and reproduced in BDok II, no. 302) has less symmetry. Hence, creating elements of balance seems to have been a special concern of Bach's as he refashioned the folk song into a fugue subject.

11. This elaboration also occurs in the subject of the "Little" Fugue in g, BWV 578, at m. 26. In the passage from the Fugue in g, BWV 542/2, quoted in Example 3, Bach may have fashioned the embellishment in the first measure (see bracket in Example 3) in the process of transposing part of the subject down an octave in order to avoid the note d‴, which was not available on many organs of the time.

12. The stretto at the conclusion of the Fugue in G, BWV 541/2, is the only instance of a learned device in Bach's *Spielfugen* for organ.

13. In the Fugue in D, m. 80, the theme starts in the bass and then moves to the soprano. In the Fugue in g, at m. 25, the subject begins in the tenor and concludes in the soprano. Thematic migration also occurs in the Fugue in a, BWV 543/2 (at m. 115, where the subject moves from the tenor to the alto), which is a dance fugue and, as such, is closely related to *Spielfugen* (see discussion below).

14. Johann Gottfried Walther, *Musicalisches Lexicon* (Leipzig, 1732), p. 598.

15. While various natural phenomena were given as measures of the *tempo ordinario* pulse, from walking (Buchner) to vegetable chopping (Hermann Finck), the human heartbeat was most frequently cited (Gaffurius, Zarlino, Zacconi, Quantz, etc.).

16. Although the authenticity of the "Gigue" Fugue has been questioned (see *The New Grove Bach Family*, where it is listed as a spurious work), the present author believes it to be a genuine, if early, Bach composition. The part writing, the Italian-derived modulatory scheme, the careful withholding of the lowest pedal entry until the end, and the technical demands are uncharacteristic of anyone other than Bach. Also lending new credibility to the piece are two recently discovered eighteenth-century manuscript copies

(Göttingen: Bach-Institut, and Braunschweig: Esser Collection), both naming Bach as the author.

17. The authenticity of the Pastorale, too, has been doubted, and unjustly so. See George Stauffer, "Bach's Pastorale in F—Another Look at a Maligned Work," *The Organ Yearbook* 14 (1983): 44–60.

18. The dance fugues in the *Well-Tempered Clavier* include five gigues (vol. I, the Fugues in G and A; vol. II, the Fugues in c♯, F, and g♯), two gavottes (vol. I, the Fugue in c; vol. II, the Fugue in F♯), two passepieds (vol. I, the Fugue in F; vol. II, the Fugue in b), one bourrée (vol. II, the Fugue in e), one minuet (vol. II, the Fugue in B♭), and possibly one allemande (vol. II, the Fugue in A♭).

19. All the dance fugues cited in note 18 have three voices, with the exception of the Fugue in A♭ from vol. II (which has four and may not be a dance fugue for that reason, among others).

20. All Bach's *pedaliter* fugues have at least four parts.

21. These metrical accents are discussed in Johann Philipp Kirnberger, *Die Kunst des reinen Satzes* (Berlin, 1771–79), part 2, pp. 113–36. Kirnberger studied with Bach in Leipzig from 1739 to 1741 and appears to have passed down the views of his teacher in his treatise.

22. Walther, for instance, defined the gigue as "an instrumental piece consisting of an English dance in two reprises, in 3/8, 6/8, or 12/8, in which the first note of each principal beat normally has a dot" (*Musicalisches Lexicon*, p. 281).

23. The strict, invertible counterpoint in the Passacaglia fugue is closely related to permutation technique. See Christoph Wolff, "Zur Architektur von Bachs Passacaglia," *Acta organologica* 3 (1969): 183–94, as well as his diagram of the fugue's structure in "Johann Adam Reinken and Johann Sebastian Bach," note 77, in the present volume.

24. Early copyists may have delayed the entry of the pedal until m. 63 because the e' in the bass in m. 57 was not available on many eighteenth-century pedal boards.

25. Examples: the concluding gigue from Böhm's harpsichord Suite in d (no. 3 in *G. Böhm: Sämtliche Werke*, edited by Johannes and Gesa Wolgast [Wiesbaden, 1952]), or the second fugue from Buxtehude's *Praeludium Pedaliter* in e, BuxWV 143.

26. Mattheson, *Der vollkommene Capellmeister*, p. 224.

27. For details of this revision see George Stauffer, *The Organ Preludes of Johann Sebastian Bach* (Ann Arbor, 1980), pp. 97–98 and 119.

28. Kirnberger, *Die Kunst des reinen Satzes*, part II, p. 119.

29. In the *Well-Tempered Clavier* Bach reserved 6/16 and 12/16 for vol. II (the Fugues in F and c♯ respectively). Vol. II was compiled and written in the late 1730s, when Bach appears to have become more interested in the newer, lighter dance forms.

30. Christoph Wolff, *Der stile antico in der Musik Johann Sebastian Bachs* (Wiesbaden, 1968), pp. 119–42.

31. Ibid., pp. 122–25.

32. While the "Dorian" Toccata and Fugue seems to have been conceived as a single work, the Toccata and Fugue in F probably originated as two separate pieces that were later paired. The evidence for this is summarized in Stauffer, *The Organ Preludes*, p. 134n11.

33. Kirnberger, *Die Kunst des reinen Satzes*, part II, p. 118; quoted from Johann Philipp Kirnberger, *The Art of Strict Musical Composition*, translated by David Beach and Jurgen Thym (New Haven, 1982), p. 386.

34. Friedrich Wilhelm Marpurg, *Abhandlung von der Fuge nach dem Grund-sätzen der besten deutschen und ausländischen Meister* (Berlin, 1753–1754), part I, p. 12. Marpurg conferred with Bach in Leipzig on matters of fugue writing (see note 5 above). In 1752, at the request of Bach's heirs, he wrote a preface for the second edition of *Art of Fugue*.

35. One is reminded of C. P. E. Bach's description of his father listening to fugues: "When he listened to a rich and many-voiced fugue, he could soon say, after the first entries of the subjects, what contrapuntal devices it would be possible to apply, and which of them the composer by rights ought to apply, and on such occasions, when I was standing next to him, and he had voiced his surmises to me, he would joyfully nudge me when his expectations were fulfilled." BDok III, no. 801; translation from *Bach Reader*, p. 277.

36. The BG and Peters Edition give ¢ as the meter of the Fugue; the NBA, ℂ. The sources do not clarify the matter. Of the twelve copies of the work (Bach's autograph is lost), nine, including the important manuscripts Berlin, SPK, *P 290* (C. P. E. Bach copyist Anonymous 303), and Berlin, SPK, *P 274* (Kellner?), show ¢. The remaining three manuscripts, which include the important source Leipzig, MB, *Poel. 32* (Penzel), show ℂ.

37. An excellent analysis of the fugue appears in Peter Williams, *The Organ Music of J. S. Bach* (Cambridge, 1980–84), vol. I, pp. 158–63.

38. In Bach's autograph (Berlin, SPK, *P 460*), the work's only source, the fugue breaks off at the bottom of a verso page after 26½ measures (see the facsimile in NBA IV/5, p. x). The fantasia with which the fugue is paired, BWV 562/1, is a fair copy in Bach's manuscript and probably represents the revision of the earlier work, BWV 562/1a. The fugue, by contrast, appears to be a first draft (see Dietrich Kilian, "Studie über Bach's Fantasie und Fuge c-moll," in *Hans Albrecht in Memoriam*, edited by Wilfried Brennecke and Hans Hasse [Kassel, 1969], pp. 127–35). Bach seems to have written more than the surviving segment, for *custi* are given for all five voices at the end of m. 26½, presumably for the continuation of the piece. There is also the possibility, however, that he left the work unfinished, as he did a number of other keyboard compositions (for example, the Fantasia in C, BWV 573, and the Fugue in c, BWV 906/2).

39. Kilian, p. 133.

40. Wolfgang Schmieder, editor, *Thematisch-systematisches Verzeichnis der Musikalischen Werke von Johann Sebastian Bach* (Wiesbaden, 1950), p. 426.

41. Georg von Dadelsen, *Beiträge zur Chronologie der Werke Johann Sebastian Bachs* (Trossingen, 1958), p. 113. Kilian ("Studie," p. 135), basing his judgment on copies of the fantasia made at its various stages of revision, believes the fugue was written no earlier than the 1740s, most likely around 1745.

42. While *Art of Fugue* has traditionally been assigned to the very last years of Bach's life, Christoph Wolff has presented persuasive arguments that it was started at an earlier date, perhaps at the beginning of the 1740s (unpublished paper).

43. Philipp David Kräuter described Bach as playing "incomparable things" (BDok III, no. 58a). G. H. L. Schwanberg wrote, "I have never heard anything like it" (BDok II, no. 239). Constantin Bellermann, in describing Bach's playing in Kassel, said, "He ran over the pedals . . . as if his feet had wings, making the organ resound with such fullness that it penetrated the ears of those present like a thunderbolt" (BDok II, no. 522).

44. Berlin, SPK, *P 287* (Johann Stephen Borsch), and New Haven, Yale Music Library, *LM 4838* (Johann Christian Rinck).

45. Stuttgart, Württembergische Landesbibliothek, *Cod. mus. II, 288* (Lorenz Sichart?).

46. The qualities of the *stile antico* are discussed at length in Wolff, *Der stile antico*, pp. 36–118.

47. Ibid., pp. 43 and 130; and in the Peters Edition and the BG, where the editors (Friedrich Conrad Griepenkerl and C. F. Becker respectively) "corrected" the meter from c to ¢.

48. Kirnberger, *Die Kunst des reinen Satzes*, part II, p. 122; translation from Beach and Thym, p. 391.

49. Admittedly, the rhythmic ambiguity and the 6/4 meter also point to the dance fugue. Thomas Harmon has suggested that this central fugue is a courante (oral communication with the author). The difficulty of a dance classification arises from the fact that Bach never set a courante in 6/4. The section may well be a *Spielfuge*–dance fugue hybrid, in which the duple qualities point back to the opening *stile antico* fugue in c and the triple qualities point forward to the concluding dance fugue in 12/8 (see below).

50. See Stauffer, *The Organ Preludes*, pp. 74–77; and Victoria Horn, "French Influence in the Organ Works of J. S. Bach," in this volume.

FRIEDHELM KRUMMACHER

❧

Bach's Free Organ Works and the
Stylus Phantasticus

Bach's organ works are filled with fantasy, and their dense structure stamps them with an unmistakable style. In Bach's art, fantasy and style are joined, but it is not immediately clear what "fantasy style" means with respect to his organ works. Even a scholar fully familiar with the *stylus phantasticus* as it appears in Baroque theory might well harbor doubts about applying this term to Bach's music. And justifiably so, for Bach's works appear to be so strictly structured that they resist classification according to theories of style that go back to the seventeenth century.

If one asks just which categories from the theory of Bach's day would be appropriate to his work, one falls victim to a certain embarrassment. If Bach's music shows one unalterable characteristic, it is that it leaves the customs and the theoretical criteria of the time far behind. For free organ works of the rank and scope of Bach's, there was no place in traditional compositional teachings, which did not assign instrumental genres a position of importance.[1] Nevertheless, if we wish to capture the true individuality of this music, we must begin with the relationship of the free organ works to the theoretical categories of their time. More precisely, we must investigate the importance of the *stylus phantasticus* for the genre of the toccata, which was one of Bach's early points of orientation. In addition, we will sketch in passing the continuing influence of this genre for Bach, since his later works continued to feed upon it even as they incomparably transformed the models upon which they were based.

I

The coupling of the terms *prelude, toccata,* or *fantasia* with *fugue* is well known to today's listeners and players, and we have come to assume that the pairing of a free prelude with a fugue is itself a genre that was representative of Bach's time. But in actuality, Bach's organ compositions scarcely corresponded to the general standards of the organ music of the high Baroque. Rather, they represented a somewhat late and very personal response to older traditions. For only in the generation before Bach do we find organ music of a comparable gravity, music that occupied a central position in the life of its composer. Only with musicians such as Werkmann, Buxtehude, Bruhns, Böhm, Reinken, and Pachelbel were such compositions part of a varied career, one not limited to organ music.

History makes it clear, therefore, what a special status we must grant to Bach's organ music, both in relationship to other works Bach composed and to the practices of his contemporaries and predecessors. While Bach's contributions to the popular genres of his day were forgotten rather quickly after his death, his keyboard music became the vehicle by which his art was handed down to posterity, in part because it was music for one player and was not written to satisfy the demands of an official function.

Analogous circumstances underline the special character of free organ works both in Bach's *oeuvre* and in the older tradition of organ music.[2] Although the organ was required to play at definite places in the Lutheran liturgy, the formal and qualitative design of the music itself was not prescribed. Thus the organist not only enjoyed a great deal of freedom in composition but also could be the sole interpreter of his music. And so it is surely not by chance that Bach first mastered the older traditions and confronted the new Italian concerto style within the context of his organ repertoire.[3] His organ music has a special place in his life work and a greater weight in his *oeuvre* than is the case for any of his contemporaries.

The relationship between the genres of organ music and eighteenth-century compositional precepts is contradictory. Theorists of the time scarcely attempted to describe the types of free organ works—from the standpoint of form or of style—as they did for other genres. For instance, we have an encompassing theory of the minuet by Johann Mattheson and exemplary definitions of the sinfonia by Johann Adolf Scheibe and of the concerto by Johann Joachim Quantz.[4] Yet compa-

rable descriptions of the toccata or the prelude for organ are lacking.
Even the fugue was neglected; it appeared as an object of theoretical
reflection only in the works of Friedrich Wilhelm Marpurg and Johann
Philipp Kirnberger, who began the formal codification of the fugue
along lines derived from Bach's works.[5] In the systematic theory of
genre drawn up by Johann Mattheson, there is hardly any room for
specific kinds of free organ music. This can be observed in *Kern melodischer Wissenschaft* (1737) and a bit later in *Der vollkommene Capellmeister*
(1739).[6] True to his motto "the paths of nature lead from the incomplete to the complete," Mattheson arranged the vocal genres on the
one hand, and the instrumental genres on the other, in series of ascending complexity, from individual movements or types of movements to composite cyclical forms. It is true that forms such as fantasia, capriccio, or toccata, as well as ciacona and passacaglia, appear
among the instrumental genres. Yet there is no place in Mattheson's
system for the coupling of a prelude or a toccata with a fugue. There
is hardly a better illustration of the small role assigned to the paired
forms that constitute the center of Bach's free organ works.

   It is not entirely surprising that treatises of the time failed to explain the variety and multiplicity of Bach's organ music, for it would
have been difficult to account for the structural characteristics of these
unusual pieces using the theoretical categories then available. Still, it is
striking just how little space was devoted to organ music. Naturally,
the vocal genres retained a certain primacy because they were vital
for the traditional method of teaching counterpoint. Nevertheless,
Mattheson's essay suggests the increasing importance accorded to instrumental genres. In fact, the cyclical forms were held up as a goal,
corresponding to the concept of "completeness." If the forms of organ
music—both those that were free and those that were based on a chorale—were left undiscussed, it was not a sign of blindness toward
Bach's achievements. It was, rather, a reflection of the fact that organ
music represented the continuation of an older tradition, and as such
it could not be counted among the more modern instrumental genres,
to which the future belonged.

II

The pairing of the prelude and fugue appeared in other keyboard
music of Bach's time, but Bach's works were structurally much weightier than those of his contemporaries. A similar gap exists within Bach's

own *oeuvre*, between the free pieces for organ and those for clavier. The former are endowed with a structural spaciousness made possible by the use of the obbligato pedal. But they benefit equally from the extraordinary variety of stylistic approaches available to the composer. In the prelude we can discern the coupling of concertante and contrapuntal procedures, and in the companion fugue, we can observe enlargement through episodes in the concertante style.[7] These expansive forms, which arise through richness of technique, cannot be separated from the richness of sonority offered by the organ.

The structural characteristics of Bach's organ works also point strongly to the tradition of the organ toccata. At first the formal differences between the early organ toccata and Bach's works seem formidable, as long as we view the paired form—which in the seventeenth century seems hardly to have existed at all—as the principal trait of Bach's compositions. But the older toccata had a latent cyclical construction, with a combination of free and fugal sections. The manuscripts of Bach's free organ works clearly indicate that prelude and fugue were never so firmly bound to one another as to exclude the possibility of their being transmitted separately. Moreover, it has come to light that certain preludes and fugues that appear to belong to one another were not composed at the same time. Since the tie between prelude and fugue in certain works is not entirely verifiable, demonstrating their structural affinities is not a simple matter.[8] But if we think beyond the external form of these paired arrangements, the internal stylistic complexities in the prelude as well as in the fugue become more important, and this differentiation in style shows the continuity of the tradition from the older toccata to the organ works of Bach.

If we seek the relationship of Bach's free organ works to this tradition, the differences and similarities in terminology tell us little. In both seventeenth-century repertoire and Bach's compositions, the titles *prelude* and *toccata* alternate without signifying a difference in construction. How a work is titled is less significant than its technical context within the tradition of a genre. During the seventeenth century there arose a type of piece characterized by an alternation of figurative and imitative sections. What bound the free organ works together, regardless of what they were called, was their function as prelude or postlude in the worship service, which, of course, did not suggest a close differentiation of form.

It is therefore significant that Michael Praetorius, in his definition from the *Termini musici* of 1619, presented—in contrast to the vocal genres—two genres of instrumental music: preludes and dances.[9] He distinguished between "preludes before dances," "preludes before motets and madrigals," and "independent preludes." To the preludes appropriate for introductions to motets and madrigals, he assigned toccatas, which the organist "makes up out of his head." In discussing the "independent preludes," which appear as autonomous forms, Praetorius differentiated among "fantasias, fugues, symphonies, and sonatas." At the top stood the "fantasia, or more properly, phantasia-capriccio," composed

> when one, for pleasure and amusement, takes up the task of playing a fugue, yet doesn't stay with it too long, but rather quickly slips over into a different fugue, just as one happens to think of it. For with proper fugues one may not put a text under them, and thus one isn't bound to words. . . . And in these fantasias and capriccios one may show off one's skill and artifice equally, since one can make use of all those things that are tolerable in music—linking the discords and meters, etc.—without having any qualms about it. However, one ought not stray too far from the mode and the melody, but keep oneself within certain bounds.[10]

Throughout the definitions of preludes the common thread seems to be the accent on the "fantastic." By the end of the sixteenth century, the growing variety of compositional possibilities had created a situation in which the concepts of contrapuntal theory no longer sufficed to classify the various types of composition. In 1558 Zarlino spoke of the *maniera* of composing, and in 1588 Pietro Pontio distinguished between the *stile* or *modo* of individual genres.[11] It became clear at the same time that the distinction between the *prima* and *seconda prattica*, which had developed from the arguments of Monteverdi with the theorist Giovanni Maria Artusi, would also have to be understood as a separation between the *stile antico* and the *stile moderno*.

At first these concepts of style aimed to describe the different ways of composing, yet since Marco Scacchi they had been linked to the social functions or uses of music. The concepts *stylus ecclesiasticus*, *teatralis*, and *cubicularis* indicate church music, theater music, and chamber music respectively. The Jesuit Athanasius Kircher, active in Rome, united these changing aspects into a complete theory in his *Musurgia universalis* of 1650. In this treatise he ordered the technical definitions of style under the individual genres and their functions.[12] Corresponding to Praetorius' description of the fantasia as a genre is Kircher's definition of the stylistic category *stylus phantasticus*:

> The fantastic style is an instrumental style. It is a method of composi-
> tion free and unrestrained in manner, and without any restriction, ei-
> ther of words or of a harmonic subject. It was established as a display of
> artifice, foreswearing the ordinary logic of harmony, in order to teach
> the ingenious joining of harmonic sections and fugues. It is divided into
> what we refer to in common speech as fantasias, ricercatas, toccatas, and
> sonatas.[13]

For Kircher as well as for Praetorius, the instrumental nature of this
type of music, the absence of words, the many possible varieties of form
and texture, and the freedom granted to the composer are the crucial
features, calling for particular skill. Peter Schleuning has defined the
older fantasia as a contrapuntal genre whose extreme demands of
compositional art separate it from the rambling freedom of the modern fantasia.[14] In this way, through its "individually structured artifice," the contrapuntal fantasy of the early seventeenth century differs from the free fantasia of Carl Philipp Emanuel Bach. In Kircher's
definition, the words "ingenious" and "display of artifice" suggest that
the older fantasia could be considered an example of mannerism in
music. Schleuning linked Kircher's stylistic concept primarily to the
genre of the fantasia, to which certain of its categories certainly seem
to refer.

Yet, such a stylistic concept obviously points toward a procedure
that can be employed in such differing genres as ricercata, toccata, or
sonata; that is to say, it points less toward a specific genre than toward
a compositional principle. This is also clear from Kircher's later remarks, which concern a fantasia by Froberger. For Kircher, this work
serves not only as a fantasia, but also as an example of a genre of composition that most people call *praeludium*. Thus Kircher establishes the
inner relationship between the forms of keyboard music. At the same
time he implies that the *stylus phantasticus* relates not only to the genre
of the fantasia but to other genres of free keyboard music as well. In
this context, however, the genre that was to become the model for the
future was not the fantasia but the toccata.

Almost a hundred years after Kircher, Johann Mattheson considered the toccata the most important model for composition in the
stylus phantasticus. It is true that Mattheson's definition presupposes
the changes in the manner of composition that had occurred in the
intervening time. His explanations of the fantastic style and its corresponding genres are confusing at first because they reflect the difficulties that had arisen from the overlap in theories of genre and style.
The *stylus phantasticus* appears in Mattheson's writings from 1713

through 1739 primarily in the framework of the *genus theatralis*, the music one hears "on the stage."[15] This apparent illogicality resulted from Mattheson's orientation toward vocal genres as well as from the many uses of the *stylus phantasticus*. It was employed not only "in plays" but also "in churches and in chamber," even though this was, Mattheson said, "all the same thing."

Even the first definition of *stylus phantasticus* in the theatrical style cites the "so-called fantasias, capriccios, toccatas, ricercatas, etc." It accords nicely with the affinity of these genres for one another, a fact that Mattheson had already noted in 1713, saying that such works, written without "exact observance of the measure," rely only on the "fancy" of the composer.[16] The corresponding paragraph from 1739 points even more closely to the North German organ toccata, and it cites the incipits of two such works—one by Froberger, the other by Buxtehude—as examples.[17]

Among Mattheson's compositional criteria for the toccata, the decisive feature is the "most free and unrestricted" way with which one "hits first upon this idea and then that." One is bound by neither words nor melody, but by harmony. Other characteristics include "unconventional progressions, concealed decorations, clever turns and garnishings." Such music remains "without actual observance of measure and key," and furthermore it is "performed without proper main and subsidiary sections, without theme and subject." It is characterized by alternation of monophonic and polyphonic sections and by contrasting tempos, to which one may also add sections in strict meter. "In this style of composition one is free to do anything except disregard the laws of harmony." Of course, one can hardly avoid the establishment of a principal theme or section, but they "should not be joined closely together, much less given a proper working-out." That is why musicians who "work out formal fugues in the context of their fantasias or toccatas have no proper concept" of the *stylus phantasticus*.

In his description, Mattheson is sketching out the multipartite form of the toccata, which becomes for him the actual and true representative of the *stylus phantasticus*. Strict meter and contrapuntal style are by no means excluded but appear as a background against which the development of fantastic elements takes place. Norms of measure, tempo, key, or compositional method are thus points of departure through which the free play of the *stylus phantasticus* is realized anew. Mattheson differs significantly from Kircher, who pointed to a concentration of contrapuntal techniques, but both writers are oriented toward keyboard music. Thus it appears that the fantasia, as a genre of the *stylus phantasticus*, has been replaced by the toccata. Accordingly, Mattheson wrote, "Fantasias therefore consist of various pieces" that can nevertheless be "comprehended under the general name of toccatas."[18] It could hardly be clearer: for Mattheson's time, the toccata as it was found in North German organ music had become the paradigm of the *stylus phantasticus*. And so it could be written: "One must know what fugues are, before one introduces them into toccatas." Analogously, ciaconas could be "woven into toccatas" even if they no longer commanded, in Mattheson's days, "as much respect" as before.[19] That means that strict procedures such as the fugue or the ciacona had to be mastered before one was able to integrate their free derivatives into the fantastic style of the toccata.

We cannot pursue here the extent to which this description fits the North German organ toccata of Buxtehude's circle. Yet as great as the difference between the North German toccata and the free organ music of Bach seems to be, it is clear that Mattheson considered the older toccata the ultimate representation of free organ music. If one wishes to find historically appropriate categories for Bach's free organ music, one must consider its connection to the tradition of the toccata in the *stylus phantasticus*.

III

Bach's free organ works do not display the *stylus phantasticus* as defined by Mattheson, for Mattheson's theories depend too much on the older toccata. But even a theorist like Mattheson, who was open to the new tendencies of the time, had to take a retrospective stance in order to discuss the possibilities of organ music. And it is significant that the traditional descriptions of style to which Mattheson turned preserved the important link between the genre of free organ music and the concept of the *stylus phantasticus*. At the same time, Bach's organ music clearly evades the criteria of contemporary theory, for it can no longer be compared directly with the old toccata in *stylus phantasticus*. It maintains very little of the tradition from which it came and rarely fulfills the norms the theories of the time define.

How far does Bach overstep the tradition defined by Mattheson? The rich variation of thematic character, idiom, and formal structure in Bach's preludes and fugues ought not to be accepted simply as a matter of fact. Rather, it is a reflection of the variety that the theory of the *stylus phantasticus*, with a look to the older toccata, describes. Only in relation to the freedom that the *stylus phantasticus* offers to the toccata does Bach's own accomplishment appear as a judicious concentration of compositional procedures.[20] The rich contrasting alternation of parts, a feature of the older toccata, gains a new visage in Bach's paired layout of prelude and fugue. In the free forms for organ—in contrast to analogous works for clavier—complete development results first and foremost from the internal flux of different elements. Not only are the mutual contrasts of parts more sharply pronounced in the organ works but also they form the basis for the large-scale structural plans. In other words Bach relinquished the multipartite structure of the older toccata in favor of a paired design, but then he integrated the traditional principle of contrasting parts into the components of his paired form. Therefore the contrasts that are part and parcel of the older toccata in *stylus phantasticus* still have an effect in Bach's free organ works: they appear to unify and give substance to the paired layout. Thus the vestiges of the early involvement with the toccata extend to the great late paired works of Bach.[21]

The full extent of Bach's fascination with the older toccata is not as marked in the early works for organ as it is in the toccatas for clavier. The dating of these works causes difficulties in some cases. In spite of their notable quality, we may assume that they were written at a relatively early period. Hence it is not by chance that the beginning of the Toccata in D for clavier, BWV 912, is taken up in the Prelude in D for organ, BWV 532.[22] This striking similarity, which appears almost to be a quotation, definitely points to an inner affinity between the initial figure of a toccata and the motivically fecund beginning of a prelude. Although the multipartite toccata and the paired organ work appear to be far apart, the two genres mirror each other in their openings.

It is all the more striking, then, that the clavier toccata, which most clearly reflects the older type of the genre, forgoes the obbligato pedal, that symbol of the rich, sonorous contrast of the North German organ toccata. Of course there were also *manualiter* toccatas in the North German tradition, but they played a subsidiary role to works with pedal. In his clavier toccata Bach therefore consciously relinquished a dimension of contrast in order to concentrate all the more on the stabilization of the inner structure. On the one hand, the contrapuntal sections undergo an expansion that allows them to appear not just as short *fugati*, but as full, independent fugues. On the other hand, the free sections show a tendency toward continuity, achieved through extension or sequential repetition of rhythmic or figural motives, a procedure that occurs only occasionally in the North German tradition.

That both tendencies were pursued systematically by Bach is further demonstrated by the Toccata in E for organ, BWV 566, which may rank as the most important example of the reception of the older toccata in Bach's organ works.[23] The formal layout corresponds throughout to the North German model, with a free opening, two fugues separated by a free interlude and a free closing. Also traditional is the process of making the themes of both fugues variations of a single model; the first fugue is in duple meter, the second in triple. The unusual thoroughness with which the two fugues are worked out gives them the appearance of independence, causing the connection between the themes to recede and the free interlude to appear as a short insertion. The free introduction also acquires continuity through the fact that its initial figure and its pedal solo are based on complementary rhythmic figures. The free conclusion presents another pedal solo, which does not contrast with the final fugue but reflects the incipit of the fugue's theme by being in the same meter. The expansive dimensions of the two fugues correspond with the relatively large proportions of the free sections. It may not be mere chance, then, that a manuscript written by Johann Christian Kittel transmits the introduction and first fugue as a prelude and fugue pair.[24] In the Toccata in E the concentration of figural and contrapuntal parts within the context of the multipartite toccata paves the way for Bach's later paired forms.

No other work of Bach's reflects the *stylus phantasticus* so unmistakably as the Toccata in E. The other early works, which George Stauffer has endeavored to place in chronological order, point from the beginning toward the paired design of prelude and fugue. It is not always certain whether a work is to be dated before or after the famous trip to Lübeck in the winter of 1705–1706, whether the piece therefore originated under the direct influence of Buxtehude's art or during a later period, when the distance from Buxtehude had increased. The early works frequently contain pedal solos and figurations, while their fugues lead into free coda sections, as in the pieces in d, BWV 549a, and C, BWV 531 (written before 1703, according to Stauffer), or the works in a, BWV 551, and g, BWV 535a (written around 1703–1704 according to Stauffer).[25] If one accepts Stauffer's interpretation of the Prelude in a, BWV 569, as a latent *ostinato* form, then this strikingly simple work can be perceived as a reflection of the *stylus phantasticus*, whose possibilities, Mattheson said, included the integration of *ostinato* techniques.

Such works as the Preludes and Fugues in e, BWV 533, and A,

BWV 536 (both written around 1704, according to Stauffer), are also related to the North German toccata, since the preludes lack motivic constancy and the fugues resolve into free conclusions.[26] Even more significant are a number of works that seem to have been written after 1706 and therefore originated mostly in Weimar. The Toccata in d, BWV 565 (written before 1706, according to Stauffer), with its tripartite form, reflects North German models: a wandering introduction is followed by a concentrated fugue, which in turn leads into a free Recitativo.

The multipartite toccata still glimmers in the paired form, even when the introduction and fugue are unified rhythmically. In the paired work in a, BWV 543, the fugue theme is related to the figuration of the prelude, according to Stauffer. That would signify that the thematic connection between the *fugati* in the older toccata has been transferred to the prelude and fugue. At the same time, the free sections in the prelude and especially in the coda following the fugue point to the North German tradition of the *stylus phantasticus*. The Prelude in D, BWV 532, displays this tradition not only in its affinity with the beginning of the Toccata in D for clavier, as has already been mentioned, but also in the way the connecting Allabreve foreshadows the toccata-like free conclusion.

The Prelude in D, BWV 532, as well as other compositions show that Bach did not take a direct, digressionless path to the paired form. At times he seems to have seriously considered a tripartite design.[27] Such deliberations surface especially in the Fantasia in G, BWV 572, and the Toccata in C, BWV 564 (composed before 1712 according to Stauffer). Another composition that belongs to this series of works is a version of the Prelude and Fugue in C, BWV 545, in which the Largo from BWV 529 (Trio Sonata no. 5 in C) was inserted between the prelude and fugue. Indeed, these works not only follow the older toccata but also reflect Bach's preoccupation with the Italian concerto. The Adagio in BWV 564 ends with a rhapsodic, free conclusion, and the fluctuating Gravement movement in BWV 572 is set up with the free Lentement as a conclusion. Even more than the three-part form, the free sections in these works point back to the toccata in *stylus phantasticus*. It has often been noted that the great Fantasia in g, BWV 542, depends to a large extent on the extreme fantasy of the North German toccata, while at the same time extending its harmonic ambitus. On the other hand, the Fantasia is regularly interrupted by episodes whose contrasting, eighth-note motive is systematically worked out in imitation. By contrast, the "Dorian" Toccata, BWV 538, and the

Toccata in F, BWV 540, correspond much more to the paired design, without harking back to the multipartite toccata.[28]

The more the late organ works of Bach represent the model of the prelude-fugue pair, the greater the separation from the older toccata and the distance from the *stylus phantasticus*. That is especially the case with five pieces that, according to Stauffer, originated in Leipzig after 1723: the preludes and fugues in e (BWV 548), b (BWV 544), c (BWV 546), and Eb (BWV 552), and the Fantasy and Fugue in c (BWV 537).[29] Nevertheless, one can still find many traces of Bach's involvement with the older tradition. His fugues use the so-called *repercussio* type of theme, which is especially characteristic of the playful *fugati* of the older toccata. Variations of the *repercussio* appear in the Fugue in G, BWV 541, as well as in the Fugue in c, BWV 537. The free expansive closing section is characteristic of the older toccata, whose image is still reflected in Bach's mature preludes and fugues. Significant in this regard are the expressive closing of the Prelude and Fugue in f, BWV 534, and the pedal-point coda of the "Dorian" Toccata, BWV 538.

In a highly sublimated way the thematic stamp of the mature prelude sometimes appears to point to the figurative material of the older toccata. Such is the case with the free passages of the Fantasia in g, BWV 542, and the rhythmic and harmonic denseness of the Prelude in b, BWV 544. Last but not least are the preludes whose figuration and pedal point derive from a certain type of older toccata: Toccata in F, BWV 540, and in a subtler way, the Preludes in e, BWV 548, and C, BWV 545. While the thematic material might be termed instrumental figures over a pedal point, its motivic profile still suggests the elementary type of the older toccata.

Bach's preference for combining antithetical prototypes, which is certainly a hallmark of his music, also derives from the toccata tradition. According to Mattheson, the joining of opposites was a characteristic of free organ music in *stylus phantasticus*, where fugue and dance, recitative and *ostinato* could be paired in equal measure in wandering exposition.[30] Even if Bach did not tolerate an aimless succession of contrasts, he did unite different types of styles into a thematic bond. In the Prelude in Eb ("St. Anne"), BWV 552, for instance, one can detect how similar rhythms are resolved in both the French style and the playful echo figures. Similar unifying devices can be found in the Prelude in b, BWV 544, or the Prelude in c, BWV 546, in which the static chords and the flowing triplet figures are linked motivically. Such complex motivic material can no longer be traced to prototypes, but Bach's desire to combine different elements may have been spurred by the variety of the older toccata.

What consequences are there for the performer in the traces of the toccata in *stylus phantasticus* that appear in Bach's work? Certainly his organ works no longer display the free alternation of meter, tempo, and manner of playing that were characteristic of music in the *stylus phantasticus*, to judge from Mattheson. Still, one must be aware that the apparently closed form in Bach's preludes and fugues is not a foregone conclusion. For his formal structures show the results of a protracted involvement with the *stylus phantasticus*, whose presuppositions are not so easily dispelled. Bach's forms can be perceived as one side of a tradition that the performer cannot ignore. The player must make it clear that the closed structure results from the relationship of its individual parts.

Stauffer shows that in the autograph of the Prelude in b, BWV 544, the formal parts in Bach's notation are dovetailed, precluding the possibility of a separation or of a change of manual or registration.[31] One must ask, however, to what extent this overlapping represents an exception, from which a generalization ought to be drawn with caution. On the other hand, it is true that the alternation of thematic and formal structures within the course of a movement also calls for a change in the manner of performance, except where one is not easily realized. The difficulties are more pronounced in works that first present such contrasts in order that they may later be balanced or combined. Even if one finds it unnecessary to change registration, one must not rule out a differentiated performance. Nuances become all the more important—nuances that can be achieved through articulation and phrasing. In any case, one must emphasize the differences between the contrasting elements, for when these elements later overlap their individual characteristics make the progress of the movement perceivable. Themes that stem from the playful *repercussio* type do not merit a ponderous articulation, and the free coda sections, into which many of Bach's preludes and fugues flow, should not be rendered to resemble what precedes them, but should be highlighted as a rich relic of the *stylus phantasticus*.

The balance of contrasting elements that is achieved in Bach's free organ music is thus accounted for from two columns of the same ledger: the continuous development of the works is balanced by the free alternation of contrasts. The structural completeness and free-

dom of fantasy that appear in Bach's organ music are equally important, since they are mutually dependent. Bach's art corresponds little
with the free fantasy, as it evolved from the classical mold, or with the
concept of the *stylus phantasticus*, as it is proclaimed in contemporary
theory.

But Bach's music shows an undeniable debt to the fantasy-filled toccata. This tradition remained active, even when Bach distanced himself from it in the extraordinary concentration of his work. His versatile craft first made the exciting relationships of this style visible. If
we wish to bring out this craft correctly, then we must give up the historical norm, which can yield but a single correct performance. No
performance standard is available for Bach. The scholarly as well as
the artistic interpreter of Bach's organ music must bear with this
difficulty.

(TRANSLATED BY THOMAS BAKER)

NOTES

1. It is no contradiction that the theorists of the time esteemed Bach
chiefly as an organ virtuoso and occasionally cited his fugue themes. See
BDok II, pp. 219 and 294. On Bach's free organ works see Hermann Keller,
The Organ Works of Bach, translated by Helen Hewitt (New York, 1967); George
Stauffer, *The Organ Preludes of Johann Sebastian Bach* (Ann Arbor, 1980); and
Peter Williams, *The Organ Music of J. S. Bach* (Cambridge, 1980–84).
2. On the use of the free organ works see Stauffer, pp. 137–53; as well as
Arnfried Edler, *Der nordelbische Organist. Studien zu Sozialstatus, Funktion und
kompositorischer Produktion eines Musikerberufes von der Reformation bis zum 20.
Jahrhundert* (Kassel, 1982), pp. 40–81.
3. On this point see Stauffer, pp. 42–77; and Werner Breig, "Bachs freie
Orgelmusik unter dem Einfluss der italienischen Konzertform," *Bach-Studien*
7 (in preparation).
4. See Johann Mattheson, *Der vollkommene Capellmeister* (Hamburg, 1739;
reprint, Kassel and Basel, 1954), pp. 224–25; Johann Adolph Scheibe, *Cri-
tischer Musicus* (Leipzig, 1747; reprint, Hildesheim, 1970), pp. 623–26 and
630–41; and Johann Joachim Quantz, *Versuch einer Anweisung die Flöte traversiere zu spielen* (Berlin, 1752; reprint, Kassel and Basel, 1953), pp. 294–302.
5. Friedrich Wilhelm Marpurg, *Abhandlung von der Fuge* (Berlin, 1753–
54), vol. 1 and 2; Johann Philipp Kirnberger, *Die Kunst des reinen Satzes*
(Berlin, 1771–79). The relevant excerpts from both works appear in BDok
III, pp. 25–71 and 216–37.
6. *Kern melodischer Wissenschaft* (Hamburg, 1737), pp. 93–126; and *Der
vollkommene Capellmeister*, pp. 210–34, esp. pp. 232–33.
7. Stauffer, pp. 31–90.
8. On BWV 543, for instance, see Stauffer, pp. 130–31.

9. Michael Praetorius, *Syntagma Musicum*, vol. 3, *Termini musici* (Wolfen-büttel, 1619; reprint, Kassel and Basel, 1958), pp. 21–25.

10. Ibid., p. 21.

11. Gioseffo Zarlino, *Le istitutioni harmoniche* (Venice, 1558; modern reprint, New York, 1966), p. 336; and Pietro Pontio, *Raggionamento di Musica* (Parma, 1588; modern reprint, Kassel and Basel, 1959), p. 153. See also Friedhelm Krummacher, "Stylus versus Opus. Anmerkungen zum Stilbegriff in der Musikhistorie," in *Om Stilforskning* (Stockholm, 1983), pp. 29–45.

12. See Erich Katz, "Die musikalische Stilbegriffe des 17. Jahrhunderts," Diss., University of Freiburg, 1926, pp. 83–89 and 132; Athanasius Kircher, *Musurgia Universalis sive Ars Magna Consoni et Dissoni* (Rome, 1650; reprint, Hildesheim, 1970), pp. 581–98; and Friedhelm Krummacher, "Stylus phantasticus und phantastische Musik. Kompositorische Verfahren in Toccaten von Frescobaldi und Buxtehude," *Schütz-Jahrbuch* 2 (1980): 7–77.

13. Kircher, p. 585.

14. Peter Schleuning, *Die freie Fantasie. Ein Beitrag zur Erforschung der klassischen Klaviermusik* (Göppingen, 1973), pp. 13–23; and Schleuning, *Die Fantasie*, vol. I (Cologne, 1971), Introduction, pp. 5–22.

15. Mattheson, *Der vollkommene Capellmeister*, pp. 87–88.

16. Mattheson, *Das neu-eröffnete Orchestre*, p. 176.

17. Mattheson, *Der vollkommene Capellmeister*, pp. 88–89 (see also the following citations).

18. Ibid., pp. 477–78.

19. Ibid., pp. 478–79.

20. See Krummacher, "Stylus phantasticus und phantastische Musik," pp. 35–53 (on toccatas by Froberger, Weckmann, and Buxtehude); and Willi Apel, *The History of Keyboard Music to 1700* (Bloomington, Indiana, 1972), esp. pp. 448–83 and 610–23.

21. See Friedhelm Krummacher, "Bach und die norddeutsche Orgeltoccata. Fragen und Überlegungen," BJ 1985: 119–34.

22. Stauffer, p. 108.

23. Ibid., pp. 102–103.

24. See Dietrich Kilian, NBA IV/5–6, KB, vol. 2, pp. 523–34.

25. Stauffer, pp. 94–103 and the table on pp. 122–25.

26. Ibid., pp. 98 and 103–105.

27. Stauffer, p. 109; and Kilian, pp. 298–308.

28. Stauffer, pp. 109–14.

29. Ibid., pp. 115–19.

30. Mattheson, *Der vollkommene Capellmeister*, p. 478.

31. Stauffer, pp. 167–70.

LAURENCE DREYFUS

The Metaphorical Soloist
Concerted Organ Parts in Bach's Cantatas

Near the end of his third annual cycle of church cantatas at Leipzig (1726), J. S. Bach composed six works that include substantial concerted solos for the organ. Although the range of instrumentation throughout Bach's cantata *oeuvre* is highly inventive, this concentrated appearance of organ solos invites a closer look. Isolated organ obbligatos surface in several earlier vocal pieces, but these six works constitute a genre without precedent in German Protestant sacred music. It is curious that concerted organ parts were not staples of German cantata orchestration, given the organ's rich solo repertoire and its emblematic identity as the sacred instrument *par excellence*. The usual role of this veritable *organum organorum* in Baroque concerted music contrasted markedly with its status as a solo instrument: while the organ possessed a solo repertoire unmatched in breadth and theological importance, it was relegated to realizing the basso continuo in ensemble music.

One reason for this dual existence was simply logistic: playing with his back to the singers and the orchestra, the organist was in an inconvenient position to take a leading melodic role and even to realize the continuo with ease. For example, Bach occasionally employed a simultaneous harpsichord accompaniment in many of his church cantatas for better coordination of the orchestral and vocal forces.[1]

A solo role for the organ in concerted music may also have appeared superfluous. First, the organ already comprised a metaphorical orchestra, seen in the range of its resources as well as in the names of orchestral instruments given to many of its stops.[2] The organ therefore represented the "instrument of instruments" not only because of its diverse tonal palette but also because it embraced (and often superseded) the forces of the contemporary orchestra. As a structural metaphor, "the organ as orchestra" made the very notion of obbligatos redundant: One orchestra is, after all, enough.[3] By a related conceptual turn, sacred concerted music already "included" the organ's indigenous repertoire. In this substitution of product for producer— replacing "organ" with its "repertoire"—the organ can be seen as represented in the sacred cantata by its fugues, chorale harmonizations, and cantus firmus settings, all of which had their generic analogues in organ music. By virtue of its status as equivalent to an orchestra as well as its embodiment via its conventional genres, the organ—one may conclude—seemed neither a desirable nor an appropriate addition to concerted church music.

These considerations may explain why J. S. Bach did not compose the organ obbligatos in the noticeable large-scale traditions of organ playing. Conspicuously absent are toccatas, fugues, chorale preludes— in short, any genres in which the organ presents itself as stylistically complete. Instead, Bach wrote for a more "minimalist" organ to signify a notion of "concentus" within figural music: the organ plays soloist to the concerto grosso, or obbligato to the singer, or cantus firmus to the *stile concertato*. But in every case, the organ contributes to but does not control the aggregate "harmonia."

This simultaneous restriction and extension of role is yet another in the myriad of experiments in Bach's cantata cycles. But what further distinguishes the organ solos is their attempt to pose as modern or even "galant." Consider the following evidence. Bach composed the 1726 solos some time before the organ trio sonatas (BWV 525–30, compiled and written ca. 1727), which, in their conspicuously light textures and veiled artifice, bear a strong resemblance to the organ solos. Writing in 1788, Carl Philipp Emanuel Bach mentions that the six trio sonatas "are written in such *galant* style that they still sound very good and never grow old, but on the contrary, will outlive all revolutions of fashion in music."[4] By "galant" Emanuel Bach can hardly have meant the thematic material in the sonatas, which is largely fugal or Vivaldian. More likely, he intended to signify the more delicate voicing, which intentionally avoids the massive textures of traditional North German organ style. The same "galant" feature in our organ obbligatos also comes in for mild censure from Johann Friedrich Reichardt in the early 1790s:

> My eyes fill with tears when I hear sacred music with an orchestra of twenty to thirty instrumentalists who play . . . together with a beautiful

but weakly voiced organ, which even with the greatest success cannot produce the great majestic effect that a true organist—a Bach, a
Homilius, a Fasch, a Hässler—was able to bring forth on a big and
beautiful organ. It js inconceivable that church composers have not yet
made greater and more lofty use of this magnificent instrument, and
that even Sebastian Bach and Handel did not better exploit it in their
movements with obbligato organ.[5]

Although Reichardt idealizes a grandiose combination of organ
and orchestra as a desideratum of sacred music, his argument sum-
mons up Bach's solo organ works rather than his concerted organ
solos for support. For he admits—somewhat perplexed—that the obbligatos in the cantatas do not live up to this imagined magnificence.
Indeed, for Reichardt, the disappointment probably lies with the light
textures, which fail to produce a "majestic effect." On the other hand,
he seems to disregard how the restraint of the organ solos figured in
their design. The pieces may therefore be understood, in part, to the
extent that they strive toward some notion of "galant" stylishness.

For whom did Bach write the organ obbligatos of 1726? The organ
trio sonatas, Forkel tells us, were written for his son Wilhelm Friedemann Bach.[6] There are no similar reports regarding the obbligatos,
and yet one reads repeatedly in the twentieth-century literature that
they, too, were composed for Bach's eldest, and apparently favorite,
child so as to distinguish Friedemann and establish his reputation.[7]
Although Friedemann, who was born in November 1710, was old
enough in 1726 to have played the obbligatos, he could not—it turns
out—have been the intended soloist. According to Marpurg:

> In his fifteenth year, [Wilhelm Friedemann] availed himself of study
> on the violin with the present Royal Prussian Concertmaster, then
> Concertmaster to the court at Merseburg, Herr [Johann Gottlieb]
> Graun, so as to be able to compose idiomatically for this instrument.
> Composition, organ and harpsichord fell under the supervision of his
> own father, as is easy to understand.[8]

Friedemann worked for his father as an auxiliary copyist more or
less regularly through the early months of 1726. His participation
ceased after May 19, when he copied a duplicate first violin part for a
cantata by Johann Ludwig Bach, *Und ich will ihnen einen einigen Hirten
erwecken*.[9] Friedemann's written lessons in his *Liber Exercitorum* at the
Thomasschule, moreover, run from May 16, 1725 through June 27,
1726, and then break off until April 30, 1727.[10] Marpurg must therefore have meant that Friedemann left for Merseburg when he was fif-

TABLE 1

Cantatas with Organ Solos

BWV	Title	First performance	Movement(s) with obbligato organ
71	*Gott ist mein König*	Feb. 4, 1708	2
161	*Komm, du süsse Todesstunde*	Oct. 6, 1715	1
70	*Wachet, betet, seid bereit allezeit*	Nov. 21, 1723	3
172	*Erschallet, ihr Lieder*	May 28, 1724	5
128	*Auf Christi Himmelfahrt allein**	May 10, 1725	4
146	*Wir müssen durch viel Trübsal*	May 12, 1726 (?)	1,2
170	*Vergnügte Ruh, beliebte Seelenlust*	July 28, 1726	3,5
35	*Geist und Seele wird verwirret*	Sept. 8, 1726	1,4,5
47	*Wer sich selbst erhöhet*	Oct. 13, 1726	2
169	*Gott soll allein mein Herze haben*	Oct. 20, 1726	1,3,5
49	*Ich gehe und suche mit Verlangen*	Nov. 3, 1726	1,2,6
188	*Ich habe meine Zuversicht*	ca. 1728	1,4
120a	*Herr Gott, Beherrscher aller Dinge*	ca. 1729	4
63	*Christen, ätzet diesen Tag*	1729 (?)	3
29	*Wir danken dir, Gott, wir danken dir*	Aug. 27, 1731	1,7
73	*Herr, wie du willt, so schicks mit mir*	1732–35	1
27	*Wer weiss, wie nahe mir mein Ende*	1737 (?)	3

*Although Bach specified "organo solo" in his score, he had the part copied for the oboe d'amore. Apparently, this organ solo was never heard.

teen years old (actually, in his *sixteenth* year). He seems to have arrived there near the beginning of July 1726 and remained through April 1727. Although he may still have been present in Leipzig on May 12, when Cantata 146 was performed,[11] he was surely away when his father composed and performed the others (Cantatas 170, 35, 47, 169, and 49) during July, September, October, and November (see Table 1).

Since Carl Philipp Emanuel Bach was only twelve years old at the time, J. S. Bach may well have played the solos himself. The sources speak for this claim, since Bach took the trouble in all the 1726 cantata scores—except in one movement of Cantata 170—to notate the organ part at its playing pitch of *Chorton*, a whole step below the normal *Cammerton* pitch of the orchestra. Normally the organ was notated at the same pitch as the orchestra in Bach's score and was transposed down in a separate performing part. In all likelihood, then, the organist played these pieces from the score and not from a performing part.[12] In view of the difficulty of realizing the solo part from Bach's composing scores—some are fraught with corrections and even *ad hoc* notation in tablature—Bach himself appears to be the most likely soloist.[13]

The solo organ parts, which Bach designates as "Organo obligato," present a qualitatively new situation for the basso continuo. For now that the organist is engaged with his concerted part, he can no longer execute the chordal accompaniment usually entrusted to him. The ensuing problem—who is to realize the continuo?—is one that apparently engaged Bach's attention, as can be seen from the manuscript sources. Explicit documentary evidence regarding the performance of these pieces is lacking, but the original scores and parts reveal that Bach experimented with different methods of substitution, although he never settled on one solution.

Since the concerted organist was usually charged with two lines of music, occupying both hands, he could not realize the continuo. The pedal alone served no useful function here. Consequently, Bach either dispensed with continuo chords in the concerted movements or replaced the organ with another instrument. The two most likely candidates were the harpsichord or a smaller *Positiv* organ.

By 1723, the year Bach arrived in Leipzig, the Thomaskirche and the Nikolaikirche each possessed one large main organ located on the choir loft. The composer undoubtedly intended the organ solos to be performed on these instruments.[14] At the Thomaskirche there was also a smaller organ on a small gallery attached to the east wall. This instrument was in use until 1740, when it was dismantled.[15] But it was so far from the main choir loft that it could hardly have participated in the performance of the solo organ cantatas. No smaller organs were permanently housed—as far as we know—in either church, but the Thomasschule, next door to the Thomaskirche, owned two *Positiv* organs that Bach may have used for continuo. According to the school inventory, one was particularly small, and it was regularly carried to wedding ceremonies in private homes. Like the main organs, both small instruments were pitched at *Chorton*.[16] Finally, in each church there was a harpsichord in the main choir loft tuned in *Cammerton*, the pitch at which Bach composed his Leipzig works and at which the singers, the strings, and the woodwinds performed.

In Cantata 170, the organ plays concerted parts in movements 3 and 5. Movement 3, as a *bassetto* aria dispensing with the continuo, presents no particular problems. Its part in the autograph score was transposed down to *Chorton*, from which we may conclude that Bach intended to play the solo from the score. On the other hand, the score notates movement 5, which requires continuo accompaniment, in *Cammerton*. (Of course, if Bach were the soloist, he would easily have managed the transposition from the score.) Two continuo parts survive to Cantata 170—an unfigured part in *Cammerton* for the cello and a completely figured, transposed part notated in *Chorton*. If the soloist sat at the main organ, the continuo player must then have played one of the *Positiv* organs brought up to the loft, because two organs are then required for movement 5. Most likely, the continuo player accompanied at the *Positiv* for the entire performance of Cantata 170.

In Cantata 169, performed a few months later, movements 1, 3, and 5 included solo organ parts, all of which Bach transposed down to *Chorton* in his score. Only two continuo parts—both in *Cammerton*—survive from this performance. One contains a complete set of continuo figures and was therefore intended for the harpsichord. (*Tasto solo* markings in movement 1 confirm further that the figures cannot have been mere cues.) The organ and harpsichord therefore played simultaneously during at least three movements, although the sources do not clarify whether the organ also played continuo together with the harpsichord during the remaining movements of the cantata.

The performance of Cantata 29 in 1731, on the other hand, provides a case in which Bach intended the "dual accompaniment" of harpsichord and organ, even when the organist was not playing a concerted part. Unlike his handling of the pieces in the 1726 group, Bach had a complete organ part copied out; it included both solos (movements 1 and 7) as well as the continuo parts to the remaining movements. Only movements 2 through 6 are figured here, so that the organist obviously played continuo when he was not occupied with the solos. However, Bach also figured one of the *Cammerton* continuo parts in its entirety. From this striking fact, it seems clear that the harpsichord filled in not only in the solo movements but throughout the cantata. Consequently, the organ and harpsichord realized the continuo simultaneously in the inner movements, which include— perhaps surprisingly—two *secco* recitatives.

More perplexing is the unique consolidation of concerted solo and continuo parts in a performance of Cantata 73 held some time between 1732 and 1735. Here the registration markings on the treble line of the solo part—alternately *Rück-Positiv* and *Brust-Positiv*—indicate the manual on which the organist's right hand was occupied in a line alternating between a chorale melody and a concerted obbligato. (The markings also suggest that someone other than Bach occasionally played the solos, for the composer would hardly have made these notations for himself.) But the bass line in the solo organ part to this opening chorus—which embraces a choral concerto, a chorale setting in addition to an accompanied recitative—includes a consistent set of continuo figures. Where are they to be realized? If the player takes the chords in the right hand, beneath the treble obbligato, they would protrude uncomfortably, compromising their accompanying function and destroying the distinct "voice" of the solo obbligato. It is likewise difficult to imagine the chords superimposed just over the bass if the continuo is played with the left hand. This manner of realization would be unusual as well as ungainly, since the bass line itself jumps around considerably. Perhaps, then, the player took the bass line in the pedal while realizing the continuo in the left hand—again, an unconventional procedure. Whatever solution was adopted, Bach apparently strove on this occasion to cast the organ in a solo role without sacrificing its usual ability to accompany.

To discuss the various styles of Bach's organ obbligatos falls beyond the scope of the present essay. Indeed, to do justice to the wealth of ideas found here would necessitate a more or less complete typology of the compositional devices Bach employed in his cantatas. Instead, let us focus on a few representative stylistic issues that figure prominently in the group of organ solos.

Certainly one of the most "galant" features of the organ solos is the clever manner in which the organ feigns identities other than its own. In the first place, it imitates melody-line instruments by imitating their range, idiom, and character. It is of course possible—and sometimes demonstrable—that Bach first substituted the organ for another instrument on an emergency basis; perhaps the intended instrumentalist became ill. But, conceptually, the notion of the organ standing for something else seems to have taken on a logic and direction of its own. Posing as a cello, for example, the organ functions as an elaborative bass decoration to a continuo aria (Cantata 70, movement 3) or as a bass concertato accompanying an alto aria with idiomatic "string crossings" (Cantata 35, movement 4). It also imitates the nimble articulations and flourishes characteristic of the *flauto traverso* (Cantata 170, movement 5) or echoes the oboe's ornate elongated phrases in an adagio aria (Cantata 63, movement 3). But the organ most often assumes the guise of a violin, as in Cantata 29, movement 7, when it explicitly replaces the violin solo of movement 3 in a transposed, intensified repetition of the earlier aria; or in Cantata 47, movement 2, when virtuoso running figures in the first section and parodied "double stops" in the second appear over an unrealized bass line.

Perhaps the most striking, if also the most problematic, of the organ solos—one that Bach used in both Cantata 29 and Cantata 120a—occurs in an orchestrated sinfonia of the Prelude to the Partita in E for solo violin, BWV 1006 (see the comparative openings in Examples 1 and 2). It is not difficult to account for the process of expansion with which Bach transformed a solo suite into a noisy orchestral display aspiring to mammoth proportions.[17] Instead, we might consider what the arrangement for organ and orchestra reveals about the nature of the original work.

Taken by itself, the violin prelude depends on no specific generic convention. One might say that preludes—particularly for Bach—are a place where genre is absent, and hence a place where a freely arranged bundle of ideas converge. Although the Prelude in E prominently features its violinistic character, it is the organ version that emboldens its reference to the violin writing in the concertos of Antonio Vivaldi. The rhythmicized arpeggios at the beginning, the *forte* and *piano* indications, and the alternation between fingered notes and adjacent open strings over a pedal point all confirm this influence. But the affect of the Italianate style—in a sense, Bach's compositional intention—only fully emerges in the orchestral version, which, by placing the soloist before a pompous background, exudes the self-assurance that accompanies virtuosity.

And yet, the content of the movement remains more, not less, ambiguous once the Prelude becomes a Sinfonia. For this piece does not resemble the keyboard preludes "in concerto style," as in the Prelude to the English Suite in g. Instead, as a kind of caprice or fantasy, it all but ignores the process of alternation that characterizes the concerto. To be sure, the movement displays features that, in concertos, distinguish the ritornello from solo episodes: it brings back opening material in different key areas and sets up medial cadences. On the other hand, it frustrates any hope that the logic of ritornello governs the composition. The signs of "concerto" thus represent an imperfect allusion.

It is hard to deny that the cantata sinfonia magnifies the visceral excitement and virtuosity to a degree unknown in a "real" concerto. And yet, because it lacks a constructive principle, the piece makes a virtue of motion without ever gaining ground. This lack of development accounts for the peculiar pedal points, which prolong what was

EXAMPLE 1. Cantata 29, Mvt. 1, mm. 1–23

EXAMPLE 2. Violin Partita in E, Prelude, mm. 1–25

never withheld, oblivious to harmonic goals. Instead, the exalted passage-work constituting much of the movement denotes no more than virtuosic presence—*Fortspinnung* raised to a higher power. The Sinfonia, to be sure, shares several insights about the Prelude. For one thing, it pompously supplies the missing opening downbeat, which the violin Prelude could not even have hinted at. Moreover, the Sinfonia gilds the final cadence with such ornate elaborations that it becomes clear that the original conception of the violin Prelude never intended the grand *ritardando* so often heard in performance; Bach meant nothing more than an unadorned grammatical marker. Ironically, though, by telling truths about its character, concretizing its fantasies of brilliance and conceit, the Sinfonia unmasks the Prelude's weaknesses, disclosing a bombastic, perhaps even empty, shell. Of course, Bach may have composed the original piece, as one eighteenth-century writer put it, to help the player "master the full resources of the instrument."[18] But the real invention of the work may lie, para-

TABLE 2

Concerto Movements Arranged for Organ Obbligato
(Date indicates first performance.)

BWV 1052   Concerto in d for harpsichord and strings
    1. Allegro = BWV 146/1   May 12, 1726   D minor
    2. Adagio   = BWV 146/2   May 12, 1726   D minor
    3. Allegro = BWV 188/1   ca. 1728   D minor

BWV 1053   Concerto in E for harpsichord and strings
    1. Allegro = BWV 169/1   Oct. 20, 1726   D major
    2. Andante = BWV 169/5   Oct. 20, 1726   B minor
    3. Allegro = BWV 49/1   Nov. 3, 1726   E major

BWV 1059   Concerto in d for oboe and strings
    1. Allegro = BWV 35/1   Sept. 8, 1726   D minor
    [2. Adagio = BWV 156/1   1729 (?)   F major]*
    3. Presto   = BWV 35/5   Sept. 8, 1726   D minor

*Never arranged for solo organ.

doxically, in neither version but in evoking an aspiration only imperfectly realizable.

Among the most fascinating movements of the organ solos are the sinfonias cast in the mold of solo concertos. Indeed, three of Bach's solo concertos known only from later sources first appear in the Bach sources in versions for solo organ and orchestra[19] (see Table 2).

It is usual to read concerto movements in ritornello style as a struggle between the soloist and the orchestra, that is, as a visually discernible competition between the players of the concertino—in our pieces, the solo organ—and the players of the *ripieno*—the orchestral tutti. However, in Bach's concertos, here as elsewhere, the real struggle is somewhat more abstract and hence more interesting. Rather than being determined by the tutti–solo contrast, the pieces are structured by significant ritornello statements cast into new and alterable guises. In other words, *who* happens to be playing matters much less than *whether* the ritornello is present. Indeed, the sense of any particular passage in these works can best be understood from a sort of measurable distance marked away from an "ideal ritornello" underlying the work.

This view has a significant corollary. For a passage may pretend, on the surface, to act like a solo section while it really remains a decorated statement of the ritornello. Compare Examples 3 and 4, in which the opening ritornello to Cantata 35, movement 1, is followed by a later ritornello statement. The second ritornello—although not a complete restatement—is clearly generated by the first. The opening segments, admittedly, are slightly expanded (mm. 98–102), but their harmonic identity is nonetheless maintained. Note, however, how the solo organ—from m. 101 until the *piano* marking at m. 103—plays the tutti theme, encouraging the belief that the solo instrument has "taken over" the ritornello. On the other hand, the ritornello has not disappeared merely because Bach gives the organ the chief melodic idea. Indeed, in mm. 103–105, the surface indicators suggest even more strongly that the ritornello is no longer present. Bach marks the passage *piano*—the traditional sign of a solo section—and thereby permits the chromatic "motive" in the organ part to pose as the leading idea of a solo episode. In fact, Bach has woven this bit of counterpoint as an enhancement—but not suspension—of the ritornello. If one needs "proof" of this assertion, then it would be a simple matter to replace the passage from m. 103 to the downbeat of m. 105 with the parallel passage from mm. 4–6. The syntax of the later passage remains identical to the earlier one; only the decoration has changed. The seeming removal of the tutti simulates no more than a wondrous mask that Bach has designed to enrich the play of identities.

With this move to the concerto proper, Bach takes the final step in extending the idea of the organ as an obbligato instrument within his sacred vocal works. And yet, this step cannot help but undermine the original enabling metaphor, which distinguished between "organ as sacred icon" and "organ as galant conversationalist." For we do not encounter just *any* melody-line instrument designated as concerto soloist in a church cantata, but precisely the organ, the traditional bearer of the divine word. Its presence as soloist, then, validates, at least in one sense, the very transfer of the secular solo concerto into the church cantata. Consistently identified in the eighteenth century by its etymology evoking "striving" and "struggle," the concerto—even with its modish Vivaldian facade—is ideally suited to stand at the beginning of a genre dedicated to repeating, week after week, a narrative of redemption and the deliverance from the earthly struggle. The cantata sinfonia masking a concerto therefore sets the stage with a more abstract but no less vivid allegory of conflict, replete with its own symbolic catharsis.

The diverse styles constituted by the spectrum of Bach's organ obbligatos, however ingenious their invention, cannot be judged equally

EXAMPLE 3. Cantata 35, Mvt. 1, mm. 1–9

EXAMPLE 4. Cantata 35, Mvt. 1, mm. 97–106

successful. As a modest melodic voice that arbitrarily replaces a more usual obbligato instrument, the organ adds little to Bach's cantata orchestration. Certain movements even tend to highlight a sense of posing, as if the composer called on the organ as a temporary, auxiliary aid. As a demure galant subject, moreover, shunning the strict style, the organ likewise appears dispensable. Thus, in Cantata 169, movement 5, in which Bach adds a text to the slow movement of a previously composed concerto, the organ—retaining the original solo line—and the alto part waver in an unhappy compromise between contrapuntal distinctiveness and galant redundancy.

On the other hand, the organ obbligatos attain a magisterial status whenever they allude—however obliquely—to the normative character of the instrument. The concerto movements in the sinfonias, therefore, by virtue of their theologically elevated debate, sound compositionally complete and not in the least like mere arrangements. Nor do the two obbligato lines assigned to the organ in Cantata 170, movement 3, appear in any way superfluous. Here, an otherworldly aura is evoked by the absence of the bass fundament and by the tortuous chromatic intertwining of the treble organ lines (located in the same tessitura). The effect is a uniquely Baroque expression of the Christian soul who, despairing of human folly, desires an end to his earthly life.[20] At best, then, Bach's organ obbligatos typify an interpretive acumen that pervades the length and breadth of a lifetime aspiration—that of a "well-regulated church music." That this massive corpus of occasional works, moreover, manages to avoid stylistic rigidity and only rarely devolves into formula testifies to a remarkable human achievement.

NOTES

1. See Laurence Dreyfus, "Zur Frage der Cembalo-Mitwirkung in den geistlichen Werken Bachs," in *Bachforschung und Bachinterpretation heute*, edited by Reinhold Brinkmann (Leipzig, 1981), pp. 178–84; and Dreyfus, "Basso Continuo Practice in the Vocal Works of J. S. Bach: A Study of the Original Performance Parts," Ph.D. diss., Columbia University, 1980. Chapter 2 of the dissertation focuses on questions of performance practice related to the cantatas with concerted organ solos.

2. J. F. Reichardt, for example, writes in 1791 that the organ is "such a resourceful instrument . . . [that] one man can represent a complete and powerful orchestra. . . ." Cited in BDok III, p. 508.

3. On this use of structural metaphors, see George Lakoff and Mark Johnson, *Metaphors We Live By* (Chicago, 1980), esp. pp. 61–68.

4. *Bach Reader*, p. 285; German text in BDok III, p. 441, citing an article appearing in 1788 in the *Allgemeine deutsche Bibliothek*. Although published anonymously, the author was almost certainly C. P. E. Bach. See BDok III, p. 444.

5. BDok III, p. 508.

6. English translation in *Bach Reader*, p. 346.

7. This view originated with Bernhard Friedrich Richter, "Über Seb. Bachs Kantaten mit obligater Orgel," BJ 1908: 58, but his guess presumed Spitta's now disproven dating of 1731 for the cantatas in question. In his *Beiträge zur Chronologie der Werke Johann Sebastian Bachs* (Tübingen, 1958), p. 32, Georg von Dadelsen corrects Spitta's dating but maintains Richter's claim that Bach composed the obbligatos for Wilhelm Friedemann. Alfred Dürr mentions the possibility most recently in *Die Kantaten von Johann Sebastian Bach* (Kassel, 1971), p. 54.

8. Friedrich Wilhelm Marpurg, *Historisch-Kritische Beyträge zur Aufnahme der Musik* (Berlin, 1754), p. 431.

9. Alfred Dürr, *Zur Chronologie der Leipziger Vokalwerke J. S. Bachs* (Kassel, 1976), p. 152.

10. Martin Falck, *Wilhelm Friedemann Bach* (Leipzig, 1913), pp. 5 and 8.

11. However, since no original sources survive, the dating for the first performance of Cantata 146 remains hypothetical. See Dürr, *Chronologie*, p. 166.

12. See Dreyfus, "Basso Continuo Practice," p. 56. Separate, transposed obbligato parts survive only from the later pieces (as of 1731). It is also possible, though unlikely, that original obbligato parts have been lost.

13. On the characteristics of "composing scores," see Robert L. Marshall, *The Compositional Process of J. S. Bach* (Princeton, 1972), pp. 3–30.

14. Richter (p. 54) raises the possibility that the solos could have been played on one of the *Positiv* organs, but in view of their limited sound, that is most unlikely.

15. See Winfried Schrammek, "Fragen des Orgelgebrauchs in Bachs Aufführungen der Matthäus-Passion," BJ 1975: 114–16.

16. Arnold Schering, *Johann Sebastian Bachs Leipziger Kirchenmusik* (1936; Leipzig, 1954), p. 69. But Schering's claim (p. 71) that this *Positiv* was pitched at *Cammerton* is untenable. On this point, see Dreyfus, "Basso Continuo Practice," pp. 75–76.

17. The accompaniment in Cantata 120a requires only strings. In Cantata 29, Bach adds the three trumpets and drums. See Marshall, p. 25.

18. J. F. Agricola, *Allgemeine deutsche Bibliothek* 32[1] (1774), p. 527. Agricola added that Bach "often played [his violin solos] on the clavichord, adding as much in the nature of a sounding harmony, such as in compositions of this sort he could not more fully achieve." One may also cite in this regard the two keyboard arrangements of other movements from the solo violin sonatas— BWV 964 and BWV 968. German text in BDok III, p. 293; English translation in *Bach Reader*, p. 447.

19. Joshua Rifkin offers the most convincing explanation of the earliest version of BWV 1059 in "Ein langsamer Konzertsatz Johann Sebastian Bachs," BJ 1978: 140–47.

20. Dürr, *Kantaten*, p. 365.

Matters of Performance Practice

But in particular the art of organ playing, which had to a great extent been learned from the Netherlanders, was already at this time in a high state of advancement. . . . Finally, the admirable Johann Sebastian Bach brought it to its greatest perfection in recent times. We can only hope that now, after his death . . . it will not again fall into decline or decay.

—*Johann Joachim Quantz (1752)*

GEORGE STAUFFER

❧ ⟨⟩ ☙

Bach's Organ Registration Reconsidered

Scholars and performers have long puzzled over the fact that Johann Sebastian Bach, a meticulous composer and an exacting performer, should have said so little about the registration of his organ works. He never set down his views on registration, and, more mysteriously, he gave only a handful of stop indications in his manuscripts. How, then, are his works to be performed?

In the past, treatment of this problem has been highly uneven. Among the first to seek a solution was Johann Nicolaus Forkel, the late eighteenth-century music historian. In gathering information for his Bach biography, Forkel asked Carl Philipp Emanuel Bach about his father's mode of organ playing. On the subject of registering, Emanuel replied:

> No one understood registration at the organ as well as he. Organists were often terrified when he sat down to play on their organs and drew the stops in his own manner, for they thought that the effect could not be good as he was planning it. But then they gradually heard an effect that astounded them. These sciences perished with him.[1]

Instead of settling the registration question then and there, Emanuel's response marked the beginning of nearly two centuries of misunderstandings. The phrase "in his own manner" appeared to separate Bach completely from the practices of his day, so much so that later writers failed to consider eighteenth-century traditions seriously. Thus in 1844, in the first widely promulgated discussion of Bach's registration, Peters editor Friedrich Conrad Griepenkerl passed lightly over eighteenth-century conventions before turning to more prac-

tical, nineteenth-century-oriented advice.[2] Griepenkerl's remarks were
followed by less-restrained speculation, ranging from Albert Schweitzer's romantic advocacy of the Swell pedal to Hermann Keller's Reger-
influenced manual-change schemes.[3] Even recent, more objective
studies, such as those by Hans Klotz and Thomas Harmon, continue
to becloud the issue, for they fail to eschew past misconceptions.[4]

Were Bach's registrational procedures as unorthodox as we have assumed them to be? To judge from the most reliable evidence—manuscript sources and eighteenth-century accounts of organ playing—
they may not have been. While Bach appears to have selected stops in
his own fashion, he does not seem to have abjured contemporary registrational conventions altogether.

When it came to registering organ pieces, the Germans were never
as dogmatic as the French. In the seventeenth and eighteenth centuries, the French evolved a very elaborate system of registration.
Since organs in France tended to be constructed along standard lines,
composers were able to write works for specific combinations, know-
ing that these combinations would be available throughout the country.[5] Registrational possibilities and compositional considerations were
closely intertwined, and pieces were conceived with specific stop combinations in mind. For instance, the hundreds of works entitled *Récit
de Cornet* were written to exploit the Cornet mixture found in the
treble range of almost every French Classical instrument.

In Germany such exactitude was not possible. Local traditions were
much stronger, and organs were built according to regional tastes.
The great diversity of instruments prevented German composers
from adopting a registrational system as codified as that of the French.
Still, several general precepts obtained. The most important, according to treatises on organ building and organ playing, was the division
of registrations into two families: the full organ (*das volle Werk, die volle
Orgel, organum plenum,* or *Organo pleno*) and all the remaining, more
colorful combinations. As Johann Mattheson explained,

> In general, organ registrations can be divided into two families. To
> the first belongs the full organ. To the second belong all the remaining
> diverse variations, which can be realized especially through the use of
> several manuals and weaker but nevertheless carefully selected stops.[6]

Central to the present discussion is the fact that specific types of pieces
were associated with each of these two registrational categories.

The Full Organ

Eighteenth-century manuals present a rather detailed picture of *organum plenum*, or, as Mattheson put it, "the full organ." They indicate it was used above all for free compositions, that is, for fugues, preludes, toccatas, fantasias, and other works not bound to a chorale melody.[7] The custom of playing free pieces "pro Organo pleno" was long standing; one can trace the practice from the mid-seventeenth century to the late nineteenth. During Bach's lifetime there seems to have been no disagreement on the matter: Theorists recommend nothing but a *plenum* sound for free works. For instance, in 1706 Friedrich Erhardt Niedt instructed neophytes to improvise free pieces "with the full organ, or something just about as strong."[8] Johann Adolf Scheibe, an organ builder's son and perhaps one of Bach's students before becoming his infamous critic, described the process in more detail:

> I have yet to talk about the second manner of preluding—that is, when one improvises freely, without being bound to a chorale. It must be remembered that this generally takes place with the full organ. One should employ good and lively invention and should crown such a prelude or postlude with a fine and magnificent fugue.[9]

Jacob Adlung, a source of information about Bach's playing,[10] went so far as to admit that the *plenum* was much abused: "Many know nothing of preluding before a concerted piece or a chorale, than to rage with the full organ." Still, he warned that the practice of performing free works with the full organ should not be disregarded.[11]

The manuscripts of seventeenth- and eighteenth-century organ music corroborate the remarks of the theorists. Most lack registrational instructions. But in the free repertoire, a significant number of sources include the phrase "pro Organo pleno" or similar expressions that confirm the use of a *plenum* sound. These registrational rubrics appear in the manuscripts of free works by Buxtehude, Johann Ludwig Krebs, Kittel, and others closely linked with Bach. To take a striking example: Krebs's Toccata in a, a work modeled directly after Bach's Toccata in F, BWV 540/1, bears the title *Toccata con Fuga ex A♮ pro Organo pleno con Pedale obligato* (see Plate 1). Would Krebs have mimicked his teacher's compositional style without borrowing his registration as well? It seems unlikely. The Krebs heading implies that Bach's Toccata in F was also written "pro Organo pleno."

Turning to the manuscripts of Bach's free compositions, one discovers that they, too, support the application of a *plenum* registration.

Johann Ludwig Krebs: Toccata and Fugue in a
(Manuscript of Johann Christian Kittel; Hessische Landes- und
Hochschulbibliothek, Darmstadt, *Mus. Ms. 562*)

PLATE 1

The autograph of the Prelude and Fugue in b, BWV 544, and the
Clavierübung III print of the Prelude and Fugue in E♭, BWV 552, include the words "in Organo pleno" and "pro Organo pleno." But the
secondary sources of many other free compositions also contain *plenum*
indications[12]—indications omitted in modern editions. The entire list
of Bach free works with a *plenum* marking in at least one source is as
follows:

Prelude and Fugue in g, BWV 535
Prelude and Fugue in d ("Dorian"), BWV 538
Fantasia and Fugue in g, BWV 542
Prelude and Fugue in a, BWV 543
Prelude and Fugue in b, BWV 544
Prelude and Fugue in C, BWV 545
Prelude and Fugue in c, BWV 546
Prelude and Fugue in C, BWV 547
Prelude and Fugue in e ("Wedge"), BWV 548
Prelude and Fugue in E♭ ("St. Anne"), BWV 552
Prelude in a, BWV 569
Fugue in g, BWV 578
Passacaglia and Fugue in c, BWV 582
Allabreve in D, BWV 589

That so many pieces can be linked with *plenum* indications suggests
that Bach adhered to the convention of setting free works for the full
organ.

An intriguing case is the Passacaglia and Fugue in c, BWV 582. The original autograph is lost, but a copy of what appears to have been a later, revised autograph carried the title *Passacalio* [sic] *con Pedal pro Organo pleno*.[13] This appellation refutes once and for all Forkel's mistaken notion that the Passacaglia was written for pedal-clavichord. But in terms of registration, it removes the Passacaglia from the crescendo category and places it where it properly belongs, in the *plenum* sphere. This characterization is not surprising, for Mattheson alluded to the extemporization of ciaconas (i.e., passacaglias) "with the full organ" in the *Grosse-General-Bass-Schule* of 1731.[14] It is reassuring nevertheless to find manuscript evidence linking Bach's composition with the practice Mattheson described.

In addition to free organ works, certain kinds of chorale preludes were intended for *plenum* performance. These pieces were invariably written in the manner of free organ compositions or in the style of vocal or instrumental genres requiring a large, rich sound. When *pedaliter*, they seem to have called for the full organ. When *manualiter*, they probably required a slightly smaller combination, perhaps the *plenum* on a secondary manual. The first two types of *plenum* chorales were developed in the seventeenth century; the third and fourth were Bach's own invention:

1. *Chorale fugues.* One of the standard methods of improvising a chorale in the Baroque was to construct a fugue or fughetta on the chorale melody. Mattheson described the process succinctly:

> As far as fugue playing is concerned, there are two types. The first type of fugue belongs to the actual working out of a chorale, in which case the fugue theme is drawn from the melody of the chorale itself. The second type concerns the prelude or postlude, for which the fugue serves as a section or a conclusion. Here one is free to borrow or invent the theme, as one wishes.[15]

As Mattheson points out, the chief difference between a chorale fugue and a free fugue is the source of the *soggetto*. In a chorale fugue, the subject is derived from the chorale tune. In a free fugue, the subject is invented by the performer. Otherwise, the two fugue types are quite alike, and both require a *plenum* registration. Representative examples of the chorale fugue in Bach's *oeuvre* are *Wir glauben all' an einen Gott*, BWV 680 (marked "in Organo pleno" in the original print of *Clavierübung* III); *Fuga sopra il Magnificat*, BWV 733 (marked "pro Organo pleno" in several eighteenth-century manuscripts); *Fughetta super Dies sind die heil'gen zehn Gebot'*, BWV 678; and *Herr Christ, der ein'ge Gottes Sohn, Fughetta*, BWV 698.

2. *Chorale fantasias.* Stylistically, chorale fantasias resemble the free prelude or free fantasia, hence their ties with a *plenum* registration. In many cases, fragments of the chorale are given in the manual voices while the complete melody is presented in the pedal as a cantus firmus. Bach's chorale fantasias include *Komm heiliger Geist, Herre Gott*, BWV 651 (marked "in Organo pleno" in Bach's autograph[16]); *Valet will ich dir geben*, BWV 736; and *Jesu, meine Freude*, BWV 713.

3. *Chorale preludes with a tutti instrumental texture.* During the Weimar years Bach transferred the instrumental writing of Corelli, Vivaldi, and other Italians to the organ, adopting their succinct melodies, incisive rhythms, strong harmonies, and transparent polyphonic textures. His sudden shift to an instrumental idiom is most easily observed in free works such as the "Dorian" Toccata in d, BWV 538/1, or the Prelude and Fugue in G, BWV 541. But many of the chorale preludes composed in Weimar, or later in Cöthen and Leipzig, display the same kind of writing. In works in which Bach imitates the style of a tutti ensemble, *organum plenum* appears to be the proper registration. Examples include *Komm, Gott Schöpfer, heiliger Geist*, BWV 667 (marked "in Organo pleno" in Bach's autograph[17]) and numerous *Orgelbüchlein* chorales: *Vom Himmel hoch, da komm' ich her*, BWV 606; *Wir Christenleut'*, BWV 612; *Wer nur den lieben Gott lässt walten*, BWV 642; and others.

4. *Stile antico chorale preludes.* As Christoph Wolff has demonstrated, during the last two decades of his life Bach developed a new type of chorale prelude based on the *stile antico*, or Renaissance vocal style.[18] In these pieces Bach took the *a cappella* writing of Palestrina and transferred it to the organ, producing a unique type of keyboard motet. Since he modeled the *stile antico* chorale preludes on the sound of a large, rich vocal ensemble, it is understandable that he wished them to be played *organum plenum*. *Kyrie, Gott heiliger Geist*, BWV 671 (marked "Cum Organo pleno" in the original print of *Clavierübung* III[19]), and *Aus tiefer Not, schrei ich zu Dir*, BWV 686 (marked "in Organo pleno" in the original print of *Clavierübung* III), are the best illustrations of this unusual style.[20]

These four kinds of chorale preludes join the free works as compositions intended for the full organ. Let us explore for a moment the constitution of the *plenum* in Bach's time.[21] Bach, an ever-reluctant correspondent, did not record his view of the *plenum* combination, but fortunately many of his contemporaries did. Their accounts suggest that the *plenum* did not call for the random use of *all* the stops; it comprised instead a judiciously chosen group of manual and pedal registers. As Mattheson outlined its composition:

> To the full organ belong the Principals, the Sorduns, the Salicionals or Salicets ["Weiden-Pfeiffen"], the Rausch-Pfeiffen, the Octaves, the Quints, the Mixtures, the Scharfs (small Mixtures with three ranks of pipes), the Quintades, the Zimbels, the Nasats, the Terzians, the Sesquialteras, the Superoctaves, and the Posaunes in the pedal, not in the manual, for the Posaunes are reed pipes which are excluded in the manual for the full organ. This is done because the Posaune rattles too much on account of its pitch. On the other hand, when there is proper wind, it sounds splendid in the pedal because of the depth of its tone.[22]

Adlung gave an even fuller description:

> Anyone who would like to know what to draw in the manual for the *plenum* need only remember this: One must have registers, which brighten. To this end the Principal serves together with all the Octaves and the Quints and Terzes and best of all the mixed voices such as the Terzian, the Sesquialtera, the Mixtures, the Scharfs, the Cymbels, and so forth. If one does not wish such a strong combination, then one should leave something out—whatever one wishes. But if one desires an even brighter *plenum* then one should pull the appropriate stops on another manual and couple it into the main keyboard. One must also have stops, however, which add gravity. For this purpose, the Gedackts act as well as the Quintaton 16', or even better, the Gedackt 16' or Rohrflute 16' or a Bourdon of similar size (according to what is available), the Gedackt 8', Quintaton 8', Rohrflute 8', Gemshorn 8', and so forth.
>
> What has been said about the manual *plenum* is also true for the Pedal *plenum*, for it must be very strong in order to be heard above the manual. One usually depends more on gravity in the Pedal, although sometimes one brightens it as well. In order to obtain gravity one should use the Contrabass 32', Subbass 16', Gedackt 8', Principal 32' and 16', Violon 16', and the Octave 8'. All these stops may be drawn together when the organ has enough wind (and especially when the Pedal division has its own bellows). Sometimes one employs bright voices in the Pedal, such as the Octave 4' and 2' and perhaps Mixtures, too. If the organ does not have such stops, then one can bring manual registers into the Pedal through the use of the coupler. If several bright ranks are already found in the Pedal, then one does not need to use the coupler at all. The Posaune 32' and 16' along with the Trumpet and other reeds can be included in the *plenum*. Often the Posaune 16' is sufficient, however, especially in rapid passages where 16' stops work better than 32' stops.[23]

The advice of Mattheson and Adlung can be reduced to several principles:

In the manuals:

1. The Principal chorus (all pitches) and Mixtures are to be drawn, plus any other stops (including 16′) that add gravity or brightness to the total ensemble.

2. Reed stops are generally excluded from the manual *plenum*.

3. The *plenum* is concentrated in the sound produced on one manual (the *Hauptwerk* in most cases); the other manuals serve to add strength or brightness to the main manual through coupling.

In the Pedal:

1. The Principal chorus (all pitches) and Mixtures are to be drawn, plus any other stops that add gravity. Thirty-two-foot stops may be used if the music does not move too quickly.

2. Reed stops may be employed in the Pedal *plenum*.

3. The manual divisions should not be coupled to the Pedal division unless the latter is deficient in some respect.

On these general points most of Bach's German contemporaries agree. In the second half of the eighteenth century the concept of *organum plenum* began to change; more and more stops were added in order to increase the volume. This development foreshadows the nineteenth-century proclivity for an extremely loud, thick sound, an ideal that contrasts starkly with the more carefully balanced combinations of Bach's day.

All the Remaining Diverse Variations

The second category of registration included all the non-*plenum* possibilities. As Mattheson explained, these registrations were best realized through the use of different manuals and with softer "but nevertheless carefully selected stops." They encompassed an almost limitless variety of flute, string, and reed combinations, used soloistically on two or more manuals, or as a small ensemble on one. The variegated registrations were employed for *bicinia*, trios, chorale partitas, and chorale preludes of many types: duets, trios, canons, and pieces with an embellished melody or cantus firmus.

On rare occasions, Bach's German contemporaries, such as Johann Gottfried Walther, Daniel Magnus Gronau, or Georg Friedrich Kauffmann, wrote specific registrations into manuscripts or prints of their

chorale preludes.[24] From these examples—especially those in Kauffmann's *Harmonische Seelenlust musikalischer Gönner und Freunde* (Leipzig, 1733–1739), which includes 98 chorale preludes written in a
great variety of styles and often with detailed suggestions for registration[25]—we gain a glimpse of the imaginative way stops were employed
in the smaller combinations. For instance, Kauffmann's indications
show that the 16′ Fagott found on the *Hauptwerk* of many German
organs was often used, along with a Principal 8′ and Kleingedackt 4′
or similar stops, for the left-hand figuration in duets in which the
right hand had a cantus firmus, outlined with a Sesquialtera or a similarly bright sound. Such employment of the 16′ Fagott corresponds
with Bach's description of the stop's function[26] and with the indications passed down in his chorale prelude *Ein' feste Burg ist unser Gott*,
BWV 720 (see below). Unfortunately, such pieces of enlightening information appear but infrequently in eighteenth-century sources.

We can assume that Bach was extraordinarily imaginative in select-
ing colorful combinations, and it was probably this skill that C. P. E.
Bach alluded to when he said his father registered "in his own manner." But like his fellow German composers, Bach was reticent to
stipulate specific registers in the manuscripts of his non-*plenum* works.
In his personal copy of the Schübler Chorales, BWV 645–50, he indicated the pitches of the stops to be used.[27] And in *Ein' feste Burg ist
unser Gott*, the *Orgelbüchlein* chorale *Gottes Sohn ist kommen* (BWV 600),
and the opening movement of the Concerto in d (BWV 596), he
named exact stops.[28] Otherwise, he granted the choice to the performer, who might have a very different instrument at his disposal.

Again, one can see national traditions at work. In France, the regu-
larization of organs allowed the almost universal realization of the colorful registrations outlined by Nivers, F. Couperin, Clérambault, and
others. But in Germany, local peculiarities of instruments prevented
the codification of the smaller combinations. Instead of outlining a
uniform set of rules, as the French did, German theorists presented
sample combinations, adding that adjustments needed to be made according to what was available.[29] Seen in this context, Bach's decision to
leave the matter of small registrations open is quite understandable.

By contrast, Bach was very exacting when it came to the question of
one- or two-manual performance. He carefully marked pieces that
were to be played on two keyboards with expressions such as "a due
Manuale" or "a 2 Claviere." Because two-manual works involved idio-
syncratic writing—a melody highlighted on a second manual, duo or
trio texture, or extensive voice crossing—Bach wished to warn the

Liebster Jesu, wir sind hier, BWV 634
(Autograph; Berlin, DstB *P 283*

Prelude in E♭, BWV 552/1, mm. 29–43
(Original print of *Clavierübung* III)
PLATE 2

performer that the pieces should not, and often could not, be played on one manual. It is worth noting that the two-manual indications are not limited to Bach's mature years, when his notation became increasingly precise. They appear throughout his lifetime, from the very earliest chorale preludes[30] to the Schübler transcriptions and the "Great Eighteen" revisions of his final decade.

In instances where the distribution of the parts on two manuals might be ambiguous, Bach frequently added further clarifications. In *Allein Gott in der Höh sei Ehr*, BWV 663, for example, the subscript "a 2 Clav. e Pedale, Canto fermo in Tenore" not only apprises the performer of the structure of the piece but also indicates that the tenor is the voice to be outlined on a second keyboard. The subtitle of the *Orgelbüchlein* chorale *Liebster Jesu wir sind hier* (BWV 634), "in Canone alla Quinta a 2. Clav. & Ped.," points to a two-manual performance. But Bach added braces in front of the incipit to show that the upper two voices are to be taken on one keyboard, the alto and tenor on a second keyboard, and the bass on the pedal (see Plate 2, top).

This notational refinement is obscured in most modern editions, which transcribe the piece onto three staves without showing precisely how Bach differentiated the parts within the confines of a two-staff system.[31] While Bach allowed freedom in the choice of stops for "all the remaining diverse variations" of registration, he did not seem to permit license with regard to the use of one or two manuals. When two keyboards were necessary, a subtitle or braces alerted the player. If no such admonishment appeared, a one-manual performance appears to have been the assumed standard.

Manual Change in the Free Works

On the question of manual change in the free works, eighteenth-century treatises are of little help, for they do not discuss the matter. Fortunately, certain clues can be gleaned from the manuscripts of Bach's compositions themselves.

Among the free works, only two pieces are handed down with indications for manual change: the Prelude in E♭, BWV 552/1, and the "Dorian" Toccata in d, BWV 538/1. In the former, Bach used manual change for the two echo passages occuring at mm. 32–40 and mm. 111–19. He notated the point of transfer by the words *piano* and *forte*, a method he employed in the Italian Concerto, BWV 971, the French Ouverture, BWV 831,[32] and other two-keyboard works (see Plate 2, bottom). The terms *piano* and *forte* do not necessarily imply a strong contrast in dynamics, but signify a change from a main manual (on an organ, usually the *Hauptwerk*; on a harpsichord, usually the lower keyboard) to a secondary one.

In the "Dorian" Toccata Bach employed a more sophisticated system of notation. First, he used the words *Positiv* and *Oberwerk* to show where one should change keyboards. Second, in passages where the transition might be ambiguous, he indicated the exact point of transfer through the beaming of individual notes. In m. 13 of the Toccata, for instance, the broken beaming of the upper voice makes it clear that the transfer from the *Oberwerk* to the *Positiv* is to take place between the first and second sixteenth notes of the third beat (see Plate 3, top).

Finally, Bach frequently used braces at points of transfer to show precisely which parts were to be taken on the new manual. One sees these three notational devices—*Oberwerk–Positiv* indications, irregular beamings, and braces—throughout the many manuscript copies of the "Dorian" Toccata.[33] In m. 32 all three methods are used (see Plate 3, middle). The irregular beaming of the right-hand chords

Toccata in d ("Dorian"), BWV 538/1, mm. 13–14
(Manuscript of Michael Gotthard Fischer; Library of the School of Music,
Yale University, *LM 4839e*)

Toccata in d ("Dorian"), BWV 538/1, mm. 31½–33½
(Manuscript of Michael Gotthard Fischer; Library of the School of Music,
Yale University, *LM 4839e*)

Fugue in E♭ ("St. Anne"), BWV 552/2, mm. 35½–38½
(Original print of *Clavierübung* III)

PLATE 3

(♪♪♪♪♪♪♪♪ instead of ♫♫♫♫) reflects the breaking necessary to transfer from one keyboard to the other. Bach appears to have evolved this most elaborate and precise system of manual-change notation in connection with his Weimar concerto transcriptions, BWV 592–96,[34] though one can see the use of broken beamings and brackets to indicate a transfer of keyboards even in his earliest surviving organ manuscript, dating from before 1707, the autograph of *Wie schön leuchtet der Morgenstern*, BWV 739.[35] In using these indications, Bach left nothing to chance as far as manual change was concerned.

None of the other free works are handed down with manual-change indications in their texts. Does that mean that Bach intended all his free compositions except the Prelude in E♭ and the "Dorian" Toccata to be performed on one manual, *organum plenum*? There is no evidence to the contrary. In the Fugue in E♭, BWV 552/2, for instance, most performers transfer to a subsidiary keyboard for the central *manualiter* fugue (the 6/4 section) at the beginning of m. 37. But the notation does not suggest such a procedure (see Plate 3, bottom). If Bach had desired a manual change at this spot, why did he not use the indication *piano*, as he had done in the Prelude in E♭ (see Plate 2, bottom)? To say that he left the manual transfer to the discretion of the performer is to disregard the meticulous notation of the composer-supervised first edition.[36]

The Prelude in b, BWV 544/1, is a second case in point. Bach's autograph of 1727–31[37] calls for a *plenum* registration but gives no indications for a change of manuals. The Prelude contains three episodes, mm. 17–27, mm. 43–50, and mm. 73–79, which are traditionally performed on a secondary keyboard. Bach notated the beginning of what is frequently termed the first "manual episode," mm. 17–18, without any signs for manual change. If he had actually intended this section to be performed on a secondary keyboard, would he not have indicated the change through the word *piano*, through braces, or, at

EXAMPLE 1

the very least, through beaming? It has been demonstrated that he consistently used one or more of these methods when notating a two-manual work. A different beaming, for example, would have indi-cated a manual change at m. 17 (see Example 1).

A close look at the autograph of the piece shows that Bach deliber-ately avoided this reading (see Plate 4, top). Initially, he broke the beams of the first two notes of the alto voice in m. 17. He then changed his mind and extended the flags downward and to the right in order to join them with those of the next note. When he arrived at the paral-lel passage at m. 43, his mind was made up, and he connected the two critical notes without hesitation (see Plate 4, middle).

Prelude in b, BWV 544/1, mm. 16–17½
(Autograph; Rosenthal Collection, Oxford)

Prelude in b, BWV 544/1, mm. 42–43
(Autograph; Rosenthal Collection, Oxford)

Passacaglia and Fugue in c, BWV 582, mm. 165–72
(Manuscript of an anonymous copyist; Berlin, SPK *P 286*)

PLATE 4

Had Bach separated the flags in m. 17, the passage would have re-sembled m. 13 of the "Dorian" Toccata, where both the beaming of the notes and the word *Positiv* delineate a manual transfer. Since no such indications are found in the autograph of the Prelude in b, one must assume Bach deemed manual change unnecessary.

The Prelude in E♭ and the "Dorian" Toccata in d appear to have been very special free compositions. Undoubtedly modeled on the technique of the concerto transcriptions, they required two manuals. The rest of Bach's free works appear to be more conventional and seem to call for no more than a one-manual performance. This con-clusion parallels the accounts of Mattheson and others, who link the use of two or more keyboards only with non-*plenum* combinations.

Would the performance of most of Bach's free works on one manual become tedious? The composer himself provided the necessary vari-ety through well-planned textural changes. A striking example occurs in the Passacaglia and Fugue in c, BWV 582. At mm. 168–69 the varia-tions end, the fugue commences, and the texture thins abruptly, from five to two parts (see Plate 4, bottom). To transfer manuals or to switch registration at this point would be superfluous. Bach has done the work for the performer by drastically reducing the number of voices.[38] As the notation suggests and the absence of a double bar implies,[39] the music should proceed without interruption. So, too, in the Fugue in E♭, the Prelude in b, and other *plenum* free works. Bach has engi-neered the textural changes with exacting care. Are we to question the logic of his design?

Bach's Concert Programming

To summarize: The principal factor in Bach's registrational practice is the distinction between *organum plenum* and the smaller combinations. Free pieces and special types of chorale preludes were written for the former; chorale preludes, chorale partitas, trios, and duos were com-posed for the latter. When Bach concertized, he appears to have taken advantage of the contrasts inherent in these two registrational genres. Forkel described his programming as follows:

> When Johann Sebastian Bach seated himself at the organ when there was no divine service, which he was often requested to do, he used to choose some subject and to execute it in all the various forms of organ composition so that the subject constantly remained his material, even if he had played, without intermission, for two hours or more. First, he used this theme for a prelude and a fugue, with the full organ. Then

he showed his art of using the stops for a trio, a quartet, etc., always upon the same subject. Afterwards followed a chorale, the melody of which was playfully surrounded in the most diversified manner by the original subject, in three or four parts. Finally, the conclusion was made by a fugue, with the full organ, in which either another treatment only of the first subject predominated, or one or, according to its nature, two others were mixed with it.[40]

To judge from this account, Bach opened and closed his concerts with free works, *organum plenum*. In between, he played more modest pieces—trios, quartets,[41] chorale preludes, etc.—in order to demonstrate the "art of using the stops." Registrationally, the result was a well-balanced, aesthetically pleasing plan: a large, full *plenum*; followed by smaller, variegated combinations; followed by a concluding *plenum*. Bach obviously had the same symmetrical scheme in mind in *Clavierübung* III:

Bach's organ recitals (according to Forkel):
⟶ prelude and fugue (*organum plenum*)
    trios, quartets, etc.
    chorale preludes
⟶ fugue (*organum plenum*)

Clavierübung III:
⟶ Prelude in E♭ (*organum plenum*)
    chorale preludes
    duets
⟶ Fugue in E♭ (*organum plenum*)

In *Clavierübung* III the Prelude in E♭, BWV 552/1, and the Fugue in E♭, BWV 552/2, serve as "pro Organo pleno" framing pieces. Between them is an extended series of chorale preludes and duets—ideal vehicles for illustrating the "remaining diverse variations" of registration. In addition, three of the chorale preludes, carefully interspersed among the others,[42] require *organum plenum*. By inserting these *plenum* pieces into the middle of the *Clavierübung* III collection, Bach was able to explore the full gamut of chorale prelude registrations while maintaining the general structure of his organ concerts. His tasteful distribution of registrations, his felicitous ordering of genres, and his use of *plenum* free works as introductory and closing pieces are principles as valid for programming today as they were in the eighteenth century.

NOTES

This article first appeared as "Über Bachs Orgelregistrierpraxis," BJ 1981: 91–105. It is reprinted here, in translation and with several additions, by permission. The essay originated as a paper presented at Harvard University and the University of Nebraska-Lincoln. Gratitude is extended to Christoph Wolff and Ernest May for their helpful suggestions on a number of points.

1. BDok III, no. 801; translation from *Bach Reader*, p. 276.

2. Peters Edition, vol. I, Foreword, pp. ii–iii.

3. Charles-Marie Widor and Albert Schweitzer, *Johann Sebastian Bach— Complete Organ Works* (New York, 1912); Hermann Keller, *The Organ Works of Bach*, translated by Helen Hewitt (New York, 1967), esp. pp. 38–58.

4. Hans Klotz, *Pro Organo Pleno* (Wiesbaden, 1978); Thomas Harmon, *The Registration of J. S. Bach's Organ Works* (Buren, 1978). For criticisms of Harmon's volume see the review by George Stauffer, *NOTES* 34 (1979): 360–62.

5. For an extended discussion of Classical French registrations see Fenner Douglass, *The Language of the Classical French Organ* (New Haven, 1969).

6. Johann Mattheson, *Der vollkommene Capellmeister* (Hamburg, 1739), p. 467.

7. For a discussion of the fugue as a *plenum* genre see Hans Musch, "Von der Einheit der grossen Orgelfuge Johann Sebastian Bachs," *Musik und Kirche* 44 (1974): 267–79. The *plenum* registration of Bach's free preludes is discussed in George Stauffer, *The Organ Preludes of Johann Sebastian Bach* (Ann Arbor, 1980), pp. 155–59.

8. Friedrich Erhardt Niedt, *Handleitung zur Variation* (Hamburg, 1706), chap. XII.

9. Johann Adolf Scheibe, *Der Critische Musicus*, Tuesday, July 14, 1739, p. 159.

10. See BDok III, nos. 692–96.

11. Jacob Adlung, *Anleitung zu der musikalischen Gelahrtheit* (Erfurt, 1758), pp. 490–91.

12. See Dietrich Kilian, NBA IV/5–6 (*Präludien, Toccaten, Fantasien, und Fugen*), KB (1978), vol. I; and Stauffer, *The Organ Preludes of Johann Sebastian Bach*, pp. 155–57.

13. See Yoshitake Kobayashi, *Franz Hauser und seine Bach-Handschriftensammlung* (Göttingen, 1973), p. 72.

14. Johann Mattheson, *Grosse-General-Bass-Schule* (Hamburg, 1731), p. 34. Mattheson gave as the sixth requirement for the 1725 *Organisten-Probe* at the Hamburger Dom: "To conclude with a quickly prepared Ciacona on the following groundbass, played with the full organ."

15. Mattheson, *Der vollkommene Capellmeister*, p. 474.

16. Berlin, DStB *P 271*, pp. 58–61.

17. Ibid., pp. 98–99.

18. Christoph Wolff, *Der stile antico in der Musik Johann Sebastian Bachs* (Weisbaden, 1968).

19. The two other parts of the *Clavierübung* III *pedaliter* setting of the Kyrie—*Kyrie, Gott Vater in Ewigkeit*, BWV 669, and *Christe, aller Welt Trost*, BWV 670—also require a full registration. They do not fall into the strict *plenum* category, however, because they are set for two manuals (see comments below).

20. An obvious question springs to mind: Why did Bach fail to label many chorale preludes intended for *organum plenum*? The answer probably lies in

the purpose of the pieces. Works earmarked for a broad audience—*Clavierü-bung* III chorales or the "Great Eighteen" Collection (if indeed Bach was pre-paring it for publication)—had to be labeled more explicitly than did works used solely within the Bach circle, such as the *Orgelbüchlein*. In the latter case, Bach could have passed along the "pro Organo pleno" instructions orally.

21. This discussion of the *plenum* registration is drawn from Stauffer, *The Organ Preludes of Johann Sebastian Bach*, pp. 159–61.

22. Mattheson, *Der vollkommene Capellmeister*, p. 467.

23. Jacob Adlung, *Musica Mechanica Organoedi* (Berlin, 1768), pp. 169 and 171.

24. These registrations are discussed at length in Gotthold Frotscher, *Ge-schichte des Orgelspiels und der Orgelkomposition*, 3d ed. (Berlin, 1966), pp. 605–14 and 1028–32; and to a lesser extent in Peter Williams, *The European Or-gan, 1450–1850* (London, 1966; reprint, Bloomington, Indiana, 1978), pp. 143–45.

25. Kauffmann was tied closely with Bach. The two competed for the va-cant Thomaskantor post in Leipzig in 1722, and it appears that three of Kauffmann's cantatas (*Komm, du freudenvoller Geist; Nicht uns, Herr;* and *Die Liebe Gottes ist ausgegossen*) were performed by Bach in Leipzig a few years later. See Joshua Rifkin, "Georg Friedrich Kauffman," in *The New Grove Dic-tionary of Music and Musicians*, edited by Stanley Sadie, vol. 9, p. 831. *Harmo-nische Seelenlust* was undoubtedly known to Bach, for it was engraved in Leipzig by the workshop of Johann Gottfried Krügner, who also worked on Bach's *Clavierübung* I and III. See Gregory G. Butler, "Leipziger Stecher in Bachs Originaldrucken," BJ 1980: 9–26.

26. "It is useful for all kinds of new ideas ('inventionibus') and sounds very fine in concerted music," Bach stated in his suggestions for improving the organ in Blasiuskirche in Mühlhausen in 1708. See BDok I, no. 83.

27. See Christoph Wolff, "Bach's Personal Copy of the Schübler Chorales," in this volume.

28. The stop indications in *Ein' feste Burg*, handed down via a secondary source, may not stem from Bach. Even if they do not, they are important, since they reflect contemporary registrational practices.

29. See, for instance, the suggestions set forth by Mattheson in *Der vollkom-mene Capellmeister*, pp. 467–68; Adlung, in *Musica Mechanica Organoedi*, vol. I, pp. 161–62; or Johann Friedrich Agricola in Friedrich Wilhelm Marpurg's *Historisch-Kritische Beyträge zur Aufnahme der Musik* (Berlin, 1758), vol. III, sec. 6, pp. 503–504.

30. The autograph of *Wie schön leuchtet der Morgenstern*, BWV 739 (Berlin, SPK *P 488*), which dates from before 1707, carries the phrase "a 2 Clav: Ped.," for example.

31. Like his middle-German contemporaries, Bach used two-staff notation for all organ works except trios. This method saved paper and reduced the number of page turns.

32. For facsimiles see NBA V/2.

33. Though the autograph of the "Dorian" Toccata has disappeared, it is safe to assume that the indications for manual change stem from Bach. The consistent appearance of the indications in the surviving sources; their close ties with the notation of the concerto transcriptions, BWV 592–96; and the unique structure of the Toccata itself support this supposition.

34. See the facsimiles of the concertos in NBA IV/8. The notational simi-larity between the "Dorian" Toccata and the last movement of the Concerto in

d, BWV 596, which survives in Bach's autograph (Berlin, SPK *P 330*), is especially striking.

35. See the facsimile (Tafel 7) in Georg von Dadelsen's *Beiträge zur Chronologie der Werke Johann Sebastian Bachs* (Trossingen, 1958). I am indebted to Russell Stinson for bringing this point to my attention.

36. Bach worked closely with the printer of *Clavierübung* III, Balthasar Schmid of Nürnberg. He made several of the *Stich-Vorlagen* for the edition and later added handwritten corrections to copies of the print. See Manfred Tessmer, NBA IV/4, KB.

37. Oxford: Rosenthal Collection.

38. By happy coincidence, Marie-Claire Alain's essay "Why an Acquaintance with Early Organs Is Essential for Playing Bach" makes precisely the same point about Bach's careful control of texture, using the Fugue in g, BWV 542/2, as an illustration. See pp. 51–52 of this volume.

39. The double bar between the Passacaglia and the Fugue found in modern editions does not appear in any eighteenth-century source. Double bars are also lacking between the three sections of the Fugue in Eb, BWV 552/2 (see Plate 3, bottom) and the Fantasia in G, BWV 572, in the original source materials. In these three instances, modern editors have sought to impose a division not advocated by Bach.

40. Johann Nicolaus Forkel, *Über Johann Sebastian Bachs Leben, Kunst, und Kunstwerke* (Leipzig, 1802), p. 40. Translation from *Bach Reader*, pp. 315–16.

41. Quartets for organ were quite common in the French repertoire, where they were considered a virtuoso vehicle for displaying an organist's registrational and digital mastery. These pieces were commonly written for three manuals and pedal, with one hand (usually the right) playing on two keyboards at the same time. One well-known example was published by Louis Marchand (whom Bach supposedly vanquished in 1717) in his *Première suite de pièces d'orgue du premier ton* (1732). The collection is reprinted in *Archives des Maîtres de l'orgue*.

42. The ordering of the chorale preludes in *Clavierübung* III is discussed in Christoph Wolff, "Ordnungsprinzipien in den Originaldrucken Bachscher Werke," in *Bach-Interpretationen*, edited by Martin Geck (Göttingen, 1969), pp. 144–67.

ROBERT L. MARSHALL

Organ or "Klavier"?

Instrumental Prescriptions in the Sources of Bach's Keyboard Works

As everyone knows, during the Baroque era the various keyboard instruments, including the organ, largely shared a common repertoire.
Most standard discussions of early keyboard music in fact begin with
a statement to that effect. For example, we read at the start of Willi
Apel's *The History of Keyboard Music to 1700*:

> The word *keyboard* in the title of this book . . . suits our purpose not
> only because of its brevity but also because it eliminates the need to
> differentiate between the organ and other keyboard instruments—a
> decision that is simply not feasible for most types of early keyboard
> music. . . .[1]

With respect to the music of Johann Sebastian Bach, however, musicians and scholars have never been comfortable with this information
and have suspected that the practical reality in Bach's case could not
have been so casual. Since at least the beginning of the nineteenth
century until quite recently, all serious editions of Bach's keyboard
music—publications that include both the *Bach-Gesellschaft* edition
and the *Neue Bach-Ausgabe*—have proceeded on the assumption (usually unstated) that it is not only possible but altogether appropriate to
separate this repertoire rather strictly into two discrete parts: one consisting of "organ" music, the other of music for the string keyboard
instruments. The scholarly literature, too, has approached the repertoire in largely the same way, i.e., with separate discussions of each
corpus of works.

Nor has it been difficult to devise simple rules to help decide in which category a given work belonged. Compositions with an independent pedal part (especially one with an obbligato character) or that make use of liturgical material (i.e., a chorale melody) are normally classified as organ works. Conversely, keyboard compositions apparently lacking a pedal part or chorale-derived material are assumed to have been conceived for the harpsichord or the clavichord. This division has the double virtue of being not only easy to implement but also eminently useful in that it has satisfied the very practical needs of the most-interested constituencies—organists and other keyboard players.

These criteria, in fact, are already implicit in the Obituary of 1754,[2] where the pertinent "unpublished works of the late Bach" are grouped as follows:

> 5) Many free preludes, fugues, and similar pieces for organ, with obbligato pedal
> 6) Six trios for organ with obbligato pedal
> 7) Many preludes on chorales for the organ
> 8) A book of short preludes on most of the hymns of the church for the organ
> 9) Twice twenty-four preludes and fugues, in all keys, for the clavier
> 10) Six toccatas for the clavier
> 11) Six suites for the same
> 12) Six more of the same, somewhat shorter

And Forkel, in his biography, not only devoted separate chapters to "Bach the Clavier Player" (chap. III) and "Bach the Organist" (chap. IV), but, in his own list of works, expanded upon the separation of the two repertoires already found in the Obituary. Moreover, in his introduction to the organ pieces, he emphasized the indispensability of the pedals, literally regarding them as the "essential part of the organ."[3]

The formal and official codification of the subdivision of Bach's keyboard repertoire is found in the pages of the *Bach-Werke Verzeichnis*, the BWV, where the "Works for Organ" occupy numbers 525 through 771, the "Works for Klavier" numbers 772 to 994. (Throughout this study, too, the modern German term *Klavier* is used to denote the string keyboard instruments only, as opposed to the eighteenth-century *clavier*, which, like the English, *keyboard*, embraces all keyboard instruments, including the organ.)

A brief scanning of these sections of the BWV will show that a discrete and systematic classification was not without its difficulties. Indeed, for the very first entry among the organ works, the six sonatas, BWV 525–30, the setting has been qualified as "Orgel. In erster Linie für Pedalclavichord oder Pedalcembalo geschrieben." The Fantasia and Fugue in a, BWV 561 (now considered to be a spurious work, perhaps by J. C. Kittel), although listed in the BWV among the organ works, carries the indication "Pedalcembalo (Orgel)". Similarly indecisive designations are offered for the Fugue in c, BWV 575: "Pedalcembalo (Orgel)"; the (presumably) spurious fugues in G, BWV 576 and BWV 577: "Orgel (Pedalcembalo?)"; the Passacaglia in c, BWV 582: "Orgel oder Cembalo"; the Pastorale in F, BWV 590: "Orgel (Pedalcembalo)"; and even the chorale partitas on *Christ, der du bist der helle Tag*, BWV 766: "Pedalflügel (Orgel)"; *O Gott, du frommer Gott*, BWV 767: "Orgel (Pedalflügel?)"; and *Ach, was soll ich Sünder machen*, BWV 770: "Orgel (Pedalflügel)."

The "Works for Klavier" evidently presented fewer ambiguities of this kind. Nonetheless, the four duets from *Clavierübung* III, BWV 802–805, are designated in the BWV for "Klavier (Orgel?)"; the Fugue in C, BWV 946, for "Klavier (Pedalcembalo)"; the Fugue in A, BWV 949, for "Klavier (Pedalflügel)"; and, finally, the Capriccio in E, "In honorem Joh. Christoph Bachii," BWV 993, for "Klavier (Pedalcembalo)".

The main reason for Schmieder's occasional uncertainty is not difficult to find. As his curiously varying formulations in these questionable instances remind us, string keyboard instruments—especially clavichords but also harpsichords—as well as organs could be equipped with pedals. But what could have prompted Schmieder to weigh this possibility seriously enough to suggest it in no fewer than nineteen instances, when he is willing to entertain the opposite alternative—the performance on the organ of a "Klavier" work requiring only manual(s)—only once: in the special case of the four duets, BWV 802–805? This tendency is particularly strange since the option of writing an organ work without an obbligato pedal part was readily available for any Baroque composer. Indeed, the notion that performance on the organ of a number of Bach's compositions calling for manual(s) alone was not only tolerated but actually preferred—i.e., that such compositions were perhaps conceived in the first instance as organ works—has not received much serious consideration.

In view of the common repertoire tradition as well as the Baroque era's uninhibited practice of transcribing virtually any work from one medium to another, it is difficult to imagine that Bach would have objected to organ renditions of most of his keyboard compositions. But this proposition cannot be proven. Moreover, there is reason to believe that he was more sensitive than many of his contemporaries to the matter of scoring. It is striking, for example, that in his chamber music he consistently avoided such typical formulations of the period as "Violino ò traverso." If it could be demonstrated that some of Bach's compositions for manuals alone were probably conceived as organ works, that fact should be of considerable interest not only to scholars but even more so to organists and keyboard players.

Heinz Lohmann is apparently the first to take advantage of the practical implications of the common repertoire tradition as it affects Johann Sebastian Bach.[4] In the Short Afterword to his edition of the complete organ works for Breitkopf und Härtel, dated "Summer, 1979" (and reproduced identically in vols. 1–3, i.e., the volumes devoted to the preludes, fantasias, toccatas, fugues, and single pieces), Lohmann remarks:

> [T]he attempt to recover many *manualiter* works for the organ—and also for the Positive—has substantially expanded [the] range [of this edition] in comparison with other organ editions of the past and present. That this recovery could only be achieved for a selection of works is self-evident.

Lohmann has in fact carried out his selection with few restraints, evidently guided by little more than personal taste and inclination. His edition includes about 50 compositions hitherto regarded as belonging to the province of "Klaviermusik." The "new" works are drawn chiefly from the larger and smaller preludes, toccatas, fantasies, and fugues. (Almost all the compositions in vol. 3 are new to editions of Bach's organ works.) But the edition also includes several of the concerto arrangements for manuals alone and, more surprisingly, such compositions as the Ouverture in F, BWV 820; the *Aria variata alla maniera italiana*, BWV 989; and even the *Capriccio sopra la lontananza del suo fratello dilettissimo*, BWV 992.

In adopting this extremely "loose" approach, it seems that Lohmann has refrained only from recruiting compositions whose identification as works for string keyboard instrument is by now apparently unshakeable: the *Well-Tempered Clavier*; the Two- and Three-Part Inventions; the French and English Suites; and Parts I, II, and IV of the *Clavierübung*.[5] Lohmann's approach to Bach's repertoire is not only bold but clearly justified by early eighteenth-century practice, although it is not entirely satisfying in its reliance on personal taste and preference. One wonders whether there may not be more-objective criteria on which to base the inclusion or exclusion of particular compositions from a conscientious edition of Bach's organ works.

Original Instrumental Designations

Perhaps the most reliable source of Bach's intentions with regard to instrumentation are in the headings or on the title pages of the primary sources: the autographs and the original editions prepared under the composer's supervision. Contrary to the impression often conveyed by the secondary literature, there are in fact a respectable number of keyboard compositions by Bach preserved in such sources (see Tables 1 and 2).

It is significant that Bach has usually troubled to provide some kind of instrumental designation along with the title or the genre indication of a composition. But it is admittedly disappointing that many of these designations, at least at first glance, are ambiguous. They usually do not contain explicit prescriptions, such as "pro organo" or "per il cembalo," but are as likely to read "a 2 Clav. et Pedal," "pedaliter," "manualiter," or, simply, "Clavier." These formulations, however, may be more informative than would at first appear. But it is advisable to proceed cautiously, even if that at times entails belaboring the obvious.

Organo; Cembalo; Clavessin

The almost invariable inclusion of a reference to the pedals in any original heading explicitly mentioning "Orgel" or "Organo," as in the phrases "Organo con/cum Pedal(e)" or "Organo pedaliter," certainly suggests (as Forkel argued) that Bach must have regarded the pedals as an "essential" part of the organ. But it also suggests that organists of the time expected to be informed (or forewarned) whether an organ composition contained an obbligato pedal part. Otherwise such phrases would be tautological. At all events, it is safer to assume that Bach had reason to add such written qualifications. (The only instances in which he apparently failed to mention the pedals in connection with an "Organo" heading are the autograph of the *Fantasia pro Organo* in C, BWV 573, preserved in the 1722 *Clavierbüchlein* for Anna Magdalena Bach; and the *Praeludium pro Organo pleno*, BWV 552/1, printed at the beginning of *Clavierübung* III. However the indications "Ped." and "Pedal" respectively are present in the first measures of these works.) As for the harpsichord, it is not surprising, but worth noting, that no Bach autograph or original print specifying "Clavessin/Clavecin," "Cembalo," or "Clavicymbel/Clavicimbal" contains an independent pedal part.[6] And, from the titles of *Clavierübung* II and IV, it seems safe to conclude that Bach normally had to reckon with a single-manual harpsichord.

TABLE 1

**Work Headings in the Primary Sources
of Bach's Organ Compositions***

BWV	Heading	Source	Date	Comment
525–30	Sonata 1[−6] à 2 Clav. et Pedal	*P 271*	c.1730	Autograph
535	Preludio con Fuga per il Organo	Lpz *III. 8.7*	c.1740–50	Apograph with autograph additions
535a	Praeludium cum Fuga— ex Gb. Pedaliter	*Mus. ms. 40644*	c.1707	Autograph fragment
541	Praeludium pro Organo con Pedal: obligat:	SPK (1983)	c.1733–42	Autograph
544	Praeludium pro Organo cum pedale obligato (Title page)	Private collection	c.1727–31	Autograph
	Praeludium in Organo pleno, pedal: (Heading)	Private collection	c.1727–31	Autograph
545	Praeludium pro Organo cum Pedale obligato (Title page)	Lost	?	Autograph
	Praeludium in Organo pleno pedaliter (Heading)	Lost	?	Autograph
548	Praeludium pedaliter pro Organo	*P 274*	c.1727–31	Partial autograph (to m.21 of Fugue; thereafter: Kellner)
550	Praeludium pedaliter	*P 1210*	?	Apograph with autograph additions
552/1	Praeludium pro Organo pleno	*Clavier-übung* III	1739	Original edition
552/2	Fuga à 5. con pedale. pro Organo pleno	*Clavier-übung* III	1739	Original edition
562/1	Fantasia pro Organo. a. 5 Vocum, cum pedali obligato	*P 490*	c.1720–30	Autograph

TABLE 1 (continued)

BWV	Heading	Source	Date	Comment
562/2	Fuga. a 5	*P 490*	c.1745?	Autograph fragment
573	Fantasia pro Organo	*P 224*	c.1722–23	Autograph
596	Concerto a 2 Clav: & Pedale	*P 330*	c.1713	Autograph
599–644	Orgel-Büchlein Worinne einem anfahenden Organisten Anleitung gegeben wird . . . sich im *Pedal studio* zu *habili-tiren*, indem . . . das Pedal gantz *obligat trac-tiret* wird.	*P 283*	1713 ff.	Autograph title added during Köthen period
645–50	Sechs Chorale von ver-schiedener Art auf einer Orgel mit 2 Clavieren und Pedal. . . .	Print	c.1748	Original edition
651–65	[From the "Seventeen Great Chorales"]	*P 271*	1740–48?	Autograph
651	Fantasia . . . in organo pleno			
652	alio modo à 2 Clav. et Ped			
653	a 2 Clav. e Pedal			
654	a 2 Clav. e Pedal			
655	Trio a 2 Clav. e Pedal			
656	Versus. manualiter [3rd verse:] Pedal			
657	a 2 Clav. et Ped.			
658	[over Staff:] Ped.			
659	a 2 Clav. et Ped.			
660	a due Bassi è canto fermo			
661	in organo pleno. Canto fermo in Pedal			
662	a 2 Clav. et Ped.			
663	a 2 Clav. et Ped.			
664	Trio . . . a 2 Clav. et Ped			
665	sub communione . . . pedaliter			*pedaliter* possi-bly added later
669–89, etc.	Dritter Theil der Clavier-Übung bestehend in	*Clavier-übung* III	1739	Original edition

BWV	Heading	Source	Date	Comment
	verschiedenen Vorspielen über die Catechismus- und andere Gesaenge, vor die Orgel			
669	à 2 Clav. et Ped			
670	à 2 Clav. et Ped			
671	a 5 Canto fermo in Bassi cum Organo Pleno			
672	alio modo manualiter			
675	Canto fermo in alto			
676	à 2 Clav. et Pedal			
677	. . . manualiter			
678	à 2 Clav. et Ped.			
679	. . . manualiter			
680	In Organo pleno con Pedali			
681	. . . manualiter			
682	à 2 Clav. et Pedal			
683	alio modo manualiter			
684	à 2 Clav. è Canto fermo in Pedal			
685	alio modo manualiter			
686	à 6 in Organo pleno con Pedale doppio			
687	à 4 alio modo manualiter			
688	à 2 Clav. e Canto fermo in Pedal			
689	à 4 manualiter			
691	Wer nur den lieben Gott läßt walten	Yale: (Clavierbüchlein WFB)	c.1720	Autograph
728	Jesus mein Zuversicht	P 224	c.1722–23	Autograph
739	Wie schön leuchtet . . . a 2 Clav. Ped.	P 488	c.1705?	Autograph
753	Jesu meine Freude	Yale: (Clavierbüchlein)	c.1720	Autograph
764	[No heading]	P 488	c.1705?	Autograph
769	Einige canonische Veraenderungen . . . vor die Orgel mit 2. Clavieren | und dem Pedal	Print	c.1747?	Original edition

TABLE 2 (continued)

BWV	Heading	Source	Date	Comment
769a	Vom Himmel hoch . . . [Var. 1, 2, 4:] a 2 Clav. et Pedal	*P 271*	c.1748?	Autograph

*See the source descriptions in the pertinent *Kritische Berichte* of the NBA and *Bach-Dokumente* I; also George Stauffer, *The Organ Preludes of Johann Sebastian Bach* (Ann Arbor, 1980), Appendix I; and Peter Williams, *The Organ Music of J. S. Bach* (Cambridge, 1980–1984), vols. 1 and 2.

Pedal Clavichord; Pedal Harpsichord

The consistent presence of pedal indications in the primary sources of Bach's keyboard compositions explicitly for organ and, conversely, their consistent absence in the primary sources of works explicitly for harpsichord would seem to support a number of corollaries: for example, that compositions with pedal indications but no instrumental designation per se—e.g., the isolated *pedaliter* indication in BWV 535a or, far more common, the prescription "a 2 Clav. e(t) Ped(al)" alone— were in fact intended for the organ and only the organ. There is absolutely no evidence that they were intended for the pedal harpsichord or pedal clavichord. These instruments are not mentioned in the original sources for any Bach compositions or in any authentic Bach document.[7] Much has been made of a statement in a document dated November 11, 1750, shortly after the death of J. S. Bach, to the effect that he had once given his son Johann Christian "3. Clavire nebst Pedal" (translated in *The Bach Reader* as "3 claviers with a set of pedals").[8] To assume automatically that the formulation must have been synonymous with "3 Pedalcembali"[9] is dangerous, since it seems most unlikely that Bach would have possessed three complete pedal harpsichords and given them all to the same son. It is far more likely that he had once owned, in addition to the various clavecins mentioned in chapter 6 of the Estate Catalogue of July 28, 1750,[10] three *claviers*, i.e., manuals (perhaps the otherwise unmentioned clavichords; see below), along with a set of pedals that could be played together with one (or more?) of the manuals in the manner described by Jakob Adlung in his *Musica mechanica Organoedi*.[11]

In any case, it seems that pedal harpsichords and clavichords served primarily as practice instruments,[12] on which a keyboard player not only practiced pedal technique but also prepared compositions that were ultimately to be performed on a full-sized pedal organ, no doubt in a church. As for Bach's use of the contraption, Forkel reports in chapter 3 of his biography that the composer used it for such private purposes as sight reading ensemble pieces at the keyboard(s) and improvising upon them.[13]

2 Clav. et Pedal; Pedaliter

There is ample evidence that Bach regarded the designation "2 Clav. e(t) Ped(al)" as a synonym for the (full-sized) organ. The title page of the Schübler Chorales mentions an "Orgel mit 2 Clavieren und Pedal," as do numerous headings of the individual chorale settings in *Clavierübung* III, the title page of which specifies "vor die Orgel." Also, the surviving autograph scores for the early chorale prelude *Wie schön leuchtet uns der Morgenstern*, BWV 739, whose heading reads "a 2 Clav. Ped.," and the "Concerto a 2 Clav: & Pedale," BWV 596, both contain the organ registration indications "BR" and "Brustpos." (i.e., *Brustwerk, Brustpositiv*), "O" and "ObW" (i.e., *Oberwerk*), and, in the case of BWV 596, "R" (i.e., *Rückpositiv*). It should be recalled, too, that even the Trio Sonatas, BWV 525–30, "a 2 Clav. et Pedal"—the works that have been suggested as candidates for the pedal harpsichord most frequently and most seriously (as, for example, in the BWV citation)—were catalogued as early as 1754, in the Obituary, as organ compositions.[14]

The use of the term *pedaliter* alone—i.e., unattached to an organ prescription—is found in a Bach autograph only once: in the pre-1707 version of the Prelude and Fugue in g, BWV 535a, preserved in the *Möllersche Handschrift*, Berlin, SPK, *Mus. ms. 40644*. Confirmation for the view that here again Bach could have had only the organ in mind (not that there was ever much doubt), is provided by a manuscript containing the revised form of the work, BWV 535 (Leipzig, MB *III.8.7*). The presence of autograph entries in the manuscript also lends the authority of a primary source to the title page, which reads, "Preludio con Fuga per il Organo."[15] *Pedaliter*, in any case, was a very common designation in the late seventeenth and early eighteenth century for North German organ works requiring obbligato pedals; for example, in the compositions of Scheidemann, Tunder, and Buxtehude.[16] In fact, of the presumed organ works in the *Möllersche Hand-*

TABLE 2

Work Headings in the Primary Sources of Bach's "Klavier" Compositions*

BWV	Heading	Source	Date	Comment
772–801	[No general title]	Yale *Cla-vierbüch-lein*	c.1722–23	Autograph
772–86	Praeambulum 1 [−15] (Headings)			Partial auto-graph
787–801	Fantasia 1[−15] (Headings)			Autograph
772–801	Auffrichtige Anleitung, Wormit denen Liebhabern des *Clavires* . . . eine deüt-liche Art gezeiget wird . . . eine *cantable* Art im Spielen zu erlangen	*P 610*	1723	Autograph
772–87	Inventio 1 [−15] (Headings)	*P 610*	1723	Autograph
788–801	Sinfonia 1[−15] (Headings)	*P 610*	1723	Autograph
802–805	Duetto I[−IV]	*Clavier-übung* III	1739	Original edition
814	Suite pour le Clavessin	*P 224*	1722	Autograph
815	Suite ex Dis pour le Clavessin	*P 224*	1722	Autograph
816	Suite pour le Clavessin ex G♮	*P 224*	1722	Autograph
825–30	Clavier Ubung be-stehend in Praeludien, Allemanden, Cou-ranten, Sarabanden, Giquen, Menuetten, und andern Galan-terien	*Clavier-übung* I	1731 (1726–30)	Original edition
	[Individual compositions:] Partita I[−VI]			
827	[No heading]	*P 225*	1725	Autograph
830	[No heading]	*P 225*	1725	Autograph

BWV	Heading	Source	Date	Comment
831a	Ouverture pour le Clavesin	*P 226*	c.1730	Apograph with autograph heading
971, 831	Zweyter Theil der Clavier Ubung . . . vor ein Clavicymbel mit zweyen Manualen	*Clavier-übung* II	1735	Original edition
846–69	Das Wohl*temperirte Clavier*, oder *Praeludia*, und Fugen durch alle *Tone* und *Semitonia* . . .	*P 415*	1722–c.1740	Autograph
870–93	[*Well-Tempered Clavier* II: No title page]	London BL Add. 35021	c.1738–41	Partially autograph
886	Fuga ex Gis dur	*P 274*	1730s?	Autograph
906/1	Fantasia per il Cembalo	Bethlehem Bach Choir	1726–31	Autograph
906/1–2	[No heading]	Dresden LB 2405-T-52	c.1735–40	Autograph fragment
924	Praeambulum 1	Yale *Clavierbüchlein*	1720	Autograph
930	Praeambulum	Yale *Clavierbüchlein*	1720–22	Autograph
953	Fuga à 3	Yale *Clavierbüchlein*	c.1724	Autograph
988	Clavier Ubung bestehend in einer ARIA mit verschiedenen Veraenderungen vors Clavicimbal mit 2 Manualen. . . .	*Clavier-übung* [IV]	c.1742	Original edition
991	Air	*P 224*	1722	Autograph
994	Applicatio	Yale *Clavierbüchlein*	1720	Autograph

---

*See the source descriptions in the pertinent *Kritische Berichte* of the NBA and *Bach-Dokumente* I, as well as in the various published facsimile editions.

schrift with any instrumental designations at all, five carry the *pedaliter* designation. (In addition to BWV 535a, they are the Prelude and Fugue in C, BWV 531; the Prelude and Fugue in d, BWV 549a; and Nikolaus Bruhns, Preludes in G and e. One also finds "con Pedale" for a Prelude and Fugue in A by Buxtehude, and "2 Clav. con Ped." for BWV 739.) None make specific reference to "organo."[17] In sum, the proposition entertained, if not quite advocated, in the pages of the BWV that any composition of Johann Sebastian Bach's could have been seriously intended for—as distinct from merely tolerated on—a pedal harpsichord or clavichord is surely nothing but a red herring.

When we attempt to determine the instrument(s) Bach had in mind for his keyboard compositions lacking obbligato pedal parts the difficulties multiply. We have only been able to establish so far that there are no pedal parts in any of Bach's compositions explicitly for harpsichord (i.e., "cembalo" or "clavecin"). Can anything more useful be learned beyond this not very surprising fact?

Clavichord

The clavichord is never mentioned in any original or early sources of Bach's keyboard music, nor—despite Forkel's well-known claim in chapter 3 of his biography that Bach "liked best to play upon the clavichord"—is the instrument mentioned in the catalogue of his estate.[18] Forkel does go on to say in the same context, though, that Bach "considered the clavichord as the best instrument for *study* and, in general, for *private* musical entertainment [emphasis added]."[19] The tacit implication of this remark is, at the least, that Bach did not regard the clavichord as the "best instrument" for his more-ambitious keyboard compositions. Indeed, Johann Gottfried Walther, in the entry "clavicordo" in his *Musikalisches Lexikon* (p. 169) notes that the instrument "is, so to speak, for all players the first grammar," that is, a "primer"[20]—in effect, a practice instrument, perhaps not substantially different in function from the domestic pedal board instruments. (This usage may be the reason that the pedal clavichord was more common than the pedal harpsichord at the time.[21] It also lends strength to the suspicion, already expressed above, that the "3. Clavire nebst Pedal" Bach gave to Johann Christian were, in all likelihood, so many clavichords, along with a pedal board.)

Manualiter

There can be little doubt that Bach had the organ in mind for the eight chorale settings in *Clavierübung* III that both lack pedals and are specifically marked *manualiter*. Not only does the title page of the collection specify the organ in connection with the "various preludes on the Catechism and other hymns" but its internal ordering—along with the occasional addition of an "alio modo" indication (in *Kyrie, Gott Vater in Ewigkeit*, BWV 672; *Vater unser im Himmelreich*. BWV 683; *Christ, unser Herr, zum Jordan kam*, BWV 685; and *Aus tiefer Not schrei' ich zu dir*, BWV 687)—makes clear that the pieces were offered as alternatives to the setting(s) of the same chorales "a 2 Clav. et Pedal." Furthermore, since in Bach's usage, keyboard works specifically intended for harpsichord have no pedal parts (almost by definition, we might say), the only meaning the *manualiter* indication could have had (beyond mere redundancy) would be in connection with organ rendition. That is, under normal circumstances the term must have been the *de facto* equivalent of an organ indication. If so—unfortunately Walther does not include entries for *manualiter* or *pedaliter* in his dictionary—then the presence of the term in reliable Bach sources could be taken as *prima facie* evidence that the compositions were conceived in the first instance as organ works.

The Toccatas, BWV 910–16

Apart from *Clavierübung* III, the *manualiter* indication appears in the heading of only one other primary Bach source: the autograph of the three-strophe chorale setting *O Lamm Gottes unschuldig*, BWV 656, from the "Great Eighteen Collection." (The third strophe, or verse, calls for "Pedal.") But the term does appear in a few early, if nonautograph, Bach sources. Many of them—such as the *Andreas-Bach-Buch*, Johann Peter Kellner's voluminous miscellany (Berlin, SPK, *P 804*), and a Preller manuscript (Berlin, SPK *P 1082*)—originated either within or reassuringly close to Bach's own circle.[22] Most significantly, the compositions involved are virtually all confined to a single genre, the toccata, and indeed include all the surviving "Klavier" toccatas, BWV 910–16 (see Table 3).[23] The clear implication is that the "Klavier" toccatas must have been intended by Bach for the organ. And there is evidence, apart from the presence of the *manualiter* indications, to support this assertion. Table 4 shows the ranges of the principal instruments at Bach's disposal throughout his career.[24]

TABLE 3

Representative Early Sources of Bach's Keyboard Toccatas
(by Key)

Key	BWV	Heading	Source	Comment
C	564	Toccata ex C♮. pedaliter	P 286	Copyist: Kellner; range: to d″
c	911	Toccata C♭. Manualiter	ABB*	Copyist: Hauptschreiber
D	912a	Toccata ex D fis	Mus. ms. 40644	Copyist: Hauptschreiber
D	912	Toccata. Manualiter del . . . Bach. Organista	P 289	Anonymous copyist; 2d half of 18th century
d	565	Toccata Con Fuga: pedaliter. ex d♯ [sic]	P 595	Copyist: Ringk
d	538	Toccata con Fuga D♭.	P 803	Copyist: Walther
d	913	Toccata Prima. ex Clave D♭ manualiter	P 281	Copyist: Joh. Christoph Georg Bach?
e	914	Toccata ex E♭ manualiter	Private collection, Germany	Copyist: H. N. Gerber
F	540	Toccata col pedale obligato	P 803	Copyists: J. T. Krebs, 540/1; J. L. Krebs, 540/2
f♯	910	Toccata ex Fis. Manualiter	ABB	Copyist: Hauptschreiber
G	916	Toccata. Manualiter	ABB	Copyist: Hauptschreiber (and Nebenschreiber)
g	915	Toccata manualiter in G mol	P 1082	Copyist: Preller

Andreas-Bach-Buch

In his study of the compass of Bach's "Klavier" works, Alfred Dürr points out that in the Toccata in d, BWV 913 (at m. 89), and the Toccata in g, BWV 915 (at m. 186), B♭₁ has been conspicuously avoided; as has d‴ in the Toccata in G, BWV 916, (at m. 134; i.e., movement 3, m. 54).[25] That is, at these points in the compositions the logical continuation of a sequential pattern has been broken, evidently because the composer was constrained by the compass limitations of his instrument. Apart from such adjustments, the keyboard ranges found in the Toccatas, BWV 910–16, are as shown in Table 5.

It is important to realize that although such range limitations do prevail in Bach's "Klavier" works up to the mid-1720s (more precisely,

TABLE 4

The Compass of the "Bach" Organs

Arnstadt (Neue Kirche)	manuals: CDE–d'''
	pedals: CDE–d'
Mühlhausen (Divi Blasii)	manuals: CD–d'''
	pedals: CD–d'
Weimar (Schlosskirche)	manuals: C–c'''
	pedals: C–e'(?)
Köthen (Schlosskapelle)	manuals: C–e'''
	pedals: C–e'
Köthen (St. Agnus-kirche)	manuals: C–d'''(?)
	pedals: CD–d'e'f'
Leipzig*	manuals: CD–c'''
	pedals: CD–d'

*The range observed in the organ works presumably composed during the Leipzig period.

TABLE 5

The Ranges of the "Klavier" Toccatas

BWV	Key	Range
910	f♯	C(B♯$_1$)–b''
911	c	CD–c'''
912/912a	D	CDE–c'''
913	d	CDE–c'''
914	e	CD–c'''
915	g	CD–c'''
916	G	CDE–c'''

until 1726—with the publication of the first of the Partitas belonging to *Clavierübung* I), they are not universal—not even in his early compositions. Most significant for our concerns is the appearance of A$_1$ in the *Aria variata*, BWV 989. Like three of the toccatas under consideration here, it is transmitted in the *Andreas-Bach-Buch*.[26]

Several other features related to keyboard range in the "Klavier" toccatas are worth noting. Bach calls for the complete chromatic range only in the Toccata in f♯, BWV 910, which is an emphatically chromatic work in every respect, a "chromatic fantasy" of sorts. None of the others contain the low C♯, not even the Toccatas in g, BWV 915, and G, BWV 916, where the pitch could have been employed effectively as the leading tone of the dominant. Bach did find ample opportunity in the Toccata in f♯, after all, to prescribe the low C several times—notated as B♯₁ and serving just this function (mm. 13, 104, and 134).

It is tempting to try to connect the individual toccatas, on the basis of their ranges, with the various "Bach" organs—associating the toccatas that omit both C♯ and D♯ (the Toccatas in D, d, and G) with Arnstadt, linking those omitting only the C♯ (the Toccatas in c, e, and g) with Mühlhausen, and ascribing the fully chromatic Toccata in f♯ to Weimar. (The latter's inclusion in the *Andreas-Bach-Buch* precludes a later origin.[27]) But this chronological placement is too bold. There was nothing to prevent Bach from composing the Toccatas in D, d, or G, despite their lack of C♯ and D♯, after the Arnstadt period, or the Toccatas in c, e, or g, despite their lack of C♯, after the Mühlhausen period.

On the other hand, the appearance of the Toccata in D, BWV 912a, in the *Möllersche Handschrift* (in close proximity to the autograph entry of the Prelude and Fugue in g, BWV 535a), along with its undeniably primitive stylistic features—conventional thematic material, stereotyped sequential patterns[28]—argues strongly for an early date of composition (before 1707, i.e., Arnstadt?). And if one assumes that Bach normally composed keyboard works for the instruments regularly at his disposal, then it follows that he would have written the Toccata in f♯ at Weimar, since the work, with its fully chromatic range, could only have been performed on the Weimar organ. Moreover, both the advanced chromatic language and the more-sophisticated organization of the composition[29] argue for such a dating.

Finally, in the case of the Toccata in G, BWV 916, there is strong stylistic as well as external evidence supporting not an Arnstadt origin, as entertained above, but one in Weimar. The deliberate avoidance of d‴ (noted by Dürr) would have been necessary only on the Weimar organ (the note was available on the Arnstadt and Mühlhausen manuals). The three-movement concerto form of the composition also provides a compelling argument (made by Schulze and others), for Weimar. It points specifically toward the later Weimar period, ca.

1713–14, when Bach seems to have been preoccupied with the Italian concerto form.[30]

The conclusion that the Toccatas, BWV 910–16, were in all likelihood conceived as *manualiter* organ pieces inevitably demands that they be considered in connection with the *pedaliter* Toccatas in d ("Dorian," BWV 538), F (BWV 540), C (BWV 564), and d (BWV 565). If one "collates" the two groups, their keys seem to complement each other (see Table 3 above). The C-major *Toccata ex C♮. pedaliter*, BWV 564,[31] corresponds, as it were, to the *Toccata C♭. Manualiter*, BWV 911; the D-major *manualiter* Toccata, BWV 912/912a, to one or the other of the D-minor *pedaliter* Toccatas, BWV 538 or 565. (But then there is also the D-minor *manualiter* Toccata, BWV 913.) The obvious tonal and even stylistic counterpart to the E-minor *manualiter* Toccata, BWV 914, would be the E-major *pedaliter* "Toccata," BWV 566, although it must be reported that the work is called "Praeludium" or "Preludio" in the eighteenth-century sources with unusual unanimity.[32]

It is particularly tempting to try to associate the *Toccata col pedale obligato*, in F, BWV 540 (thus headed in *P 803*), with the Toccata in f♯, BWV 910. We have seen that both the range and the mature style of the Toccata in f♯ argue for a Weimar origin. As for the Toccata in F, its unique pedal range—to f′ (and including e♭′)—makes it virtually certain that the work was written for the organ at Weissenfels.[33] And since the copy of the work entered into the Walther manuscript, Berlin, DStB *P 803* (by Johann Tobias Krebs), seems to be dateable to ca. 1714,[34] one can conclude that Bach composed at least the toccata section of BWV 540 during the Weimar years, almost certainly in connection with his visit to Weissenfels in February 1713, at which time the "Hunting" Cantata, BWV 208, was composed and performed in honor of the birthday of Duke Christian.[35]

Whatever principle of alternation between *manualiter* and *pedaliter* settings may have been operating—intentionally or not—in the surviving corpus of toccatas, it was evidently abandoned by Bach when he composed the Toccatas in G and g, BWV 916 and 915, for manuals alone.

"Alio modo" Settings; Concerto Arrangements

Other keyboard works by Bach seem to be related to one another according to what may be called an "alio modo" principle based on the alternation of *manualiter* vis-à-vis *pedaliter* settings of similar material. For example, the Toccata in D, BWV 912/912a, not only exists in two alternative *manualiter* settings but shares its striking opening flourishes with the Prelude and Fugue in D, BWV 532, a work dated by Stauffer to the early Weimar period or perhaps even earlier.[36] The general resemblance between the clavier Fugue in a, BWV 944, and the organ Fugue in a, BWV 543/543a, has often been noted.[37] (In the *Andreas-Bach-Buch*, the fugue of BWV 944 is preceded by a free prelude in arpeggio style with the heading "Fantasia in A♭ pour le Clavessin."[38] It is not clear whether the harpsichord prescription is meant to apply to the Fugue as well as to the "cembalistic" Fantasia. The Fugue contains rather long sustained notes in the bass and has a range of CD–c‴.)

Finally, among the keyboard transcriptions of concertos five are *pedaliter*, BWV 592–96,[39] and sixteen are *manualiter*, BWV 972–87— seventeen, if one includes the questionable Concerto in G, BWV 592a. If the concerto is authentic, then there are two instances of "alio modo" settings in the strict sense (i.e., alternative versions based on the same material) within this repertoire. The first is the pair of arrangements of Duke Johann Ernst's Violin Concerto in G, consisting of BWV 592 and BWV 592a. The former is preserved in the manuscript Berlin, SPK, *P 280*, where it has the heading "Concerto a 2 Clav. et Ped." The latter apparently survives in a single source, Leipzig, MB *Poel. mus. MS 29* (a manuscript that has been dated ca. 1780/90), with the heading "Concerto per il Cembalo Solo."[40] The second "alio modo" pair, both members of which are certainly authentic, consists of alternative settings of another work by Johann Ernst, the Violin Concerto in C. The heading of the *pedaliter* arrangement, BWV 595, in a copy found in the Kellner-circle manuscript, Berlin, SPK *P 286*, reads "Concerto . . . appropriato all Organo à 2 Clavier: et Pedal." The *manualiter* arrangement, BWV 984, copied into the Kellner miscellany, *P 804*, by Johannes Ringk,[41] contains no instrumental designation.

With the exception of the arrangement of Vivaldi's Concerto in d, Op. 3, No. 11, "a 2 Clav: & Pedale," BWV 596, discussed earlier, none of the concerto transcriptions survive in autograph. The concertos, BWV 972–82, along with BWV 592, are contained in the copy prepared by Bach's cousin, amanuensis, and house guest, Johann Elias Bach. (The manuscript, in *P 280*, carries the inscription "J. E. Bach. Lipsiens. 1739.") The title page, which, like the rest of the manuscript, is in J. E. Bach's hand, reads *XII. CONCERTO di Vivaldi*. [sic]

elabor: di J. S. Bach.[42] Neither the title page nor the headings of the individual concertos contain any instrumental indication except for the "a 2 Clav. et Ped." indication for BWV 592 (see above). Nor are there any instrumental designations in the principal source for BWV 983–87, the Kellner manuscript, *P 804*.[43] In contrast to the *manualiter* arrangements, the five *pedaliter* settings, BWV 592–96, are scattered over a number of manuscripts, each concerto having its own source constellation.[44] Like the headings of the principal sources for BWV 592 and 596 cited earlier, the copy of BWV 594 in *P 286* mentions "2. Clavier et Pedal." (As we have seen, the heading for BWV 595, which is also contained in *P 286*, specifically mentions the organ.) The late eighteenth-century source for BWV 593 originally read only "Concerto." (A later hand added "pro organo."[45])

The prevailing assumption—one apparently never really challenged until Lohmann included the *manualiter* concerto transcriptions BWV 973, 974, 978, 984, and 986 in vol. 5 of his edition—has been that only the five concertos "a 2. Clav. et Pedal" were meant for the organ, the other sixteen (or seventeen) for the harpsichord. Once again, there can be no doubt that Bach would have condoned harpsichord performances of these pieces. But whether he actually intended them for the harpsichord in the first place is not at all clear. There is, after all, no explicit indication for the harpsichord in the best sources for BWV 972–87 (*P 280* for BWV 972–82, *P 804* for BWV 983–87). And, as Hans-Joachim Schulze has convincingly demonstrated, Bach's arrangements must have been prepared, on commission from Johann Ernst, during the period from July 1713 to July 1714, i.e., on the Duke's return to Weimar from a tour of the Netherlands. During the journey the duke acquired numerous concertos and became familiar at first hand with the Dutch practice of performing transcriptions of Italian concertos in church—on the organ—as part of a tradition of nonliturgical concert entertainments.[46] In 1713, and until March 1714, Bach's official position in Weimar was as court organist at the Himmelsburg Chapel. In the spring of 1713, the Weimar court was eagerly awaiting not only the return of the duke from his travels abroad (with his cache of Italian and French instrumental music) but also the completion of the renovation of the organ in the Himmelsburg Chapel.[47] Johann Gottfried Walther, the duke's instructor in music and the Weimar town organist, as well as Bach produced a number of concerto transcriptions for the organ, some of them *manualiter*.[48]

Finally, as Alfred Dürr notes, the keyboard range of BWV 592a and

972–87 largely stays within the four octaves C–c'''. The only exceptions are the B₁ in BWV 979, a single B♭₁ in BWV 982, and
an isolated d''' in BWV 975—a pitch otherwise regularly avoided in
the work. Dürr points out that the only source for BWV 975 is Johann
Elias Bach's copy of 1739, and that it is possible that here (and in the
other instances as well?) the source "does not reflect the original reading of the Weimar arrangement in every respect."[49] All this suggests
that not only the concerto transcriptions "a 2 clav. et pedal" but the
manualiter settings as well may have originally been intended for the
organ.

The Duets from *Clavierübung* III

Whatever one ultimately concludes about the toccatas and the concerto transcriptions, there can hardly be any doubt that Bach must
have reckoned with organ performance of the four duets, BWV 802–
805, published in *Clavierübung* III. A *manualiter* designation, however,
is notably absent from the headings of these pieces in the print: they
are simply called *Duetto* [I–IV]. Nonetheless, since only the organ is
specifically mentioned on the title page, the burden of proof is surely
on anyone who would maintain that the duets were written for some
other instrument. One could point out, of course, that the title page
refers only to the chorale settings as "vor die Orgel." But the monu-
mentally organistic Prelude and Fugue in E♭, BWV 552, is not mentioned on the title page either. Neither that omission, then, nor the
remark by Johann Elias Bach (in a letter of January 1739) that *Clavierübung* III was only "*principally* for those who play organ"[50] seems sufficient to challenge the *prima facie* case favoring the organ as the instrument of choice for the entire collection. Indeed, the range of all four
duets keeps within the limited organ compass of CDE–c'''. As the
other parts of the *Clavierübung* abundantly testify, Bach was rather
keen at this time on extending the range of his harpsichord works well
beyond this compass (from G₁A₁ to d'''). It would thus seem that Bach
was concerned that the duets be playable on almost any organ.

Clavier

There was surely more involved in Bach's self-imposed restraint. A
keyboard composition that was restricted to a single manual and to a
C–c''' compass could have been played on virtually any keyboard instrument of the time, especially if it also largely avoided the low chro-

matic pitches C♯ and/or D♯. In other words, the absence of the pedal and the restriction of the range to C–c''' were the two—and the only two—"universal characteristics" common to both the organ and the string keyboard instruments, i.e., to the *clavier*. During the Baroque era *clavier* was the general designation for all keyboard instruments; and Bach confirmed that usage when, following the precedent of Johann Kuhnau, he chose *Clavierübung* as the title for his ambitious series of keyboard publications.

But in his practical realization of this project, Bach provided explicit instrumental designations: in Parts II and IV for a Clavicymbel/Clavicimbal with two manuals, in Part III for an organ. Needless to say, he felt free—though not obliged—to take advantage of the specific capacities of each; but he could not ignore their limitations. Thus, Part III of the *Clavierübung*, "vor die Orgel," keeps within the four-octave range throughout, even though it does not always prescribe the pedal; and the harpsichord works of the remaining parts necessarily dispense with a pedal part even though they do not necessarily exploit the complete G_1A_1–d''' range.[51] Part I contains no instrumental designation, but both the genre to which the collection is devoted (the suite, with its strong identification with the harpsichord) and the expansive compass of the pieces make it clear that only the harpsichord was intended. Furthermore, since these suites can all be played on a single manual, there was no need for any additional prescription, as was the case in Parts II and IV. (The presence of the designation "pour le Clavessin" in the headings of the French Suites, BWV 814–16, in the 1722 *Clavierbüchlein* for Anna Magdalena Bach provides explicit confirmation—if any were needed—that Bach associated the suite genre with the harpsichord. The formulation "Suite . . . pour le Clavessin" itself was obviously borrowed from French publications of the time.)

The term *clavier* also appears in the titles of the *Clavierbüchlein* volumes for Anna Magdalena and Wilhelm Friedemann Bach. Since these books are eminently personal documents, which reflect the particular needs, tastes, and instrumental resources of their recipients and owners, it would be rash to generalize too much from them. But they do reveal, as Dürr notes, that until ca. 1730 Anna Magdalena must have had at her disposal a *clavier* with a range of C–c''', and thereafter an instrument that extended at least from B♭₁ to d'''. Similarly, the presence of B₁ in both original sources of the Two- and Three-part Inventions and Sinfonias—that is, in both the *Clavier-Büchlein vor Wilhelm Friedemann Bach* and the fair copy, Berlin, DStB

P 610—suggests that Bach must have assumed that these avowedly preparatory compositions would be studied at home, no doubt on one of the domestic keyboard instruments. The most likely candidate was surely the traditional "practice" instrument, the clavichord, whose low strings, of course, could also be retuned from one piece to another.[52]

Bach's most enigmatic use of the term *clavier* perhaps is in the title *Das Wohltemperirte Clavier*. The *Well-Tempered Clavier*, of course, cannot properly be compared either to the *Clavierbüchlein* volumes or to the Two- and Three-part Inventions, even in their fair-copy version with its elaborate title page. Unlike the former, the *Well-Tempered Clavier* is clearly addressed to a general audience; unlike the latter it is not limited to relative beginners but also intended for more advanced students ("also for those who are already skilled in this study," in the words of the title page). Despite the technical difficulties of many of the compositions, it is remarkable that Bach rigorously observes the four-octave compass C–c‴, even though in the more than twenty years, beginning in 1722, during which he repeatedly refined the fair copy of the *Well-Tempered Clavier* (Berlin, DStB, *P 415*),[53] he gradually expanded the compass of his other keyboard works. This process, by the way, is not only observable in the Partitas in *Clavierübung* I but also in the French and English Suites.[54]

As in the case of the duets, BWV 802–805, the range restriction in the *Well-Tempered Clavier*, taken together with the absence of an obbligato pedal part throughout the work, must mean that the composer was determined to keep the work "universally" accessible to all keyboard players, including organists, and that is confirmed by Bach's choice of the "generic" term *clavier* in the title. (Whether the long pedal points in some of the compositions should be taken as a hint that performance on an organ was more than merely "acceptable" is a question best left unasked. They do suggest that such pieces, e.g., the Prelude and Fugue in a, BWV 865, may have originally been conceived as organ pieces before their incorporation in the *Well-Tempered Clavier*.)

Dürr notes that the few instances in WTC II in which the four-octave range is exceeded seem to be "exceptional cases, while the compass, on the whole, is retained here as well."[55] However, one should add that, whereas we have Bach's explicit description of WTC I, no autograph title for WTC II, much less an elaborate title page stating its precise purpose, has come down to us.

Let us return now to Heinz Lohmann's edition of the Bach organ works and attempt to assess the validity of his selection in the light of

Bach's own instrumental prescriptions and the principles we have been able to derive from them. It would seem that Lohmann was justified in including in his edition not only the toccatas and the concerto arrangements for manuals alone but also the various keyboard preludes and fugues that respect the normal C–c‴ compass (so long, of course, as the authenticity of the works is otherwise secure). It is at the least questionable, however, whether it was appropriate to include in an edition of organ works compositions for which the earliest sources carry an explicit prescription for harpsichord, as is the case with the Fantasia in a, BWV 904.[56] And there was little or no justification to include compositions that belong to the clearly secular genres, such as the *Fantasie sur un Rondeau*, BWV 918; the *Aria variata*, BWV 989; the *Capriccio sopra la lontananza del suo fratello dilettissimo*, BWV 992; or the *Ouverture* in F, BWV 820—certainly not if (as is the case with BWV 989) the four-octave range is clearly exceeded. Ironically, Lohmann has resisted the boldest stroke of all—one which, as we have seen, there is reason to believe would have been in conformity with Bach's intentions: the inclusion of the preludes and fugues of the *Well-Tempered Clavier* in an edition of Bach's organ works!

The possibility that compositions such as the Toccatas, BWV 910–16, were conceived as organ pieces raises another issue: What occasion would the young Bach have had to perform such virtuosic and manifestly "public" display pieces on a harpsichord? Whether *manualiter* or *pedaliter*, Bach's toccatas seem designed for large audiences and large rooms which at that time would only have been found in a church. The toccatas presumably composed in Weimar (those in f♯, BWV 910; G, BWV 916; and perhaps c, BWV 911[57]), like the concerto arrangements, could conceivably have been performed at court. But given Bach's position in Weimar as court "organist," it seems more reasonable that he would have made his public appearances in that capacity rather than as a "chamber musician" at the harpsichord, either in the ballroom or in some other "chamber." We know about a number of occasions on which Bach "made himself heard" in public at the organ as a solo recitalist—e.g., in Hamburg in 1720, Kassel in 1732, and Dresden in 1736—but there is no evidence that he ever did so as a harpsichordist. Rather, whenever he performed for an audience on the harpsichord it seems to have been in the context of ensemble music and under the auspices of an institution like the Leipzig *collegium musicum*, playing the obbligato cembalo parts in his violin, gamba, and flute sonatas, perhaps, or the solos in his harpsichord concerti. Harpsichord "recitals," to the extent that such things existed at all, apparently were private or quite exclusive occasions: for example, the aborted contest with Marchand, which, according to the Obituary, was to take place "in the home of a leading minister of state [identified by Forkel as one Count Flemming], where a large company of persons of high rank and of both sexes was assembled";[58] or the well-known anecdote, related by Forkel, about Count Keyserlingk, Goldberg, and the origin and purpose of the famous variations; or the command performance at the court of Frederick the Great.

We know very little about concert performance during the Bach era. But the functional division of music at the time into the realms of "church, chamber, and theater" as it applied to keyboard music (and keyboard players) suggests that not only chorale settings but also grandiose compositions like the toccatas and similarly large, serious, and technically demanding works among the preludes and fugues, regardless of whether they invariably contained obbligato pedal parts, were written with a view to church performance. The only keyboard compositions clearly intended for the "chamber," i.e., the aristocratic salon or ballroom, were dance suites and such secular entertainments as program pieces or variations on popular tunes. The keyboard parts, both continuo and obbligato, in instrumental ensemble works ("chamber music" in our sense), would normally have been performed on the harpsichord. The theater was of marginal significance in the career of J. S. Bach. The keyboard's role here would have been limited to continuo accompaniment on the harpsichord in the orchestra pit. This picture of Baroque musical practice is in accord with that drawn by commentators of the era, from Marco Scacchi to Mattheson and Heinichen; and it is largely borne out (and certainly nowhere contradicted) by Bach's own instrumental prescriptions in the original and early sources of his keyboard and chamber compositions.

A fourth sphere of musical activity, one that was fundamental to all the others, was instruction in the art of music itself, both its performance and its creation. It was here that the musicians of the time came as close as they ever would to producing music "for its own sake," where it served no purpose other than self-understanding and self-perfection. The only appropriate instrument for such a purpose was a keyboard, because of its contrapuntal and harmonic capacity. The most appropriate keyboard, paradoxically, was no particular instrument at all but rather the *clavier*, with its "universal characteristics": a single manual with a range of C to c''', regardless of whether it was attached to pipes or a set of strings. It was for this ideal yet "universally" available medium that Bach created works that were to serve, as he put it on the title page of the *Well-Tempered Clavier*, "For the Use and Profit of the Musical Youth Desirous of Learning as well as for the Pastime of those Already Skilled in this Study."

NOTES

1. Willi Apel, *The History of Keyboard Music to 1700* (Bloomington, Indiana, 1972), p. 3. See also the introduction to the article "Keyboard Music," in *The New Grove Dictionary of Music and Musicians*, vol. 10, p. 11.

2. See BDok III, p. 86; also *Bach Reader*, p. 221.

3. *Bach Reader*, p. 345.

4. Johann Sebastian Bach: *Sämtliche Orgelwerke*, 10 vols., edited by Heinz Lohmann (Wiesbaden, 1968–79).

5. The following is the complete list of "appropriated" works in Lohmann's edition, in the order of their appearance: vol. 2: BWV 900, 947, 894; vol. 3: BWV 910–16, 904, 944, 918–19, 961, 992, 993, 963, 820, 833, 989; vol. 4: BWV 899, 901, 902, 895, 943, 946, 952, 953, 948, 945, 956, 962, 949, 950, 947, 958, 951, 1079/1, 1079/5, 950a, 951a; vol. 5: BWV 984, 974, 978, 592a, 973, 985, 986, 917.

6. Bach reserves the French term, reasonably enough, for compositions in French style—overtures and suites.

7. It would be most interesting, but beyond the scope of this paper, to know whether they are mentioned explicitly in any practical sources of keyboard music of the late seventeenth or early eighteenth century.

8. See BDok II, p. 504; and *Bach Reader*, p. 197.

9. As in Alfred Dürr, "Tastenumfang und Chronologie in Bachs Klavierwerken," in *Festschrift Georg von Dadelsen zum 60. Geburtstag*, edited by Thomas Kohlhase and Volker Scherliess (Stuttgart, 1978), p. 76.

10. *Bach Reader*, p. 193; BDok II, p. 492.

11. Jakob Adlung, *Musica mechanica Organoedi* (Berlin, 1768; reprint, Kassel and Basel, 1961), vol. 2, pp. 158–62.

12. See the articles "Pedal Clavichord" and "Pedal Harpsichord" by Edwin M. Ripin in *The New Grove Dictionary*, vol. 14, p. 327.

13. See *Bach Reader*, p. 311.

14. BDok III, p. 86; *Bach Reader*, p. 221; see also Peter Williams, *The Organ Music of J. S. Bach* (Cambridge, 1980–1984), vol. I, pp. 8–9.

15. See NBA IV/5–6, KB, p. 131.

16. See George Stauffer, *The Organ Preludes of Johann Sebastian Bach* (Ann Arbor, 1980), p. 2.

17. See the description of the *Möllersche Handschrift* in NBA IV/5–6, KB, pp. 100–103.

18. See *Bach Reader*, p. 193.

19. *Bach Reader*, p. 311.

20. Ibid., p. 311 fn.

21. See Ripin, "Pedal Harpsichord."

22. See Ernest May, "J. G. Walther and the Lost Weimar Autographs of Bach's Organ Works," in *Studies in Renaissance and Baroque Music in Honor of Arthur Mendel*, edited by Robert L. Marshall (Kassel and Hackensack, N.J., 1974), pp. 264–82.

23. The only other use of the *manualiter* indication that I have discovered

so far is in the heading of the Fugue in A on a Theme of Albinoni, BWV 950. The heading in Berlin, SPK *P 595*, copied by Johannes Ringk, reads "Fuga. ex A. Dur. Manualiter."

24. Summarized in NBA IV/5–6, KB, pp. 183–86.

25. Dürr, "Tastenumfang," p. 79.

26. Ibid., esp. pp. 79–82.

27. See Hans-Joachim Schulze, *Studien zur Bach-Überlieferung im 18. Jahrhundert* (Leipzig, 1984), pp. 45–50.

28. See Hermann Keller, *Die Klavierwerke Bachs* (Leipzig, 1953), p. 66; also Schulze, *Studien*, p. 47.

29. See Keller, *Klavierwerke*, pp. 66–67.

30. See Schulze, *Studien*, esp. p. 163.

31. Thus the title page in the Kellner manuscript, *P 286*. There are similar headings in other sources. See Stauffer, *The Organ Preludes*, p. 227.

32. See Stauffer, *The Organ Preludes*, pp. 228–29.

33. See NBA IV/5–6, KB, p. 404.

34. See Hermann Zietz, *Quellenkritische Untersuchungen an den Bach Handschriften P 801, 802, und 803* (Hamburg, 1969), p. 213.

35. See NBA I/35, KB, pp. 39–43.

36. Stauffer, *The Organ Preludes*, p. 108.

37. See Williams, *The Organ Music*, vol. I, p. 127; and especially Reinhard Oppel, "Die grosse A-moll-Fuge für Orgel und ihre Vorlage," BJ 1906: 74–78.

38. See NBA IV/5–6, KB, p. 128.

39. The Concerto in E♭, BWV 597, is now considered spurious. See Hermann Keller, "Unechte Orgelwerke Bachs," BJ 1937: 66.

40. See Peter Krause, *Handschriften der Werke Johann Sebastian Bachs in der Musikbibliothek der Stadt Leipzig* (Leipzig, 1964), p. 10.

41. See NBA IV/5–6, KB, p. 199.

42. See Schulze, *Studien*, p. 59, and his discussion in general regarding these arrangements.

43. The headings here, like those for BWV 972–82 in *P 280*, indicate at most the tonality of the concerto along with an attribution to J. S. Bach. See NBA V/5, KB, pp. 30–33.

44. See Lohmann, ed., *Sämtliche Orgelwerke*, vol. 5, Preface.

45. See NBA IV/5–6, KB, p. 62.

46. See Schulze, *Studien*, pp. 154–63.

47. See the document, dated April 10, 1713, quoted in Schulze, *Studien*, p. 156–57.

48. See Johann Gottfried Walther, *Gesammelte Werke für Orgel*, edited by Max Seiffert, *Denkmäler deutscher Tonkunst*, vol. 26/27 (Leipzig, 1906).

49. Dürr, "Tastenumfang," p. 80.

50. See BDok II, p. 335; also Williams, *The Organ Music*, vol. I, pp. 321–22.

51. Part II is particularly modest in its range demands. See Dürr, "Tastenumfang," p. 83.

52. Ibid., pp. 77–78.

53. See the critical notes in the Wiener Urtext edition, edited by Walther Dehnhard (Vienna, 1977), p. xi.

54. See Dürr, "Tastenumfang," pp. 80–83.

55. Ibid., p. 83.

56. Published in vol. 3 of the Lohmann edition. The heading in *P 804*, in J. P. Kellner's hand, reads "Fantasia in A mol pro Cembalo." See NBA V/5, KB, p. 29.

57. See Keller, *Klavierwerke*, pp. 67–68.

58. See the pertinent passages in *Bach Reader*, pp. 218 and 304.

LUIGI FERDINANDO TAGLIAVINI

Bach's Organ Transcription of Vivaldi's "Grosso Mogul" Concerto

Johann Sebastian Bach's arrangements of Vivaldi concertos[1] have often given rise to vehement controversies and misunderstandings. Indeed, there are sharply diverging views even about the importance of the Vivaldi models. Thus the Concerto in a for Two Violins, Op. 3, no. 8 (arranged by Bach as the Organ Concerto in a, BWV 593), is extolled as exemplary by Einstein[2] and even termed "*the* masterwork of 18th-century Italian orchestral music" by Della Corte and Pannain.[3] But the brilliant final movement of this work, deemed by Einstein to contain "one of Vivaldi's—and not just Vivaldi's—greatest inspirations," is judged extraordinarily "weak in invention" by Hermann Keller.[4] Vivaldi's musical stature is taken to task most harshly, perhaps, by Johannes Schreyer.[5] Schreyer's attempt to prove the lack of craftsmanship and musical worth in Vivaldi's concertos lies at the heart of his arguments against Bach's authorship of the organ and harpsichord arrangements.

After all, Vivaldi's humorous ideas, the frequent flightiness and unaffectedness of his writing style, and the conceit of his rhythmic and tonal play bewildered even his contemporaries. Quantz, as a youth, was "impressed in no small way" by Vivaldi's concertos,[6] but later reproached the Venetian composer for his "thoughtlessness and impertinence, both in composing and in playing."[7]

Even certain aspects of the Bach transcriptions have offended some scholars and musicians. As Ferdinand August Roitzsch published the four concertos, BWV 592–95 (the models for these concertos were two works by Vivaldi and two by Johann Ernst von Sachsen-Weimar), for vol. 8 of the Peters Edition of Bach's organ works in 1852, he could not conceal his amazement that such compositions, particularly the Vivaldi concerto arrangement, BWV 593, "were considered idiomatic for the organ, despite runs and arpeggios which normally would not be acceptable to present-day tastes."[8]

More recently Keller has similarly reproached Bach for having transcribed several passages in the third movement of his arrangement of Vivaldi's Concerto in d, Op. 3, no. 11, "with all too much fidelity to the violin and too little to the organ." Thus Keller even proposes an "improvement" for Bach's text.[9] For his part, Schreyer sharply criticizes the "un-Bachian" treatment of the double pedal and the "barbarous conclusion" of the Concerto in a, BWV 593.[10]

Striking misunderstandings have plagued Bach's transcriptions. Until 1910 the Organ Concerto in d, BWV 596 (the only organ transcription for which Bach's autograph exists[11] and which is therefore the best evidence to counter Schreyer's doubts about authenticity), was not considered an arrangement of Vivaldi's Op. 3, no. 11, but was thought to be an original composition by Wilhelm Friedemann Bach.[12] With this attribution the work was admired and viewed as an expression of "love's sweet melancholy and tender sensibility"[13] and even as a dramatic reflection of the "restless soul" of Johann Sebastian Bach's eldest son.[14]

The Organ Concerto in C, BWV 594, represents an especially interesting case. For many years its model was considered to be Vivaldi's Violin Concerto in D, Op. 7, Book 2, no. 5 (RV 208a).[15] In actuality, only the outer movements of Vivaldi's composition correspond with those of Bach's organ transcription; the middle movement of the printed concerto, a short *Grave*, is unrelated to the *Recitativo* of the organ version. Thus it was thought that Bach had taken the liberty of composing a completely new middle movement[16] as well as decorating each of the outer movements with an extensive cadenza.

The long cadenza of the third movement is one of Schreyer's key arguments against Bach's authorship of the concerto arrangements. How could Bach really have composed "this musical monstrosity— such a pitiful piece of street-organ playing?"[17] In truth, even a superficial consideration of this lengthy "epilogue," which was supposedly appended by the arranger, reveals that it could not have been conceived expressly for the organ. The style is 100 percent violinistic, as is that of the cadenza for the first movement.

Even the view that the *Recitativo* middle movement is an addition by the arranger was dropped some time ago. In fact, Bach's source (we say Bach's, since Schreyer's doubts about authenticity can no longer be taken seriously [18]) was not Vivaldi's Op. 7 publication, but another version of the violin concerto that has the same *Recitativo* for the middle movement as the organ version. This version, RV 208, is found in three manuscripts, one at the Biblioteca Nazionale in Turin,[19] another at the Wissenschaftliche Allgemeinbibliothek in Schwerin,[20] and a third at the Archivio Capitolare in Cividale (Friuli).[21] The Schwerin and Cividale copies are sets of parts, the first written by Peter Johann Fick (d. 1743);[22] while the Turin source[23] is a score in Vivaldi's hand.[24] The Schwerin manuscript gives the work the strange name "Grosso Mogul"—a humorous reference to the extraordinary size of the work or to Venice's connections with the Far East?

Until recently the Schwerin source has been known only partially. It was overlooked even by the Vivaldi Institute, which published two editions of the concerto, based on the Turin autograph and the Op. 7 version respectively.[25] However, the Schwerin material is especially interesting, since its extensive cadenzas for the outer movements are the same as those in Bach's organ transcription.[26]

The Schwerin set of parts (*Violino Prinsipalo* [sic], *Violino 1mo*, *Violino 2do*, *Viola*, and *Bassus Continuo*)[27] is incomplete, for the continuo part consists solely of a *Basso di ripieno*. Lacking are all passages in which the bass part accompanies the solo episodes, a participation that is clearly visible in the Turin autograph and the Op. 7 version.[28] Only the bass part for the middle movement (solo recitative) is provided. Up to now, these gaps were considered odd, but no attempt was made to explain them.[29] It is not a question of gaps or deletions in the extant bass part, which is only a *Basso di ripieno* or *Basso spezzato* and, as such, should be considered complete. Rather, it is a question of absence of the true *Basso continuo* or *Basso di concertino* part.

Although the cadenzas in the Schwerin source are written with typical Vivaldian gusto and fully suit the virtuosic style of the concerto, the question of whether they were composed by Vivaldi or by a virtuoso familiar with his style (one thinks especially of Pisendel) cannot be answered with certainty.[30] It is interesting that several humorous "impertinences" of the cadenzas are overemphasized in an amusing fashion by Bach; we need only note the chromaticism Bach adds to the descending arpeggio figures of the final cadenza.[31]

A comparison of the organ arrangement with the sources for the violin concerto leads to even more conclusive results. The presence of cadenzas is not the only thing that ties the organ concerto to the Schwerin source. Evidence indicates that the *Basso di concertino* part was missing from the copy of the concerto used by Bach, just as it is lacking in the Schwerin source, at least as it exists today. One can even ask whether this exact Schwerin source served as Bach's model.[32] In any case, the version used by Bach corresponds to that in the Schwerin manuscript as it is handed down to us, that is, without the bass part for the *soli*.

In several solo passages the organ transcription exhibits exactly the same gaps as does the Schwerin copy, while in other passages Bach has reconstructed the bass part, sometimes intuitively restoring the Vivaldi version but usually adding a new bass line that differs substantially from the original. The relationship between Bach's reconstructed bass and Vivaldi's original can be summarized as follows:

In three solo episodes Bach's transcription lacks the bass found in Vivaldi's original:

> Movement 1: mm. 51–57 and 64–77
> Movement 3: mm. 158–59

In two places Bach's reconstruction of the bass agrees entirely (or almost so) with Vivaldi's original:

> Movement 3: mm. 89 and 141–42

In a number of passages Bach's reconstructed bass (or countermelody) differs from Vivaldi's original:

> Movement 1: mm. 93–111 and 118–25
> Movement 3: mm. 32–63, 76–81, 90–111, 126–29, and 159–63

In most instances Bach's newly reconstructed bass lines are more subtly worked out than are the originals. One episode, mm. 96–111 of the closing movement, receives an entirely new visage, thanks to the lively bass figures Bach composed in place of Vivaldi's long pedal point. In several spots—particularly movement 1, mm. 105–11 and 118–24, and movement 3, mm. 159–63—Bach composed a truly contrapuntal voice in place of Vivaldi's simple, harmonically supportive bass line (see Examples 1 and 2).

In one instance, however—mm. 76–81 of the final movement—Bach seems not to have fully understood Vivaldi's thinking, for his solution is more rigid and more schematic than Vivaldi's, which is elegant despite the parallel octaves in m. 80 (see Example 3).

One difficulty encountered in transcribing instrumental concertos to the keyboard is that the upper range of the violin parts often exceeds the normal compass of the organ and the harpsichord. Bach solved this problem by transposing entire pieces a second or even a third lower[33] and by altering melodic turns and making octave transpositions. A fine example of octave transposition occurs at the begin-

EXAMPLE 1

ning of Vivaldi's Concerto in d, Op. 3, no. 11, where both solo parts are notated one octave lower in Bach's organ transcription. The original tessitura is respected, however, by prescribing a 4′ registration.

In the case of the "Grosso Mogul" Concerto transcription, the problem of range was particularly serious: the solo violin ascends to b‴, while the upper limit of Bach's organ was only c‴. The transposition from D major down to C allowed Bach to accommodate the introduc-

EXAMPLE 2

tory tutti *ritornello*, which rises to d''' in the original, as well as a few other tutti and solo passages (first movement, mm. 120 and 122; third movement, m. 120) within the confines of his organ manual. However, the majority of solo episodes, including the entire middle movement, required transposition to the lower octave.

The extant copies of the Concerto in C (Bach's autograph is lost)[34] do not provide any special indications for registration, as does, for instance, the autograph of the Concerto in d, BWV 596. Thus, present-day organists generally do not hesitate to use 8' pitch for the manuals throughout the entire composition, thereby playing most of the solo passages one octave (more precisely, a ninth) lower than Vivaldi's original version.

EXAMPLE 3

Serious questions about performance practice arise if Bach's text is critically examined with Vivaldi's. With regard to the solo episodes, it can be established that Bach treated them in three ways:

1. Solo and accompanying part(s) on the *Rückpositiv*, with occasional use of the pedal:

    Movement 1: mm. 40–58, 105–11, 126–28, and 137–73

    Movement 3: mm. 32–63, 89–111, 142–63, and 180–283

2. Solo part on the *Rückpositiv*, accompanying part(s) on the *Oberwerk*, with occasional use of the pedal:

Movement 1: mm. 26–40, 93–105, and 128–37
Movement 2: entire movement
Movement 3: mm. 76–89 and 126–41
    3. Solo part on the *Oberwerk*, accompanying parts on the *Rückpositiv*, without pedal:
Movement 1: mm. 64–80 and 117–26

All the solo parts on the *Rückpositiv* have been notated one octave lower, while those on the *Oberwerk* remain at normal pitch. The accompanying parts are treated in a similar fashion: the parts Bach took over from the Vivaldi model and assigned to the *Rückpositiv* (movement 1, mm. 64–80 and 125–26) are transposed down one octave, while passages for the *Oberwerk* have been notated at actual pitch. The only exceptions are in the first movement, at mm. 93–104, where the accompanimental figure has been transposed down to the lower octave, and in the third movement at mm. 130–41, where, by contrast, the figure has been transposed up an octave.

Thus we conclude that each movement of the Concerto in C requires a 4′ fundament on the *Rückpositiv*.[35] Comparison with Bach's other concerto arrangements, in which the original register is quite faithfully followed, appears to confirm this supposition. The several exceptions to this rule are easily explained. For example, in the middle movement of the Concerto in a, octave transposition was the only satisfactory way of transferring the dialogue of the two solo violins to a single manual.

A striking parallel to the 4′ registration in the Concerto in C is the obbligato organ arrangement of the first two movements of the Harpsichord Concerto in d in Cantata 146, *Wir müssen durch viel Trübsal in das Reich Gottes eingehen*. Here Bach transposed the entire right hand of the organ part down one octave because the keyboard lacked d‴. In this respect, particularly for *colla parte* passages, it again seems evident that Bach intended that 4′, not 8′, pitch be used.

If one wishes to play the devil's advocate, one can mention two passages in the "Grosso Mogul" transcription that seem to contradict the presumed 4′ registration for the *Rückpositiv*. In m. 130 of the third movement, 4′ registration produces a six-four chord, and in m. 21 of the recitative it makes parallel fifths. The first case can be juxtaposed with the situation in m. 81 of the third movement, where a six-four chord occurs no matter what registration is used, 8′ or 4′. Here is evidence that Bach did not entirely avoid this unusual harmony (that is, the use of the six-four chord as if it were a normal perfect chord in

EXAMPLE 4

root position) in a particular context. With respect to the recitative, we cannot rule out the possibility that 4' stops were also to be employed on the *Oberwerk* in this movement. If such were the case, the accompanying chords would sound in a register most natural for the normal realization of a figured bass.

In light of the above observations, several passages seem especially instructive. In Vivaldi's first solo episode, the *ripieno* violins underscore the figures of the *violino principale*. Such an effect is successful in Bach's transcription only if a 4' registration is used on the *Rückpositiv* (see Example 4).

If we take several solo passages that are to be played on the *Oberwerk* (mm. 64–80 and 125–26 in the first movement) and compare them with the corresponding places in the violin concerto as transmitted by the Turin and Schwerin sources, we once again establish that only a 4' registration on the *Rückpositiv* allows the accompanying parts to correspond properly with the *ripieno* violin and viola lines (see Example 5).

While a comparison of Vivaldi's violin concerto and Bach's organ transcription leads to fruitful conclusions about the latter, it also offers interesting hints about performing the former. Bach actually treated the *Recitativo* according to the conventions of vocal recitative, which as a rule were not written down but left to the performers. Today these practices are all too frequently ignored. The long, held

EXAMPLE 5

RV 208-Mvt. 1

in Ms. Schwerin
missing B.c.

BWV 594-Mvt. 1

B.c.

Ped.

EXAMPLE 6

tones in which composers habitually notated the bass part must be shortened and separated with rests[36] (see Example 6). Bach himself presented a most convincing illustration of this convention in the *St. Matthew Passion*.[37] An equally instructive confirmation of the practice is his realization of the figured bass in the *Recitativo* of his arrangement of Antonio Vivaldi's "Grosso Mogul" Concerto.

(TRANSLATED BY BRUCE C. MACINTYRE)

NOTES

This article originally appeared as "Interpretatorische Probleme bei Johann Sebastian Bachs Orgel-Transkription (BWV 594) des 'Gross-Mogul'-Konzertes von Antonio Vivaldi (RV 208)," in *Orgel, Orgelmusik, und Orgelspiel—Festschrift Michael Schneider zum 75. Geburtstag*, edited by Christoph Wolff (Kassel, 1984). It is reprinted here, in a version substantially revised by the author, by permission.

1. In light of recent research, Bach's arrangements for organ and harpsichord appear to have originated during the period 1713–14 at the request of Prince Johann Ernst of Sachsen-Weimar. See Hans-Joachim Schulze, "J. S. Bach's Concerto-Arrangements for Organ—Studies or Commissioned Works?" *Organ Yearbook* 3 (1972):4-13.

2. Alfred Einstein, Preface (dated 1932) to the Eulenburg miniature score (no. 762) of Vivaldi's Concerto in a, Op. 3, no. 8.

3. Andrea Della Corte and Guido Pannain, *Storia della musica*, 2d ed. (Turin, 1942), vol. 2, p. 947.

4. Hermann Keller, *The Organ Works of Bach*, translated by Helen Hewitt (New York, 1967), p. 86.

5. Johannes Schreyer, *Beiträge zur Bach-Kritik*, vol. 2 (Leipzig, 1913), pp. 8–31.

6. "Herrn Johann Joachim Quantzens Lebenslauf, von ihm selbst entworfen," in Friedrich Wilhelm Marpurg, *Historisch-Kritische Beyträge zur Aufnahme der Musik* (Berlin, 1755), vol. 1, p 205.

7. Johann Joachim Quantz, *Versuch einer Anweisung die Flöte traversiere zu spielen* (Berlin, 1752), Section XVIII, Item 58. There can be no doubt that the two "famous Lombardy violinists" cited by Quantz but not directly named are Vivaldi and Tartini.

8. Ferdinand August Roitzsch, Foreword to vol. 8 of the Peters Edition of Bach's organ works.

9. Keller, p. 89. Even as this organ transcription was published for the first time in 1844 as a composition of Wilhelm Friedemann Bach (see note 12, below), an anonymous reviewer in the *Allgemeine Musikalische Zeitung* (vol. 48, 1846, col. 57) was surprised to find a good number of passages and figures "nicht orgelmässig."

10. Schreyer, pp. 21–22.

11. Berlin-West, SPK *P 330*, described in detail by Karl Heller in NBA IV/8 (*Bearbeitungen fremder Werke*), KB, pp. 21–25.

12. The concerto was published in 1844 by Friedrich Konrad Griepenkerl as Wilhelm Friedemann Bach's composition, a work "which the father copied out in his own hand and supplied with the applicable registration and manual indications" (W. F. Bach, *Concert für die Orgel mit zwei Manualen und Pedal*, Leipzig, Preface). The concerto was recommended as an instructive example of Bach's art of registration (see Griepenkerl's Preface of the same year to vol. I of the Peters Edition). Carl Friedrich Zelter had already suspected in 1829 that the concerto was a composition by Vivaldi, but not until 1910 did Ludwig Schittler establish this fact (see Heller, p. 28). The authorship question for the original composition and the organ arrangement was conclusively cleared up one year later by Max Schneider in "Das sogenannte 'Orgelkonzert d-moll von Wilhelm Friedemann Bach'," BJ 1911:23–26.

13. See Griepenkerl's remark on the inside of the front cover of the autograph of the transcription (reproduced in Heller, pp. 21–22).

14. From such a standpoint August Stradal arranged the concerto for piano, providing it with two "stormy" cadenzas. See *Concert für die Orgel von Wilh. Friedemann Bach für Pianoforte zu 2 Handen bearbeitet von August Stradal* (Leipzig, 1897; rev. ed., 1906).

15. See Paul Graf Waldersee, "A. Vivaldi's Violinconcerte unter besonderer Berücksichtigung der von J. S. Bach bearbeitet," *Vierteljahrsschrift für Musikwissenschaft* 1 (1885):356–80; and Ernst Naumann's critical commentary in BG 38, p. xlvii. Vivaldi's Op. 7 was published by Roger and Le Cène in Amsterdam between 1716 and 1721 and reissued by Walsh in London ca. 1730. The fifth concerto of Book 2 of Op. 7 is listed as 208a in Peter Ryom's *Verzeichnis der Werke A. Vivaldi—Kleine Ausgabe* ("RV"; Leipzig, 1974).

16. This view led Hans David to move up the date of the Organ Concerto to the Leipzig period. According to David, Bach would have composed such an instrumental recitative only after becoming acquainted with Francesco Antonio Bonporti's Op. 12, a work that David dated between 1718 and 1725. David's hypothesis rests on two suppositions that are no longer tenable: that Bonporti's Op. 12 contains the first pronounced instrumental recitatives, and that Bach had composed the recitative in the Concerto in C *ex novo*. See Hans David, "Die Gestalt von Bachs Chromatischer Fantasie," BJ 1926:23–67, esp. p. 63n1.

17. Schreyer, p. 23.

18. Arnold Schering had already energetically refuted Schreyer's arguments. See "Beiträge zur Bach-Kritik," BJ 1912:124–33. On the authenticity of the concerto transcriptions, see, among others, Heller, p. 11.

19. Turin, Biblioteca Nazionale, R. Giordano Collection *29*, pp. 167–81. A detailed description of this source is presented by Peter Ryom, "Un concerto d'Antonio Vivaldi transcrit par J. S. Bach," in *Dansk Aarborg for Musikforskning 1966–67*, edited by N. Schiørring and S. Sørensen (Copenhagen, 1968), pp. 91–111 (cited hereafter as Ryom 1968). See also Heller, p. 47.

20. Schwerin, Wissenschaftliche Allgemeinbibliothek, *Mus. 5565*, described in Ryom 1968, p. 101, and Heller, pp. 47–48. The version in Turin and Schwerin is no. 208 in Ryom's catalogue.

21. The manuscript source of Cividale was discovered only after the present article was prepared for the Schneider *Festschrift*. See Maurizio Grattoni, "Una scoperta vivaldiana a Cividale del Friuli," in *Informazioni e studie vivaldiani—Bollettino annuale dell'Istituto Italiano A. Vivaldi*, no. 4 (Milan, 1983), pp. 3–19.

22. On P. J. Fick, see Ryom 1968, pp. 101–102; and Heller, p. 48.

23. The existence in Turin of a version of this violin concerto that corresponds in all movements with Bach's organ transcription was already evident from the 1939 thematic catalogue of Vivaldi's instrumental works preserved in Turin. See Olga Rudge, "Catalogo tematico delle opere strumentali di Antonio Vivaldi esistenti nella Biblioteca Nazionale di Torino," in *Antonio Vivaldi—Note e documenti sulla vita e sulle opere* (Siena, 1939). Study of this catalogue enabled the present author to point out the relationship between the Bach transcription and the Turin manuscript in 1947 (in the introductory remarks to a broadcast of an organ concerto by Ireneo Fuser for Italian Swiss Radio on March 25, 1947). Otherwise, this important source of information remained remarkably unnoticed. Only in 1956 was the version that served as a basis for Bach's transcription conclusively reported by Rudolf Eller, in "Zur Frage Bach-Vivaldi," in *Bericht über den Internationalen Musikwissenschaftlichen Kongress Hamburg 1956* (Kassel, 1957), pp. 80–85. However, Eller's source was

not the Turin score but the Schwerin parts. Actually, the presence of Vivaldi's concerto in the former Mecklenburgische Landesbibliothek at Schwerin has been known since the publication of Otto Kade's catalogue *Die Musikalien-Sammlung des Grossherzöglichen Mecklenburg-Schweriner Fürstenhauses aus den letzten zwei Jahrhunderten* (Schwerin, 1893). This catalogue supplies the musical incipit for the first movement only (vol. 2, p. 293), and it is not clear that the Schwerin source is not the Op. 7 version.

24. Peter Ryom has proven indisputably that it is an autograph. See Ryom 1968, as well as his *Les manuscrits de Vivaldi* (Copenhagen, 1977), p. 338. In the former work, Ryom carefully compares the Turin autograph with the Schwerin manuscript, the Op. 7 version, and Bach's transcription. Among other things, Ryom is puzzled by the fact that four measures crossed out in the first movement of the Turin score (mm. 130–33) were included in the Schwerin manuscript, the final version of Op. 7 and the Organ Concerto in C. Since the ink of the crossing out is different from that of other improvements and corrections, there is a strong possibility that the change did not originate with Vivaldi.

25. A. Vivaldi, *Concerto in re maggiore per violino, archi e cembalo F. I n° 138*, edited by Gian Francesco Malipiero, Istituto Italiano A. Vivaldi, Tomo 314 (Milan, 1960). This edition is based on the Turin score. The Bortoli print of the twelve violin sonatas, Op. 2 (Venice, 1709), is erroneously given as a source. Malipiero did not include the above-mentioned four measures crossed out in the autograph (first movement, after m. 129; see note 24, above). The Op. 7 version appeared as Tomo 452 of the edition of the same Istituto (Milan, 1968) and also as Eulenburg miniature score no. 1237, edited by Felix Schroeder (London, 1961). In the Preface of his edition, Schroeder—who used the Schwerin source for purposes of comparison—stated the un-acceptable hypothesis that the *Recitativo* of the Schwerin version is a "re-arrangement for violin" of the "second movement added by Bach."

26. Although the presence of both cadenzas in the Schwerin manuscript was announced by Eller in 1956 (Eller, p. 82), Walter Kolneder, in *Antonio Vi-valdi—Leben und Werk* (Leipzig, 1965), p. 142, asserts that this source includes the cadenza for the first movement, "though not the cadenza for the final movement." Schroeder, on the other hand, who examined the Schwerin manuscript for his edition of Vivaldi's Concerto, Op. 7, no. 11 (see note 25, above), refers only to the cadenza for the final movement. The Cividale manu-script also contains two cadenzas. The cadenza for the first movement is iden-tical to that in the Schwerin manuscript, while the extended cadenza of the third movement (126 measures, designated "Cadenza del Vivaldi per il Sig'. Pontoti") agrees with the Schwerin source only at the beginning and end (completely for the first nine measures, but only partially for the final 22). Grattoni (see note 21), published facsimiles of the Cividale and Schwerin ca-denzas for the third movement.

27. I am grateful to Dr. Antonio Fanna, who graciously made available to me photographs of the Schwerin parts.

28. The only exceptions are the three bass notes in mm. 41, 43, and 44 of the first movement. These notes could be considered a continuation of the *ripieno* instruments' participation during the first solo (see Example 1).

29. The bass passages lacking at Schwerin were noted in Schroeder and Ryom 1968 (p. 104). Ryom determined that "a number of basso continuo pas-sages from the two allegros had been done away with, something that might appear odd since the omissions affect the accompaniment for all the soloist's

episodes." The "pausing" of the bass part is also stressed by Heller (p. 51; see note 32, below). It is interesting that in the set of parts recently discovered in Cividale the *Basso di concertino* part is also missing (see Grattoni, p. 6n2).

30. As proof that the cadenza of the first movement stems from Vivaldi, Eller, p. 83, maintains that this cadenza is "an organically integrated part of the movement" and "cannot be easily removed"—by no means a sound argument (as Ryom 1968, pp. 102–103, also remarks). Eller has compared similar cadenzas for the Vivaldi concertos RV 212 and 562, which are preserved in Dresden, Sächsische Landesbibliothek, *Mus. 2389–0–74* and *–94*. But, as Ryom asserts (p. 103), the problem of the cadenzas' authenticity is still not resolved because the Dresden copies are attributed to none other than J. G. Pisendel. See the remarks about RV 212 and 562 in the Ryom catalogue, pp. 152 and 155. See also Rudolf Eller, "Über Charakter und Geschichte der Dresdener Vivaldi-Manuskripte," *Vivaldiana*, vol. 1 (Brussels, 1969), pp. 57–63.

31. The cadenzas of the Schwerin manuscript have been published by Heller in the appendix of NBA IV/8, KB, pp. 100–104.

32. Eller (p. 82) rules out such a hypothesis: "Comparison of the sources leads to the sure conclusion that Bach worked not from the Schwerin manuscript but from a third copy." Eller's view is shared by both Ryom (1968, p. 108) and Heller (p. 51). A comparison of the Schwerin source and Bach's arrangement does not lead to the same radical conclusion, since the discrepancies can be interpreted as Bach's changes or additions. In fact, the greatest differences are to be found in the bass part of the *soli* passages, which is missing in the Schwerin manuscript and which (according to the thesis presented in this article) has been reconstructed by Bach. Serious doubts about the direct dependence of Bach's arrangement on the Schwerin manuscript begin to surface, however, if the comparison is enlarged to include the Turin score (a source not available to Eller). At two places in the *Recitativo* (mm. 7 and 8), the Schwerin copy deviates slightly from the Turin autograph. At these spots Bach's text is closer to the Turin version (see Example 7). In Heller's edition the rhythm of Bach's version of this passage was made to fit that of Vivaldi's autograph (see Heller's KB, p. 55).

EXAMPLE 7

33. Vivaldi's Concerto in G, Op. 3, no. 7 (=BWV 978 for harpsichord), and Concerto in b, Op. 3, no. 10 (=BWV 1065 for four harpsichords and strings), were transposed down a whole step; Concerto in B♭, Op. 4, no. 1 (=BWV 980 for harpsichord), down a minor third; and Concerto in E, Op. 3, no. 12 (=BWV 976 for harpsichord), down a major third.

34. On the source situation for the Concerto in C see Heller's KB, pp. 43–50.

35. In 1958 Ulrich Siegele remarked that the Concerto "by its relatively low notation for the *Rückpositiv* appears to take into consideration the fact that its sonority usually lay one octave above that of the *Oberwerk*." See Siegele, *Kompositionsweise und Bearbeitungstechnik in der Instrumentalmusik J. S. Bachs* (Neuhausen-Stuttgart, 1975), p. 91.

36. As early as the start of the nineteenth century this practice was no longer clearly understood in Germany. See the anonymous article "Welche ist für die Bässe die beste und zweckmässigste Art, das einfache Rezitativ zu begleiten?" *Allgemeine musikalische Zeitung* 12 (1810): col. 969–74. The article presents a discussion between a representative of the newer tendencies, named *Neulieb*, and a supporter of tradition, *Altlieb*. While *Neulieb* asserts that *recitativo secco* bass lines "must be performed as notated by the composer," i.e., with long, held notes, *Altlieb* replies that "Italian composers as well as Graun and particularly Hasse . . . used this manner of writing almost like an abbreviation." They did it "partly to spare themselves and their copyists the writing out of numerous rests, partly to facilitate keyboard accompanists' note reading by means of a reduction in the number of symbols and through the continuous visual presence of fundamental chord tones," and, even more, because the "incessant rumbling of the bass parts would eventually become unbearable to the ear."

37. In his fair-copy score of the late version of the *St. Matthew Passion* Bach used long, held notes for the bass part of the Evangelist's recitatives. In the original continuo part, by contrast, he wrote short notes separated by rests. He did so not, as Alfred Dürr maintains, "to distinguish more effectively the accompaniment of the Evangelist from that of Jesus with its sustained string chords," but to present the continuo player with a more exact text, one that conformed with the usual performance practices. See Alfred Dürr, NBA II/5 (*Matthäus-Passion*), KB.

VICTORIA HORN

French Influence in Bach's
Organ Works

French style in the organ works of J. S. Bach has always been a somewhat awkward subject. Discussions invariably begin with an identification of the pieces from Bach's *oeuvre* that are modeled on French
themes or concepts. Then comes the uncomfortable realization that
Bach's pieces really do not do a convincing job of being French. They
do not resemble French music to the ear, and closer inspection of the
most "typically" French passages reveals a less than unequivocal French
orientation. At this point the discussion is usually left unresolved, or it
ends with an apologetic note that perhaps the French influence is not
so important in Bach's works after all.

There is no need to form such timid conclusions if we look at the
question from a slightly different viewpoint. We can begin quite confidently, pointing out that C. P. E. Bach, the most authoritative chroni-
cler of Bach's career, tells us in the famous Obituary of 1754 that his
father studied and valued the works of the old French masters.[1]
There is a wealth of evidence to substantiate C. P. E. Bach's rather general remarks, including his father's personal copies of French music,
other French pieces Bach would have known from the collections of
his close colleagues, and, of course, the references to French music
and style in his own compositions.

As for the works themselves, there is no reason to expect Bach's music to conform to a style so radically different from his own. Bach was
not, after all, French, nor was he engaged in writing exercises in mim-
icry. When he made use of French musical elements, they were completely reworked to serve his designs for the piece in question. The
ways in which he did so offer some insight into his compositional aes-

thetic, and it is on this level that the subject must ultimately be pursued. With this end in view, let us summarize the French musical traditions important for Bach's development and look at a few selected examples where French style seems to emerge in his works.

I

Bach's use of foreign musical traditions was always grounded in a thorough knowledge of representative compositions, and the case of French style is no exception. Every serious German musician of the time was expected to have a general acquaintance with French music. It enjoyed tremendous popularity throughout Germany during the years of Lully's fame (ca. 1680–1710). French and French-influenced opera was much more in vogue than Italian, court establishments of all sizes had orchestras modeled after Lully's famous Vingt-quatre violons, and keyboard players commonly copied French keyboard suites or transcriptions of opera excerpts into their manuscript books.[2]

Among German composers, Bach was hardly the first for whom French style was a shaping force. Consider, for example, the French-like melodic writing of Georg Böhm,[3] which in turn was so influential for Bach's own early organ works. Even Buxtehude was not immune to the spirit of France—some of his thicker chordal textures are indebted to French orchestral homophony.[4] Hence Bach's similarly orchestral five-part writing in the middle section of the Fantasia in G, BWV 572, may well be French via Buxtehude.

In short, French music was enough a part of the public domain that "French style" easily brought to mind the sounds of the French overture, dotted rhythms, and five-part string writing. What one might call the "spirit of the age," then, constituted a somewhat intangible yet highly important source for Bach's knowledge of French style. A few compositions that are definitely traceable to Bach's library are of particular interest here because they are organ works: a scrupulously faithful copy of the entire *Livre d'orgue* of Nicholas de Grigny made by Bach himself, and a similar copy of the two *livres d'orgue* of Jacques Boyvin made by one of Bach's students.

The de Grigny manuscript, now located in the Frankfurt Stadt- und Universitätsbibliothek under the signature *Mus. ms. 1538*, contains six keyboard suites by François Dieupart and a table of ornaments from D'Anglebert's *Pièces de clavecin* of 1689 as well as de Grigny's *Livre d'orgue*. Bach appears to have written out the de Grigny manuscript

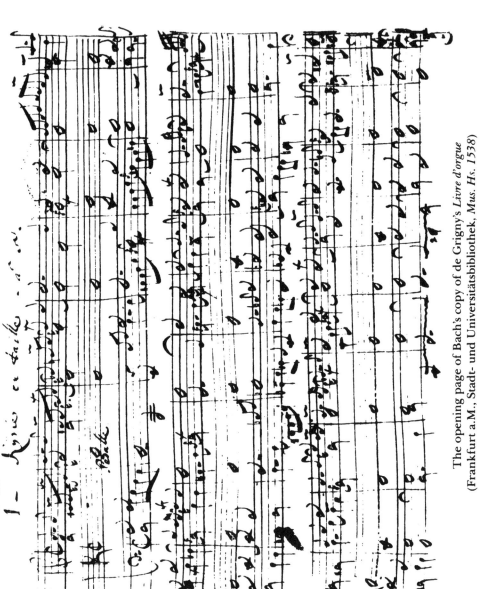

The opening page of Bach's copy of de Grigny's *Livre d'orgue*
(Frankfurt a.M., Stadt- und Universitätsbibliothek, *Mus. Hs. 1538*)

PLATE 1

(see Plate 1) during the middle years of his Weimar tenure. Customarily, scholars rely on handwriting analysis to date Bach's autograph manuscripts. In this case handwriting criteria alone are inconclusive, since there are too few autographs from the period before 1713 to pinpoint the year of the de Grigny copy. The paper of the manuscript, however, is a common type employed by Bach in Weimar and is found in sources datable between 1714 and 1716.[5] Thus the period 1714–16, or just before, seems the most likely time for Bach to have written out the de Grigny collection.

The Boyvin copy (see Plate 2), Berlin SPK, *Mus. ms. 2329*, clearly seems to be related to the de Grigny. The manuscript paper is the same, and the handwriting is the youthful script of the Bach student Johann Caspar Vogler,[6] who no doubt penned the volume during his instruction with Bach at Weimar, 1710–15.[7] Vogler, born in 1696, was still a teenager at the time in question, and though he did the writing, we can safely assume that he was working under Bach's supervision.

During this same general period, Bach was also privy to the compositional and copying projects of his cousin and close colleague at Weimar, Johann Gottfried Walther. French music was well represented in Walther's extensive library of *musicalia*.[8] Of particular interest here are some miscellaneous keyboard suites which come down to us in the manuscript Berlin, DStB, *P 801* (see Table 1). This music was penned by Walther between 1712 and 1714–15,[9] at the same time that Bach was displaying interest in a similar repertoire. Although most of these compositions are not organ works, they are still important for our discussion. When considered in conjunction with the de Grigny and Boyvin manuscripts, they demonstrate an intensive involvement with idiomatic French keyboard writing at just the moment when Bach was working with and absorbing other stylistically significant repertoires. His initial copies of *stile antico* sacred works,[10] the Vivaldi concerto transcriptions, and even a written copy of Frescobaldi's *Fiori musicali* (now lost)[11] were all projects of this same period.

In addition to these reliable primary and secondary sources, which precisely document both Bach's involvement with French music and his general style awareness, there is some firm but less-specific evidence linking Bach with the French tradition. It includes references in the documents, anecdotes about Bach's life, and even thematic quotations in his music that imply a familiarity with particular French works.

For example, Bach used part of a bass melody from a Chaconne by André Raison as the basis for his own Passacaglia in c, BWV 582.[12]

The opening page of a copy from the Bach circle (Johann Caspar Vogler)
of Boyvin's *Livre d'orgue*
(Berlin, SPK, *Mus. ms. 2329*)

PLATE 2

TABLE 1

French Music Copied into *P 801* by Johann Gottfried Walther

Composer	Work	Publication
Jean-François Dandrieu (1682–1738)	Suite in g	No printed source
Jean-Henri D'Anglebert (1635–1691)	Suite in d	*Pièces de clavecin*, livre I, Paris, 1689
Charles Dieupart (d. 1740)	Suite in A	*Six suittes de clavecin*, Amsterdam, n.d.
Gabriel Nivers (c. 1632–1714)	Prelude and Fugue in a	No printed source
Louis-Nicolas Clérambault (1676–1749)	Suite in g	No printed source
Louis Marchand (1669–1732)	Suite in g	*Pièces de clavecin*, livre II, Amsterdam, n.d.
Nicolas LeBègue (1630–1702)	Suite in g	*Les pièces de clavecin*, Paris, 1677
Gaspard LeRoux (fl. 1675–1700)	Suite in d	*Pièces de clavecin*, Paris, 1705

The source might quite reasonably have been a copy of the Raison *Premier livre d'orgue*, which was also available at Weimar. Perhaps Bach also knew the works of another classical French organist, Pierre Du Mage. Johann Abraham Birnbaum, writing for Bach in response to criticisms from Johann Adolph Scheibe, mentions the name Du Mage along with de Grigny as composers respected by Bach.[13]

Should the Aria in F, BWV 587, be accepted in the Bach canon, we have another example of a work based largely on a preexisting French model. The Aria is an arrangement of a trio from François Couperin's *Les Nations* (from the fourth *Ordre* of that work, entitled "L'Imperi-ale"). However, there are serious doubts about Bach's authorship of this arrangement.[14] His familiarity with Couperin's music is docu-mented with more certainty by the copy of the Rondeau, "Les Bergeries," from the *Second livre de pièces de clavecin* (1717) in the *Clavier-büchlein* for Anna Magdalena Bach of 1725.

Personal experience with music making in the French style apparently began for Bach with visits to Celle while he was a student at St. Michael's in Lüneburg, 1700–1703. In the Obituary of 1754 we read:

> From Lüneburg Bach journeyed now and again to Hamburg to hear the then famous organist of the Catherine-Kirche, Johann Adam Reincken. And here, too, he had the opportunity to go and listen to a then famous band of musicians kept by the Duke of Celle, consisting for the most part of Frenchmen. Thus he acquired a thorough grounding in French taste, which in these regions, was at the time something quite new.[15]

Thus Bach's ideas of French rhythmic gestures may well have been gleaned from hearing the French manner of articulating the highly stylized dance and orchestral music performed by the Duke's "band." This aurally derived knowledge was acquired early in his career and probably contributed to the sensitivity with which Bach later "read" French texts he encountered at Weimar.

The above description of Bach's early exposure to French music includes only keyboard sources and styles, but even within these limits it is surely incomplete. Bach undoubtedly knew a good deal of French music for which there is no longer any evidence.[16] Still, even as a partial account, the list is impressive, showing that Bach had a broad exposure to idiomatic usage of both the organ and the harpsichord as well as a personal acquaintance with such large-scale designs as the suite and the organ mass. Though the slate of composers is more heavily weighted in favor of the older generation (D'Anglebert, de Grigny, Boyvin, and Raison), younger composers, closer to Bach in age and proponents of a lighter, less-majestic style, figure as well (Dieupart, Dandrieu, and François Couperin).

II

Of course Bach's engagement with French musical models, no matter how extensively documented, is only of secondary interest compared with the way this knowledge manifested itself in his works. French organ textures figure prominently here. From even a casual perusal, the French *livres d'orgue* cannot help but impress us with their unusual range of texture and voice combinations; and Bach, similarly impressed, must have looked to these different textural models as a means of adding greater character to his scores. Furthermore, typically French textures were often closely associated with specific French genres; when employed, they could evoke the "parent." Bach may well have seen that as a way of expanding the scope of those works—preludes, fantasias, fugues, and chorale settings—that were by function and influence so completely molded by an almost exclusively Central and North German tradition.

One of the most distinctive compositional features to occur in the French organ works is the rich sound of five-part texture. (Fuller-voiced textures were distinctive of other French repertoires, of course. Lully's scoring for five separate strings became an ideal for much French orchestral music. Hence organists, in search of the richness of a thick, five-part sonority, were responding to a more general French trend.) In French organ music, this textural ideal was sometimes realized by distributing two imitative voices on two manuals, each requiring a different registration, with a pedal voice that alternated in function between sustained-note harmonic underpinning and more active, thematically significant interplay with the upper parts. A favored registration was the soloistic Cornet for the upper pair and the Cromorne for the lower; the range of the lower pair itself is quite high, with the bottom line rarely dipping below e.[17]

None of Bach's five-part examples are entirely faithful to this model. Textural parody is rarely the sole goal for Bach, and hence the textural plan becomes submerged beneath other aspects of the compositional fabric. The closest Bach comes to the French model is in the Fantasia in c, BWV 562/1, especially in the first twenty bars or so. Not only does the pairing look typical, but the parallel thirds and sixths that arise contrapuntally within the voice pairs help to emphasize the "Frenchness" of the material. However, these thirds and sixths result from the initial pattern of entries and become less frequent as further development affects this pattern. The differentiated treatment of subject and countersubjects, rather than the novelty of the texture, commands the listener's attention (see Example 1). As we shall discuss later, qualities other than texture make this piece an interesting study of French influence, and it is perhaps his overall concern with the Gallic style that accounts for the care Bach took in establishing a French fabric so faithfully at the outset.

Another example reflecting the French model is the *Orgelbüchlein* chorale, *Liebster Jesu, wir sind hier*, BWV 634. Here the voice pairing is critical to the design of the piece.[18] The top voices paraphrase the chorale melody in canon and are thus tightly connected. The second pair

EXAMPLE 1

is also highly unified by an upbeat figure of three rising or falling
eighth notes (see Example 2). The pervasiveness of this motive in the
second pair (a particularly Bachian device) gives the middle voices
greater melodic prominence—something Bach must have admired in
the French counterparts. In addition to the frequent occurrence of
thirds and sixths, this chorale setting is further "Frenchified" by the
light, dancelike rhythmic treatment of the chorale melody. Once again,
however, much of the Gallic nature of this piece exists on the surface.
The French qualities add character, certainly, but they are to be
appreciated within the context of a fundamentally German chorale
harmonization.

The remaining examples of the five-part scoring are more removed
in concept from the original French formulation. In the two five-part
settings from *Clavierübung III, Diess sind die heil'gen zehn Gebot'*, BWV
678, and *Vater unser im Himmelreich*, BWV 682, the texture hardly
sounds like five true voices. That is because the two canonic parts

EXAMPLE 2

(the chorale melody) overlap so little, and the pauses between phrase statements are so lengthy, that all five voices are rarely heard simultaneously.[19]

This is not to say that the French tradition is totally absent from Bach's conception. In the *Vater unser* setting at least, even the visual image of the five parts helps to reinforce the reference to France conveyed by the decidedly French melodic writing. France, or more particularly, the majesty of the French court, is no doubt one object of the Gallic references, used here as a symbol for the heavenly kingdom, the *Himmelreich*.[20]

Of the wealth of textures and sonorities so characteristic of the French organ works, five-part writing was perhaps the most novel to interest Bach, but it was certainly not the only one. Surely it was his predilection for inner-voice prominence that drew his attention to the French Cornet de dessus and Tierce en taille settings, each with its highly stylized use of the middle register. The Tierce en taille features a florid middle voice, registered soloistically, with two less highly profiled upper parts in imitation, fashioned after wind writing. The Cornet de dessus is defined by a floridly written top line with a fully conceived duet in the middle register. Both types of pieces include a pedal bass.

Bach must have been captivated with the novel color quality that resulted from the texture of the Cornet de dessus, in particular. It is

clearly to this type that we owe the three highly unusual chorale settings of the "Great Eighteen" Collection—*Komm heiliger Geist, Herre
Gott*, BWV 652; *Schmücke dich, o liebe Seele*, BWV 645, and *Allein Gott in
der Höh sei Ehr'*, BWV 662. The musical material, too, shows many
French elements, to a degree most unusual for Bach. Dance rhythms
characterize *Komm heiliger Geist* and *Schmücke dich*. Moreover, the particularly sensitive use of ornamentation emphasizes the important
stresses of each measure. The Tierce en taille genre is less-vividly represented, although *An Wasserflüssen Babylon*, BWV 653, from the same
collection is close to the French model in many respects.

Another piece in the Bach organ literature is all the more striking
because it demonstrates the use of a textural idea further afield than
French and German organ music. *Nun komm, der Heiden Heiland*,
BWV 599, of the *Orgelbüchlein*, displays a *style brisé* opening that points
to the French harpsichord tradition. Bach was certainly not trying to
achieve the sound of a harpsichord; the *brisé* writing is not present
throughout, nor is the organ capable of articulating the *brisé* texture.
Rather, it is likely that he wished to allude to the French harpsichord
genre most often associated with the broken style, the *prélude non me-
suré*. Such pieces often headed the suites of the *clavecinistes*, and Bach
perhaps wanted this initial chorale of his most-ambitious collection to
date to be identified in this way with an opening-piece genre.

All the foregoing examples demonstrate that while aspects of Bach's
compositional fabric are often shaped by French musical ideas, the
French influence only partially accounts for a work's sound, expres-
sivity, musical material, and developmental plan. No work better illus-
trates the complexity that characterizes Bach's experiments with other
styles than the Fantasia in c, BWV 562/1, in which Bach's command of
the musical material produced a work that went far beyond the sum of
the contributing elements.

Most notable in this Fantasia, aside from the five-part texture, is the
striking thematic connection with the first fugue from the Gloria in de
Grigny's *Livre d'orgue* (see Example 3). Bach's theme—we might almost
say his subject, since the writing is so fugal—is not, as might be expected, a direct copy of the Frenchman's. But the two are melodically
similar and rhythmically identical. Also identical is the use of French
ornamentation on the first and third beats, which serves more to add
rhythmic emphasis than to provide melodic embellishment. Bach's
melodic line differs from de Grigny's chiefly in its initial upward semitone; this semitone not only helps to emphasize the third beat by a

EXAMPLE 3

change in melodic direction, but also eliminates any possibility of the cross-relation between G and G♯ occurring in de Grigny's second measure.

Other aspects of the composition, notably its structure and harmonic language, have a strong Italianate cast. For instance, Bach makes frequent use of the sequences so typical of early Italian concerto writing. Even where he does not use actual harmonic sequences, he sometimes constructs long phrases that give the impression of sequential structure. Consider, for example, mm. 4–12, where the soprano descends, with brief interruptions when it has the subject, in a simple minor scale from A♭ to B♮, the two notes necessary to define the key of C minor.

This type of large-scale planning imposes strict limits on the kinds of harmonic surprises that are permissible. Perhaps Bach's avoidance of a cross-relation like the one in de Grigny's second measure reflects this concern for longer lines. As used by de Grigny, the cross-relation provides a harmonic "jolt" that occurs throughout the fugue almost as a characteristic of the subject material. Such jolts, so typical in French organ music, would only obscure Bach's long-range design. In a later revision of this work Bach does make use of a cross-relation for dramatic effect, but not until the cadenza, where it cannot interfere with his basic harmonic plan.

III

After the 1720s, Bach was less interested in simply augmenting his compositional vocabulary with elements of French or Italian style. He was very much involved with old music and new, French music and Italian. But his approach to style became more systematic, emblematic, and in some cases, even "confrontational." His burgeoning systematic outlook is seen in works such as *Clavierübung* I, which contains a plethora of suite movements in old and new dance styles. Bach's desire to distinguish the introductory preludes by names as well as style underlines his concern with encyclopedic diversity. His movement toward the emblematic, that is, toward the use of stylistic aspects to represent nonmusical images, can be seen in *Clavierübung* III, where he uses French style in the *pedaliter Vater unser im Himmelreich* to symbolize the *Himmelreich* of the text. And, finally, the juxtaposition of Italian and French styles in *Clavierübung* II can only be viewed as a sort of musical confrontation, epitomized by the "mi contra fa" of the work's key scheme: the F major of the Italian Concerto and the B minor of the French Overture.

It is within the framework of this extreme style consciousness that one must view *Clavierübung* III, Bach's most-consequential compositional project for the organ from the years of his maturity. A casual glance at the cycle's contents reveals at most the basic plan of the opus: an opening prelude; the Kyrie, Gloria, and catechism chorales; and a final fugue.[21] The dual settings of the catechism chorales, the multiple versions of the Kyrie and Gloria pieces, and especially the *plenum—non-plenum* alternations hint at one of the basic themes of the work: the exploration of style elements in juxtaposition. The central nature of the drama is explicitly heralded in the first number, the famous "St. Anne" Prelude in E♭, BWV 552/1, in which Bach intertwines elements of both the French and the Italian styles, the two national traditions most often treated as polar opposites.[22]

Bach begins with.a French overture, an aptly chosen musical model since the Prelude serves as an introduction to the entire cycle. His evocation of the classical French overture is especially realistic—even the five-part scoring supports the genuineness of the copy. Perhaps the only atypical aspect in this allusion is the absence of the ascending upbeat flourish so characteristic of the Lullyian models. Bach's deliberate descending flourish will be taken up shortly.

As the Prelude progresses, its structure begins to emerge, and it is not the form of the French overture, as one might expect, but that of the Italian concerto. The overture segment (mm. 1–32) serves as a *ritornello*, which alternates in whole or part with two episodic sections. The first episode begins with the upbeat to m. 32 and features an echo exchange between two manuals. At m. 71 the other episode appears. It is longer than the first, imitative, and has typical keyboard figuration.

If viewed as a concerto, the Prelude is surprisingly un-Italian, and not only because of the French material of the *ritornello*. The strong differentiation that exists between the three basic sections (*ritornello* and two types of episodes) is highly unconventional for a concerto. In each of the segments not only are rhythmic, melodic, and textural elements quite different, but the sound or style of each belongs to a separate sphere. Consider, for example, the old-fashioned majesty of the *ritornello* material and the lighter, almost *galant* sound of the echo passages of the first episode. Such sharp differentiation and highly individual characterizations of musical material, while atypical of the Italian concerto, are essential elements of French music.

From an aesthetic point of view, the effect of this French characterization of sections is to stretch the formal limits of the Italian concerto. Indeed, before concluding that these limits are stretched too far, we must remember that the work is not, after all, a concerto. Rather, it is a prelude that in one facet of its complex personality pays homage to the concerto form and Italian style. If this form is stretched in atypical ways, Bach uses other forces to hold it together. We noted earlier that the *ritornello* employs a descending flourish in place of the ascending one common in French models. Having thereby made a point of the gesture, Bach then uses it as a unifying element, for both episodes also prominently feature a descending upbeat motive.

Clavierübung III is not devoted entirely to the juxtaposition of French and Italian style elements. In fact, this feature seems purposely confined to the Prelude, where it serves as a possible metaphor for the contrast and confrontation theme. Later in the cycle we find two works that dramatize the difference between the old style and the new. Interestingly enough, this exploration of widely different types of writing takes place within the parameters of essentially French idioms. Both the *manualiter Wir glauben all' an einen Gott*, BWV 681, and the *pedaliter Vater unser im Himmelreich*, BWV 682, owe their melodic conceptions to French influences. Each, however, is derived from a radically different repertoire. In *Wir glauben all'*, occurring on p. 39 of the original edition, the dotted rhythms of the French overture clearly bring to mind the older classical French tradition. On the next facing page we find the antithetical short–long French snap rhythms, a well-known feature of the new *galant* style, dominating the two melodic voices of the *Vater unser*. Also underscoring the contrast of old and new is the fugal idiom of *Wir glauben* versus the trio-sonata texture of *Vater unser*. Bach also mixes characteristics of the two idioms: brevity, often associated with the new style, is the property of the "older" *Wir glauben*, while long-windedness, of which the older contrapuntists were accused, characterizes the *Vater unser* setting. Then, too, the treatment of the chorale tune, paraphrased and highly embellished in *Wir glauben*, is more modern in concept than the cantus firmus treatment of the tune in *Vater unser*.

IV

After discussing so many examples in a theoretical way, we should conclude with a few remarks on practical matters of performance. General questions of performance practice in the organ works of Bach, especially with regard to registration, have been dealt with elsewhere in the Bach literature.[23] Here we will focus on just one aspect: To what extent does Bach's use of typically French material invite a more French interpretive treatment?

This question has particular relevance to our discussion of French textures, since the very concepts of the five-part organizations of the Tierce en taille and Cornet de dessus pieces were so intertwined with the registration for each. Bach was never as specific as the French when it came to instructing performers about registration;[24] and it is no surprise that he did not indicate in his five-part works Cornet for the upper manual and Cromorne for the lower. However, in view of his shaping of the musical material (see the earlier discussion of voice pairings in Bach's works), it is only reasonable to suppose that Bach desired a registration that would produce similar results.

One should, though, exercise considerable caution in the literal application of French registration practice to Bach's works. There was, after all, no way that Bach could have known how specific French registrations sounded. French organs in the style perfected by the Silbermanns were unknown to Bach before 1717[25]—after many of his own works had been composed. Furthermore, German organs were not designed to have the same soloistic clarity as the French. The German

Krummhorn, for example, was quite different in sound from the French Cromorne. Nor could another combination of stops on a German organ have reproduced the French effect. Therefore, instead of slavishly imitating French registrations, performers can work with the character possibilities of their instruments toward the same ideals sought by the French: light, clear stops, with a sharp differentiation between manuals.

As for other interpretive matters, such as ornamentation and *inégal*, a conservative approach seems wisest. Bach indicates French ornaments fairly explicitly when he wishes them used.[26] Naturally, it is essential for the performer to study enough of French ornamentation to understand the application and proper execution of these embellishments. But any attempt to add substantially to the ornamentation indicated is probably unwarranted.

Bach's use of the French musical language is highly selective; elements of French style are well intermixed with Italian characteristics and Bach's own. Therefore, it would seem misguided to treat one of Bach's melodic lines with an *inégal* articulation for example, merely because it occurs in a piece with five-part texture. The decision must be made on the basis of the melodic material itself and what role this material plays in the composition as a whole. In short, such choices are best made after studying the piece as a Bach work, which it is, rather than a French work, which it is not.

NOTES

1. The text of the Obituary reads: "In the year 1703 he came to Weimar, and there became a musician of the Court. The next year he received the post of Organist in the Neue Kirche in Arnstadt. Here he really showed the first fruits of his application to the art of organ playing, and to composition, which he had learned chiefly by the observation of the works of the most famous and proficient composers of his day and by the fruits of his own reflection upon them. In the art of organ he took the works of Bruhns, Reinken, Buxtehude, and several good French organists as models." See BDok III, p. 82; English translation from *Bach Reader*, p. 217.

2. The practice of making transcriptions of opera excerpts is even documented within the Bach circle. Transcriptions of pieces from Marais's *Alcide* can be found in the *Andreas-Bach-Buch* (Leipzig, MB, *III.8.4*) and a Chaconne from Lully's *Phaeton* occurs in the *Möllersche Handschrift* (Berlin, SPK, *Mus. ms.40644*). Both of these manuscript books, the work of the same principal scribe, were undoubtedly known to J. S. Bach, since he himself copied his Prelude and Fugue in g, BWV 535a, into the *Möllersche Handschrift*. For details on these important sources, which contain works by Buxtehude, Böhm, Bach, and some French suites by Marchand and LeBegue, see NBA IV/5–6,

KB, vol. 2, pp. 180–83; and Hans-Joachim Schulze, *Studien zur Bach-Überlieferung im 18. Jahrhundert* (Leipzig, 1984), pp. 30–55.

3. Böhm's chorale partita *Ach wie nichtig, ach wie flüchtig* is a relevant example. See Georg Böhm, *Sämtliche Werke: Klavier- und Orgelwerk*, rev. ed., vol. 2 (Wiesbaden, 1952).

4. See Dietrich Buxtehude, *Sämtliche Orgelwerke*, vol. 2 (Copenhagen, 1952). The Praeludia in f♯ (BuxWV 146) and g (BuxWV 149) and the Toccata in F (BuxWV 157) contain such chordal writing.

5. The paper is of the type "Blankenburg I." For details about its use see Alfred Dürr, *Studien über die frühen Kantaten Johann Sebastian Bachs*, 2d ed. (Wiesbaden, 1977), pp. 232–33.

6. I came across this manuscript in the Staatsbibliothek Preussischer Kulturbesitz in Berlin while doing research in 1979. I am indebted to Hans-Joachim Schulze of the Bach-Archiv in Leipzig for identifying the scribe and for answering my numerous queries on the source.

7. This assumption is based on the fact that the handwriting is less mature than the otherwise earliest-known example of Vogler's hand, a copy of the French Suites penned in 1723. For further details on Vogler see Hans-Joachim Schulze, "'Das Stück in Goldpapier': Ermittlungen zu einigen Bach-Abschriften des frühen 18. Jahrhunderts," BJ 1978: 19–42.

8. For details on Walther's copying activities in Weimar, see Ernest May, "Johann Gottfried Walther and the Lost Weimar Autographs of Bach's Organ Works," in *Studies in Renaissance and Baroque Music in Honor of Arthur Mendel*, edited by Robert L. Marshall (Kassel, 1974), pp. 267–68.

9. Walther's participation in the manuscript *P 801* is discussed in Hermann Zietz, *Quellenkritische Untersuchung an den Bach-Handschriften P 801, P 802, und P 803* (Hamburg, 1969), pp. 111–13.

10. See Christoph Wolff, *Der stile antico in der Musik Johann Sebastian Bachs* (Wiesbaden, 1968), pp. 17–29.

11. BDok III, p. 634.

12. The theme in question is that of the Christe from Raison's *Premier livre d'orgue* (Paris, 1688). Modern reprint in *Archives des Maîtres de l'Orgue*, vol. 2.

13. BDok II, p. 304; *Bach Reader*, p. 246.

14. For a thorough summary of the controversy surrounding this work, see Ulrich Siegele, *Kompositionsweise und Bearbeitungstechnik in der Instrumentalmusik Johann Sebastian Bachs* (Neuhausen-Stuttgart, 1975), pp. 77–78.

15. BDok III, p. 82; *Bach Reader*, p. 213.

16. Bach made it his business to keep abreast of all the newest musical developments, and we can assume that he would not have missed Couperin's important publications.

17. For an excellent discussion of this and other matters related to the music of the classical French organists, see Fenner Douglass, *The Language of the Classical French Organ* (New Haven, 1969), esp. p. 97.

18. In the autograph for this piece Bach brackets each voice pair. See the facsimile of the incipit, reproduced as Plate 2 in George Stauffer, "Bach's Organ Registration Reconsidered," in this volume.

19. Another similar example is *Christe, du Lamm Gottes unschuldig*, BWV 619, a five-part piece with two slow-moving voices carrying the chorale mel-

ody in canon. The full texture remains consistent throughout the work. Because of the brevity of the setting, the chorale is stated once without internal pauses. Despite the consistent presence of five voices, this example is not quite representative of the French model, mostly because of its atypical voice pairing.

20. Bach similarly used the dotted material of the French overture to symbolize the heavenly kingdom in Cantata 61, *Nun komm', der Heiden Heiland*, composed in 1714.

21. I have omitted in this context the four Duets because they are only loosely connected with the cyclical plan. See Christoph Wolff, "Ordnungsprinzipien in den Originaldrucken Bachscher Werke," in *Bach-Interpretationen*, edited by Martin Geck (Göttingen, 1969), pp. 144–67.

22. For a similar discussion of concerto and French overture elements in the Prelude and Fugue in E♭ see George Stauffer, *The Organ Preludes of Johann Sebastian Bach* (Ann Arbor, 1980), pp. 74–77.

23. Among the more important monographs dealing with Bach's registration are Hermann Keller, *The Organ Works of Bach*, translated by Helen Hewitt (New York, 1967); Jacobus Kloppers, "Die Interpretation und Wiedergabe der Orgelwerke Bachs," Diss., Frankfurt University, 1965; Thomas Harmon, *The Registration of J. S. Bach's Organ Works* (Buren, 1978); Stauffer, *The Organ Preludes of Johann Sebastian Bach*; and Peter Williams, *The Organ Music of J. S. Bach* (Cambridge, 1980–1984), vol. 3.

24. See Stauffer, "Bach's Organ Registration Reconsidered," pp. 194 and 201.

25. See the interesting article by Winfried Schrammeck, "Johann Sebastian Bach, Gottfried Silbermann, und die französische Orgelkunst," *Bach-Studien* V (1975): 93–108.

26. For example, ornaments in the Fantasia in c, BWV 562, are carefully notated in Bach's autograph score, Berlin, SPK, *P 490*. See Dietrich Kilian, "Studie über Bachs Fantasie und Fuge c-moll (BWV 562)," in *Hans Albrecht in Memoriam*, edited by Wilfried Brennecke and Hans Hasse (Kassel, 1969), pp. 127–35.

PETER WILLIAMS

❦

The Snares and Delusions
of Notation
Bach's Early Organ Works

It is a curious irony that the uniform appearance presented by any edition of Bach's organ works distorts them in that it does not give a true impression of the disparate nature and origins of the pieces themselves. The first printed collection of the free organ works (Vienna, 1812)[1] already had this characteristic, giving a visual uniformity to BWV 543–48 (the Preludes and Fugues in a, b, C, c, C, and e) and making them look like roughly similar compositions. Once one gets behind the notation, it is clear that BWV 543 is a much older piece than BWV 544–48 and that BWV 545 and 546 have much more complicated histories than do BWV 544, 547, and 548. Even the BWV numbers ultimately derive (via BG 15) from the order of this print, since the putative manuscript sources for the print (finally *AmB 60*) had a different order. Of course, one could make the same point about this manuscript source; it, too, disguises the disparateness, and the only reasons that printed editions come in for more "blame" is that they are more thorough and systematic, they more directly influence players, and they are more up-to-date and therefore apparently reliable. In giving pieces of edited music to the public, editors misrepresent them, despite earnest endeavors to do the opposite.

One of the most obvious elements in the uniformity of modern editions is the number of staves: three, if pedals are, or could be, or might be used. While in general it must be true that as editing procedures progress the degree of conventionality increases, in this case the convention is as old as editing itself. The Peters volumes use three

staves as a matter of course, reserving two for those works Griepenkerl saw as doubtless without pedal or—and this is an interesting exception—as being less important (e.g., unlike the Prelude and Fugue
in D, BWV 532, the small-type variant BWV 532a is on two staves). It
looks as if three staves were seen as a kind of "full dress," and the result of the convention was that works were stamped as either *manualiter* and *pedaliter*, as indeed so many are. But the convention took
(and still takes) no account of those works in which the pedal is op-
tional or ambiguous.

The presence or absence of a third staff is simple, but many other
conventions are far subtler and even insidious. Thus a scribe's well-
intentioned habit of marking the close of a work with a long chord
(with or without a fermata) can be the result of an unconscious anach-
ronism (the assumption that a work ends with a long chord being
characteristic of the scribe's period, not the work's), a deliberate alteration (the practice of his day suggesting to the scribe that a short chord,
much less a single note, does not work well), or a literal transcription
of a tablature (which, however, has its own conventions not necessarily
to be transferred to stave notation). If it is only through the labors of
such a copyist that we know the piece, we can only conjecture what the
composer's final chord (or note) had been. The best modern edition,
moreover, would not be justified in rejecting the copyist's big, long
chord-with-fermata as inauthentic, for the editor could not know for
sure that it was so and could do no more than print the chord as the
copyist had it. But the result would be that the editor was then reserving for some editorial addition (in the form of a footnote, small-type
alternative, or critical note at the end or even in a separate book) an
observation so crucial that an organist or scholar ignoring it would
quite misunderstand that moment in the piece of music—perhaps
even all of it.

Furthermore, the composer himself was subject to conventions that
are not to be taken literally. The subtlest of these conventions is that
he was making a score at all (a "literate model"), and sometimes details are left open. An obvious example is *In dulci jubilo*, BWV 608,
which can only be performed if the player *interprets* the autograph
score, i.e., by playing the tenor cantus firmus down an octave and
drawing a certain stop. The ease with which the notational puzzle of
this piece can be solved should not deflect us from seeing that the
composer's only known copy of *In dulci jubilo* is a kind of model short
score to be realized as the organist finds best. In this instance, there
may not be much of an alternative, but in at least two of the Schübler

Chorales, pedal and manual can be exchanged despite the rubrics given by the composer in a copy of the edition.[2] In fact, the composer's rubrics here can lead us to conclude something important about all notational details (signs, slurs, manual distribution, etc.): *The effect of every detail in any notation is to limit the performer's choice.* Naturally, in certain directions the composer does wish to limit the player's choice— the notes themselves, their meter, and their rhythms. But limiting the player to producing this line on pedals and that on manual, or pre-scribing when to use pedal (which is what a third staff automatically does) or when to change manuals, or telling the player to slur the notes in a particular way at a specific tempo: these instructions are a different order of "limiting choice," and they occur both infrequently and ambiguously.

The following examples of questions raised by the sources as we have them are not meant to be a review of current editions[3] or a kind of speculative, ersatz *Kritischer Bericht.* They are meant only to serve the organist who wishes to question his assumptions and is "Desirous of Learning" about the inadequacies of notation as well as solving the familiar problems of scarce articulation, ambiguous ornaments, un-certain manual changing and speculative registration.

Tablature Originals

If the composer's original score was written in tablature, it is easy to imagine several kinds of misinterpretations creeping into the manu-script tradition. For example, in some sources of the Passacaglia in c, BWV 582, certain notes or passages are displaced an octave.[4] In the anonymous Fantasia in c, written in tablature in the *Andreas-Bach-Buch* (Lpz MB *III.8.4*, ff. 72'–72a) and now attributed to J. S. Bach, the scribe-composer has closed the work with a "big, long chord-with-fermata," in fact, seven fermate (one for each note in the six-part chord plus one below the whole). The final chord of the chorale *Gott, durch deine Güte*, BWV 724, also in tablature in the *Andreas-Bach-Buch*, in the hand of Johann Christoph Bach, is similar, though there is an interesting difference: Johann Christoph Bach gives no rhythmic sign for the last chord and *replaces* it with a fermata for each note. His younger brother J. S. gave both but cannot have meant anything dif-ferent. They both meant "NB: this is the end of the piece"; and other fermate had the same meaning, whether written above the final long chord, or above the double barline itself (a common convention), or over a final chord written short (quarter note followed by a rest). The last two can be seen in other pieces copied by Johann Christoph Bach in this manuscript (C. F. Witt's Capriccio in e on f. 73 and the close of the Fantasia in c, BWV 921, on f. 72).

However, tablatures can have subtler characteristics. There is an inherent abstraction about tablature layout: Unless there is a specific cue, nothing shows what belongs to each hand or pedal, and while a two-stave score is often similarly ambiguous (or versatile), it is not even clear from tablature that it is organ music at all. Both tablature pieces in the *Andreas-Bach-Buch* are written in a kind of "open score," and in neither one does the lowest part look at all like a pedal line typical of c. 1705, except for the fragmentary cantus firmus in the chorale (cued in in m. 34, a cue not given in the BG or the NBA score[5]). Similarly unidiomatic (i.e., "open") are the Fantasias in b, BWV 563, and C, BWV 570, which though copied in stave notation in the *Andreas-Bach-Buch* (like the Passacaglia) might well have been originally in tablature. Had the Prelude and Fugue in C, BWV 531, or the Prelude and Fugue in c, BWV 549, also been originally in tablature, some of the later accretions (thick chords, long finals, unsuitable pedal lines, meaningless pedal leap in BWV 549, m. 29; corrected in Example 1) would be more easily identified. One might suspect that unusual details in other early works—minor infelicities (awkwardnesses for the hands) in the Fugue in g, BWV 535/535a, and in the Passacaglia; and some empty moments in the final fugue of the Capriccio in B♭, BWV 992—might derive from the transferring to stave notation of fair-copy tablatures. It could well be—though this is frankly speculative—that the occa-

EXAMPLE 1

a. BWV 549/1

b. BWV 549/2

sional "empty moments" in the sixth movement of the Capriccio are a sign not so much of immaturity on the composer's part as that the piece (being quite a strict fugue) was conceived on paper, in tablature, the parts having there a logic that in stave notation would more easily be seen as insufficient to "carry" the piece at those moments.

Stave Notation

Three examples show the scope of questions raised: the notation of pedal points, of sectional breaks, and of ties.

The notation of pedal points is not always clear. A harmonic phrase can often be a pedal point in spirit without the bass note actually being held. The source for the Legrenzi Fugue, BWV 574a, has a long note at mm. 100–103 for a passage that in the versions BWV 574 and 574b has pedal rests. Not dissimilar passages in Buxtehude (*Gelobet seist du, Jesu Christ*, BuxWV 188; Praeludium in G, BuxWV 147; and the Praeludium in d, BuxWV 140) have partially held pedal points (i.e., stave sources, probably derived from tablatures, partially write out a long pedal note), suggesting that the Protestant German organist varied the performance from occasion to occasion. Although the fact that the Legrenzi Fugue, BWV 574a, breaks off at this point does not necessarily "explain" the pedal point; it might suggest that the anonymous, late-eighteenth-century copyist was interfering. Either way, it could be hinting that implied pedal points were sometimes made explicit by the player. The question of the pedal points at the close of BWV 574 (mm. 117–18), the close of the fugue of the Toccata in C, BWV 564, and the opening of the Prelude in a, BWV 543/1, is unclear in all the sources. Is the pedal to hold its note right through, while the left hand completes the figuration (Legrenzi Fugue, Toccata in C)? Is the pedal really to be taken off completely (Toccata in C)? Is the left hand to hold its *point d'orgue* while the pedal completes the figuration (Legrenzi Fugue)? Is the pedal to bring in its *point d'orgue* half a measure earlier, as the left hand reaches the tonic (Prelude in a, m. 9)?

The notation of sectional breaks is often ambiguous because composers, their copyists, their modern editors, and even those editors' publishers each have their own conventions, which may or may not be meaningless. Presumably the double bar before the toccata-coda of the Legrenzi Fugue, BWV 574 and 574b, has the same purpose whether it is drawn singly through each staff (*Andreas-Bach-Buch*) or through both of them (NBA). But does the absence of double bars in the sources for the Prelude and Fugue in G, BWV 550, the Prelude in a, BWV 551, and the Prelude and Fugue in D, BWV 532 (m. 16), mean that the break is not so marked by the player? The Prelude in D (at m. 9) and the Prelude in a (at m. 29) have double bars in the same way as in the Legrenzi Fugue, i.e., quite unnecessarily, since the rests and change of direction already make the gap clear. The various types of sectional breaks suggest that the composer had what may be called "varying degrees of separateness" before a fugue subject was announced:

No break but an overlap: Passacaglia in c, BWV 582.

No break, fugue continues *a tempo*: Prelude and Fugue in G, BWV 550.

A long chord preceding the fugal subject played *a tempo*: Prelude in a, BWV 551 (sources disagree as to whether the chord is held over).

A long chord, then a complete break: Adagio of Toccata in C, BWV 564.

The notation of ties is a problem for editors and players, usually because the sources have too few, both for long tied notes (e.g., the Fantasia in C, BWV 570) and for those little notes that convention, often stretching back far into the seventeenth century, would have expected to be tied (see Example 1). There are many such instances. Occasionally an organist could well suspect that a copyist got carried away and put in ties where they do not belong (arrows in Example 2a and 2b, and no fermata in Example 2b). In the case of the great Prelude in e, BWV 548/1, one copyist's ties in the main theme itself[6] are easily enough discounted because of the existence of good copies (in-

EXAMPLE 2

a. BWV 579

81

b. BWV 550/2

cluding an autograph fair copy) that do not have them. But for other works, we are not so fortunate.

Wrong Notes, Etc.

It goes without saying that there are many cruxes in any composer's music, but it is important to distinguish between error and misunderstanding on the part of the copyist. Although the result may be the same, a misunderstanding may turn out to be more influential because we do not detect it. An error can be seen, for instance, in the top part of m. 13 in the BG edition of the Fantasia in b, BWV 563. Although the *Andreas-Bach-Buch* does read this way, the copyist must have gotten the third beat wrong. A good example of a misunderstanding is not as easy to find. One possible case is that of mm. 10 and 39 of the Prelude in G, BWV 550/1. The sources make perfect sense here (Example 3), and the second of these passages is paralleled a few

EXAMPLE 3

BWV 550/1

bars later in the home key; but there is an obsessive, Buxtehude-like quality to the figuration in mm. 37–50 that makes an unresolved quasi pedal point more than possible (NB the pedal!). That may also be true of m. 10 (see Example 4). This is speculation, of course, but such "obsessive" harmonies occur elsewhere in early Bach, such as in the Passacaglia in c (from m. 153),[7] and ultimately they allude to old habits of not resolving the fourth degree of the scale to the third at a perfect cadence (there is a fine example in Frescobaldi's *Cento partite*).

EXAMPLE 4

Many organists must have been struck from time to time by a hiatus or inconsistency in a contrapuntal passage that would have been quite easy for Bach to avoid. For example, something odd happens in the bass line of the Prelude and Fugue in c, BWV 549 (Example 5). The

EXAMPLE 5

a. NBA

b. BG

D-minor version, BWV 549a, has the same disposition as Example 5a, and since this is almost certainly the original form of the work,[8] the "misunderstanding" goes back to the Möller manuscript. Perhaps it, too, was transcribed from tablature and the part writing was obscured; one can only guess what the composer intended (Example 6).

EXAMPLE 6

A similar moment occurs at the end of the C-minor version of the fugue, BWV 549/2, at mm. 55–56, where one can confidently assert that either the left hand plays the bottom E or the pedal plays it *plus* the previous two notes; a sudden break seems impossible.

Of the solutions suggested for the Prelude, Example 6a is the least problematic and, perhaps, most likely to conform to *Orgelpunkttokkaten* conventions in Central Germany (compare the pedal entry in the

Fugue at m. 40). Example 6b is unlikely if the pedal is indeed to be used in the previous six measures (i.e., after its opening solo), but perhaps it does not have to be. Examples 6c and 6d complete the motive in its own right but require a major rewriting that, particularly in the case of Example 6d—new octave imitation—is not very likely. BG's solution (Example 5b) is also, alas, unlikely, even were a tenor d to be added and held; such motives would be out of character with pedal parts of the early works. In other instances, it could be important for the pedal to preserve the identity of motives, especially in those chromatic *durezze* moments (e.g., the end of the Prelude in D, BWV 532/1, mm. 96–107; or the end of the Adagio of the Toccata in C, BWV 564, mm. 23–31) when the motives are easily lost sight of. The NBA edition of the Prelude in D (complete with putative double pedal) is in this respect superior to the NBA edition of the Toccata in C (where the lines are confused in mm. 29–30).

Being consistent with a motive is often impossible. Measures 99–101 of the Corelli Fugue, BWV 579, may have begun as shown in Example 7, but had to be changed (alto g′ to b′) to avoid a parallel octave.

EXAMPLE 7

Unfortunately, in the process, a promising motive (marked *x* in the example; see also mm. 79–81 of the same fugue) had to be sacrificed. One can imagine the mature Bach finding another solution. For one thing, a marked slurring of the two notes of the motive would create another promising detail in the interests of "counterpoint by articulation"; one can imagine that by the time of the *Orgelbüchlein* (in which many pieces have a marked similarity to the four-part writing of the Legrenzi Fugue) such a detail would not have been lost.

One can often see the composer not being able to find fully satisfactory part writing when some incident makes it awkward. Were it not that the left hand has to be cleared for its bass solo, it is probable that m. 13 of the Prelude in C, BWV 531/1, would have been written as shown in Example 8a (as one copyist has it)[9] but not as in Example 8b

EXAMPLE 8

(NBA, etc.). The copyists, too, seemed to appreciate that the bass solo was not a pedal line (as BG guessed), because it does not conform to the alternate-foot idiom of mm. 1–9 and 21–22, and they attempted various solutions at this spot.

Of course, in the case of an actual transcription, especially one perhaps unauthorized by the composer, many comparable situations can arise. But in the "Fiddle" Fugue in d, BWV 539/2, the "misunderstandings" often became "errors" when the original harmonies, implicit and explicit, were incorrectly taken over into the new idiom. There are many moments in this arrangement that the organist should have no qualm in "improving" in the light of the Violin Sonata. The work as we know it in the editions merely reflects one eighteenth-century way of transcribing a very complex movement and has no limitless authority for today's organist, who would surely want to make the violin's original echo passages clear on the organ.

As with transcription, so with transposition: if the Fugue in f, BWV 534/2, is, like its Prelude, the result of transposition, the authority of such questionable details as the number of parts in certain chords, the notation of the cadenza, and the final tonic minor chord is accordingly less reliable. Only accident of extant sources makes it so much clearer that the following are the composer's original keys:

Prelude and Fugue, BWV 532: D major rather than C or F major
Fantasia and Fugue, BWV 542: G minor rather than F minor
Prelude and Fugue, BWV 545: C major rather than B♭ major
Prelude and Fugue, BWV 549: D minor rather than C minor
Toccata, BWV 566: E major rather than C major

But there are distinct problems outstanding about BWV 534 (G minor?), BWV 566 (D major?), and, of course, the Pastorale, BWV 590, which is so unlikely a collection of pieces that finding the "proper" key for the second movement (F major?) begs too many questions.

Beaming of Small Notes

The opening *passaggi* figures of the Prelude and Fugue in e, BWV 533, and of the Prelude and Fugue in g, BWV 535, immediately evoke not only the playing method of those figures but also the rhetorical articulation that results from correct hand distribution. That is clear to any organist who compares the opening of BWV 535 in the NBA with its early variant, BWV 535a, whose source (the Möller manuscript) gives a plain "open score" presentation. The dividing of *passaggi*, arpeggios, and scale runs between the hands was obviously a crucial factor in the organist's understanding of them, and it is in this respect unfortunate that NBA so often gives no separate beaming (other passages in the Prelude and Fugue in g; and in the Prelude and Fugue in c, BWV 549; the Prelude and Fugue in a, BWV 543; the Toccata in E, BWV 566; and the Toccata in C, BWV 564). It does so because the composer's authority is not usually assured for them. But J. T. Kreb's beaming of the C-major version of the Toccata in E (see BG) and J. C. Oley's for the Prelude and Fugue in g (NBA IV/5–6, KB, p. 449) are of sufficient relevance that editions should show them. The power of notation is such that both a student and a very experienced player faced with editions whose collations are only partial (e.g., the NBA) will have a less-evocative impression of the piece concerned than from an edition based on a less-rigorously selected collation: for example, the BG version of the opening of the Toccata in C, BWV 564, whose 32nd-note beamings are based on a nineteenth-century copy.

That beamings, indicating hand distribution, did and are meant to have a bearing on articulation is clear from the arpeggio beaming in sources for the Passacaglia in c (Example 9, as in the *Andreas-Bach-Buch*). Hand distribution is not technically necessary, particularly for present-day players, whose training (exercises, scales, arpeggios, etc.) far exceeds that of any early eighteenth-century composer-player; but it is a question of motivic articulation. The distribution of the triplets in the Prelude in a, BWV 543/1, is clear enough; but the sudden introduction of 32nd notes in m. 22 must have been characterized by a marked articulation quite different from the smoothness suggested by continuous beaming. The anonymous copyist in Berlin, DStB *P 803*

EXAMPLE 9

EXAMPLE 10

had a different understanding of the triplet passages in the variant BWV 543a, but distributed the hands in his equivalent of m. 22 as shown in Example 10.

Similar points could be made about the opening arpeggios of the Prelude in A, BWV 536/1, and especially about those *passaggi* that vary between arpeggio and scale pattern (e.g., in the Toccata in E, BWV 566), whose meaning is lost if the line is played evenly and unbroken. The organist should assume that such passages involve both hands and that one of the likely articulations of the period will result if the hands are given alternating figures.

Added Parts

It is clear from authentic copies that the composer himself sometimes added a part to the closing bars of preludes and fugues (e.g., in both the Prelude and the Fugue in g, BWV 535). But it is also characteristic of pieces known from less-reliable sources that the part writing is sometimes inconsistent.

A good example is the Prelude and Fugue in f, BWV 534. Quite apart from questions of key and authenticity of the work, it is suspicious that starting at m. 24 the number of parts suddenly goes from four to six (Example 11a). Nor should corrupt sources or changing tastes allow us to assume that either the sudden eleven-part diminished seventh or its continuation into a cadenza is reliable (Example 11b; "extra" notes crossed out). Increasing the drama of an unexpected or striking chord by increasing the number of parts it contains is certainly something known to J. S. Bach (e.g., the Preludes in D and d in WTC I), but organ music had by nature a higher level of consistency. One thinks of the modest addition of a part here and there in the *Orgelbüchlein* and of the very varied texture of the Prelude in E♭, BWV 552/1. Besides, it is a question of how the extra parts are added. In the Prelude in A, BWV 536/1, the new or "extra" part in m. 30 is more credible than the thickened chords in m. 29 (see Example 12).

There are many examples in which one might suspect the extra notes in chords: the fattened seventh in the coda to the Legrenzi Fugue, BWV 574 (NBA, m. 113; A♭–e♭′–g′–c‴ only?); the seven-

EXAMPLE 11

BWV 534/1

EXAMPLE 12

part tonic in the Prelude in D, BWV 532/1 (NBA, m. 16, on which the copyists disagree); in three sections of the Toccata in E, BWV 566; in the throbbing chords of the Prelude in d/c, BWV 549 (NBA, mm. 20 and 24: five parts only?); and again in its Fugue (NBA, mm. 40–46, *et seq.*: five parts only?). Of course, one may imagine certain full chords to be fully authentic as far as they are thematic (a good example is in the Prelude in e, BWV 533/1, and, less convincingly, in the Prelude in G, BWV 568). But doubt is cast on the thick chords of the Fugue in c, BWV 549/2 by the Möller manuscript's giving a "trem." ornament to each note in one of the eight-part chords; that is hard to take seriously or to regard as anything but copyist's guesswork (see NBA IV/6, p. 105).

Pedals

In looking at the early works of J. S. Bach or those of a composer like Buxtehude, an organist today might be able to decide whether the bass part is intended for pedal by asking three questions about the bass line: Is it a *point d'orgue*? Is it a (virtuoso) solo? Is it thematic (cantus firmus in a chorale, subject entry in a fugue)?

None of these three cases necessarily requires pedal, of course; that depends on context or genre. But since so much keyboard music is ambiguous—or versatile—and was so often copied long after the date of origin, the three questions serve as a good starting point. On the one hand, copyists sometimes gave pieces a form that makes them suitable as harpsichord music (hence the B_1 notes occasionally slipped in, for instance, at the close of the fugue of the Toccata in C, BWV 564, in two copies); on the other, they sometimes saw an organ pedal contribution as so important that it could be doubled (e.g., the close of the Prelude in D, BWV 532/1; and *An Wasserflüssen Babylon*, BWV 653b). These vicissitudes merely reflect the "versatility" characteristic of the period; judging by its layout alone, one cannot even be certain that the chorale *An Wasserflüssen Babylon*, BWV 653b, is an organ piece.

Clearly, in the case of the Prelude and Fugue in e, BWV 533, pedal not only allows all the notes in the manual to be played but also makes a contribution (in the form of powerful if brief pedal solos) without which the work loses a dimension. However, it is difficult to see how either of these conditions could be upheld as "necessary." The piece makes perfect musical sense if the manual parts are rearranged and the left hand plays the bass solos; both adjustments can be done *ex tempore*, though sources for BWV 533a show that such things have been notated at some moment in the work's history. In fact, the *ad hoc* treatment of organ music in either tablature or stave notation may have been so much a part of organ art that uncertainties over what or where precisely the pedal plays in closing sections of the Prelude in C, BWV 531/1, or the Fugue in d/c, BWV 549/2, are really not important. Players would be true to the music if they had different methods or approaches on different occasions. For example, on most organs they could not have played some important bass motives that go as high as e', in such pieces as the Preludes in A, BWV 536, and G, BWV 550.

Assuming that a "versatile" piece is to be played on the organ, and that any *point d'orgue*, pedal solo, or bass cantus firmus is to be played by the pedal (if there is one), how much does it play? In the Prelude and Fugue in C, BWV 531, does it play either the bass solo at m. 13 of the Prelude (see Example 8) or the subject entry in the Fugue (mm. 36–41)? After all, the latter is a true subject, unlike the previous pedal entry, which was given a pedal-like character, i.e., the subject was drastically altered for the sake of alternate-foot pedal technique. Characteristic motives,—rather than *points d'orgue*, which may well have been treated with some license[10]—suggest that pedal certainly took an active part in the codas of the C-minor Fugues BWV 549/2, 574, and 575. Of course, the pedal's repertoire of effects gradually increased in the work of an inventive composer. The Prelude and Fugue in A, BWV 536, is already a subtle advance on the Toccata in E, BWV 566, in this respect; and it is striking how that most un-pedal-like of motives, the diatonic scale, grows from an incidental (if happy!) idea in the Prelude in C to a rhetorical virtuoso element in the Prelude in D (see Example 13). But on the whole, scales or scalelike figures are not a "normal" part of Baroque pedal playing. Awareness of this factor may make us also doubt some pedal entries in certain early fugues, since the lines do not conform with accredited pedal styles.

EXAMPLE 13

a. BWV 531/1

b. BWV 532/1

The most striking example is the Canzona in d, BWV 588, whose opening "pedal subject" is not authenticated by the sources. It commits the player to a bigger pedal part throughout than was characteristic of "versatile" keyboard music and produces a line that is quite unlike a pedal part of the period and a necessarily slower tempo than the fugue itself would suggest.

Finals

Often in matters of performance practice, one learns by comparisons between different situations. For example, in the Fugue in D, BWV 532/2, the nature of the subject and the succinctness of the close do not require any extra notes or a long final. The four parts continue without letup or hindrance to the final drop, and it is difficult to see how any copyist or player could have thickened it.

But the same is not true for the close of such Fugues as the E minor, BWV 533, or F minor, BWV 534. If the fugue had a toccata-like coda (e.g., the Legrenzi Fugue, BWV 574), one can imagine the fugue itself ending with its correct number of parts but being followed by a coda that introduces others. Compare the strict close of the first fugue in the Toccata in E, BWV 566 (four-part final, not five as in the NBA?), with the freer close of the second fugue of the same piece (BWV 566/4). This distinction may often be lost on the twentieth-century ear; it was certainly lost on good copyists, and in mature works, too. Thus the rather similar cadences at the ends of the Fugue in E♭, BWV 552/2, and the Fugue in C, BWV 545/2, are not conveyed in the same

EXAMPLE 14

a. BWV 552/2

b. BWV 545/2

Ped.

way by the sources. The former (composer's fair copy, engraved under supervision) keeps its five parts strictly; the latter (J. P. Kellner, etc.) expands its four to six or seven (see Example 14). In comparison, therefore, the latter is untrustworthy and indeed gave the copyists considerable trouble.[11] Even the fermata has a different shade of meaning, since the Fugue in E♭, BWV 552/2 (like its Prelude) ends on a middle beat and therefore needs a *signum finalis*.

The kind of succinct close (with *rallentando?*) implied by the famous final eighth-note chord of the Fugue in C, BWV 547/2, may well have been a norm as *one* way of closing a piece.[12] Such closes certainly support the final cadence of the Fugue in A, BWV 536/2, as given by NBA rather than in BG. That is, the final chord is very short (eighth note) and the (or any) fermata appears only as a *signum finalis* afterward, on a rest (NBA) but not on the chord itself (BG). Recognizing fermate to be no more than *signa finales* is important. For example, according to the sources used in the NBA, both finals in Examples 1a and 2b above have fermatas over them, but it is unlikely that either meant "hold this chord beyond the beat" (quarter note in the first, *al-labreve* half note in the second). While some succinct closes are clear enough, both at the ends of pieces (Fugue in D) and at the ends of sections (Legrenzi Fugue, before the coda), others are less so. Doubt arises also when the cadence proper is not at the end of a piece but actually a bar or two from the end (leaving what follows to be an "unwinding" over a tonic *point d'orgue*), as is the case with the Fugue in C, BWV 547/2; the fugue to the Toccata in C, BWV 564; the first prelude in the Toccata in E, BWV 566; and the chorale *Wie schön leuchtet der Morgenstern*, BWV 739. The first and last of these are clear, but should the opening section of the Toccata in E also be treated succinctly—i.e., the whole-note fermate and even extra parts (as in the NBA) treated with caution and not played literally?

In the case of the Toccata in C, it is clear that copyists could not quite understand what to make of the close, any more than many organists today can.[13] Even if the good copy in Berlin, DStB *P 803* (c. 1729) is based on the composer's manuscript (a tablature?[14]), it would not mean that the way he notated it—with the familiar "petering-out" close—necessarily conveys the effect intended. How can one know? Any difficulty today's organists may feel in obeying the notation literally comes from the mutables of music history: their *organo pleno* is of the wrong kind (so the falling lines become duller), their assumptions are not those of c. 1705 (so they think the close an "anticlimax"), etc. Harpsichord players familiar with well-restored examples of "early"

EXAMPLE 15

a. BWV 1080 (as in *P 200*)

b. BWV 1080/8 (as in 1751 ed.)

and "late" harpsichords frequently find a crucial difference when it comes to cadences: The earlier instruments convey succinct closes much better, for there is something about the changing aesthetic and ideals of musical tone that compel players to linger more and more over closes as music changed and instrument technology developed.[15]

Some succinct closes that copyists could not easily interfere with are those in *Ein feste Burg'*, BWV 720; the last movement of the Concerto in G, BWV 592; the Fugue in D, BWV 532/2; and *Erstanden ist der heil'ge Christ'*, BWV 628. The effectiveness of the single note or open octave at the end of certain compositions makes one question whether other examples once existed but did not survive the copyist's desk. Succinct closes sometimes puzzled copyists. For example, Bach wrote a short final to the dashing three-part Fugue in *Art of Fugue*, BWV 1080/8, but the engraver (assuming he used this or a similar source) added a fermata to the chord itself. He may not have intended anything significant; but it certainly looks different to a player alerted to such details (Example 15).

(IN MEMORIAM CHARLES FISK)

NOTES

1. See Dietrich Kilian, NBA IV/5–6, KB, pp. 256–57.
2. Described in Christoph Wolff, "Bach's Personal Copy of the Schübler Chorales," in this volume.
3. For example, in the manner of Emery's implied criticisms of the cadences in NBA IV/5–6; see Walter Emery, "Cadence and Chronology," in *Studies in Renaissance and Baroque Music in Honor of Arthur Mendel*, edited by Robert L. Marshall (Hackensack, 1974), pp. 156–64.
4. See Dietrich Kilian, "Zu einem Bachschen Tabulaturautograph," in *Bachiana et alia Musicologica*, edited by Wolfgang Rehm (Kassel, 1983), pp. 161–67.
5. Perhaps this cue was a guess on the part of the copyist, Johann Christoph Bach. The pedal presumably does not continue to play through to the end of the piece (whatever NBA, BG, Breitkopf und Härtel, and others suggest) but was cued in here to bring out a canonic cantus firmus that was in any case more fully dealt with in *Gott durch deine Güte*, BWV 600 (where an extra rubric had to be added to clarify the pedal canon).
6. See NBA IV/5–6, KB, p. 396.
7. See Peter Williams, *The Organ Music of J. S. Bach* (Cambridge, 1980–84), vol. 1, p. 261; and Williams, "The Harpsichord Acciaccatura: Theory and Practice in Harmony, 1650–1750," *Musical Quarterly* 54 (1968): 503–23, for further references. One could go on to speculate that at the home key version of Example 4b (mm. 45–46) the figure is no longer obsessive and does indeed

resolve in the given way. Did the copyists argue back from this passage and rewrite the earlier passages?

8. Kilian (NBA IV/5–6, KB, p. 319) shows clearly how likely it is that the C-minor version was not J. S. Bach's work.

9. Kilian, NBA IV/5–6, KB, pp. 295 and 655.

10. One has to think only of the "held" notes in the bass of contemporary Italian recitatives—such as the tied whole notes in many a cantata of Handel—to see that keyboardists, i.e., organists who were harpsichordists, who were continuo players, etc., were familiar with various *points d'orgue* conventions. In the case of recitatives, those "held" notes could be held, restruck, dropped, or picked up again as the logic of the harmony suggested.

11. See NBA IV/5–6, KB, p. 660.

12. See Williams, *The Organ Music of J. S. Bach*, vol. 3, pp. 236–41.

13. See NBA IV/5–6, KB, pp. 492 and 691.

14. See NBA IV/5–6, KB, p. 489.

15. Hence the popularity today, among those of unrefined taste, for the late-Baroque harpsichord, particularly the French and its proto-pianistic tone. Of course, there are succinct closes in Beethoven and at the end of an act in many Wagner operas, but an exceptional gesture or a consciously rhetorical element of this kind is quite different in principle from a performance "norm."

CALENDAR OF EVENTS IN BACH'S
LIFE AS ORGANIST

1685 March 21	EISENACH Born the last of eight children of Johann Ambrosius Bach and Maria Elisabeth Lämmerhirt.
1696	OHRDRUF Studies with his brother Johann Christoph Bach. This training was "designed for an organist and nothing more" (BDok III, no. 803). Copies a book, by moonlight, containing works by Pachelbel, Kerll, and Froberger (BDok III, no. 666).
1700	LÜNEBURG Student at the Michaelisschule, where he sings in the choir (BDok II, no. 5). Makes several trips to Hamburg to hear Reinken (BDok III, no. 666). May have studied organ with Böhm (BDok III, no. 803).
1702 July?	Candidate for organist post at Jakobikirche, Sangerhausen (BDok I, no. 38).
1703 March–September	WEIMAR Employed as court musician for Duke Johann Ernst (BDok II, no. 6).
July	Tests and "plays for the first time" the new organ (built by Johann Friedrich Wender) in the Neue Kirche, Arnstadt (BDok II, no. 7).
August	Named organist of the Neue Kirche in Arnstadt (BDok II, no. 11). ARNSTADT Shows "the first fruits of his application to the art of organ playing, and to composition" (BDok III, no. 666).

The principal sources for this calendar are the *Bach-Dokumente* and the *Kalendarium zur Lebens-Geschichte Johann Sebastian Bachs*, edited by Hans-Joachim Schulze, 2d ed. (Leipzig, 1979).

1705
November?   Three- to four-month trip to hear Buxtehude in
1706 ↓   Lübeck, "in order to comprehend one thing and
February   another about his art." The journey was "not
                         without profit" (BDok II, no. 16; III, no. 666).
February 21   Reproved by the Consistory for his long absence in
                         Lübeck, and for his "strange" hymn playing (BDok
                         II, no. 16).
November   Requested, by the Consistory, to take part in
                         instrumental music making (BDok II, no. 17).
November 28   Tests, along with Johann Kister, the new organ (built
                         by Johann Albrecht) in the town church, at
                         Langewiesen (BDok II, no. 18).

1707
April   Auditions for the organist post at the Blasiuskirche in
                         Mühlhausen (BDok II, no. 19).
June 15   Appointed organist at the Blasiuskirche, Mühlhausen
                         (BDok II, no. 22).
June 29   Returns "the keys to the organ" to the Council in
                         Arnstadt.

1708   MÜHLHAUSEN
February   Submits recommendations for rebuilding the organ in
                         the Blasiuskirche (BDok I, no. 83).
June   Invited to serve as organist and chamber musician at
                         the court of dukes Wilhelm Ernst and Ernst August
                         in Weimar (BDok I, no. 1).
June 25   Released from service by the Mühlhausen Church
                         Council (BDok I, no. 1).

                         WEIMAR
                         During the Weimar years "the pleasure his Grace (the
                         Duke) took in his playing fired him with the desire
                         to try every possible artistry in his treatment of the
                         organ. Here, too, he wrote most of his organ works"
                         (BDok III, no. 666).
1710
October 26   Tests and inaugurates the new organ (built by Heinrich
                         Nicolaus Trebs) in the town church in Taubach (BDok
                         II, no. 50).

1711
February 16   Writes testimonial for organ builder Heinrich
                         Nicolaus Trebs (BDok I, no. 84).

1712
September 27   Stands as godfather at the baptism of Johann
                         Gottfried Walther, Jr. (BDok II, no. 54).

1713

April	Bach student Johann David Kräuter says his teacher will play "incomparable things" on the newly rebuilt Himmelsburg-Kapelle organ when the instrument is completed (BDok III, no. 58a).
July?	Duke Johann Ernst returns from the Netherlands with new music that may have spurred Bach to write his concerto transcriptions for organ, BWV 592–96 (Schulze, *The Organ Yearbook* 1972: 8–10).
November 11	Stands as godfather at the baptism of Johann Gottfried Trebs, son of organ builder Heinrich Nicolaus Trebs (BDok II, no. 61).
December?	Begins work, around Advent (?), on the *Orgelbüchlein*, a project that continues until Lent (?) 1716 (Arfken, BJ 1966: 41–58).
December	Auditions in Halle for the organist post at the Liebfrauenkirche and is offered the job (BDok I, no. 4; II, no. 62).

1714

	Owns a copy of Frescobaldi's *Fiori musicali*, marked "J. S. Bach. 1714" (BDok I, p. 269).
January	Negotiates with the Church Board of the Leibfrauenkirche in Halle over terms of organist position (BDok I, no. 2; II, no. 65).
February–March	Declines the call to Halle (BDok I, no. 4).
March 3	Named Konzertmeister in Weimar, with increase in salary and opportunity to write cantatas (BDok II, no. 66).

1716

April 29–May 1	With Johann Kuhnau and Christian Friedrich Rolle examines the new organ (built by Christoph Cuntzius) in the Liebfrauenkirche, Halle (BDok I, no. 85).
July 3	With Johann Anton Weise examines the organ (built by Johann Georg Schröter) in the Augustinerkirche, Erfurt (BDok I, no. 86).

1717

August 8	Appointed Kapellmeister to Prince Leopold of Anhalt-Cöthen (BDok II, no. 128).
Fall	Wins, by default, a contest of improvisation with French organist Louis Marchand in Dresden (BDok I, no. 6; II, no. 441).
November 6– December 2	Incarcerated in Weimar for "stubbornly forcing the issue of his dismissal" (BDok II, no. 84).
	KÖTHEN
December 16	Examines the organ (repaired and rebuilt by Johann Scheibe) in the Paulinerkirche, Leipzig (BDok I, no. 87; II, no. 87).

1719

May–July   Attempts, without success, to meet with Handel in
                    Halle (BDok III, no. 927; Erich Deutsch, *Handel—A
                    Documentary Biography* [London, 1955], pp. 86–87).

1720

January 22   Begins *Clavierbüchlein* for Wilhelm Friedemann Bach.

November 21–23   Competes, in Hamburg, for organist post at the Ja-
                    kobikirche. Wins applause of Reinken by improvis-
                    ing, for a half hour, on *An Wasserflüssen Babylon.*
                    Position awarded to Johann Joachim Heitmann,
                    who—according to Mattheson—"was better at pre-
                    luding with his thalers than with his fingers" (BDok
                    II, nos. 102 and 253).

1722   Begins *Clavierbüchlein* for Anna Magdalena Bach.

1723

April   Requests release from his post in Köthen (BDok II,
                    no. 128).
                    Accepts position of Thomaskantor in Leipzig (BDok
                    II, no. 131).

                    LEIPZIG
May 22   Moves to Leipzig
November   Examines and inaugurates the new organ (built by
                    Zacharias Hildebrandt) in the town church, Störm-
                    thal. Cantata 194, *Höchsterwünschtes Freudenfest* is
                    performed (BDok II, nos. 163 and 164).

1724

June 25   Examines and inaugurates the new organ (built by
                    Johann Georg Finke) in the Johanniskirche, and
                    tests the new organ (also by Finke) in the Sal-
                    vatorkirche, Gera (BDok II, nos. 183 and 183a).

1725   Begins second *Clavierbüchlein* for Anna Magdalena
                    Bach

September 19–20   Presents two concerts on the Silbermann organ in the
                    Sophienkirche, Dresden (BDok II, no. 193).

1726

May–November   Writes Cantatas 146, 170, 35, 47, 169, and 49, all with
                    obbligato organ parts (Dreyfus, p. 175 above).

1729

March   Assumes directorship of the Leipzig Collegium Musi-
                    cum (BDok I, no. 20).

May   Recommends Carl Gotthelf Gerlach for the organist
                    position at the Neue Kirche, Leipzig (BDok II,
                    no. 261).

June   Attempts, for the second time, to meet with Handel in
                    Halle (BDok III, nos. 912 and 927).

December   Serves on jury for the organist position auditions at
                    the Neue Kirche, Leipzig (BDok II, no. 446).

1731

September 14   Presents a concert on the Silbermann organ in the
                Sophienkirche, Dresden, "in the presence of the
                court musicians and virtuosi" (BDok II, no. 294).

November 12   Tests the new organ (built by Johann Christoph
                Schmieder) in the Stadtkirche in Stöntzsch (BDok
                II, no. 298).

1732

February 4   Reexamines the organ in the Stadtkirche in Stöntzsch,
                in order to test several newly added registers (BDok
                II, no. 298).

September 22–28 With Carl Möller examines, tests, and inaugurates the
                new organ (rebuilt by Nicolaus Becker) in the Mar-
                tinskirche, Kassel. Plays Toccata and Fugue in d
                ("Dorian"), BWV 538 (BDok II, no. 316).

1733

June 22   Wilhelm Friedemann Bach is appointed organist of
                the Sophienkirche in Dresden (BDok I, no. 25).

1735

June   Is present as his son Johann Gottfried Bernhard suc-
                cessfully auditions for the organist position at the
                Marienkirche, Mühlhausen. Also tests the organ
                and gives advice on necessary repairs (BDok II,
                nos. 365 and 393).

August 24   Writes letter of recommendation for his organ student
                Johann Ludwig Krebs (BDok I, no. 71).

1736

October–
November   Writes to the Town Council of Sangerhausen, hoping
                to procure an organist position for his son Johann
                Gottfried Bernhard (BDok I, nos. 37 and 38).

December 1   Presents a two-hour concert on the Silbermann organ
                in the Frauenkirche in Dresden, "in the presence of
                the Russian Ambassador von Keyserlingk and many
                Persons of Rank, as well as a large attendance of
                other persons and artists" (BDok II, no. 389).

1737

January 1   Johann Gottfried Bernard Bach is appointed organist
                at the Jakobikirche in Sangerhausen (BDok II,
                no. 396).

1739

June   Requests a positive organ for the Thomaskirche (or
                the Thomasschule?; BDok II, no. 445).

September   Plays and judges the new organ (built by Gottfried
                Heinrich Trost) in the Schlosskirche, Altenburg. Also
                plays the organ for the Sunday service, and transposes
                the verses of the Creed from d to e♭ to e (BDok II,
                no. 453; Hans-Joachim Schulze, "Über die 'unver-
                meidlichen Lücken' in Bachs Lebensbeschreibung,"

	in *Bachforschung und Bachinterpretation heute*, edited by Reinhold Brinkmann [Kassel, 1981], p. 38).
October	*Clavierübung* III, newly completed, is sold at the St. Michael's Fair (BDok II, no. 456).
1742	
December?	With Zacharias Hildebrandt examines the new organ (built by Johann Scheibe) in the Johanniskirche, Leipzig (BDok II, no. 519).
1746	
April 16	Wilhelm Friedemann Bach is appointed organist of the Leibfrauenkirche in Halle (BDok II, no. 63).
August 7	Examines and dedicates the new organ (built by Johann Scheibe) in the Stadtkirche in Zschortau (BDok II, no. 545).
September 27	With Gottfried Silbermann examines the organ (built by Zacharias Hildebrandt) in the Wenzelskirche, Naumburg (BDok I, no. 90; II, no. 547).
1747	
May 8	While visiting Frederich the Great, plays the organ in the Heiliggeistkirche, Potsdam (BDok II, no. 554).
May 25	Writes recommendation for organ student Johann Christoph Altnikol (BDok I, no. 81).
June	Beginning of the organ repair in the Thomaskirche (BDok II, no. 561).
June	Completion of the Canonic Variations on *Vom Himmel hoch*, BWV 769, which is used as a presentation piece for Bach's admission into Mizler's Society of the Musical Sciences (BDok III, no. 665).
November?	With Johann Gottlieb Görner tests the organ (repaired by Johann Scheibe) in the Thomaskirche, Leipzig (BDok II, no. 561).
1748	Publication of the Schübler Chorales, probably in 1748 or 1749 (Wolff, NBA VIII/1, KB, pp. 108–109).
January 1	Writes recommendation for organ student Johann Christoph Altnikol for the organist post at Niederwiesa (BDok I, no. 82).
January 12	Writes recommendation for the organ builder Heinrich Andreas Cuntzius of Halle (Hobohm, BJ 1977: 137).
1750	
July 28	Dies, after two unsuccessful eye operations, in Leipzig (BDok II, no. 606).

INDEX